THE WOMEN OF RENDEZVOUS

The Women of Rendezvous

A TRANSATLANTIC STORY OF FAMILY AND SLAVERY

Jenny Shaw

The University of North Carolina Press

CHAPEL HILL

Designed by Lindsay Starr
Set in Dante by codeMantra

Cover art: map courtesy Wikimedia Commons;
ocean courtesy Adobe Stock / sean824

Library of Congress Cataloging-in-Publication Data
Names: Shaw, Jenny, 1977– author.
Title: The women of Rendezvous : a transatlantic story of
family and slavery / Jenny Shaw.
Description: Chapel Hill : The University of North Carolina Press, [2024] |
Includes bibliographical references and index.
Identifiers: LCCN 2024029891 | ISBN 9781469682754 (cloth ; alk. paper) | ISBN 9781469682761
(pbk. ; alk. paper) | ISBN 9781469679082 (epub) | ISBN 9781469682778 (pdf)
Subjects: LCSH: Peers, John, 1645–1689—Family. | Women—Barbados—Biography. |
Enslaved women—Barbados—Social conditions—17th century. | Women—Great
Britain—Social conditions—17th century. | Women—Great Britain—Colonies—
Social conditions—17th century. | Patriarchy—History—Social aspects—Great Britain. |
White supremacy (Social structure)—Great Britain—Colonies—History. |
Slavery—Barbados—History. | Slavery—Great Britain—History. |
BISAC: HISTORY / Europe / Great Britain / General | SOCIAL SCIENCE / Slavery
Classification: LCC HQ1525.43 .S53 2024 |
DDC 305.4097298109 / 032—dc23 / eng / 20240716
LC record available at https://lccn.loc.gov / 2024029891

For Mum

Contents

Illustrations

MAPS

ILLUSTRATIONS

Acknowledgments

I SAT DOWN TO WRITE these acknowledgments many times and found myself inexplicably stuck. I feel so supported, both personally and professionally, that finding the words to articulate my appreciation has proven close to impossible. What follows is my best attempt.

Everyone at the University of North Carolina Press has been unfailingly enthusiastic and supportive. Special thanks to Debbie Gershenowitz, editor extraordinaire, and JessieAnne D'Amico, whose positive energy kept me on track. The entire production team made the process of turning this manuscript into a book much smoother and less fraught than I could possibly have hoped. That it looks as good as it does is entirely down to Mary Caviness, Madge Duffey, Kathleen Kageff, and Lindsay Starr. Sonya Bonczek's enthusiasm and advice are second to none. Sharon Block and Sarah Pearsall read this manuscript twice for the press. Their generous and generative feedback made the book so much stronger, and I am so grateful for the time and care they took, and that they "outed" themselves to me, allowing me to thank them properly here. I first worked through some of the ideas and sources in chapters 2, 3, and 6 in articles published in 2018 in *Slavery and Abolition* ("Birth and Initiation on the Peers Plantation: The Problem of Creolization in Seventeenth-Century Barbados"), and 2020 in the *William and Mary Quarterly* ("In the Name of the Mother: The Story of Susannah Mingo, a Woman of Color in the Early English Atlantic"). I thank both journals, and editors Gad Heuman and Josh Piker, respectively, as well as Gretchen Gerzina, Ann Little, Daniel Livesay, Lorena Walsh, and the anonymous readers for their advice and close engagement with my work. In 2014 Jennifer Morgan helped me see that there was a book here, despite my fears that there was not. Her encouragement provided much-needed confidence, and I am so grateful for that conversation. Thanks also to Simon Newman for his sage advice and continued support over these many years.

At the University of Alabama (UA) a small Office for Research and Development (ORED) Grant and several Capstone International Travel Grants helped support my time overseas. My chair, Josh Rothman, and colleagues in the history department helped facilitate a sabbatical year of research and the "adult aspire" semester that enabled me to complete the project. Special thanks to fellow early modernists Dan Riches, Lucy Kaufman, Heather Kopelson, and Juan Ponce Vázquez. Dan has been a model of true friendship and collegiality. Lucy endured my insistent requests to "look at this word and tell me what you see" with patience and a smile. Heather was always willing to lend a book, an ear, and an eye. Having a fellow Caribbeanist in Juan just down the hall is a luxury. Much appreciation to our wonderful administrative staff, Kayla Key, Morta Riggs, and Marla Scott, who make life easier in so many ways. I will always miss Morta's big smile and warm welcome first thing in the morning.

In ways large and small the students in my Caribbean; Comparative Slavery and Emancipation; Atlantic World; and Early Modern Black Britain classes shaped the ideas contained in this book. I am so grateful for their curiosity and questions, especially the graduate students in my Comparative Slavery course in the springs of 2020 and 2024, the UA@Oxford crew, and undergraduates Isabela Morales, Mark King, and Johanna Obenda, whose research projects I was fortunate enough to supervise. Conversations with Aaron Hoggle and Tagen Haga opened up new lines of research and inquiry. Toward the end, Kara Hutchinson and Mary Peake jumped on board as undergraduate research assistants. Their tenacity and energy helped take me over the finish line.

I owe a debt of gratitude to the many archivists and librarians at the Barbados National Archives; the National Archives, Kew, England; the Westminster Archives; the London Metropolitan Archives; the Herefordshire Archives and Records Centre, Hereford, England; the East Riding Archives, Beverly, Yorkshire; the Bodleian Library at Oxford University; and the Amelia Gayle Gorgas Library at UA, who made my job immeasurably easier. At Kew, Liz Hore explained how to get the most out of Chancery Court records. University of the West Indies at Cave Hill professor emeritus Pedro Welch was a wonderful guide to both the archives and the vegan food in Barbados. John W. Brown, the parish archivist at St. Leonard's Church, gave up his afternoon to poke around in his shed and share his knowledge on the church and Streatham. I thank them all for their generosity and patience.

I first presented on this project at an Omohundro Institute conference in Barbados in March 2013. Since then, I have received excellent suggestions, feedback, and questions from participants at the annual conference of the Association of Caribbean Historians, the Omohundro Institute Annual Conference, the

Society for Early Americanists conference in London, the Berkshire Conference of Women Historians, the American Historical Association, the Southern Historical Association, the New York University Atlantic History Workshop, the Beniba Centre for Slavery Studies at Glasgow University, Edinburgh University's Global History and Diaspora Seminars, the University of Illinois Urbana-Champaign Premodern Workshop, UA's Early Modern Faculty reading group, and the Children of Empire symposium hosted by Glasgow University and National Trust Scotland. A sincere thank-you to everyone who attended these sessions for their engagement, and especially to Peggy Brunache, Michelle Dowd, Nikki Eustace, Claire Hammond, Emma Hunter, Craig Koslofsky, Diana Paton, Dana Rabin, Christine Whyte, and Nuala Zahedieh for organizing and facilitating these events. The list of people who read parts of the work in progress, listened to me talk about it, or offered advice over the last decade and more is long. A big thanks to Margaret Abruzzo, Lauren Beck, John Beeler, Julia Brock, Catherine Chou, Sarah Cornell, Richard Dunn, Anne Eller, Ada Ferrer, Charles Foy, Billy Gérard Frank, Heather Freund, Katharine Gerbner, Hilary Green, Dalia Griñan, Victoria Hepburn, Rana Hogarth, Nate Holly, Alicia Hughes, Stefanie Hunt-Kennedy, Tara Inniss, Sara Johnson, Frederick Knight, Jane Landers, Mark Leggett, Stephanie McClure, Melanie Newton, Jennifer Palmer, Sue Peabody, Keiara Price, Catherine Roach, Briana Royster, Cassie Smith, Ellen Spears, Rachel Stephens, Elizabeth Tavares, George Thompson, John Thornton, Sasha Turner, and Karin Wulf.

Across the pond a slew of friends continue to be enthusiastic and supportive in equal measure. A special shoutout to my Norn Iron crew, Fay Ballard, Caroline Bates, Kathy McMaster, Olwyn Roberts, and Melanie Scott: I don't think I've ever laughed or cried as much as I do when I'm in your company, which is only ever a good thing. I know I'd have to go a very long way to find people so generous with their time and with their hearts. For reminding me where I'm from and what really matters, I thank you all. Glasgow also holds a special place in my heart. Hayley Rothwell has always made me feel like part of the family. I feel so lucky that the serendipity of student flat assignments put us together almost thirty years ago. At different moments Frank Jarvis, Alan Paul, Stephen Phelan, and Graeme Virtue have let me bend their ears without complaint. Their good company means a lot.

On this side of the ocean Andrew Huebner talked me off many ledges. Among many other things, I thank him for reminding me that telling good history means staying true to your subjects. Sarah Moody made a pandemic writing retreat in Birmingham more fun than it had any right to be and always makes trips to the big city worthwhile. Matt Orndorff and Dan Sweaney might could be the best company a girl could wish for. The Cocktail Goddesses provided much-needed commiseration and camaraderie. Lillian Anderton, Harriet Cabell, and Suzanne Horsley are few but precious. The many neighborhood friends, two and four legged, made both pandemic walks and happy hour hangouts such fun.

These brilliant women and wonderful friends read the whole manuscript: Karen Ordahl Kupperman, Holly Grout, Jolene Hubbs, Kristen Block, Christian Crouch, Marisa Fuentes, and Elena Schneider. From the very first time I met her in 2000, Karen has been a fantastic mentor. Her energy for new work and new paths is inspiring. While she read every chapter as it was written, I owe her special gratitude for enduring the many versions of chapter 1. Without her honesty, I would not have found this book's voice. It doesn't often happen that an office neighbor turns out to be a fast friend, but Holly has been that for me for almost fifteen years. When the chips were down, she was there to pick me up, dust me off, and make me laugh. Her ability to cut to the heart of what I'm trying to say is an absolute gift. How I write, how I think, and how I teach have been immeasurably changed for the better because she is my friend. Jolene's sharp eye and incisive comments were key: that the introduction reads as it does is almost entirely down to her sage advice. But her quick wit and big heart have been just as important in seeing this project through.

When Kristen suggested a weekly writing group—two hours, short excerpts read in real time—in the spring of 2020 I jumped at the chance to spend time every Friday with some amazing longtime friends who also happen to be phenomenal scholars. That I ended up writing most of this book as a result of "The Coven" still doesn't quite seem real. I don't think there is a single idea in what follows that they haven't helped me shape and hone. I cannot thank Kristen enough for bringing us together, nor her, Christian, Marisa, and Elena for their kindness, brilliance, and fearless honesty. I could not ask for better sister scholars. Spending time with each of you on various research and recreational trips over the last decade (and more) has been one of the great joys of writing this book. But it will always be those pandemic Fridays at noon Central (1 p.m. Eastern; 10 a.m. Pacific) that I will cherish most.

Writing a book about a complicated and difficult family has made me very grateful for my own. In the hot summer of 2018 Ray and Helen and Esther and Barry opened their homes to me as I traveled England to visit the birthplaces of John's two wives. I'm so sorry that Esther isn't here to see the finished project. My grandmother, Jean, also passed away as I was writing this book. I will always be grateful for her lessons in storytelling and how to be true to yourself. In Belfast, Roz continued to be an amazing auntie, always ready with an ear, and a good glass of wine. Colin, crucially, made sure our glasses stayed topped up. Richard and Victoria help keep me young: I'm so happy that Hudson and Eden are now part of the crew. That Gareth and I finally got to hug this past August after almost twenty years made my summer. Thanks also to Mervyn, Isabel, Ryan, Mark, Cara, Margot, Jim, Nicola, Kieran, Mike, and Richard for taking time and time together.

The best role I'll ever have is auntie to my nephew, Leon, and niece, Freya. Twice-weekly zoom history lessons with Leon in the spring and summer of 2020 took some of the sting out of not being there in person and was some of the most rewarding teaching I've done. I'll never be able to talk about pirates in the same way again! I'm in awe of Leon's talent and kindness and the person he is becoming. Meanwhile Freya never ceases to amaze me. She's taught me a lot about facing my own fears and being direct and honest. She may also be one of the funniest people I know. I can't wait for more adventures with them both. I thank my brother, Kevin, and his partner, Maxine, for their continued support, and for bringing two amazing people into my life.

My mum and dad read each chapter of this book as it was written. "Supportive" doesn't do their faith in me justice. Dad, I hope you know how much I value the way you take people as you find them. You've taught me a lot about how to have a big heart—and, also, how to become obsessed with something to the point of pathology! I'm still holding out for that research trip to Barbados with you. Mum, writing a book about mothers has made me think a lot about how lucky I am to have you as mine. You are one of the most resilient people I know. Thank you for teaching me to trust my instincts and for encouraging me to be generous and kind, even when I don't hit the mark. But mostly, thank you for showing me what unconditional love looks like. I would not be who I am without you. And so, as a small token, I dedicate this book to you.

Author's Note

I HAVE MODERNIZED DATES THROUGHOUT, beginning the year on 1 January, rather than on 25 March, as was the practice in England and Barbados under the Julien calendar until 1752. Original spelling and punctuation when quoting from sources remains, except when doing so would confuse the meaning of the quotation. I have also expanded archaic contractions and replaced "ye" with "the." While "Peers" is the most common spelling of the family's name, in some documents it is rendered as "Piers," Peirs," or "Pears," and less frequently as "Peeres," "Pearse," or "Pearce." To avoid confusion, I use "Peers" consistently throughout. First names repeat frequently within this family for both free and enslaved individuals. When necessary, I have chosen to identify children by their mothers' first names to make their identities clear. For example, Richard, son of John Peers and Susannah Mingo, is most commonly referred to in the text as Susannah's Richard, rather than Richard Mingo. Similarly, John Peers's second son is Hester's John, rather than John Peers II. I continue this practice down the generations. John Peers's grandson, and namesake, is therefore Hannah's John, rather than John Peers III.

THE WOMEN OF RENDEZVOUS

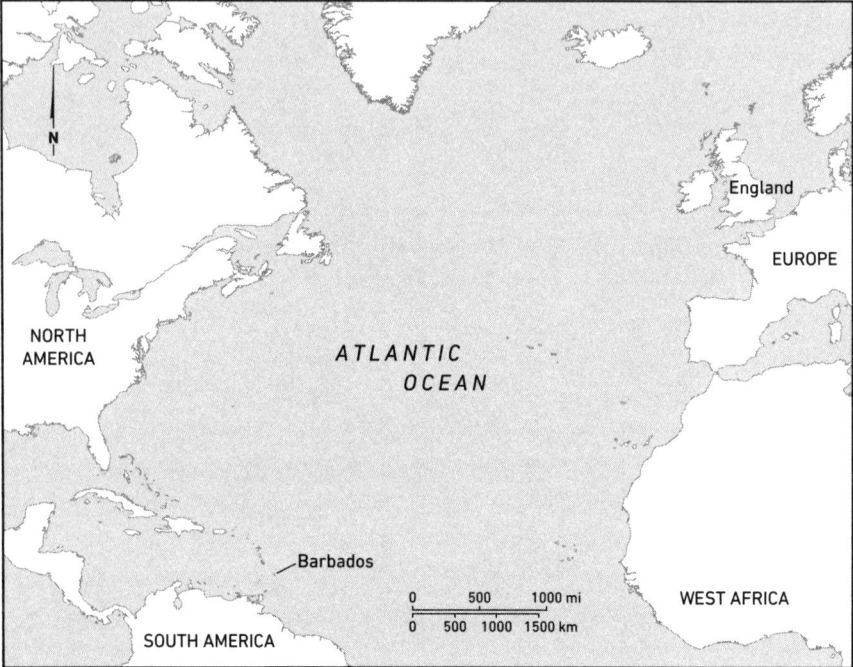

The North Atlantic World

Introduction

A BARBADOS FAMILY

THE WOMAN LATER KNOWN AS Susannah Mingo probably crossed the Atlantic Ocean twice. The first time, she would have been in her early adolescence, squeezed aboard a Portuguese slaver, crammed below decks with hundreds of others, some of whom spoke her language, most of whom did not. Before her forced march in shackles to the West African shoreline, she might not even have seen the ocean. Trapped in an overcrowded vessel rolling and roiling with the swell of the sea's unpredictable waves, she would not have known where she was going or what would happen to her. Inside the cramped ship rumors undoubtedly circulated among the shackled captives, who spoke different languages and who had been ripped away from their homes and torn apart from their families. Nothing about the experience would have suggested that anything other than continued suffering or death awaited her.

If it was like most Middle Passage voyages, she would have tossed for weeks on the forbidding dark waters, the empty expanse stretching to the horizon in every direction. Marking time would have been hard, but the people on her ship may have watched the moon move through its phases, using its waxing and waning to count how many weeks or months had passed before land finally came into view.[1] Drawing close to the coast as darkness fell, Susannah might have made out tall palms on the hills above the shoreline. The saltwater likely splashed her face as a small boat carried her and about twenty others from their ship to the shore. The men in charge would have jumped out and pulled the vessel forward onto the sand. When Susannah stepped out of the boat the warmth and humidity of the still air would have enveloped her. This was Barbados, the place where Susannah would be bound in slavery for the next two decades.

The second time Susannah Mingo crossed the Atlantic Ocean she headed east. Permitted to move around the ship and no longer shackled, this time she was accompanied by her three young children—Judith, Richard, and Hester. A fellow enslaved woman, Elizabeth, a white servant, Dorothy Spendlove, and eight other children—some enslaved, some free, all under the age of twelve— completed the traveling party. The children's father was there too. John Peers, Barbados's largest landowner, enslaver of almost 200 people, and member of the island's council, was making his way back home. With his second wife dead and buried, and both wives' older children already in England for their educations, business affairs demanded his return to London. And so, in the summer of 1686, he set sail for the metropole, bringing his "great and numerous family" with him.[2]

This time Susannah knew her destination. On this voyage she could understand what the sailors said to one another and to her. The cargo on this vessel likely comprised sugar, indigo, and other colonial goods, not human beings.[3] For almost twenty years Susannah had known a life in bondage on Barbados. Now she found herself headed for foreign soil yet again, surely uncertain about what that future might hold. In the Caribbean she and her children were enslaved and had no expectation of ever living a life in freedom. Would the same be true in England?

WE KNOW ABOUT Susannah's journeys from a series of disparate archives located in Barbados and England. The surviving parish records for seventeenth-century Barbados are held in the National Archives, which sit halfway up a hill, just below the University of the West Indies campus, in the southwest of the island. Housed in a nineteenth-century stone building are four thick, heavy, red-leather-bound ledgers that include records of the births, deaths, and marriages of island occupants who lived almost four centuries ago. Inside the Christ Church Parish register a churchwarden recorded in tidy looped handwriting how few people of color (free or enslaved) were baptized between 1650 and 1700.

Only fifty-seven of the roughly 4,000 baptisms were marked with the word "negro" or "mulatto." Even less frequently was the additional adjective "free" attached to a name.[4] And yet, in the middle of the compendium, a series of entries clustered at the top of the right-hand page listed six enslaved children baptized on the same day, 13 August 1683. Their names appeared just after another three presumably white children, all nine fathered by the same man, prominent Barbados planter and enslaver John Peers:

> Frances 6 yrs, Ann 4 yrs, John 2½ yrs, children of John Peers
>   begotten of Dorothy Spendlove
>
> Judith 8½ yrs, Richard 5 yrs, Hester 2½ yrs, children of John Peers
>   begotten of a mulatto woman named Susannah
>
> Richard 7 yrs, Elizabeth 4 yrs, Edward 1½ yrs, children of John Peers
>   begotten of a mulatto woman named Elizabeth.[5]

That John Peers fathered children with women he enslaved was unremarkable in Barbados's slave society. His recognition of his paternity, however, was unusual. Barbados prohibited Christianizing enslaved people by the early 1680s, so this act, at best, directly contravened those rules.[6] The inclusion of John's name meant that he could not hide his offspring. Perhaps, as one of the island's most eminent enslavers, he saw no need to adhere to social norms. From his opulent "Rendezvous Mancon House" (the larger of his two plantations and his primary residence) John wielded considerable political and social capital.[7] His prominence on the island meant that the three women who bore his children lived and labored in close proximity to the epicenter of colonial power.

Other truths about John and his relationships with the women emerge from the Christ Church Parish register. The ages of the children reveal that they were conceived in rotation—first Susannah, then Elizabeth, then Dorothy gave birth. The cycle repeated a second time, and then again once more. John moved among the three in what seemed to be a deliberate pattern. And these were not the only women who bore John's offspring. Other entries in the baptism records reveal two additional women—John's English wives. Between 1668 and 1676 five children of "John and Hester Peers," were born in Barbados. Four years later three children, born to "John and Frances Peers," arrived in quick succession in 1682, 1684, and 1685.[8]

Hester had her last child after the birth of Susannah's and Elizabeth's first. She could not have been ignorant of the fact that her husband was their father. By September 1678 Hester was dead, buried "in the Chancell" of St. Michael's

John Peers's entry in the 1680 Barbados census showing the 910 acres, 180 enslaved people, and 8 white servants he claimed as his property. CO1/44 fol. 47.
Image reproduced by permission of the National Archives, London.

Church in the colony's capital. Frances was pregnant with her middle daughter in August 1683, when the baptisms of the other women's children took place. Like Hester she must have been aware of John's paternity. Frances died shortly after the birth of her third child in 1685. She was buried alongside Hester in a manner befitting the wife "of the Honorable Jno Peers Esqr."[9]

But what of the three women in the 1683 baptism record? The 1680 Barbados census (held 4,200 miles away across the Atlantic Ocean in the National Archives in Kew, England), reveals that Susannah, Elizabeth, and Dorothy were part of a labor force of 180 enslaved Africans and eight white servants who toiled on John's estates. Unlike the majority of the enslaved workers on Rendezvous who were tasked with the backbreaking work of producing sugar, these women worked inside the plantation home as domestics. Dorothy was white, possibly island born, and likely a servant. Susannah and Elizabeth were enslaved women most probably from West Africa. Given John's propensity for illegally trading with Portuguese slavers, their Middle Passage may have ended in a cloak-and-dagger transaction on the island's east coast.[10] Because they labored inside the Rendezvous "Mancon House," Susannah, Elizabeth, and Dorothy were forced into close proximity with each other and, while they were alive, with John's wives, Hester and Frances. Inside the Peers household, these women reckoned daily with the fact that their children were the half siblings of free boys and girls. They also had to navigate John's sexual predation at every turn.

In 1689 John died. His will, written and processed in London, with a copy sent to Barbados, made provisions for the women and children. While leaving money to Dorothy was not an altogether uncommon move, the bequests to Susannah, Elizabeth, and their sons and daughters were extremely unusual.[11] In most cases enslaved individuals appeared in the wills of Barbados enslavers as property to be disbursed, not as inheritors of property themselves. The document also revealed second names for the enslaved women and their children: Elizabeth was "Elizabeth Ashcroft"; Susannah, "Susannah Mingo, a Black." It remained silent, however, on their bonded status. John did not refer to their manumission, but neither did the document suggest that he considered them or their children to still be enslaved. The second names provide additional clues about the women's backgrounds and, just as importantly, allow the lives of their daughters and sons to be traced beyond John's household.

John's will was produced in England where he died. In April 1686 his fellow council members granted him permission to travel to London to settle some pressing business affairs. It was on this trip that Dorothy, Susannah, Elizabeth, and their children left the Rendezvous plantation. Later Chancery Court records explain how, upon their arrival in London, the large group first lived in the city's new and fashionable West End before taking up residence in a grand manor house five miles south in the small village of Streatham. In his will, John left each of his "naturall born" children—the term used to describe illegitimate offspring in the seventeenth century—a small inheritance and the right to an apprenticeship. These transplants found ways to survive and perhaps even thrive in the capital city.

Drawing on scattered transatlantic records, *The Women of Rendezvous* tells the story of five women—Hester Tomkyns, Susannah Mingo, Elizabeth Ashcroft, Dorothy Spendlove, and Frances Knights (née Atkins)—all linked through the Barbados plantation where they first encountered one another. Together they bore at least eighteen children fathered by John. These women labored in enslavement and servitude, served John as wives, died early, sailed to England, raised their own daughters and sons as well as their half siblings, and fought for their legacies. Understanding their experiences thus reveals how patriarchy and power intersected in the early modern English world. Their lives also show the multivariant ways that enslavement and freedom manifested not only in Barbados, but at the center of England's empire itself.

John Peers

1645–1689

Hester Tomkyns	Susannah Mingo	Elizabeth Ashcroft	Dorothy Spendlove	Frances Atkins
(English)	(enslaved "negro"/	(enslaved "negro"/	(English, status	(English)
b. ?	"mulatto"/ "black")	"mulatto")	unclear)	b. 1660
m. ca. 1664	b. ?	b. ?	b. ?	m. ca. 1682
d. 1678	d. 1726	d. 1729	d. sometime	d. 1685
			after 1719	

b. born
ca. circa
d. died
m. married

———

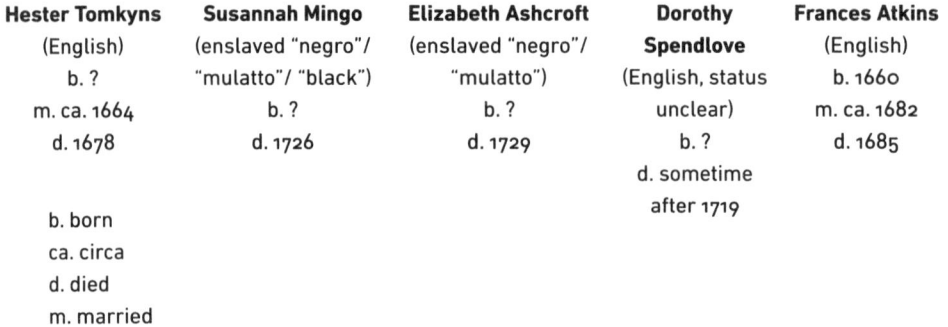

The women with whom John Peers had children.

BARBADOS WAS ENGLAND'S first slave society. Located on the easternmost edge of the Caribbean Sea, the tiny island (fewer than 170 square miles) was often the first land that ships sailing west from Africa sighted after their long transatlantic voyage. For this reason, captains found it both an important first port of call for restocking fresh water and food supplies, and a much-needed geographical marker on entering the tropics. Although the Portuguese named the island in the sixteenth century, other European powers largely ignored Barbados until the English staked their claim to the territory in 1627. Unlike the islands of the Greater Antilles, or even those of the Leeward Lesser Antilles, Barbados is, by Caribbean standards, relatively flat. Presumed to be uninhabited at the time the English began their colonization project, the colony's terrain was covered in dense forest that proved challenging to clear. Within a few years, small English settlements sprang up in Holetown on the west coast, Oistins on the south coast, and Bridgetown (the eventual location of the capital) in the southwest.

In its first decades, colonial leaders and colonizers struggled to identify a successful crop. First tobacco then cotton failed to meet expectations. Sugar—brought to the island by Native Americans from Suriname—grew exceptionally well, however processing it into a sellable commodity proved beyond coloniz-ers' abilities. By the second half of the seventeenth century, however, these early setbacks were forgotten. In the 1640s, enslaved Africans with experience in Per-nambuco, Brazil, were brought to Barbados by Dutch enslavers, carrying their know-how on refining sugar with them. Soon Barbados produced more wealth than all of England's American colonies combined.[12] It became the prime desti-nation for Englishmen seeking to get rich quickly.

Initially indentured servants from England, Ireland, and Scotland provided the labor needed to produce sugar. Soon, English landowners turned to captives from West Africa who toiled in the production of the "murderous" crop that consumed new arrivals' bodies, and in turn accelerated demand in the transatlantic slave trade.[13] By 1680 enslaved individuals of African descent outnumbered white settlers at least two to one, and women constituted the majority among both the enslaved and the free populations. As a result, white planters invented a legal apparatus of slavery in the colony to instill fear in the enslaved population and assert their dominance. Between the drive for profit and the disregard for human life, Barbados became the place where racial capitalism was practiced and perfected.[14]

If racial capitalism drove imperial economies in the early modern era, then, as Jennifer Morgan has shown, women's bodies were the vehicles through which the system was born. The concept of maternal inheritance, *partus sequitur ventrem* (that which is brought forth follows the belly), adopted in practice in the Caribbean—although not codified into law—flipped European ideas about lineage on their head.[15] In this practice one's mother, not one's father, defined a person's status. This meant that white women reproduced freedom while enslaved women reproduced bondage. Linked by the patriarch the women (enslaved and free) had in common, both lines of inheritance operated in the Rendezvous household.

Historians of the English Caribbean have usually focused on the family to explore how complex networks of obligation and affection shaped politics and society in the English Empire and at home. Other scholarship that draws on genealogy in less explicit ways examines planters within their households, centering their roles as patriarchs to uncover the racial and gendered dynamics of the plantation. Beyond these works, scholars of Atlantic history have asked how family as a category of analysis helps illuminate the intimate spheres of colonialism, offering new perspectives on the development of empires that center personal and kinship relationships rather than focusing on imperial policies alone.[16]

Meanwhile historians of slavery generally approach the family with an understanding of the difficulty (if not near impossibility) of tracing genealogical connections among enslaved Africans. For people taken captive in West Africa and sold into slavery (like those who labored on the Rendezvous estate), maintaining, restoring, or creating familial ties was curtailed by the trauma and dislocation engendered by the Middle Passage. In the colonies, the practice of maternal inheritance additionally impeded enslaved individuals' ability to pursue family. In such circumstances, blood did not always connote belonging.[17]

Weaving these disparate threads of enquiry together, *The Women of Rendezvous* reveals the multiple ways that family could both mend and tear apart the social fabric of the early modern English world. Within the Rendezvous household the presence of John's enslaved children meant that their father would find it extremely difficult to ignore the implications of the inheritability of slavery. He understood that Susannah's and Elizabeth's progeny increased his property, potentially in perpetuity. At the same time, his decision to recognize his "naturall born" sons and daughters put his "legitimate" children's inheritance at risk. Although he bequeathed to his children with Hester and Frances significantly more than he did to his sons and daughters with Susannah and Elizabeth, by providing for their half sisters and brothers at all, John placed his paternity over the Barbados custom of maternal inheritance.

And yet, maternal inheritance, especially in a colony where women (African and English) made up the majority of the population, was central to building England's empire.[18] Mastery and control in Barbados were managed through elite white women's bodies in the legitimacy they brought to husbands when they wed, and on the freedom guaranteed to their children when they gave birth.[19] In this way, they were the vehicles through which whiteness was reproduced and maintained in the colonies. Frances and Hester birthed *only* white, free children. When he fathered children with Susannah and Elizabeth, John's offspring were not white and were, by virtue of their mother's status, enslaved. His mixed-race progeny imperiled whiteness on Barbados. Frances's children (and Hester's before her) protected it.

At the same time, Susannah's, Elizabeth's and Dorothy's children's decision to take their mothers' names directly challenged the concept of patriarchal power. While all the children inherited property from their father, none of them sought to benefit from the use of his family name. Once John had died and the question of enslavement faded, for Susannah's and Elizabeth's offspring, their mothers were the source now of their freedom rather than of their enslavement.[20] For Dorothy's children, their determined use of "Spendlove" turned their illegitimate start in life on its head.

Much of John's power lay in the women who helped him build his household. His wives provided money, respectability, and "legitimate" heirs. The enslaved women's productive and reproductive labor enhanced his property. The English servant's presence sustained a hierarchy of raced labor on the Rendezvous plantation. As these relationships suggest, family reveals the perverse and insidious nature of colonialism when it is reduced to its most intimate setting.[21]

WHEN ENGLAND BEGAN its Atlantic colonial endeavors in the sixteenth century, the small nation on the edge of Europe had little clout on the international stage. Spanish efforts in the Americas and Pacific and Portuguese incursions along the western coast of the African continent and into the Indian Ocean made these nations dominant among western European would-be colonizers. Although the Elizabethan era marked the beginning of England's ventures in slaving and settler colonialism, it would not be until the mid-seventeenth century that they were able to challenge their Iberian counterparts. Failure, more than success, was the hallmark of attempts to establish footholds in Nova Scotia, the Carolinas, and Virginia.[22]

Despite these early setbacks and a violent and bloody civil war in the 1640s, by the time the Crown was restored in 1660, England was on the cusp of becoming a major player on the imperial stage thanks (in no small part) to its recent success in the West Indies. John, who was born on Barbados, but who received his education in England, returned to the island in the mid-1660s. Perfectly positioned to take advantage of the sugar boom and recent advances in the slave trade, and with familial business partners in London who facilitated trading networks, his success was all but guaranteed.

Testifying to the rise of England's imperial ambition was the rapid expansion of its capital city. In 1600 there were about 200,000 people residing in London, doubling its population since 1550. By a century later that figure had skyrocketed to almost 600,000.[23] Several factors account for the rise. First, widespread outbreaks of plague were effectively nonexistent after 1665. Second, a general rise in birthrates and a drop in mortality fueled population growth. At this time, thousands of people migrated to London from around the country. And an increased demand for sailors, shipwrights, caulkers, ropemakers, carpenters, sailmakers, and dockworkers to service the colonial trade resulted in new faces at the quays along the Thames. Migrants from the Netherlands and France as well as North Africa and sub-Saharan regions of the continent made London an increasingly cosmopolitan city. Merchants, traders, and laborers from the Middle and Far East also contributed to the heterogeneity of the metropole.

By 1700 the non-white population of England's capital stood at around 20,000. Other important sites of colonial trade like Bristol had similarly diverse populations. Thus, when the women and children of Rendezvous arrived in London in 1686, they entered a world with its own racial and gendered frameworks, ones that were developed in England itself.[24] The structures of hierarchy and power that shaped the metropole were no less insidious than those in Barbados and similarly dictated the relative positions of John, the women, and his many children.

We might assume that in bringing his "great and numerous family" with him to England that John literally brought the colonies home. Such an assumption ignores the fact that race-based hierarchies and the practice of slavery permeated the metropole.[25] Barbados may have been England's first slave society, but England had been a society with slaves for some decades before Susannah, Elizabeth, and their children arrived on London's docks.[26] A careful accounting of the infrastructure of enslavement in England itself—fine metal collars around the necks of young Black boys, runaway advertisements in the newspapers, royal masques centered on Black or African characters, slave ships crowding the quaysides, the king gifting enslaved children to his many mistresses—demonstrates the ways that slavery was a persistent and unremarkable institution in the heart of empire.[27]

IF THE MEANS through which the story of the women of Rendezvous and their children came to light is atypical, the lives of Susannah, Elizabeth, Dorothy, Hester, and Frances were not.[28] While many scholars have written about the relationships among and between enslavers and enslaved women across the Americas, few are centered on the seventeenth-century English world. In large part this is because of false assumptions about the kinds of evidence available in English-language archives whose colonial holdings tend to focus on administrative papers, population censuses, and statutory law. The personal stories, especially those that center marginalized women, seem almost impossible to reconstruct from such records. While the women in this book are not anonymous and in fact have both first and last names, their stories remain full of gaps and ambiguities. It is much harder to tell their stories than it would be to write that of John Peers.

The paragraphs that open this book are a perfect demonstration of the difficulty of narrating enslaved women's lives. The first two are written in the subjunctive and are full of the "likelys," "would-haves," and "possiblys" that make clear all that we cannot know about Susannah's journey to, and arrival in, Barbados. The second two are in the simple past tense because the evidence for her travel to London is more definitive. The certainty is possible in no small part because at the time Susannah was intimately connected to an elite white man who left a much clearer trail of his movements, and what precipitated them, in the records. Because we know about him, we learn more about her.[29]

When the prism through which we explore colonialism is the family, sources beyond those devoted to imperial management become more significant. These records were collected and maintained because they document inheritance and genealogy. They are the means through which men, especially fathers, exercised dominance in life and extended their control over the family in death. In this instance, a series of cases in England's Chancery Court—a relatively archaic and complicated civil legal system that mostly adjudicated inheritance disputes—exposes the complex relationships among those involved in the conflict over the Barbados estate. Because these documents obscure the racial backgrounds of some of the plaintiffs and omit the fact that many of them began their lives in slavery, the Chancery records would remain useless if they were not read in conjunction with church registers, wills, and deeds generated in Barbados. Putting these archives into conversation, *The Women of Rendezvous* confronts questions of generational wealth and inheritance (of property and of enslaved status), examines the operation of race and slavery in the colonies *and* in the metropole, and considers how intimate relationships underwrote imperial hierarchies. In short, it shows how family made England's first empire.

But focusing on family alone distorts reality. In Barbados, women—enslaved *and* free—constituted the majority of the population, and yet many histories of colonialism on the island push women to the margins. Other work on relationships between white planters and enslaved or servant women centers the perspectives of white men and fails to fully address the underlying issues of consent that marked their intimate encounters. In these works, women are acted on, rarely actors themselves.[30] By framing this story from the women's viewpoint, *The Women of Rendezvous* flips the dominant scholarly narrative on its head. Inverting perspective by centering women highlights the gendered power dynamics of enslavement and servitude. Not only does it force a reckoning with questions of consent, but it reveals how gendered and racial hierarchies shaped the women's encounters with the planter and their interactions with one another. By fully addressing the positions elite, servant, and enslaved women occupied in Barbados *and* in England, this book shows how women, more than men, were the vehicles through which colonialism, slavery, and the whiteness that undergirded it all were built and maintained.

THE WOMEN OF RENDEZVOUS is organized around the lives of the women who birthed children fathered by John Peers. The first half of the book is set in the Caribbean. Introducing Barbados through Hester's eyes—the land, the enslaved population, the labor they performed, and the organization of the household—reveals plantation hierarchies and underscores how power operated at every level on the estate. Susannah's perspective centers the tensions and pressures of the forced intimacy that connected the women through their shared status as bearers of John's children. Conception, pregnancy, and parturition looked very different for each of the women, all of whom experienced some degree of coerced sex. Married, widowed, and remarried in Barbados, and birthing three daughters before succumbing to death herself, Frances lived a life that offers an opportunity to explore how the reverberations from such personal life events shaped the largest forces of colonialism. Emphasizing the making and breaking of familial ties and kin relationships in both enslaved and enslaver communities shows how the construction of intimate bonds on the one hand, and inheritance and loss—of blood, kin, or property—on the other, underpinned England's imperial ambitions.

The second half of the book familiarizes readers with late seventeenth-century England through Dorothy's eyes, establishing that far from importing ideas about race and hierarchy into the metropole, the heart of empire was already steeped in anti-Black racism. It shows that enslavement, while not the experience of all people of African descent in London, was nevertheless deeply engrained and normalized in the city. Following Elizabeth on her quest to secure control over her inheritance through the Chancery Court challenges our expectations of what marginalized and raced figures could achieve in early modern England. Finally, Susannah's mixed-race daughter, Judith, illuminates the lives of the children's generation in London and highlights the ways their mothers' status shaped their opportunities. Focusing on the persistence with which the women and their children pursued their inheritances, their experiences beyond Barbados, and the ways their lives continued to mingle in the metropole reveals the precarity of freedom at the center of Britain's rapidly expanding empire.

Barbados's slave society and England's society with slaves were deeply intertwined. Moving from one to the other shifted the possibilities for the women who bore John's children and their progeny. Slavery in Barbados shaped every aspect of society—for those brought to the island as captives, or born to enslaved mothers, there was no relief. In England, slavery was one among many forms of labor, and African heritage did not equal a lifetime of bondage. That fact, however, did not make anti-Black sentiment or hierarchies of race less extreme.

In the fissures between these two worlds, Susannah, Elizabeth, Dorothy, and their children forged lives very different from those they might have anticipated when they lived in the Rendezvous household. Hester and Frances, as wealthy, well-connected women, made good wives. In marrying John they cemented his prominence and used their capital to grow the Barbados estates. They lived on Rendezvous at a time when England's investment in the transatlantic slave trade grew, and as the country's imperial ambitions reached new heights. They, just as much as the man they married, were key to their family's, and therefore the empire's, success. Between them they bore nine children, six of whom survived to adulthood, together creating the next generation of legitimate Peers heirs. And yet no son or daughter of Hester or Frances would ever take charge of the Rendezvous estate. As much as *The Women of Rendezvous* demonstrates that family, patriarchy, and the rise of racial slavery intersected to create the early modern English transatlantic world, it also reveals how the intimacies of empire sometimes created unexpected outcomes for the women and children caught in its web.

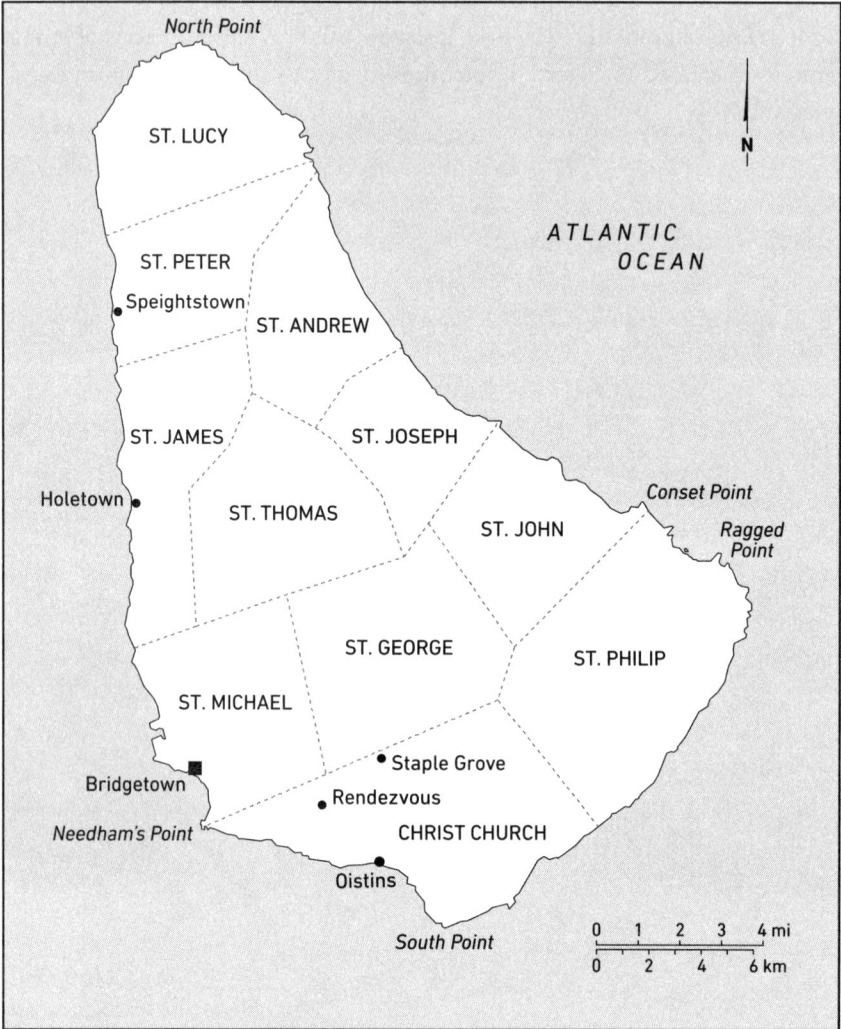

North Point

ST. LUCY

ST. PETER

Speightstown

ST. ANDREW

ST. JAMES

ST. JOSEPH

Holetown

ST. THOMAS

ST. JOHN

Conset Point

Ragged
Point

ST. GEORGE

ST. PHILIP

ST. MICHAEL

Staple Grove

Bridgetown

Rendezvous

Needham's Point

CHRIST CHURCH

Oistins

South Point

ATLANTIC
OCEAN

N

| 0 | 1 | 2 | 3 | 4 mi |
| 0 | 2 | 4 | | 6 km |

Barbados

CHAPTER 1

The Place Called Rendezvous

WHAT HESTER PEERS made of Rendezvous when she first arrived on the plantation in 1666 is unclear. She may have been transfixed by its location on a hilltop overlooking the southern coast of Barbados with clear views of the white sandy beaches that ringed the island's shores, contrasting dramatically with the translucent turquoise Caribbean Sea. She might have compared it to the lush green rolling hills and oak forests of the Herefordshire of her childhood, and wondered at the heat, humidity, and palm trees that marked this new and foreign landscape. In place of neat fields of wheat, oats, and barley were acre upon acre of sugarcane that seemed to run as far as the eye could see. Perhaps the scale of the estate—600 acres—seemed impossibly grand.

The "Mancon House," however, was not nearly so well maintained as her family's Tudor-era residence in Weobley, and its condition was precisely why she found herself 4,000 miles from home on the western side of the Atlantic Ocean. Just a few years prior, Hester, daughter of a Knight of the Realm and member of Parliament, married John Peers, heir to the Rendezvous plantation. As "a person of very great quality," she brought a considerable dowry to her

marriage, one specifically dedicated to improving the ramshackle sugar plantation and providing "all things suitable" for the newlyweds' "appearances in
the sayd Island of Barbadoes." If the plantation needed work when she arrived,
soon renovations would transform "the seate or dwelling house" into a "very
large and Beautifull" home.[1]

Hester could not have failed to note that nearly all the people whom she
observed laboring in the sugarcane fields were enslaved Africans. She may have
been familiar with people of African descent before she arrived in the Americas,
as she probably sailed from London or Bristol when she traveled with John to
Barbados, and both cities had African inhabitants, especially men who labored
at port docks.[2] But the demography she encountered on Barbados was very different from that of England. With a growing enslaved majority, the island was
increasingly West African.[3]

On Rendezvous, Hester encountered only a handful of European servants
and scores of enslaved Africans. These were the women, men, and children who
weeded, manured, and harvested the sugar growing in the fields. They were the
workers who put the canes through the sugar mills, squeezing the robust, thick
stalks to release the sweet juices that would run into the hot and suffocating
boiling house. These were the laborers who skimmed impurities from the tops
of the boiling cauldrons of liquid, waiting for the precise moment at which to
begin the cooling process and shape the soft brown crystals into cones to be sold
as muscovado sugar back in England.

The sugar that supported the Rendezvous plantation, and Hester and her
family by extension, was the "liquid gold" that ensured the success of England's
transatlantic endeavors in the seventeenth century. More significant than the
tobacco that was coming out of Virginia, or the rice that would soon be grown
on vast plantations in the Carolinas, sugar provided the capital that drove
England's imperial ambitions and created almost unimaginable wealth for the
families who claimed land on the small island. The eye-popping profits engendered by sugar production were made possible only by a simultaneous and
more insidious investment in human property. The system of enslavement that
was built on the commodification of people and the forced transportation of
millions of West and West Central Africans to the Americas was the bedrock on
which the plantation complex, and therefore the English Empire, rested.[4]

Rendezvous was no different from most Barbados sugar estates. Paying
attention to how it came to be the place that Hester encountered in the mid-
1660s reveals the early modern Atlantic world in microcosm. The shift to a sugar
monoculture on the Peers plantation was mirrored around the English West
Indies. Millions of enslaved people were forcibly transported to the Caribbean

through the same means by which they arrived on Rendezvous. The innumerable repetitive and tiring tasks that enslaved laborers performed in the sugarcane fields, in the artisan workshops, and in the plantation house were replicated across Barbados. And the hierarchies that developed among and between enslavers, servants, and the enslaved on the Christ Church Parish estate were the very ones that shaped England's first slave society.

THE LAND

Rendezvous entered the historical record in August 1640 as the property of a Captain Lancelot Pace. Appraised at "360 acres of land," much of the estate was under construction. The property's inventory noted that it included "one dwelling house boarded," "one cotton house boarded all over," "one frame house," and one unfinished "Mancon house two storeys high." In addition, there were two store houses, forty and fifty feet long respectively, a mill house, and a pigeon house occupied by six pairs of pigeons. Also listed as part of the Rendezvous estate were hoes, lamps, axes, iron pots, weights, benches, wood, lathes, water tubs, thirteen "old cowes," "sixteene heifers," two bulls, and seventeen servants with anywhere between three and a half months, and six years still to serve.[5]

Sometime thereafter, Rendezvous switched hands. It became the property of John's father, Richard Peers. Richard, one of the earliest English settlers on Barbados, married Marie Pace, a female relation of Lancelot Pace, in 1640. At some point, the property transferred from one man to the other, and by the time of Richard's death in 1661, Rendezvous had increased considerably in size, to 600 acres. Its labor force had also radically transformed. No longer did the workforce comprise only indentured servants. Now the overwhelming majority of those who worked the land were enslaved men, women, and children from West Africa.[6]

The transformation of Rendezvous mirrors the general transition Barbados plantations underwent between the founding of the colony in 1627 and the 1650s. Initially, English settlers worked to grow tobacco and cotton, but their crops rarely brought the kinds of profits they desired. For one thing, in its first decade the island remained dominated by rainforest that had to be cleared in order to plant—no small hardship given that many of the hardwoods were more than ninety feet tall.[7] Richard Ligon, who visited the island in the 1640s and managed a sugar plantation, wrote that "the Woods were so thick and most of the Trees so large and massive, as they were not to be falne with so few hands." These same trees had branches "so thick and boisterous, as required more help" and demanded "strong and active men to lop and remove them off the ground," many of whom would have been enslaved.[8] This topography meant that the acreage of land that could be devoted to growing cash crops was small.

Any tobacco that colonists did succeed in growing was generally considered to be of poor quality and no match for Virginia- or Bermuda-produced tobacco. In 1637 planter Peter Hay realized that a change was necessary when his brother in London informed him, "Your tobaco of Barbados of all the tobaco that cometh to England is accompted the worst." About a decade later, Ligon concurred, noting that "the Tobacco that grew there, so earthy and worthlesse, as it could give them little or no return from *England*, or elsewhere." When English settlers switched to cotton, they fared little better. In 1640, the same year that Lancelot Pace had Rendezvous assessed, Hay lamented the poor state of the return on cotton when he wrote to his brother, "This yeare hath beene so baise a cotton yeare that the inhabitants hath not maide so much cotton as will buye necessaries for there servants."[9] The "cotton house" on Rendezvous no doubt reflects the shift to growing the fiber, but like Hay, Pace may have found his profits lacking.

During the following decade, Barbados underwent a complete transformation in what some scholars have dubbed the "Sugar Revolution."[10] In the space of ten years, sugarcane transformed from a marginal crop grown by a handful of planters for the purpose of making a "refreshing drink" to the only plant that landowners on the island were interested in cultivating. The reasons behind the shift were myriad, but changes on the ground were precipitated by the skyrocketing demand for sugar in Europe. Once a luxury enjoyed primarily by society's elites, by the seventeenth century sugar was fast becoming an opiate of the masses. Used as a condiment in both savory and sweet dishes, sugar was also utilized as a medicinal cure for all kinds of ailments, and it became ubiquitous as the sweetener of bitter colonial beverages such as coffee, tea, and chocolate.

Sugarcane was first introduced to Barbados in 1627 by Native Americans from Suriname who knew how to grow the cane although the means to process it into highly profitable sugar appears to have remained a mystery. In the 1640s, Dutch settlers with experience in Pernambuco, Brazil, came to Barbados, bringing their enslaved workforce, who had the necessary know-how on refining, with them. This knowledge spread quickly, and planters soon turned fields dedicated to tobacco and cotton into sugarcane zones. In a climate perfectly suited to year-round planting and harvesting, and with Europe's insatiable demands exacerbated by warfare that reduced the supply of sugar from Brazil, planters in Barbados were perfectly placed to step into the market and to profit on a scale scarcely imaginable only a few years previously.[11] By 1661, when Richard Peers died, Rendezvous had grown to 600 acres, and the property included "cogs and

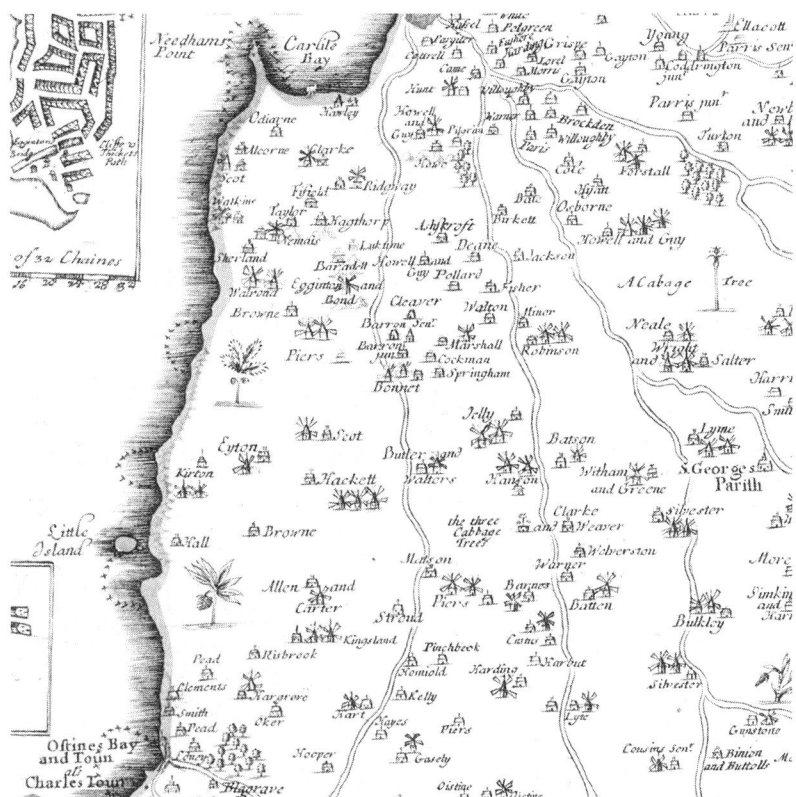

Detail from Richard Ford's 1674 map of Barbados showing the location of the plantations held by John Peers (spelled "Piers" on the map). Rendezvous is the more westerly plantation, and Staple Grove is slightly to the east. Peers also held land on the coast and in Bridgetown. Courtesy of the John Carter Brown Library, Providence, RI.

stills" and "sugar pots," indicating the plantation's full conversion to sugarcane production. Moreover, Richard bequeathed over 120,000 pounds of sugar to various family members, executors, and servants, to be paid out within two years of his death, demonstrating that by 1661 Rendezvous was one of the most productive and profitable estates on the island.[12]

Richard Peers came to own Rendezvous through familial ties that made him kin to some of England's most ambitious and formidable colonial entrepreneurs. While his birthplace in England and where he lived in the early years of his life are unknown, in 1623 he married Susan Hawley, the daughter of a prominent Middlesex gentleman, in St. Clement Danes Parish in London. Susan was the sister of Henry Hawley, one of Barbados's earliest settlers, who sailed to the island in 1629 intending to stake a claim for his patron, the Earl of Carlisle, to whom Charles I had recently granted a land patent. After successfully fighting off a competing claim from the Earl of Pembroke, Henry reaped his reward, becoming governor in 1630. That same year, Richard and Susan arrived in the colony, where shortly thereafter Richard secured a prominent political role of his own. He served as lieutenant governor of Barbados between 1631 and 1638 and acted as interim governor when his brother-in-law traveled to England in 1633 and 1635.[13]

In 1636, Henry appointed Richard president of the Barbados Council. The council was the most prestigious political body in Barbados, its membership conferred in the name of the king (and approved by the monarch) rather than by election in the manner of members of the island's colonial assembly. The council assisted the royal governor in ruling the island and ensured that the interests of large landowners were protected by approving legislation passed by the assembly. During his tenure Richard adjudicated personal disputes (sentencing one council member to death for murdering another), approved land grants, and presided over the decision made by the council in 1636 "that Negroes and Indians, that came here to be sold, should serve for Life, unless a Contract was made before to the contrary."[14] At the same time, he (like other close confederates of Henry Hawley) amassed a property portfolio that would eventually make him a very wealthy man.

Richard's marriage to Susan Hawley certainly placed him in close proximity to early Barbados powerbrokers, but it was his marriage to his second wife, Marie, that appears to have given him access to Rendezvous. Sometime between 1630, when Susan and Richard arrived in Barbados, and the end of the decade, Susan died. In January 1640 Richard married Marie Payce in St. Nicholas Cole Abbey in London. Peers returned to Barbados with his new wife shortly thereafter, arriving in the midst of an investigation into the means through which Hawley and his intimates had secured their colonial property. Among those listed in a 1640 assessment of Barbados land claims was Captain Lancelot Pace and his 360-acre plantation named Rendezvous. Pace died sometime between 1647 and 1655, leaving a will that he allegedly dictated but did not sign. While the document did not mention Rendezvous, Marie was a relation of Lancelot, and it appears the connection accounts for how the plantation ended up in Richard Peers's possession.[15]

Richard's wives gave him political connections and access to property, but just as significant were their roles as mothers to at least five children.[16] Susan gave birth to her first daughter, and namesake, in London, just one year after she married Richard. Between 1624 and her death, she bore at least two more daughters, Mary and Elizabeth. Marie birthed two sons in Barbados, John and

Edward, born in 1645 and 1648, respectively. Richard's daughters all appeared to marry well. His eldest child, Susan, was residing on thirty acres in Barbados with her husband when her father died. Mary married Nicholas Boate and lived on an estate in Braintree, Essex. Elizabeth, the youngest child, probably born on Barbados, married another Barbados planter, John Ashcroft, with whom she had a daughter, Peirce in 1659. Their family resided in the same parish as Rendezvous, Christ Church.[17]

Meanwhile John and his brother Edward, both born in Barbados, appear to have been educated in England. They would have resided in the metropole during the turbulent years of the English Interregnum (1649–60). In this decade, King Charles I was beheaded, and the parliamentarian and puritan Oliver Cromwell ruled the Kingdoms of England, Scotland and Ireland, adopting the title "Protector." These countries were riven by the split between those who continued to support the monarchy (Cavaliers) and those who thought England should be a republic ruled by politicians (Roundheads). Although John and Edward were being trained to be the primary inheritors of Richard's Caribbean property, they could not have failed to note the dangerous political circumstances their family had to navigate.[18]

During this period Richard took on an important diplomatic role as part of the efforts to quell factional fighting in Barbados following the English Civil War. Although colonists in the West Indies initially sought to remain neutral and avoid further conflict, by the early 1650s Royalist Francis Lord Willoughby (a former supporter of parliamentarian forces) became governor of Barbados. When Parliament sent Sir George Ayscue to blockade the island in late 1651 in an attempt to bring it under Roundhead control, Richard, now "Sir Rich. Pearce" was sent as one of the emissaries "with full powers to treat and conclude" a peace that would "prevent the calamities and effusion of Christian blood which follow a civil war." By 1656, Richard, now serving in the Barbados Assembly, signed his name to a joint "Address to the Protector" that sought to demonstrate the Barbados government's loyalty to Cromwell. When Charles II was restored to the throne in 1660, he appointed Richard to the Barbados Council once again.[19] As a man with a knighthood and as a shrewd navigator of colonial politics during decades of turmoil and war, Richard possessed a political savvy allowing him to remain in the highest echelons of power in Barbados. It also ensured that he maintained his ever more profitable plantations.

When Richard died in 1661 his older son, John, was left the bulk of his estate, including Rendezvous and a manor in Livers Ocle, Herefordshire, that Richard recently purchased from Walter Pye, Hester Tomkyns's maternal grandfather. Described by his father as "my well beloved son," John was to be Richard's "lawful heyre and Executor," once he reached the age of seventeen. In the meantime, to account for his "young years," a provision in the will stated that Henry Hawley, Col. Edmond Read, and James Hawley were to be "guardians to both my sonnes John and Edward during their nonage." The next five years were eventful for John. He married Hester Tomkyns, became a father, mourned the death of his younger brother, and in 1666, at the age of just twenty-one, set sail with Hester for Barbados. [20]

Hester not only brought a considerable dowry to her marriage; she also connected John to a prominent colonial agent, Robert Chaplin, who was married to Hester's sister, Ann. The relationship between the two couples was so close that when John and Hester departed for the Caribbean, they left their first daughter, Mary, to be reared by her aunt and uncle.[21] When the young couple arrived in the colony, they were well placed to improve Rendezvous, set up a household, and build a life for themselves in what had recently become the most sparkling jewel in England's imperial crown.

THE PEOPLE

Hester's arrival in Barbados coincided with a demographic shift that saw the enslaved population of Barbados first match that of European settlers, and then radically outstrip it. By the time of her death in 1678, there were at least two enslaved Africans for every white person on the island, a statistic more than reflected on Rendezvous itself, which, according to the 1680 census, had 180 enslaved laborers and only around a dozen white inhabitants. According to those who knew John, during his time on the island he stocked his estate with "slaves . . . beyond any plantation in the whole Island."[22] Inventories taken fifteen years after John's death demonstrate that almost twice as many enslaved women as men lived and worked on the plantation.

These statistics marked Hester's home as somewhat unusual among large Barbados estates. While women made up a majority of the enslaved population from relatively early in the island's history as a sugar-producing colony, they generally did not outnumber enslaved men two to one. In the 1640s, Ligon noted that planters purchased captives "so as the sexes be equal." A 1673 estimate by Governor Jonathan Atkins bore out Ligon's findings: enslaved men accounted for 31 percent of the population, while enslaved women constituted almost 36 percent in his report.[23] The numbers of women on Rendezvous were in all likelihood higher, given the huge sex-ratio imbalance by 1705. The insatiable demand for labor was not the only factor driving the importation of Africans into Barbados. Extremely high mortality rates and low birth rates accelerated the process.

In the second half of the seventeenth century, the greater part of the enslaved population on Barbados came from West Africa. The vast majority of those who found themselves trapped in this violent system of commodification departed from a region of the continent that stretched from Senegambia to the Bight of Biafra. These captives were transported in ships largely owned by Portuguese, Dutch, and English traders, who loaded their cargoes in the ports of Allada, Ouidah, Anomabu, Grand-Popo, Elmina, Cape Coast, Bonny, and Old Calabar.[24] Ligon noted that captives "are fetch'd from severall parts of *Africa*, who speake severall languages. . . . Some of them are fetch'd from *Guinny* and *Binny*, some from *Cutchew*, some from *Angola*, and some from the River of *Gambra*."[25] The men, women, and children who sailed into the unknown did not come only from the Atlantic littoral. The slave trade drew captives from across the region and from well into the interior. This meant that the diversity of captives transported across the Atlantic was greater than records from departure ports alone suggest.[26]

These trends held true for the Rendezvous plantation. While the specific origin points for the captives purchased by John are unknown, records indicate that he engaged in contraband trade with Portuguese slavers active on the Gold Coast in the middle years of the seventeenth century. John's relationship to these slavers suggests that men, women, and children originally from the Lower Guinea region were well represented on his plantations.[27] However, it was not only through illegal deals that John built his property in people. In 1680 Royal African Company vessel the *John Bonaventure* arrived in Bridgetown from "the Gold Coast and Arda." "John Peers Esquire" purchased sixteen men and five women from this ship at £20 each.[28] The locations are imprecise—the Gold Coast covered a broad swathe of the West African coastline in present-day Ghana, while "Arda" was surely Ardra (also known as Allada), in Benin. Collectively these sources indicate that John purchased captives from a fairly small region of West Africa.

There are other clues that suggest this region's dominance among the enslaved people on Rendezvous. Combining the demography of the trade with naming trends on the plantation indicates the origins of many of the women and men John bought. Inventories from fifteen years after John's death confirm that a large number of enslaved people on Rendezvous had names that were West African in origin—a full half of all those listed in the 1705 enumeration of the estate. Akan day names, such as "Quashy," "Quaco," "Cuffey," "Quasheba," "Cubah," and "Phibbah" (male and female names for Sunday, Wednesday, and Friday, respectively), accounted for around one-quarter of all West African names, suggesting strong links to the Gold Coast region, which correlates both with John's contraband and official trading and with broader demographic trends on Barbados.[29]

The journey to Rendezvous from West Africa was a long and arduous one for captives. Those who traveled on the *John Bonaventure* spent seventy days traversing the Atlantic Ocean. The ship first moved south, toward Cape Lopez in present-day Gabon before heading west to Barbados.[30] These ten weeks at sea were at the upper end of journey times for slave ship crossings to the Caribbean. There are few accounts of these journeys from African perspectives, and none from the seventeenth century. Those from the eighteenth century, such as Olaudah Equiano's, Venture Smith's, Florence Hall's, and 'Sibell's reveal some commonalities that were probably true a century before. Unlike a ship log or sale register, these first-person narratives reveal the full horror of the trade. They recount initial captures, often far from the coast, journeys to the slave forts and castles, first encounters with Europeans, and the continual separation from loved ones and friends (old and new) at every stage in the terrifying process.

Florence described how as a child she was playing in the evening "while at a distance from our houses" somewhere "in the Country of Eboe," when she and her friends were taken. She remembered with pain how "our hands were tied—while in vain our cries and screams were raised, but raised unheard, if heard, unattended."[31] Olaudah had a similar story about being kidnapped by slave raiders as a young boy, being held in bondage in West Africa, then being sold to traders who took him to the coast.[32] Venture recounted how warfare against his father's kingdom had led to his captivity and march to Anamaboo.[33] In an ethnographic account transcribed by a white man named John Ford, 'Sibell remembered being kidnapped by her brother-in-law and how he "carry, carry, carry, carry, carry me all night and day, all night and day way from my Country," to sell her to "de Back-erah [white] people."[34]

Whether taken prisoner in war or snatched from their places of birth by local traders, women, men, and children were marched in coffles to the coast. Many did not survive the journey. Ripped from their places of birth and often separated from family, kin, and friends, most found themselves shackled to a stranger with whom they may or may not have been able to communicate, only to eventually be corralled into one of the sixty or so slave castles that dotted the

---

Facing: *John Bonaventure* sale. John purchased sixteen enslaved men and five enslaved women from the *John Bonaventure* in 1680. The ship's information suggests that they came from the Gold Coast of West Africa. T70/939. Image reproduced by permission of the National Archives, London.

London the 21th October 1680

Barbados the 20th July 1680

Accompt of Sales of neg. on board the John
Bonadventure Capt John Woodfins Comand
from the Gold Coast and Arsta for Acco
of the Royall African Company of England
Viz:

	M	W	B	G	Sugar	£	s	d
Sold Cornwall Somers to pay at Xmas at £30 p head	4					80	00	—
Sold Richd Adamson to pay in 2 mo		1				19	00	—
Sold Coll Sam Newton 9 men & 2 women at £20 p head & 3 boys & girls at £17 Bills by the Ship at 30 daies	14	6	2	1		451	00	—
Sold mr Robt Rivers at £22 p head bills by the Ship at 30 daies	2					44	00	—
Sold Capt John Davies at £21 p head 9 men & 2 women 4 boys and Arsta at £17 p head bills now to goe by the Ship at 30 daies for £200 the Remainder bills payable the Last May next	8	3	2	5		350	00	—
Sold Zacharias Hardstaff to pay in Jan						10	00	—
Sold Abell Poyar to pay on demand	2					28	00	—
Sold Coll Edwd Stedwos at £18 p head bills to goe by the Ship pay at 60 daies	5					90	00	—
Sold Thos Walrond Esq at 20 p head	4					80	00	—
Sold Pett Evans at 20 p head to pay the first of March next	4	2				120	00	—
Sold Jno Hooker at £20.10 p head to pay in 2 months	4					82	00	—
Sold Saml Woodward at £18 p head Bills now to goe the first of April next pay at 30 daies	5	3	2	1		198	00	—
Sold Jno Sommers to pay in March	3	1			10000	19	00	—
Sold Robt Walke to pay in 10 daies	2					38	00	—
Sold Thos Downes Jnr at 20.10 p head to pay the first of March	2	1				61	10	—
Sold John Sput to pay the 15th March	3	1			15000			
Sold John Peers Esq p Bond to pay in 12 mo at £20 p head	16	5				420	00	—
Sold John Reid Esqr p Bond to pay the Last of July 1681	4					80	00	—
Sold Thos Corley to pay Presintly	1					19	00	—
Sold Cap Elisha Mellich to pay the beginning of the Cropp	1	1		1	10000			
Sold Chro Mellowey at £17 p head Bills by the Ship at 30 daies	5					85	00	—
Sold Rogr Starkey to pay in 4 mo	2					39	00	—
Sold Hugh Williams to pay y 1 Mar	1			1	7000			
Sold John Waite to pay ready mony	1					18	00	—
Sold Jno Vaughan to pay on demand		1				10	00	—
Sold Coll Jno Frere 1 men at 3600 p head & Woman at 3000 to pay the Last of March	5	1			21000			
Sold Sam Wood to pay in Mar next	1				3500			
Sold mat Gray to pay y Last of Mar next	6				21000			
Carried over	105	26	7	9	875 00 4			

shores of the West African coast. Venture remembered how "all of us were put in a castle and kept for market."[35]

Inside such fortresses (like Elmina or Cape Coast Castle in modern Ghana), women and men were separated and taken to a series of large underground holding cells where they were confined for anywhere from a matter of weeks, to several months.[36] French Huguenot slave trader Jean Barbot who traveled "between Senegal and Gambia" as a representative of the Compagnie du Senegal in the 1670s described the "large vaulted cellars divided into several apartments which can easily hold a thousand slaves" that he observed at Cape Coast.[37] 'Sibell shared her vivid memory of how these cellars were filled and how they "keep me in dere long time and bring two, three ebbery day, 'till de long House bin full."[38] Petrified about the possibility of revolt, those who managed the castles believed that "the keeping of the slaves thus underground" would protect them "against any insurrection."[39] Those captives who proved especially recalcitrant, defiant, or otherwise troublesome were separated from the rest and condemned to die, shut away in a small, airless, pitch-black cell constructed for that very purpose.

When a slave ship, like the *John Bonaventure*, arrived at the coast to purchase captives, the ship's captain and his surgeon entered a castle, surveyed the people for sale, and chose those they deemed the healthiest and most likely to survive the transatlantic voyage and fetch the highest price in the Caribbean. In order to make their assessment, traders stripped men, women, and children of all clothing, while a surgeon painstakingly examined every part of their bodies, poking and prodding orifices and limbs, vigilant for any sign of disability or disease. "Such as are good and sound are set on one side," noted Barbot, and then each was "marked on the breast with a red-hot iron, imprinting the mark of the French, English, or Dutch companies so that each nation may distinguish their own property, and so as to prevent their being changed by the sellers for others that are worse."[40]

Once branded, the captives were taken out of the castles, through "the doors of no return," placed in small canoes and transported to the awaiting slave ship, anchored in deeper waters. Local merchants, traders, sailors, and castle slaves engaged in or supervised the purchase and exchange of captives at every step along the way. As Florence noted, "the enemies of our Country seized and sold us to the White people."[41] In this way, African elites profited from the slave trade and protected their own populations from being sold across the Atlantic.

A voyage on a slave ship was a terrifying and brutal affair. As in the castles on the West African coast, captives were segregated and chained together. When the *John Bonaventure* departed the West African coast its cargo comprised

560 captive women, men, and children. Men were generally held in the hold, while women and children were often afforded space on deck. Always under the watchful eyes of the white sailors and other captives, these women were responsible for cooking much of the food consumed on board and were expected to yield to every urge of the crew. These demands included dancing, singing, and otherwise providing entertainment. They were also subjected to sexual assault and violence of all kinds.[42]

Florence and Olaudah noted the ways in which, as young children, they were allowed more mobility on board. Both also recounted the horrors of the slave ship. Florence remembered "our punishment was frequent and severe, and death became so frequent an occurrence, that at last it pass on, without fear, on the dying, or grief on those left behind, as we believed that those who died, were restored to their people and Country."[43] On his voyage Olaudah described the numerous whippings that enslaved people (including himself) received for everything from trying to throw themselves overboard to refusing to eat.[44] Meanwhile 'Sibell, who had been so isolated in the slave castle, found "my Country woman Mimbo, my Country man Dublin, . . . my Country woman Sally, and some more," on board the ship that transported her to Barbados. Communicating with fellow captives seems to have brought her some solace.[45] For many, such communication was impossible.

Conditions on board ship, like those in the slave castles, were extremely unsanitary. When he was briefly taken below deck, Olaudah recalled "such a salutation in my nostrils as I had never experienced in my life," thanks to the vomit, feces, and urine that together accounted for "the loathsomeness of the stench." He noted that "I became so sick and low that I was not able to eat," and like some of his fellow shipmates, Olaudah "wished for the last friend, death, to relieve me."[46] These conditions meant that disease was widespread aboard slave ships, and death tolls were high. Almost sixty of the 260 enslaved people who departed on Venture's transatlantic voyage died from smallpox by the time they reached Barbados two months later. Including suicides, punishments, and disease, death also took its toll on the voyages that Olaudah, Florence and 'Sibell endured.

Ships that headed to Barbados in the last half of the seventeenth century also had high mortality rates. At least 200,000 women, men, and children left West Africa for Barbados between 1650 and 1700, but only a little over 150,000 arrived in the colony, meaning that almost a quarter of all transported Africans in this era died on the transatlantic voyage.[47] The percentage on the *John Bonaventure* was higher still, at almost 30 percent. Only 401 captives arrived in Barbados: 200 men, 160 women, 21 boys, and 20 girls. Of their fellow prisoners 159 had died during the ten-week voyage. By the time these captives landed at Bridgetown, they had already endured trauma on an almost unimaginable scale.[48]

The enslaved women, men, and children who were brought to Rendezvous from the slave ships took a variety of routes across Barbados. Those whom John purchased illegally from Portuguese slavers were brought to the island on ships financed by John and some of the colony's wealthiest inhabitants. They were secreted off ships in the middle of the night on the eastern, less populated, side of the island. From there they would march in the dark over inhospitable terrain to the Rendezvous estate, no doubt shackled together to prevent any of their number trying to escape. Those he purchased through legal means—sanctioned English merchants in the 1660s and Royal African Company vessels like the *John Bonaventure* from 1672 onward—were brought through Bridgetown, the island's chief port.[49]

Most recorded sales of enslaved people in this period occurred aboard ship, with planters and other prospective enslavers brought out on small skiffs to inspect the human cargo. In an effort to ensure the highest prices possible, captives were conditioned for around a week with "Fresh water to wash & palme oyle and tobacco and Pipes," and given a nutritional boost from citrus fruit, potatoes, and yams. Having their hair shorn to remove lice, their bodies washed to remove the corporeal effusions excreted during the Middle Passage, and their limbs massaged with "Negro Oyle" to give their skin a luster and shine, captives endured days of invasive inspection by men like John, who purchased those they identified as the most well suited for labor on their plantations.[50] It was at this point that many of the bonds created aboard ship were once again broken. 'Sibell remembered how upon arrival in Barbados she was torn away from the country men and women who she spoke to aboard ship: "but dey sell dem all about and me no savvy where now," she recalled, before bursting into tears.[51] The purchased captives were then transported to shore on the same small skiffs that had brought their new enslavers to the auction.

Stepping off the skiffs onto the docks at Bridgetown, these new arrivals immediately encountered a bustling urban space filled with scores of fellow enslaved Africans. Men loaded boats with sugar and rum to take to the larger merchant vessels waiting to make the return voyage across the Atlantic Ocean, while market women sold "produce, meats, and household wares to the passersby." What those who had just endured a Middle Passage made of the scene is unknown—perhaps the landscape reminded them of the port towns by the West African slave castles from which they had first been sold. Those urban spaces were also full of life and movement.[52] The newcomers might also have recognized cultural markers or understood snippets of language from enslaved people at the docks.

As they moved from Bridgetown toward Rendezvous, around four miles distant, the captives purchased by John would have noticed the buildings falling away. On their left were endless sugarcane fields. To their right, the sparkling water of the Caribbean Sea. The tall island palms that hugged the shoreline offered little shade from the intensity of the tropical sun. It may have been another isolating experience if they could not communicate with those they marched alongside. Whether they walked with someone who spoke their language or not, they could not have failed to notice that almost every person working in a cane field looked more like them than like their new owners.

When the new captives arrived atop the hill where the Rendezvous plantation stood, they were taken to the slave "houses," where an overseer divided the new arrivals into task-oriented working groups. Field hands were supposed to be given essential clothing—men were handed "three pair of Canvas drawers," and women "two petticoats a piece," to last the whole year. [53] Whether it was canvas, cotton, or (more likely) coarse osnaburg that clothed their bodies, these few basic items would wear quickly. When the rest of the enslaved population returned from their day in the fields, there would have been an opportunity for the new members of the group to seek out someone who might be from the same place as them, to be able to speak in a language they understood, to ask questions about what this new stage of life would bring, and perhaps, to temper or exacerbate the fear and anxiety they surely felt.

If Hester observed their arrival, she may have wondered if any among their number would make suitable additions to the workforce that kept the Rendezvous plantation house running smoothly. Most likely she assumed that those who had come directly from Africa would not be experienced in the kinds of work performed in the "Mancon House" and that they were better suited to the field. In any case, it was best not to make specific plans for the recent acquisitions until they survived a "seasoning" period, which would reveal whether their constitutions could withstand the disease environment and brutal labor conditions on Barbados. [54]

Around a decade into Hester's time on the island, another factor might have influenced John's decisions as he purchased more saltwater slaves for his estate: the supposed ethnic background of the captives for sale. In 1675 a suspected slave revolt shook the island to its core. According to English authorities, the plot had been "hatched by the Cormantee or Gold Coast Negroes," who planned to make one of their own king of the colony. [55] "Cormantee" was a category invented by Europeans originally used to describe Akan speakers from West Africa. Governor Jonathan Atkins (John's future father-in-law) described this group as "a warlike and Robust . . . sort of People" in dispatches to London, but prior to this moment, elites considered enslaved captives from the Gold Coast region among the most loyal and hardworking of the island's enslaved laborers.[56]

Following interrogations and torture, seventeen enslaved men were found guilty of plotting to overthrow the Barbados government. They were executed in dramatic and brutal public fashion, their broken bodies displayed both as a spectacle of colonial power and as a deterrent to future insurrections.[57] Given the large numbers of West Africans on Rendezvous, and the Akan speakers among them, we can only imagine the discussions enslaved people had about these events. John, as a member of the Barbados Council, was involved in the decisions surrounding the repression of the revolt. He might well have reconsidered the locations from which he purchased enslaved Africans in its aftermath.

THE WORK

Hester understood that the main function of Rendezvous was to produce sugar. Insofar as she observed the enslaved people she and John owned, she knew that the majority spent most of their lives in the cane fields, planting, hoeing, weeding, manuring, and otherwise tending the labor-intensive crop. All enslaved field workers were involved in planting. Men dug the rows in trenches "six-inches broad and as much deep, in a straight line, the whole length of the land." Meanwhile women planted the sugar, laying "two Canes along the bottom of the trench, one by another," before covering them with earth. This pattern was repeated "at two foot distance," all the way along the designated field.[58] At every knot on the canes, a new sugar plant sprouted, and because of the method of planting, each was well rooted.

Enslaved women performed the "stooping and painfull worke" of weeding, which had to be conducted regularly over the early months of growth because, as Ligon noted, "the ground is too vertuous to be idle," and conditions were perfect for other invasive plants to take root and strangle the sugarcane.[59] Cane was hard on the soil, so fields had to be constantly manured, which as one observer noted was "a mighty Labour." Just one acre of ground "well dress'd will take thirty loads of Dung." To amass sufficient fertilizer, enslaved men and women made constant collections from "Cattle Pens," and they also supplemented the bovine manure's strength with "the Urine of their People (both whites and Blacks) to increase and enrich their Dung."[60] The use of human waste required enslaved people to collect full chamber pots from the Rendezvous plantation house, as well as their own quarters. Field work therefore held intimacies of its own.

Not only did sugar require constant tending to ensure high yields, but it took longer than an annual cycle to mature. Planters on Barbados learned that leaving the canes in the ground for fifteen months, rather than twelve, resulted in higher-quality sugar and therefore more substantial profits. To maximize their returns, landowners introduced staggered planting, in November and May, to allow for more than one harvest a year. Of course, these agricultural innovations only served to intensify burdens on enslaved laborers, who now found themselves enduring the exhausting and dangerous harvesting period with ever-increasing frequency. As Thomas Tryon, an English Anabaptist critical of slavery, put it, toiling in sugarcane fields like those on Rendezvous meant that enslaved people's "nerves are enfeebled," their "Bones fall under their Burthens," their "Spirits are consumed," and their "Souls in Weariness and Anguish, wish for Death rather than Life."[61]

When the sugarcane of Rendezvous was of "a deep Popinjay," a blue-green color, the plant was deemed ripe and ready for processing, for this was when it would "yeeld the greater quality, and fuller, and sweeter juyce." At harvest time, enslaved workers cut canes, which, "with their tops or blades, doe commonly grow to be eight foot high . . . the bodyes of them, about an inch diametre, the knots about five or six inches distance one from another." Enslaved men and women used "little hand-bills," a sort of short knife, to sever canes about six inches from the ground, work that was hard on the back and strenuous on the limbs. Adult workers discarded the sharp tops of the canes, which children gathered into bundles to be used as food for plantation horses and cattle. The canes themselves were "likewise binde up in faggots," and taken by donkeys to the mill, where they were unloaded by enslaved workers, who quickly sorted them into the order in which they would be processed.[62] At Rendezvous, as at most Barbados plantations, children as young as six followed the carts with keen eyes to ensure that any accidentally discarded stalks of cane made their way to the mill.

Mature cane stalks had to be sent through the sugar mill within forty-eight hours of cutting, "for if they should be more then two days old, the juyce will grow sower."[63] This timeline meant that enslaved workers were forced to keep a tempo one contemporary described as "perpetual noise and hurry."[64] First the canes were squeezed through rollers moved by oxen, enslaved workers, or the wind, to extract the juice. In most mills, "a *Negre* puts in the Canes of one side, and the rollers draw them through to the other side, where another *Negre* stands, and receives them; and returnes them back on the other side of the middle roller." This double-pass was thought to ensure that every last drop of juice was squeezed from the plant.[65]

The enslaved women and men who fed the canes did so at great risk to themselves, often "forc'd to work so long at the Wind-Mills" that they became "so Weary, Dull, Faint, Heavy and Sleepy," that they risked falling "into danger" when "Hands and Arms are crusht to pieces."[66] On a 600-acre plantation like Rendezvous, the volume of cane produced meant that the harvesting process continued for weeks at a time, increasing the likelihood of injury or death for enslaved workers. It also required multiple mills—Rendezvous had "Two Wind-mills" and a "Cattle mill."[67] When the trade winds for which Barbados was famous died down, the cattle mill could be brought into operation to ensure the grueling pace of production did not wane.

The liquid extracted from the canes ran directly into the boiling house, where a series of successive copper cisterns were heated around the clock by enslaved men; women were not deemed able for skilled work of this kind.[68] Rendezvous had "a Boyling house (with stoke holes adjoining)" and fifteen cisterns that could be switched in and out as necessary.[69] The "stock holes" were used to fire the furnaces, which probably burned, as Ligon described, "from Munday morning at one a clock, till Saturday night . . . all houres of the day and night, with fresh supplies of Men, Horses, and Cattle." Inside the suffocating structure there were "six or seven large Coppers or Furnaces kept boyling" during the week.[70]

Stoking the fires and gathering sufficient fuel to keep them alight was another task meted out to enslaved workers. The atmosphere of "hot sulpherous Fumes" made for perilous conditions, especially given that anyone laboring within the boiling house got very little rest. Between the oppressive work environment, the lack of sleep, and the constant removal of impurities from the boiling sugar using skimmers, accident rates were high. Enslaved people regularly suffered scalds and permanent skin damage as molten sugar splashed on their exposed limbs. In the most extreme cases of exhaustion they could slump into the bubbling cisterns and be boiled alive.[71]

The boiling house was the domain of the "master boiler," an enslaved man or a European servant with the skill to mark the exact moment when sufficient impurities had been removed from the sugar to begin a rapid cooling. According to Ligon, to produce the highest-quality yield, toward the end of the process the molten sugar was tempered with "a liquor made of water and Withs . . . without which, the Sugar would continue a Clammy substance and never kerne." At just the right moment, "two spoonfulls of Sallet Oyle" were poured

The sugar works on a seventeenth-century Caribbean plantation similar to the one on Rendezvous. Jean Baptiste du Tertre, *Histoire Generale des Antilles* (Paris, 1667). Courtesy of the John Carter Brown Library, Providence, RI.

into the final copper, and if the liquid bubbled sufficiently it was ready for "the cooling Cisterne."[72]

In the time that Hester lived on Rendezvous, John Daniel, an Englishman, was the master boiler. He may well have been indentured, or perhaps a hired servant—the 1680 census noted the presence of both kinds of laborers on Rendezvous—but eventually he became a small landowner himself. In 1682 John granted his "sugar Boyler . . . and his heires and assignes for ever one piece or parcell of Land or Ground conteyning by estimation fower acres and a half," on ground abutting the Rendezvous estate. In addition, Daniel received "all & singular the houses Edifices Structure and buildings thereon."[73] No doubt this deal was in part a reward for the many years of service and expertise that Daniel gave at Rendezvous. His specific singling out masked the fact that the vast majority of the work, skill, and knowledge that ensured the smooth running of the sugar production process belonged to the plantation's enslaved women and men.

The by-products of sugar production did not go to waste—they were quickly transformed into extremely high-proof, not very refined rum. On Rendezvous "three stills" as well as "wormes" and "cisterns" converted the impurities skimmed from the tops of the copper boilers and the residue left after the refining process into hard liquor. Ligon described how this liquid was left "in the Still-house, till it be a little soure," and that "the first spirit that comes off, is a small Liquor, which we call low-Wines." After this initial distillation process, enslaved workers put the "low-Wine" back into the still until it was ready to be decanted into the several dozen "butts" that held the primitive rum. At this point, it was "so strong a Spirit, as a candle being brought to a close distance to the bung" that plugged the container will set it "a flame, burning all about it that is combustible matter."[74]

Conflagrations begun in rum stills were common occurrences, sometimes resulting in serious burns or the loss of life for enslaved people charged with supervising distillation. These were not the only dangers exhausted enslaved workers confronted in sugar production. Barbados planter Edward Littleton observed the peril associated with the production of spirits, noting that drowning in a vat was a distinct possibility for a skilled enslaved man pushed to his limit: "If a Stiller slip into a Rum-Cistern, it is sudden death: for it stifles in a moment."[75] The collective price for John's profits, and Hester's comforts, was a high human cost among the enslaved population of Rendezvous.

John Daniel was not the only white worker on the Rendezvous estate. John's plantations had at least eight servants laboring on them in 1680, and later inventories note the presence of a tiled dwelling reserved for the estate's overseer. While John Daniel and the overseer were the white men in charge of all laborers, white servants also held positions that elevated them above enslaved workers. With the knowledge that they would eventually end their term of servitude, servants understood that even though they might perform tedious and lowly labor in the present, in the future they had the potential to become landowners, even enslavers themselves.[76] Their immediate day-to-day existence may have looked similar to the experience of enslaved Africans in terms of work, but their outlook could not have been more different. These differences also emerged in the food they ate and in their sleeping arrangements. While servants got "bone meat" twice a week and "lie in Hamocks, and in warm rooms," enslaved Africans only occasionally ate fish, and they slept on "boards" with no coverings.[77]

The most emphatic distinction between workers came in the violence intended to keep laborers in line. In the middle of the seventeenth century, both enslaved and servant workers were "treated very badly," according to Father Antoine Biet, a French Catholic priest who visited Barbados incognito in the

1650s.[78] Ligon concurred, describing an event he witnessed where an overseer "beat a servant with a cane about the head, till the blood has followed."[79] The demographic shift that occurred shortly after Biet's and Ligon's visits changed attitudes about who could receive the most brutal punishments. By the end of the century Hans Sloane described how enslaved laborers who did not work to their fullest potential were "whipt . . . with Lance-wood Switches till they be bloody." After such beatings, overseers rubbed salt or pepper into the open wounds or dripped hot melted wax onto broken skin.[80] Tying the use of the whip and racist English perceptions of Africans together, Thomas Tryon described how "unmercifull Overseers" would "Whip and Beat" enslaved workers, while calling them "Damn'd Doggs, Black Ugly Devils, idle Sons of Ethiopean Whores, and the like."[81] Viewed by the English as heathen savages, West Africans continued to encounter the whip while white servants increasingly escaped it.[82]

On Rendezvous, the overseer and John Daniel were the men who meted out, or threatened, violence on a daily basis. Clues in estate inventories reveal how workers were brutalized and controlled. For example, Rendezvous had "three pairs old ammunition and pistolls," "seven Jamaica guns," seven "musquetts" and at least two "Carbines" among the firearms on the plantation. At least a dozen swords and a number of bayonets added to the arsenal. Enslaved men, women, and children were well aware of the dangers such armaments posed. Not only were enslaved men specifically "not suffered to touch or handle any weapons," but according to Ligon, "hearing their Gun-shot . . . their spirits are subjugated."[83] Even the threat of being shot helped enforce order on the plantation and no doubt added to the anxiety and trauma of the enslaved. On Rendezvous, as on other plantations in Barbados, the dividing line between white and Black was further drawn as servants were allowed to handle firearms while enslaved people were not.

One weapon that some enslaved people were permitted to use was the whip, the implement most commonly brandished to inflict violence on enslaved bodies. While whites in supervisory positions mainly wielded such power, on plantations the size of Rendezvous, a good deal of the immediate supervision in the cane fields was performed by enslaved workers—the men and women in charge of the different work gangs. Called drivers, they could decide to punish fellow workers who were not working to full capacity, or who failed to complete their tasks well. The ultimate authority rested with overseers and the plantation owner, but a certain degree of autonomy in punishment was delegated to enslaved drivers, creating divisions within the enslaved population. Despite the tensions and problems generated by these hierarchies, enslaved people seem to have agreed that time away from whites' watchful eyes, even at the expense of supervision by one of their own, was preferable to the alternative.[84]

There were other divisions in the enslaved population that developed as a result of the different roles that enslaved women and men performed on the plantation. To make Rendezvous function smoothly, enslaved men fulfilled a whole host of skilled positions. Stable hands managed the estate's "stable" and "six horses," as well as bridles, saddles and other riding equipment. Rendezvous also had "a Smiths Shop," where an enslaved blacksmith produced horseshoes and repaired other instruments. There was also a space "for the negroe Carpenters to worke in," as well as carts that had to be fastened to horses or cattle and driven accordingly "for the plantation service."[85] The barrels that held the rum had to be made or repaired, and maintaining or building the Rendezvous home and its outbuildings required masonry skills. The enslaved men who occupied these roles all had come with, or been trained in, the skills necessary to perform these tasks. Having such skills, they were more valuable to John than some of his field hands, and they also had fewer restrictions on their movement, and less structure to their workday.[86] Skilled enslaved men were hired out to other planters in need of the services they could provide, and they sometimes got to keep a small amount of their hiring-out price. Their experiences and their mobility thus set them apart from the rest of the enslaved population of Rendezvous.

In addition to its vast sugar acreage, Rendezvous had a "Garden Tenement," where by 1705 nine enslaved Africans labored. Whether "Black Tom," "Bucky," "Rose," or "Quaquo" were the workers in the 1670s, they, or others like them, grew a variety of crops, most probably to supplement the food imported to feed Hester, John, and their children. By the middle decades of the seventeenth century, enslaved energies were focused almost solely on sugar production, so planters relied on provisions brought from outside Barbados to feed themselves and their workers. Moreover, elites wanted to eat food reminiscent of England, importing wheat flour for bread (despite the fact that it frequently arrived spoiled and full of weevils) and disdaining local crops like cassava.[87]

Despite these preferences, some fruits and herbs grew more successfully in the tropics and were considered delicacies among the population. The anonymous author of *Great Newes from the Barbadoes* published in 1676 noted the "Excellency of their Fruits" especially the pineapple, and also remarked on the "Musk-Melons, Grapes, Figs, Prickle Pears, Guavers, Pomegranets, Citrons, Sour Sops, and sweet Lemmons of a vast bigness, and delicate pleasant taste." He also noted the "Kitching Garden-Herbs" that were "better and more fragrant than in *England*" and the "Medicinal Plants . . . and several other Medicinal Herbs" that were commonly grown in plantation gardens.[88] In the "Garden Tenement" at Rendezvous, knowledge about how to cultivate, and also how to prepare, these fruits and herbs was the purview of the enslaved men and women who worked the small holding, even as Hester and the rest of the Peers family benefited from their labor and expertise.

When Hester arrived in Barbados the Rendezvous house was in serious need of repair. While there is no contemporaneous account of the furniture and furnishings, the 1705 inventory provides a sense of the kinds of decoration that adorned the home. There were three tables in the dining room, including one made from wood from the local, and deadly, manchineel tree. In the parlor were at least two "double armed chaises" and "a Prospect of Bridge Towne in Barbados in an old frame" on the wall, along with eight other pictures—perhaps portraits of the inhabitants or landscapes of Herefordshire or London. There were feather beds and bolsters, and bed frames on the second floor, and the windows were framed with white curtains. These were just some of the "furnishings" that were necessary to ensure that Hester and John's "appearances in the sayd Island of Barbados" were on par with other elites in the colony.[89]

Emulating their planter peers meant, no doubt, feeding their guests well. Rendezvous was a "Plantation near the Sea," which had a "seaside" dwelling, and so was "the best seated for a Feast," because of the ease with which goods could be transported to the estate. Ligon described how a planter with a similar location and aspirations of grandeur had "all rareties . . . brought to the Island, from any part of the world."[90] Over a period of about twenty years John elevated himself to such standards and allegedly "very much Improved his estate." Although Hester might have provided the finances to do so, the labor that made such a transformation possible was performed by the enslaved women who worked within the walls of Rendezvous.

Domestic labor was not the common experience for most enslaved women, but those who did perform such work found themselves doing repetitive, labor-intensive tasks. Laundry, cooking, and cleaning were dangerous, time-consuming, tiring, and physically taxing. Maintaining a fresh supply of linens, for example, was exhausting and included time spent hauling water, building a fire to heat the water, making soap to wash the linens, and then soaking, stirring, wringing, drying, starching, and mending the cloth itself. Moreover, while access to better food and clothing were potential perks of working in the home, the price to pay for these "benefits" was constant surveillance by masters and mistresses who often expected their enslaved domestics to be available around the clock to tend to their every wish. For men like John these whims included fulfilling their sexual desires.[91]

Enslaved domestics tended to live in the plantation house or adjacent to it, meaning that they were more isolated from the rest of the enslaved population and even less likely to escape an owners' notice.[92] On Rendezvous, Susannah and Elizabeth performed tasks inside the "Mancon house" that brought them into contact with Hester, with her children, and with other domestic workers. In this capacity, they made the feather beds, set and cleared the dining tables, swept the rugs and floors, carried wood, made fires, hauled and heated water, and completed a thousand other tasks throughout the day and sometimes the night.

Just as a handful of white workers labored in the fields, or in supervisory positions, so too did whites perform domestic work. At Rendezvous, Dorothy Spendlove worked alongside Susannah and Elizabeth in the plantation home, but her English status elevated her within the domestic hierarchy. Dorothy was probably brought into the Rendezvous home because of her family's connection to John. Throughout the early decades of English colonization in Barbados, Spendloves or "Speedloves" lived in Christ Church Parish. In contrast to John, they were fairly small landowners who could only dream of attaining his status. Despite their subordinate position, one of Dorothy's male relatives acted as a witness to several business transactions conducted by John in the 1670s and 1680s—perhaps an indication of his trustworthiness. Whether it was as a result of these connections, or perhaps through a decline in the Spendloves' fortunes, it is probable that Dorothy was one of the "hired servants" counted among John's property in the 1680 census.[93]

Hester's position as John's wife and as mistress of Rendezvous meant that she was the one who made demands of her subordinate charges, even as she likely treated Susannah and Elizabeth differently from Dorothy. Whether Dorothy and Hester knew one another, they were both English, and so Hester may have felt less need to issue her instructions or to be as precise in her directions. Their common origin or their familiarity with English household customs does not preclude the possibility that their relationship was fraught— in fact their ease of communication might well have meant that Dorothy was subjected to far more micromanagement than her enslaved counterparts.[94] Then again, Dorothy's apparent experience in the colony could have resulted in Hester turning to her for advice, and perhaps even comfort, as she adjusted to this new environment. Although we do not know when Hester was born, she was likely in her late teens, or at best her early twenties, when she arrived in Barbados. She would have had scant experience running a household in the familiar confines of England, let alone managing one on a tropical island 4,000 miles from home.

The enslaved women in the Rendezvous home were expected to heed Hester's every call, but they might have had to listen to Dorothy as well, given that she was white and free. Dorothy may have found a ready audience in Susannah and Elizabeth for her complaints about how Hester treated her. It is conceivable that Susannah and Elizabeth bit their tongues and marveled at Dorothy's inability to understand how good she had it. Or they may have vented to her in return about their own ill treatment. After all, many of the domestic tasks they performed, like laundry and cooking, required collaboration as women pooled resources and coordinated their actions to reduce the onerous nature of the tasks at hand.[95] Another possibility is that Susannah and Elizabeth recognized that their positions allowed them to earn the trust of their mistress. In 1675 they may have been aware that it was an enslaved domestic, a woman named Anna, who had informed her enslavers about the alleged plot to overthrow white rule in Barbados. Whatever they thought about Anna's actions, if they knew she was ultimately rewarded with freedom, they might have considered themselves to be similarly well placed to demonstrate their loyalty and possibly find their own way out of bondage.[96]

Constantly on call, Susannah and Elizabeth likely slept inside the Rendezvous home. In fact, one of them probably lay down to sleep at the foot of John and Hester's bed, or perhaps rested "in the passage before the door" of their bedroom, as Mary Prince, a West Indian slave in the eighteenth century, did in her enslavers' home when she was sold as a domestic in Bermuda.[97] If either one of their enslavers became thirsty in the night, it was Susannah or Elizabeth who would fetch refreshments. If they required the chamber pot, it was Susannah or Elizabeth who made it available, took the putrid vessel away, and cleaned out its contents.

In the morning, it was Susannah or Elizabeth who opened the white curtains that framed the bedroom's windows to let in the morning sunlight, and it was one of them who remade the bed, plumping the pillows, and smoothing the counterpane once John and Hester arose.[98] Susannah and Elizabeth had to tend to John and his family under circumstances from the most mundane to the most intimate and extreme. They cooked, cleaned, and bathed them, removed chamber pots and scrubbed rags and clothes soiled with effluvia and blood. When John's white children were ill, Susannah and Elizabeth nursed them. If John and Hester were poorly, Susannah and Elizabeth did the same for them.

Domestics like Susannah and Elizabeth, who labored in the homes of their enslavers, were shielded from the harsh and unforgiving environment of the fields. But working in the Rendezvous plantation home increased the level of surveillance. Domestic work necessitated greater exposure to their enslaver and his wives. There were very few moments when they were not expected to be at John's and Hester's beck and call. The enslaved women may have been less familiar with the running of an English colonial household, but they no doubt quickly learned how to meet Hester's expectations, as they would have been subjected to various forms of "correction" if their efforts failed.

As did so many women enslavers, there is reason to suppose that Hester committed acts of violence against the enslaved women herself.[99] White women could be just as cruel and mercurial as their husbands when it came to those who labored closest to them, as Mary Prince explained. She described how her mistress educated her in "the exact difference between the smart and the rope, the cartwhip, and the cow skin, when applied to my naked body by her own cruel hand," as well as the effects such punishments had on her psyche.[100] Hester was unlikely an exception, and when she died and John's second wife, Frances, took her place as mistress, no doubt the dynamic repeated itself all over again. Neither wife could have failed to note that it was Dorothy, Susannah, and Elizabeth who made the Rendezvous house run. It was these women who provided the Peers family with the comforts of home.

THE RENDEZVOUS PLANTATION was one of Barbados's largest, most productive, and most elaborate estates by the time Hester gave birth to her last child in 1676. She had now lived in the colony for a decade and had come to learn what life in a slave society meant for her and her family. Her deceased father-in-law acquired the land on which Rendezvous stood, but it was the money Hester brought to her marriage to John that provided the impetus to improve the "Mancon House." The couple were able to live well because of the arduous labor performed by enslaved men and women in the sugarcane fields, in the Garden Tenement, and in the house where they lived. It is unlikely, however, that Hester recognized that the dilapidated home she encountered on her arrival had been transformed into one of Barbados's most opulent and decorous homes through their efforts, not hers.

The enslaved population's path to Rendezvous differed greatly from Hester's. Their experiences of life in a slave society were shaped by unrelenting labor, exhaustion, and the never-ending threat, and actual execution, of violence. Forcibly removed from their homes and transported thousands of miles across a vast ocean to an inhospitable colony, their lives were dictated by enslavers, overseers, and a colonial regime that emphasized its power and exerted its control at every turn. The system of enslavement shaped everything enslaved women, men, and children did. The daily grind of sugar production filled John's coffers, even as the toil drained life out the people he enslaved. Death haunted the sugarcane fields of Rendezvous, and new captives arrived regularly off the slave ships, a resupply of labor that brought new West Africans to the plantation every year.

At something of a remove from the enslaved field workers whose sweat ensured her status, Hester had more intimate ties to the women who worked inside her home. Their close proximity meant that she might have come to know more about their backgrounds and perhaps made assumptions about their personalities, capabilities, or suitability for particular kinds of work. Hester probably came to know how to ensure that each woman expended every last bit of energy in her chores. She watched them age, learn skills, and reach milestones—including becoming mothers themselves, for Susannah, Elizabeth, and Dorothy provided more than simple productive labor in the Rendezvous home. Each woman also performed reproductive labor for John, birthing at least three children apiece by Hester's (and then Frances's) husband, the man who claimed their time, and owned their bodies.[101]

CHAPTER 2

Household Intimacies

THE DISCOVERY OF A PREGNANCY does not necessarily bring an expectant mother joy.[1] Susannah was likely overcome by countless conflicting emotions when she realized that she was pregnant for the second time in early 1678. Should this child survive it would surely, like its older sister, experience a lifetime of bondage. For that was the sole legacy that Susannah could pass on. At the moment of birth, her infant would become John's property, and Susannah would legally be a mother in name only.[2] Giving birth was dangerous, and Susannah no doubt worried about the threat to her health, even to her life. Although her first child thrived, she had probably witnessed other women, enslaved and free, watch their sons and daughters perish a few weeks after taking their first breaths. If she made it through childbirth this time, there was no guarantee that her infant would survive.

The months before this second pregnancy became visible provided Susannah with a brief moment where she alone knew of the changes wrought on her body. She was intimately aware of how the birth of her child, far from a private matter, would become a public event. Every child Susannah produced added to John's property—a birth had ramifications for his account books, his ledgers, and even the colony's census.[3] Once Susannah's hips widened and her belly swelled, everyone in the house and in the enslaved quarters would know she was pregnant. This knowledge might well have brought anxiety, fear, and dread, possibly even a degree of shame. Is it possible that she also felt some measure of pleasure or hope in her pregnancy? Or would her newborn only further symbolize the inhumane violence and financial calculation of her enslavement?[4]

The Rendezvous plantation home exhibited almost all the hallmarks of a polygynous household, one where a man kept multiple women as wives or sexual partners.[5] In different ways, John exerted power over Susannah, Elizabeth, Dorothy, Hester, and Frances. In the slave societies of the Americas, enslaved women and servants frequently birthed their master's offspring. They did so in an environment that seriously limited consent in the case of servant women and legally precluded it altogether for those who were enslaved. Even John's wives had little recourse when it came to rejecting his sexual advances because marital rape was inconceivable in this period.[6]

Under John's dominion the women had to find ways to navigate the Rendezvous home even while they did not have equal control over their actions or each other. Hester's and Frances's children were freeborn English subjects who would never have to suffer the brutalities of bondage. Moreover, the wives' power over the subordinate women in their household allowed them to distance themselves from their own supposedly dependent status.[7] Although Dorothy was a servant and so had to follow orders, she knew that her status was temporary, and that her whiteness provided her additional protection. Most importantly, Dorothy's children were born free.[8] As enslaved women, Susannah and Elizabeth were subjected to Hester's (and later Frances's) demands. Unlike John's wives, or Dorothy, their bodies produced property: their children could be bought and sold on the open market.[9] Despite these differences, the women's lives were intertwined in the domestic work they performed and in the complicated reproductive labor they endured for John.

While England had strong prescriptions against bigamy, this did not prevent men from impregnating women who were not their wives. Among the highest echelons of English society illegitimate children marked a man's virility. Although Charles II and Catherine de Braganza, queen consort, did not have children together, he infamously fathered around a dozen offspring with numerous mistresses, each of whom he recognized and ennobled. Wives, whether queen consorts or mere mistresses of the household, had these children thrust under their noses. Often, they were forced to accept their inclusion in their families, however much they may have wished to feign ignorance of their existence.[10]

It was not only in Europe that elite men fathered children with multiple women: polygyny was a prominent feature of many West African societies. Because wealth and power in these polities resided in people, not in land, elites often married multiple women, producing numerous children to underscore their status.[11] As in England, such children were not always openly celebrated, and men who were not of sufficient rank to create families of their own often resented others' polygynous practices. As the circumstances on Rendezvous closely resembled an elite domicile in West Africa, Susannah may have found the set up familiar, if not welcome. In fact, as a young girl she might even have been trained in the "skills of being a wife and a mother" in a polygynous household.[12]

Centering the women, paying attention to the practices surrounding pregnancy, childbirth, and the postpartum period in England and West Africa, and examining the broader Barbadian context in which events on Rendezvous played out: these focuses make clear the opportunities for some of the women, and the limitations, dangers, and dread of others. Examining how each of the women—wife, servant, slave—navigated the control (or lack thereof) of her body, and how their relationships developed and changed as they aged or in the period between Hester dying and Frances joining the family, lays bare the ways in which race and patriarchy intertwined to dictate the parameters of all the women's lives, but especially of those least empowered: Susannah and Elizabeth. In short, it reveals the horror and complexity of practical polygyny at Rendezvous.[13]

SEXUAL COERCION AT RENDEZVOUS

The many claims made by her enslavers required Susannah to be alert and on guard at all times, not least with John, whose demands were often sexual in nature. Elite white men seized women's bodies with impunity, and enslaved women were especially vulnerable. Because of racist beliefs that women of African descent possessed voracious sexual appetites and willingly used their sexuality to bend enslavers to their will, white men's sexual coercion of enslaved women was an extension of their belief that all serving women were willing and accessible prey.[14]

Did John view Susannah and Elizabeth in this way? It is possible that, like Richard Ligon, he had complicated views of women of African descent. Ligon infamously viewed the women of the Cape Verde islands as exquisitely beautiful while damning enslaved women in Barbados as savage beasts.[15] John may well have found himself similarly torn. Perhaps he arranged Susannah's and Elizabeth's baptisms to assuage his concerns about their origins. Or maybe this was merely another way to exert control over their bodies and their souls. More to the point, John might have believed them to be seducing him, using their feminine wiles to better their own positions on the Rendezvous plantation.

If John did think like this, he would not have been alone, either then or now. Too often scholars explain enslaved women's suffering in deliberately titillating and salacious ways, describing their sexuality in overtly racist terms, and casting enslaved women as literal master manipulators who used sex to gain preferential treatment (better food or clothing, fewer punishments, a higher status among their fellow slaves, or perhaps even freedom itself).[16] Reading evidence of agency into enslaved women's sexual coercion is dangerous, not least because it suggests that every action by an enslaved woman can be reimagined as resistance.[17] This assumption turns the trauma and coercion enforced by enslavers into narratives of power wielded by the enslaved.

Equally problematic are the ways that historians reproduce the patriarchal order of colonial society by focusing on what women like Susannah and Elizabeth "gained," using records created by the women's enslavers. Probate records showing freedom or financial support conferred, plantation journals that documented better treatment, personal diaries that note affectionate feelings on the part of the author toward his conquest—these can only show the intent and desires of men like John. They reveal neither what enslaved women thought about their circumstances, nor whether enslaved women even desired the supposed benefits their enslavers bestowed.[18] Equating agency with capital accumulation suggests that women could resist enslavement only by working within the institution's framework, and it assumes that the acquisition of goods and money is the only reliable evidence of an enslaved woman's self-determination.[19] As Emily Owens points out in stark and devastating terms, "when sex is understood as a transaction, women are imagined as responsible for their own violation."[20]

On Rendezvous, Susannah and Elizabeth were in a bind that rendered their ability to refuse or escape John's predation extremely limited. Barbados's slave society considered them property, and so they were devoid of legal standing. They could not, even if they had wanted to, accuse John of rape and expect to receive any kind of institutional justice: the de facto understanding in the English Caribbean was that enslaved women could not be sexually assaulted. They also—like any other enslaved woman on Rendezvous, Barbados, or in British North America—found it almost impossible to refuse their perpetrator even if the attack was physically violent, sadistic, or intentionally humiliating.

Given their reality, what words should we use to describe what they endured? To call what Susannah and Elizabeth experienced "sex"—which implies a level of consent that could not, and did not, exist—is misleading. Scientific in origin and deployment, "copulation," "coitus," and "intercourse" are too technical, suggesting a measure of objectivity that did not exist in the perpetration of these acts and cannot be applied to how they were experienced by women.[21] Such clinical language not only sanitizes the encounter but also conceals its inherent brutality. As a qualifier attached to the words "relationship," "encounter," and "interaction," "sexual" is equally troublesome as it falls on a spectrum from overly romantic to insidiously benign. Regardless of how Susannah and Elizabeth might have perceived their interactions with John, we should be mindful of the inescapable power dynamics at play.

Faced with these realities, Sharon Block's use of "coerced sex" is a productive way to understand the circumstances that Susannah, Elizabeth, and even Dorothy found themselves in. The verb "coerce" places the burden of the interaction on John and has the added benefit of inverting contemporary descriptions that depict serving women as aggressors. By making the perpetrator's intent active, Block ensures that our encounter with coerced sex highlights women's lack of power in these situations, and she provides us with a potent vocabulary that cuts through the complexity and crystalizes the stakes of such acts. Her construction lays bare the ways that women's racial and class identities shaped their exposure to sexual assault by men. John's position as an elite white man meant that he could wield his power without resorting to physical force.[22] Framing the interaction this way also reveals how "sexual violence was not primarily spectacular," for enslaved and servant women, or at least not necessarily so. Rather, it emphasizes how mundane, ordinary, and everyday such encounters were without reducing the likely trauma of the coercion.[23]

Although Dorothy was a servant, and so had more choices and opportunities on Rendezvous, refusing John's sexual advances was something she had to approach with care. In England, it was common for elite men to view servant women's bodies as disposable and available at all times. The rooms that live-in servants slept in, for example, did not lock, allowing masters unfettered access to women. In the Americas, this kind of behavior continued. Across the colonies men impregnated servant women, increasing their indentures to recover lost labor, and sentencing their offspring to eighteen or twenty-one years of service in the process. Even hired servants like Dorothy were subjected to the "sexual mastery" of men like John.[24]

Elites sometimes masked their paternity, but the frequency with which illegitimate children appeared meant that often they did not bother to do so. In Dorothy's case, it seems that John acknowledged his responsibility for his children and bequeathed them the same amount of money as his sons and daughters with Hester and Frances. Unlike Susannah or Elizabeth, Dorothy could have sued John if he refused to recognize his paternity. Whether she would win her case was less clear. Nonetheless she, like other servant women, could make such a claim, her whiteness granting her standing in court that neither Susannah nor Elizabeth could ever have.[25]

Despite their high social status, even John's wives had trouble rejecting his sexual advances as technically they could not rebuff their husband's demands. Historically there were a number of days in the year when husbands were supposed to refrain from sex, but by the seventeenth century these holy days were rarely honored in England. The month following the birth of a child was probably the only period of abstinence that John's wives could expect.[26] The frequency with which Hester, and especially Frances, had children indicates that neither had much respite when it came to sex with John. Hester probably gave birth to her first daughter with John in 1665, one year before the couple departed for Barbados. The Christ Church Parish baptism records show that she bore five more children over the next decade before she died in 1678.[27] Birthing children every two years was in keeping with European norms, but at least six pregnancies and births in eleven years stressed Hester's body. Frances was even less fortunate. She married John in 1682 and gave birth to three daughters in three years before dying in 1685 just two weeks after the arrival of her youngest.[28] Neither woman had much control, it seems, over her body.

Although all the women with whom John fathered children had difficulty refusing his sexual advances, they were by no means in equal positions. As his wives, Hester and Frances were elite: both came from prominent families and brought considerable capital to their marriages. Moreover, the "rigid gender and sexual expectations" that constrained their lives "did not destroy their sexual agency." Hester and Frances understood their wifely duty to provide heirs; despite the toll their pregnancies took on their bodies, it is possible that they enjoyed sex with John. In the seventeenth century, refinement and subversion of desire was not yet part of a prominent woman's performance of femininity. Sex, whether to conceive and bear children, or with wives who were past menopause or who were infertile, was not just allowed, but a duty born by both partners, with the understanding that "good sex made for domestic harmony." Moreover, people presumed that to increase the likelihood of successful procreation, women had to enjoy themselves; sexual pleasure was not only for men.[29]

While it is impossible to know how Susannah, Elizabeth, and Dorothy felt about their circumstances, clues in the baptism records divulge how John approached their interactions. Susannah and Elizabeth were likely in their adolescence when they were baptized in 1670, given that they were described as

John
1645–1689

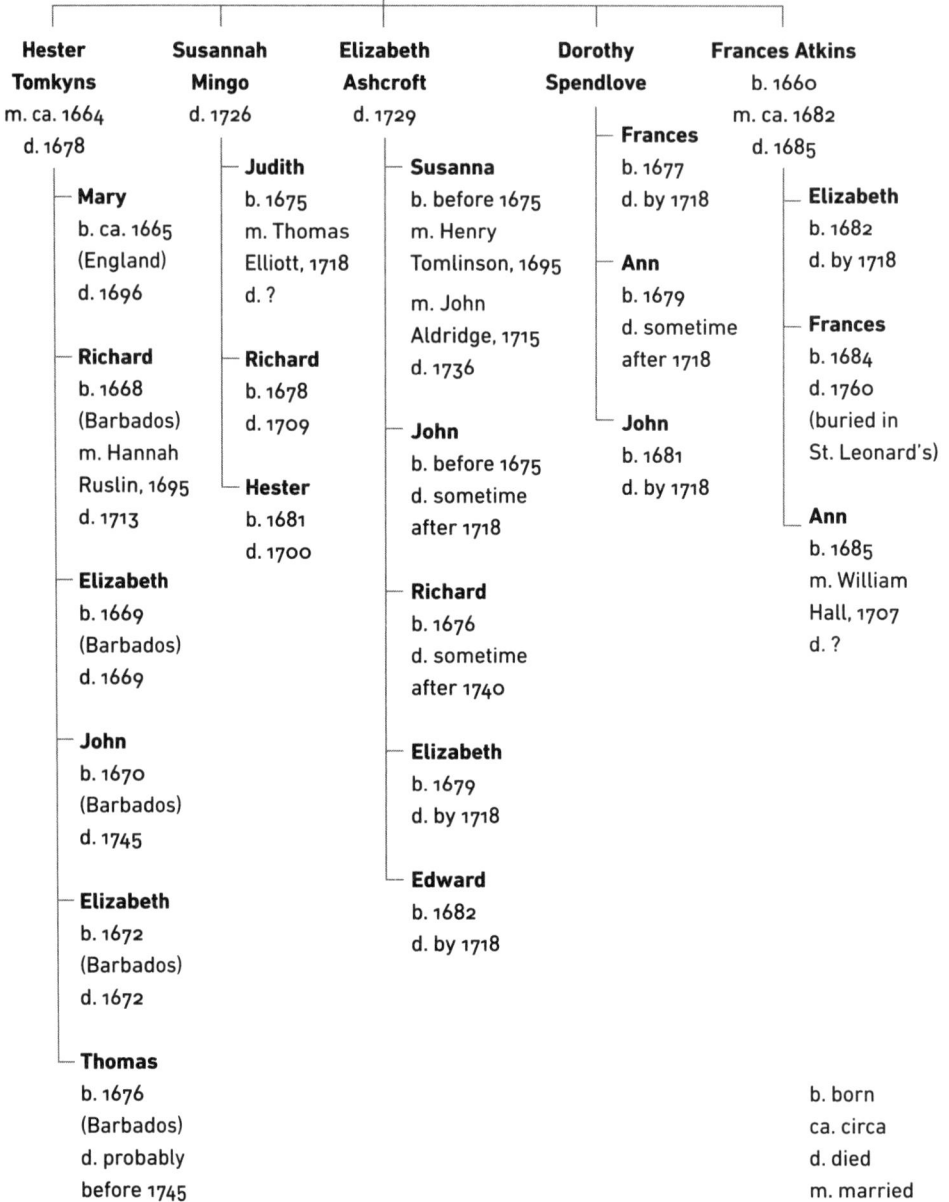

Hester Tomkyns
m. ca. 1664
d. 1678

- **Mary**
  b. ca. 1665
  (England)
  d. 1696

- **Richard**
  b. 1668
  (Barbados)
  m. Hannah
  Ruslin, 1695
  d. 1713

- **Elizabeth**
  b. 1669
  (Barbados)
  d. 1669

- **John**
  b. 1670
  (Barbados)
  d. 1745

- **Elizabeth**
  b. 1672
  (Barbados)
  d. 1672

- **Thomas**
  b. 1676
  (Barbados)
  d. probably
  before 1745

Susannah Mingo
d. 1726

- **Judith**
  b. 1675
  m. Thomas
  Elliott, 1718
  d. ?

- **Richard**
  b. 1678
  d. 1709

- **Hester**
  b. 1681
  d. 1700

Elizabeth Ashcroft
d. 1729

- **Susanna**
  b. before 1675
  m. Henry
  Tomlinson, 1695
  m. John
  Aldridge, 1715
  d. 1736

- **John**
  b. before 1675
  d. sometime
  after 1718

- **Richard**
  b. 1676
  d. sometime
  after 1740

- **Elizabeth**
  b. 1679
  d. by 1718

- **Edward**
  b. 1682
  d. by 1718

Dorothy Spendlove

- **Frances**
  b. 1677
  d. by 1718

- **Ann**
  b. 1679
  d. sometime
  after 1718

- **John**
  b. 1681
  d. by 1718

Frances Atkins
b. 1660
m. ca. 1682
d. 1685

- **Elizabeth**
  b. 1682
  d. by 1718

- **Frances**
  b. 1684
  d. 1760
  (buried in
  St. Leonard's)

- **Ann**
  b. 1685
  m. William
  Hall, 1707
  d. ?

b. born
ca. circa
d. died
m. married

Lineage of the women and their children.

"negro *women*" in the records, a status that meant they were at least fourteen. Whether John began coercing them immediately or not, we know that Susannah conceived a child with him in 1674, and Elizabeth did the same in 1675. Dorothy's age is harder to ascertain, although she conceived her first child with John in 1676. If she was the average age of an Englishwoman giving birth for the first time she would have been in her early twenties, although it is possible that she was younger.[30]

The births of their children prove that each of the women was coerced into sex for at least five to seven years. In all likelihood they endured John's claims on their bodies for much longer: taking them to England suggests that he probably had the ability to demand sex from each of them for well over a decade.[31] Whether John was violently coercive or used the power of his mastery to coerce the women into sex is unknowable. It is equally impossible to tell if Susannah, Elizabeth, and Dorothy believed that acquiescing to John's sexual control was part of their duties as enslaved and servant women. John's privileged position as a white man with considerable political and social power allowed him to act with impunity.

The children's ages suggest how John moved among the women in a rotation, coercing sex from each in turn. First Susannah, then Elizabeth, then Dorothy birthed a child. The pattern repeated itself three times, indicating that each woman had a period when she did not become pregnant or carry children to term while she was in the early stages of childrearing. This spacing raises a range of questions: did the women know when they were going to be subjected to John's attentions? Were they able to anticipate his approaches, or was he entirely unpredictable? Was there a particular location or space that John favored?[32] Did his actions in the days or weeks beforehand or his treatment of them offer some indication that they were about to be coerced into sex, or was his pursuit of them so relentless that there was no way to tell?

We do not know the precise layout of the Rendezvous plantation house, but the women labored and slept within its walls and would have been within earshot of John and Hester or Frances to attend to their every need, so his access was a given. So too were the myriad opportunities John had to assign each woman a task or an errand that contrived to leave them alone in his presence. At the same time, and despite every advantage John had in coercing the women, Susannah, Elizabeth, and Dorothy may also have employed strategies to thwart his desire for sexual control. They may even have worked in concert with one another. Perhaps they shared knowledge about how to deflect John's attentions or did their best to make sure that John had few opportunities to isolate them on the plantation.[33]

Even when one of the women did find herself alone, and on the receiving end of John's advances, she might have worked hard to change the terms of the encounter. Although she lived 150 years after the events at Rendezvous, Harriet Jacobs recalled her response to a similarly coercive relationship. In her auto-biography she painstakingly described the tactics she employed both to feign ignorance of her enslaver's pursuit, and to transform the nature of their inter-actions. Rather than allowing him to pretend that they lived in a world where she could freely choose to consent to sex, Harriet's persistent refusal meant that her enslaver had to resort to overt force—angry words, a razor at her throat—to achieve his goals. That he interspersed these violent moments with persuasive bribes and even the language of love and affection did not change the coercion at their center.[34]

Perhaps Susannah, Elizabeth, and Dorothy deployed similar methods to deter John. It is likely that their varied status shaped their actions. Dorothy's whiteness and the temporary nature of her bondage probably dictated both John's attitude toward her and the scope of what she could do to avoid his atten-tions. Meanwhile, as enslaved women, Susannah and Elizabeth had options that were more constrained. The threat of being sold away, being separated from children, or being whipped or maimed was always present. John may have wanted to believe that the women welcomed his advances, but if they said or did things to dissuade him, his certainty might have wavered. He still probably saw his access to the women's bodies as his right. Even so, John would not have been able to fully ignore the implications of the women's challenges, however carefully they were couched.

There are more definitive clues in the records that speak to how the women exercised control over their bodies: the birth dates of the nine children bap-tized on 13 August 1683. Identifying the precise month of each child's birth is difficult because their ages are listed as estimates in the baptism register. For example, Susannah's elder daughter is described as being "8½," while both Eliz-abeth's and Dorothy's youngest children also have "halves" in their listed ages. It is not likely that they were all born in February or March, and it is equally unlikely that the children described with round ages were all born in or around August in their respective birth years. Nonetheless, it is clear that Susannah and Elizabeth each birthed children three years apart, whereas just two years sep-arate the births of Dorothy's children. The gaps for Dorothy are in keeping with European customs, while those of the enslaved women are consistent with child-spacing practices in West Africa.[35]

What did it mean to practice West African child spacing on Rendezvous? Although the accounts of European observers are filled with racism and disdain, evidence that West African mothers and fathers ensured the well-being of their children by engaging in ritual abstinence for a period following birth comes through. Ignorant of the reasons behind such reproductive choices, most Europeans credited "seldom pregnancy" or mothers who produced only "two or three [children] in their whole lives" to diseases contracted through sexual promiscuity rather than calculated spacing. When they offered other explanations, writers attributed abstinence to supposed West African customs that prohibited men from having sex with lactating women, with the average West African woman breastfeeding for two to three years.[36]

Many West Africans also appeared to believe that birthing children too close together resulted in higher rates of infant mortality. By working to ensure the health of mothers and a manageable space between births, West African parents "increased the probability that their child would survive infancy." Jennifer Morgan notes that such abstinence required cooperation between women and men and suggests that West African men understood "the physical demands of childbirth and nursing," and so partnered with women in this practice. Is it possible that Susannah and Elizabeth worked to do the same on Rendezvous?[37]

Complicating matters was the women's enslaved status. Adhering to abstinence over a long period of time would have been next to impossible given the issue of their inability to refuse or to consent to sex. If Susannah and Elizabeth wished to follow West African pregnancy precepts, John, despite his clear pattern of rotating through the women, was not familiar with (nor likely cared about) such practices.[38] It is also probable that he coerced, or attempted to coerce, sex from all three women in the periods between the births of their children. Perhaps Susannah and Elizabeth used their knowledge to deter John's coercion by explaining the importance of abstinence to him. Or contraception, abortion, miscarriage, stillbirth, or no conception might account for the gaps. Environment affected fertility: hard labor and disease could significantly reduce one's ability to bear children, and malaria rendered men temporarily infertile.[39] These factors were beyond Susannah's and Elizabeth's control.

Devices to actively prevent pregnancy, such as contraceptives and abortifacients, were well within the women's grasp. Among the African plants transported to the Americas were okra and aloe, both of which were used to induce abortion. Knowledge about the abortifacient properties of snake root and cotton root also traversed the Atlantic Ocean, while plants from European and American medical knowledge joined these to help women control reproduction. In addition to leaves, roots, and vegetables inducing miscarriage, there were a number of relatively effective contraceptives available in the seventeenth and eighteenth centuries, including vaginal suppositories made of gum, camphor, and rue, which could be used without the knowledge of men.[40] Susannah and Elizabeth might well have employed some of these tactics to ensure they did not give birth more than every three years.

The practical polygyny on Rendezvous might provide some of the explanation for the birth spacing among the women with whom John had children. In West African societies polygyny facilitated abstinence following childbirth. Under this system, the father of the child left the mother to recover from childbirth while seeking out sexual partners from among the other women in his household. European accounts of these practices in West Africa focused on the supposed deviancy involved and exaggerated the numbers, often conflating wives and slaves.[41] Pieter de Marees, a Dutch explorer on the Gold Coast, noted that "for three months . . . they do not sleep with these wives or make love to them . . . because they have enough wives who will oblige their desires."[42] In 1684 Johann Nieman, a Brandenburg engineer at Fredericksburg, remarked that "a caboceer sometimes has as many as twenty or thirty wives," while just a few years later Johann Peter Oettinger, a surgeon in the Dutch West India Company, claimed that the size of the "residence of the King" at Ouidah was due to the number of rooms "occupied by his wives, seven hundred in number."[43]

Other observers, like Jean Barbot, assumed that beliefs about purity were affecting men's behavior: "The men never lie with their wives who have given birth until three or four months later—either because they fear it will spoil their milk, or because they have sufficient alternatives, having so many wives."[44] The circumstances on Rendezvous were very different, but they nonetheless offer one way of understanding the pattern of births among Susannah, Elizabeth, and Dorothy. They also raise questions about the relationships among and between the women, especially as Susannah, and perhaps Elizabeth too, might have been schooled in how to navigate such interactions as young girls in West Africa.[45]

Hester and Frances must have been aware that John fathered Susannah's, Elizabeth's, and Dorothy's children. Proximity made secrets almost impossible, and given that Hester lived in a fully developed slave society, there was no need to keep her in the dark. Thomas Tryon, who spent time on Barbados in the 1660s and 1670s and who was a noted critic of the immorality of slavery, recorded how enslavers "gratifie their raging Lusts" by approaching enslaved women and girls "and make them their Concubines . . . upon whom they beget mungril Children, that are neither White nor Black but between both."[46] If Hester was ignorant of such relationships before she traversed the Atlantic Ocean, the almost decade she spent on Rendezvous before Susannah gave birth to

Judith would have schooled her in the common practice of enslavers sexually coercing subordinates.

Frances had at least four years in Barbados to learn about the kinds of perverse intimacies that dominated plantation culture before she married John in 1682. In fact, she may well have been bequeathed the daughter of such a coerced encounter when "my mollatto Girl Franke" was left to her by her first husband, Benjamin Knights.[47] The possessive "my" might only have indicated that Benjamin considered Franke to be his property. Her description as a "mollatto" suggests that her father was white. In this context, the "my" could confer not merely ownership on the part of Benjamin, but paternity too.

Hester's and Frances's presence in the Rendezvous home, just as much as John's, "fostered a coercive and vulnerable form of intimacy."[48] All nine "naturall born" children were baptized while John was married to Frances: she might have encouraged him to acknowledge his offspring or forced the issue herself. Whether they approved or disapproved of Susannah, Elizabeth, and Dorothy, both of John's wives had the authority to dictate how they would spend their days. First Hester, then Frances, was able to reward or punish. Hester was probably around a decade older than Susannah, Elizabeth, and Dorothy, but Frances was closer to their ages, possibly even younger. These age differentials would also have influenced the dynamics of the Rendezvous house.

Once Frances died, Dorothy may have assumed a more dominant role herself. Although it is more indicative of John's attitudes than anything else, the fact that Dorothy and her children received the same financial remuneration in John's will as his children with Frances and Hester demonstrates that her position was elevated far above that of Elizabeth and Susannah. Whether that translated into Dorothy's behavior toward the enslaved women is less clear, but she could not have failed to understand the relative power her whiteness brought, even if she simultaneously saw herself in a precarious and degraded position.

We should not, however, assume solidarity between Susannah and Elizabeth. They may have found common ground given their enslaved status; equally they might have resented each other. John's will marked a divide: Elizabeth and her children received twice as much money as Susannah and hers, even if the amount was one-fifth of what Dorothy and her children were bequeathed. Again, these differences reveal more about John than about the women, but it is possible that this financial discrepancy played out in how he acted toward Susannah and Elizabeth, which might, in turn, have shaped their interactions with one another. Following John's death, when they were all in England, Susannah appeared to set out on her own: it was Elizabeth and Dorothy who attempted to recoup their inheritance together. The enslaved women's split in the metropole is not evidence of their dislike for one another, although perhaps whatever prompted them to go their separate ways in London had its roots in their relationship on Rendezvous.

PREGNANCY AND CHILDBIRTH

Susannah was undoubtedly introduced to childbirth rituals on Rendezvous years before she bore her first child. She was on the plantation at least as early as her own 1670 baptism. This event occurred within ten days of the baptism of two infant boys: Hester and John's second son, and the son of an enslaved couple named Judith and Nocke.[49] It is possible that Susannah witnessed both births. As a domestic laboring in the Rendezvous home, Susannah likely attended Hester's childbed. Given the baptism of her enslaved son, Judith probably also worked in a skilled domestic position at Rendezvous. Although Judith most likely gave birth in her own quarters, there is reason to suppose that Susannah, who moved through the same spaces, would have been close by even if she wasn't present at the birth. And of course, Judith was far from the only enslaved woman to have a child at Rendezvous during Susannah's time on the plantation.[50] Aiding in the birth of Hester's child and witnessing the labor of other enslaved women, Susannah encountered cultural practices imported from both England and West Africa.

Hester first gave birth in England—her eldest daughter, Mary, was born before she and John departed for Barbados. Hester most likely bore her child in her family home in Herefordshire, with her mother and married sister, Ann, on hand for support. Traveling late in pregnancy was popular among first-time mothers, who found comfort in the familiar environs of their childhood residence. At least one of the local midwives from Weobley would have been present too, taking command of the birthing room and orchestrating everyone in it.[51] Ann, who was likely declared Mary's godmother upon her birth, probably assisted the midwife during labor and supported Hester through its aftermath. Together these women passed on remedies for helping Hester through childbirth, including various salves and caudles (a kind of thick, sweet beverage) that would assist "Women in Labour," "expell the afterbirth," and "increase Milk abundantly."[52]

During her labor, Hester may well have used the childbed linens that had belonged to her mother. These laundered bedclothes would have displayed the faint stains of childbirths past. In the dark and stifling birthing room the sheets would soon be soaked in "the blood, waters, and other filth which is voided in

Labour."[53] The closed, suffocating atmosphere of the chamber would have contrasted starkly with the sharp cries of pain wrenched from the woman writhing on the childbed. Of course, not all women gave birth in the same way. According to medical treatises of the time "some are best Deliver'd lying in their Beds, others sitting on a Chair or Stool, or on the side of the Bed others on their Knees, being supported by People under their Arms."[54] Parturition laid bare the limits of Hester's body, both the marvel of birthing a human, and the ways that expelling an infant might tear it asunder.

A shrill wail elicited from unpracticed lungs marked Mary's arrival into the world. If Hester's experience followed English norms, the midwife would quickly ensure that the infant's body was intact, determine the child's sex, and cut the umbilical cord before bathing and swaddling it. Mary would then be laid beside Hester for a brief moment, before being presented to her father, who up to this point would have been absent from the room.[55] Within hours Hester's Mary would have been settled with a wet nurse, getting her sustenance from another woman while Hester's body recovered from her ordeal.[56] Recuperation would begin immediately after birth, as the midwife concocted broths and drinks to restore Hester's strength while using herbal remedies and cloth dressings to reduce pain, bleeding, and inflammation. After a month of lying-in (during which time Hester would have been entertained by her mother and sisters) would come Hester's "churching," to give thanks in Weobley's parish church for her, and her daughter's, safe passage through childbirth.[57]

In the colonies, Englishwomen like Hester and Frances followed many of the same practices that guided childbirth among elites back home, even as the distance from England meant that complete replication was impossible. In the weeks before they gave birth the women would have sequestered themselves from John and the outside world, seeing only their closest domestic attendants. Unlike in England, however, Hester was not attended by her mother or sister but by members of the plantation household, including enslaved women. In addition to Susannah and Elizabeth, perhaps Judith was present or acted as a wet nurse for Hester's younger children.

Far removed from England, it is unlikely that Hester had heirloom childbirth linens at her disposal unless she had carried them from Herefordshire. Frances does not appear to have birthed any live children with her first husband, but she did bring all the "household Lynnen" with her to Rendezvous upon her marriage to John, which might have included some as yet unused childbirth cloths. Regardless of where the material came from, the childbirth bed had to be prepared, the white linen sheets laundered and laid by enslaved domestics.[58] Washing and starching was a time-consuming process at the best of times; it must have taken on new meaning, as the enslaved women worked to remove the stains of blood, amniotic fluid, and other effluvia associated with childbirth.

Another significant difference between childbirth in England and childbirth in Barbados was the climate. Birthing rooms were already cloistered and suffocating spaces, and the heat and humidity of the tropics would have rendered the atmosphere even more unbearable. The "Mancon House" at Rendezvous was equipped with feather beds that, while more comfortable than their straw counterparts, were hard to keep clean in tropical settings. Moreover, feather beds absorbed heat, making an already uncomfortable environment hotter for the woman in labor. If either Hester or Frances wished to avail herself of a birthing stool, she was likely to be out of luck—despite their prevalence in England, few appear to have made it to the colonies.[59]

Some medical pamphlets suggested that the warm climate was conducive to giving birth, citing the supposed ease with which enslaved women produced children as evidence of their claims.[60] Certainly Hans Sloane seemed to believe that childbirth was easier for women in the Caribbean when he noted that "a great many White Women, all Indians and Negroes, keep not their Beds over a Week after having brought forth [the child], when they return to their ordinary Business."[61] Whether the women believed these assertions or not, it is likely that the experience of giving birth contested theories of easy deliveries espoused by mostly male writers. They might well have turned to manuals written by women midwives like Jane Sharp who not only had attended numerous births but had firsthand experience of bringing a child into the world.[62]

John's wives probably did not have family members on hand to provide comfort during lengthy labors, or for the period of lying-in that followed. Friends may have stepped in to fill the void, though given how removed planters' wives were from public life, it is equally likely that they instead relied even more heavily on enslaved and servant women to tend them. Without the support of white peers, the convivial atmosphere that followed a successful birth was curtailed. In England, the sisters and friends who entertained new mothers were known as "gossips," a term that originally referred to the women who would act as godmothers to the newborn. Over time, "gossip" came to refer generally to the women who attended the birth, and more pejoratively to the discussions that took place in this woman-only space.[63] At Rendezvous, Susannah, Elizabeth, and Dorothy may well have been the women who performed the role of "gossips" in the weeks after Hester or Frances gave birth. They would not have been granted the privilege of being named godmothers, even while they were the women on hand to provide distraction, comfort, and perhaps conversation to

THE
MIDWIVES BOOK.

Or the whole *ART* of
MIDWIFRY
DISCOVERED.
Directing Childbearing Women
how to behave themselves

In their {
Conception,
Breeding,
Bearing,
and
Nursing
} of **CHILDREN**.

In Six Books, *Viz.*

I. *An Anatomical Description of the Parts of Men and Women.*

II. *What is requisite for Procreation : Signes of a Womans being with Child, and whether it be Male or Female, and how the Child is formed in the womb.*

III. *The causes and hinderance of conception and Barrenness, and of the paines and difficulties of Childbearing with their causes, signes and cures.*

IV. *Rules to know when a woman is near her labour, and when she is near conception, and how to order the Child when born.*

V. *How to order women in Childbirth, and of several diseases and cures for women in that condition.*

VI. *Of Diseases incident to women after conception: Rules for the choice of a nurse; her office; with proper cures for all diseases Incident to young Children.*

By Mrs. *Jane Sharp* Practitioner in the Art of
MIDWIFRY above thirty years.

London, Printed for *Simon Miller*, at the Star at the West End of St. *Pauls*, 1671.

Title page of Jane Sharp, *A Midwives Book. Or the Whole Art of Midwifry Discovered* (London, 1671), 476851, the Huntington Library, San Marino, CA.

the recovering mother. They would have been responsible, however, for meeting every need or desire of Hester and Frances.

The gulf between the experience of pregnancy for the working women, on the one hand, and that of Hester and Frances, on the other, was likely wide. Neither of John's wives had to expend much energy while pregnant; indeed, they had enslaved and servant women to wait on them hand and foot. For Susannah, Elizabeth, and probably Dorothy, the travails of pregnancy would have been exacerbated by the labor they had to perform to keep Rendezvous clean and its occupants fed, clothed, and watered. If Hester and Frances felt nauseous or tired during their first trimesters, they could take to their beds, or sit quietly. Medical manuals of the day encouraged husbands to be "very tender over their wives and helpfull to them in all things needfull," in the months after conception. These prescriptions included taking on more responsibility for running the household, and so it is likely that John became the prime interlocutor on domestic matters while his wives were pregnant.[64] The working women within the Rendezvous home would have had no such reprieve. They continued to attend to their duties regardless of whether or not their bodies cooperated, although the fact of their pregnancies may have caused disruption to exacting household timetables.[65] Domestic labor was exhausting; the months of pregnancy made it especially so. In the first trimester, when signs of their pregnancies would be invisible, the women might well have battled fatigue and nausea, all the while wondering if they would get enough sleep and, when they felt able to eat, food.

As Hester and Frances entered the latter part of their pregnancies, they might have hoped to follow practices in England surrounding rest and relaxation. John Oliver's *A Present for Teeming Women* allowed that women, "when they begin to grow big and unwieldy, must be taken off from such manual imployments in which they were busied before, and must allow for some rest and retirement." Taking to one's bed in the weeks before childbirth was a common practice among elites, who viewed time away from husbands and other visitors as a respite before the arduous hours or days of labor.[66]

Likely no such relief was available to Susannah and Elizabeth, who would have been expected to perform their regular tasks right up to the moment they experienced their first contractions. Englishman Thomas Tryon, who adopted the perspective of an enslaved man in his critique of slavery in Barbados, noted how enslavers "make our Wives, during the time of the Pregnancy, work equally with the rest, even until the very day of their delivery."[67] As Susannah's and Elizabeth's bellies expanded and their hips widened, household duties that had once been familiar and practiced would have become new and ever more draining challenges. Maneuvering bodies that were weightier, broader, and no longer fully agile meant that the women would likely have been more aware of their bodies and more conscious about how they moved through space. Swollen ankles, aching backs, and broken sleep would only serve to make the daily grind more unbearable.

Enduring substantial and continuous physical labor was not the only way that Susannah's and Elizabeth's pregnancies differed from those of Hester or Frances. As in England, in West Africa it was common for women to return to their home village to give birth, something that was impossible for enslaved women in Barbados.[68] Each time the enslaved women realized they were pregnant, they might have marked the occasion with a ritual bath, something foreign to their English counterparts. For West Africans, bathing and cleanliness took on new and special meanings during pregnancy. On the Gold Coast, women participated in bathing as soon as they knew they had conceived, a ritual that also included adorning their bodies with protective devices to ensure a safe pregnancy. In the advanced stages of pregnancy these practices were repeated to prepare the woman for labor. The final bath occurred around nine days after birth and coincided with the naming ceremonies that officially welcomed the infant into the community.[69]

From available sources, it is difficult to determine whether these specific practices continued in the West Indies. Richard Ligon noted what he deemed enslaved African's unusual dedication to "washing themselves in the Ponds, in hot weather." Although Barbados lacked streams and springs, Ligon assessed that by collecting rainwater—the means by which most inhabitants gathered potable water—enslaved Africans could manage to wash themselves.[70] If they did follow the bathing rituals around conception, pregnancy, and childbirth, Susannah and Elizabeth likely deployed these water-catching methods in order to cleanse themselves. As girls in West Africa, they may have witnessed other women engaging in the same kinds of practices or had been trained by women relations in the appropriate way to approach birth.

Removed from familiar West African contexts, and with few sources that illuminate enslaved experiences, it is impossible to know how Susannah or Elizabeth experienced the birthing process. Richard Ligon noted that for enslaved couples, "at the time the wife is to be brought to bed, her husband removes his board (which is his bed) to another room . . . and leaves his wife to God and her good fortune, in the room, and upon the board alone, and calls a neighbour to come to her." Ligon suggested that this neighbor "gives little help to her deliverie," but he could not have known what came to pass in the birthing room, and his account is no doubt inaccurate.[71] It is more likely that women called on to assist in childbirth did a great deal to help the woman enduring parturition. Enslaved midwives were feted for their expertise and knowledge. It is possible Judith was the midwife on Rendezvous given the way she, her son, and his father were marked out for special recognition in the Christ Church Parish baptism register. At the same time, given the work they had to perform in the household, and the inability to abandon their enslavers, it is possible that Susannah and Elizabeth had to give birth alone.[72]

If Judith or another enslaved woman on Rendezvous performed the role of midwife for Susannah and Elizabeth, her job was to assist the women through labor and following birth to "make a little fire nere her feet and that serves instead of Possets, Broaths, and Caudles."[73] Women with experience of childbirth knew not simply how arduous labor could be but also how to remedy difficult birthing situations, including those where the fetus was breech. Enslaved midwives also prepared medicines and soothing compresses designed to alleviate aches and tenderness, and they advised on which positions would ease the pain of contractions or otherwise reduce the stress of childbirth.[74] By the time they underwent their third births, Susannah and Elizabeth would have gained their own understandings of their bodies. While every pregnancy is different, this experiential knowledge might have provided some comfort to the women insofar as the process was no longer completely unfamiliar.

English observers assumed that enslaved women, whether laboring in sugar fields, or performing domestic work, like Susannah and Elizabeth, needed no recovery from childbirth. Ideas about Black women's bodily strength had a long history among European observers, who often commented on the supposed lack of pain that African or Indigenous American women experienced when birthing children.[75] Most European men in the sixteenth and seventeenth centuries did not witness childbirth by their own wives, mothers, and sisters, let alone attending when African or Indigenous American women gave birth. Nonetheless, their racist presumptions about the innate strength of non-white women's bodies informed their ideas about these women's ability to recover quickly from labor.

Ligon, for example, noted that two weeks following birth, an enslaved woman was "at worke with her Pickaninny at her back, as merry a soule as any is there."[76] In the 1660s Thomas Tryon also noted the lack of "lying-in, for alas! they have no monethly Nurses, nor groaning Cheese, none of the Comforts of Ale, or Wine, or Caudles, or rich refreshing Suppings." He put the space between birth and a return to labor at "two or three dayes rest."[77] By the 1670s white enslavers and overseers expected the postpartum period to have no deleterious effects on enslaved women at all. Susannah and Elizabeth (and the other enslaved women on Rendezvous) had their own understandings and lived experience of what recovering from childbirth really looked like.

MOTHERING IN A SLAVE SOCIETY

When Susannah gave birth to Judith, Richard, and Hester, she became a mother, yet her children were not hers to parent. In legal terms she could "convey nothing but bondage to her progeny."[78] While many of her circumstances placed Susannah apart from the rest of the enslaved women on Rendezvous, this was the one experience they all shared in common. Customary and statutory laws defined all enslaved people as chattel and denied them the ability to pursue family.[79] Susannah expanded John's property, which further highlighted the vast gulf between her condition and the status of her white cohabitants.

Enslaved mothers like Susannah knew that surviving childhood was an uphill struggle for their progeny: Black children were twice as likely to die as white children in the colonies. The precarity of life affected enslaved women's reactions to motherhood. In the early months of their infants' lives, some enslaved mothers worried about whether they had sufficient food to sustain a strong milk supply while others might well have tried to keep an emotional distance from their children lest they die or be sold away.[80] As domestic laborers, Susannah and Elizabeth had more access to food than the enslaved women who worked in the fields, and they might have been able to secure more sustenance for themselves and their offspring. Proximity to their enslaver did not ensure a less stressful childhood for Judith, Richard, Hester, Richard, Elizabeth, and Edward, nor did it necessarily mean that their mothers had greater access or rights to their children. Susannah and Elizabeth navigated the Rendezvous home under a set of circumstances different from those of field workers. They had to get their daughters and sons safely through infancy while continuing to labor in a domestic space that put their children in close proximity to their father and enslaver, his wives, and his other, white children.

Given these challenges, could enslaved women ever look positively on their reproductive capacities? We have few accounts from enslaved women in the Caribbean discussing their views regarding motherhood, and none from the seventeenth century. On the one hand, an enslaved woman's "maternity wrenched parenting out of the realm of the domestic and into the marketplace," bringing into sharp relief the conflicting emotions that mothering in slavery must have produced.[81] When enslaved children were entered into a plantation ledger, thus establishing their monetary value, they were stripped of their personhood, acquiring instead the status of chattel, property exchanged among Europeans, bought and sold to the highest bidders. On the other hand, even in the face of unrelenting planter power, having a child provided an enslaved woman with the opportunity to assert her autonomy as a mother, and perhaps to call on her enslaver to recognize the importance of her maternity. Despite knowing that her child would inherit her status, there were reasons for enslaved women to not always choose to avoid motherhood.[82]

Recognizing a variety of responses to enslaved motherhood does not require adopting an overly romantic view of enslaved mothers, but nor should we minimize the importance of women who regarded motherhood positively. It is possible that some enslaved women hoped that giving birth might make their present circumstances more bearable. Having children created familial connections and made kinship ties anew, mimicking, if not replacing, those broken by the Middle Passage. Susannah, who was probably born in West Africa, had to reckon with the fact that her daughters and son would grow up not only in enslavement, but in a different culture from her own. They probably would not speak the language she learned as a child, nor would their first names evoke her homeland.[83] This reality did not mean that she found mothering an unattractive proposition.

One way for an enslaved woman to keep her own West African childhood present and real was to teach her children about life beyond the Barbados plantation. Stories from the past that invoked memories of her own parents, siblings, cousins, aunts, uncles, and friends may have sparked laughter or joy or might have been painful to recall depending on the context in which they were told. Perhaps Susannah sang lullabies in her own language to calm her infant children or to soothe them to sleep. She might even have had names for them that their father did not acknowledge or recognize. For example, an enslaved girl named Nell who lived on Rendezvous in 1705 also went by the Akan day name Cubenhah (Tuesday). Scores of others had two names registered in the estate's inventories.[84]

Lessons from the past were not the only ones that enslaved children on Rendezvous learned from their mothers. As they moved from infancy into childhood, Susannah's children would come to understand life in a slave society. Susannah and Elizabeth may have hoped that John would not sell his own children away, but they would equally have understood that if he chose to do so, neither mother would have been able to prevent their sale. Even though the women and their offspring shared space with John and his family, it was his needs, and those of his white wives and children, that dictated his actions. John illegally moved enslaved people from Frances's first husband's estate to Rendezvous, separating family and kin in the process.[85] The women might have feared

Rendezvous plantation inventory, 1705. Bodleian Libraries, University of Oxford, C/WIN/BAR 1–4.

that he would do the same to their sons and daughters, either selling them on, or moving them to his other plantation, Staple Grove.

Susannah and Elizabeth also knew that they had no control over the punishments their children might face for any infractions committed against the household. As they grew older, part of their education would have been based on ensuring that they did not anger or disappoint their father or one of his wives. We have no way of knowing whether John, Hester, and Frances were capricious and erratic or clinical and predictable when it came to enacting violence on their enslaved property for perceived slights or alleged misbehavior. In fact, it is likely that they were all these things, and that their attitudes on one day did not affect their behavior on another. And an enslaved person's never knowing exactly how an enslaver might react was part of the enslaver's power. Regardless of how the children were punished, Susannah and Elizabeth could not intervene. As Mary Prince reflected on her own experience in enslavement, "mothers could only weep and mourn over their children, they could not save them from cruel masters."[86]

The lessons that Susannah's children—Judith, Richard, and Hester—and Elizabeth's offspring—Richard, Elizabeth, and Edward—learned regarding expected behavior and deferential comportment would have been supplemented by the instruction they received about the labors they were expected to perform. By the time enslaved children were around six years old, they began to take on small domestic tasks. Some of the earliest roles they played probably included acting as playmates for their white half siblings. It was not unusual for enslaved children, especially those whose mothers were domestics, to spend the first years of their lives in the company of their free counterparts.[87]

John's enslaved offspring would be deployed in household labor soon after Hester's children were sent to England for their educations. Daughters learned how to do laundry, clean rooms, and prepare beds. Sons became the kitchen runners and dining-room servers at the Rendezvous "Mancon House."[88] As they aged, the jobs they performed necessarily increased in scope and scale. Although all of Susannah's and Elizabeth's children were under the age of twelve while they lived on Rendezvous, they gained an important education regarding the work they performed, and they learned how to behave around white people, including their half siblings.

The vast gulf that separated mothering in enslavement and mothering in freedom divided the experiences of Susannah and Elizabeth from those of Hester, Frances, and Dorothy. It is likely that both Susannah and Elizabeth performed wet-nursing duties for John's younger children with Hester and Frances. In England lower-class women were commandeered to ensure that elite Englishwomen did not have to endure the "bodily claims of maternity."[89] Choosing a viable wet nurse was a serious process. *The Birth of Man-Kinde*—a manual on pregnancy and childbirth first published in 1540 and repeatedly reprinted over the following century—suggested that an appropriate candidate would "be of good colour and complexion, and that her bulk and breast be of good largeness," and "that it be two months after her labour at the least" that she take on the duty. It was also preferable, according to the author, that the wet nurse had birthed a son.[90] So commonplace was wet-nursing that contemporaries suggested all but the lowest orders of English society could afford to hire a woman to nurse their newborns.[91]

Wet-nursing carried over to the Caribbean, except that now enslaved women most frequently took on the role. Although some poor European women, including those from Ireland, might have continued to act as wet nurses in the West Indies, the vast majority now occupied a space where they too could draw on the labor of enslaved women to perform these duties. This shift fed into assumptions about white women's weakness and the "thin gruel" they produced from their breasts as a result. Racist ideas about the brute strength of African-descended women meanwhile informed English attitudes toward their innate suitability for the task.[92] Anglo-Irish naturalist Hans Sloane noted that in Jamaica "Blacks are as often taken for Nurses as Whites, being much easier to be had." This casual explanation of the use of Black women to feed white children—that they were present, and more available than poorer white women—speaks to Sloane's attitude toward enslaved people in general, and women more specifically.

Sloane couched his descriptions of Black women's bodies in the same gendered, racist language found in the writings of myriad fellow elite European travelers.[93] So effective were these writings that some planters became wary of employing enslaved women as wet nurses "for fear of infecting their Children with some of their ill Customs." Sloane declared that he "never saw any such Consequences," but he did not deny the fact of the "ill Customs" themselves. Moreover, in his appraisal of the value of enslaved women's breast milk, he used both white women and cattle as his markers to begrudgingly admit that he was "sure that a Blacks Milk comes much nearer the Mothers than that of a Cow."[94] Although Sloane did not modify "Mothers," it is clear that for him mothers were white. Thus, their milk was most desirable. Meanwhile his placement of enslaved women like Susannah and Elizabeth as barely above cattle underscored their perceived inferiority and justified their exploitation.

It is difficult to know which of the enslaved women on Rendezvous wet-nursed Hester's and Frances's children. Given that most enslaved women breastfed for at least two years, and often for longer, they could act as wet nurses for a substantial amount of time after they gave birth, even though this timeline did not necessary conform to English preferences. It is possible that Judith, the enslaved woman who birthed a baby boy in May 1670 around the same time that Hester's John was born, acted as his wet nurse.[95] Susannah probably played this role for Hester's final child, Thomas, who was born in January 1676, about ten months after she birthed her first daughter. It is also conceivable that Elizabeth acted as a wet nurse to Hester's Thomas following the birth of her first son in August 1676. Elizabeth is the most likely candidate for wet-nursing Frances's three daughters. She gave birth to her final child with John in the same month, February 1682, that Frances conceived her first child. The birth dates of Dorothy's daughters and son meant that either Susannah or Elizabeth could have fulfilled this role for her. This form of "delegated mothering" created another layer of coerced intimacy on plantations "shot through with the violence of the slave system."[96]

If they nourished their children's half siblings, Susannah and Elizabeth no doubt experienced complex emotional responses to this chore. It is possible that as a result they had to turn the feeding of their own children over to other enslaved women on the plantation. This kind of "othermothering" that involved cross-feeding babies had long roots among African-descended women in the Americas, driven by the demands of enslavement. Susannah might have asked Elizabeth to step in and breastfeed her toddler and vice versa. In 1712 English army officer Thomas Walduck described an enslaved grandmother who took responsibility for feeding her grandchild for two years.[97] And although the evidence comes from the late eighteenth and the nineteenth centuries, this practice was also common in other American plantation settings.[98]

We do not know for sure that these demands on enslaved women's breasts occurred on Rendezvous, though it would be surprising if they did not. Such a system might have helped develop camaraderie among the women who shared the task of sustaining infants. Working in concert with one another would have provided opportunities to disrupt or even circumvent the broader rhythms that dictated physical labor on the plantation. It might also have been occasion for Susannah and Elizabeth to feel more enmeshed in the larger enslaved community on the estate if they relied on women outside the plantation house to nurture their sons and daughters. Scholars often emphasize the distance (physical and experiential) between domestics and enslaved field workers, and shared feeding of infants may well have been one instance when the gap narrowed or disappeared altogether. Equally, in feeding their enslavers' white children, Susannah and Elizabeth might have become less connected to their own.[99]

The distance created between mothers and children by wet-nursing also played out for John's wives. Their status meant that Hester and Frances were conditioned to hand their newborns to a wet nurse. These societal expectations did not necessarily prevent either Hester or Frances from finding separation from their infants painful. But they did set the parameters of what was possible for elite English mothers in the Caribbean. In Hester's case, employing a wet nurse was not the only way she expected to be distanced from her children.

From the very beginning it appears that Hester understood that her offspring would not remain in Barbados past the first few years of their lives. Before she departed England she left her firstborn with her sister, Ann, and her husband, Robert Chaplin. With no children of their own, Ann and Robert took Mary in, and in the next decade Hester's three Barbados-born sons, Richard, John, and Thomas, crossed the Atlantic Ocean at a young age, following their older sister into the Chaplin household. In a deposition given by Hester's second son, John, in 1698, he recalled how because his father was "living beyond the seas" he "did not know him." Hester's John noted how he "came over to England from the Barbadoes very young," so young, in fact, that while he believed his father had a "farme or Plantation there called the Rendezvous," he learned this information from his father only when John arrived in England in 1686. John's son and namesake had no recollection of the place where he was born.[100]

If Hester and Frances were not well placed to mother their own children, this fact did not prevent them from extending their power over Susannah's and Elizabeth's offspring. The presence of enslaved daughters and sons, especially in the early years, had the potential to disrupt household work, angering white mistresses, who had no compunction about asserting their authority over children who they viewed as their property to discipline. Neither did their shared status as mothers automatically result in maternal bonding with Susannah, Elizabeth, or even Dorothy. For Hester and Frances, maintaining their domination over the women who served them far exceeded any common ground they shared from the fact that all five women had given birth.[101] Their whiteness, combined with their elite status, made John's wives every bit as invested in shoring up plantation hierarchies as was their husband.

Like their mothers, John's enslaved and servant children had to navigate racial, gendered, and economic hierarchies in the Rendezvous household. It is likely that Hester's two eldest sons had departed for England before Susannah gave birth to her first daughter with John. But Hester's Thomas was born when Susannah's Judith was one year old, and they, along with Elizabeth's Richard and Dorothy's Frances probably spent their first few years together in the Rendezvous house. That they all shared the same father may or may not have been common knowledge among the children, although it was surely something their mothers understood.

Knowing that their sons and daughters would have markedly different lives from those of Dorothy's offspring must have been especially difficult for Susannah and Elizabeth. They might have believed the best way to deal with the situation was to be honest and forthright about their paternity, and their enslavement. After all, the children may have worn the family resemblance on their bodies.[102] Or perhaps they tried to shield the youngsters from the truth altogether. At some point, however, Susannah's Judith and Elizabeth's Richard would have realized that their status was very different from that of their white half brother and half sister.[103]

By the time Susannah's third child arrived in 1681, it is likely that Hester's Thomas had been sent to England for his education. This meant that there were one or two years during which Susannah's, Elizabeth's, and Dorothy's children lived at Rendezvous without any of their legitimate half siblings. It also meant that the relationships among the mothers likely changed. There were four years between Hester's death and John's marriage to Frances, during which time hierarchies within the "Mancon House" may well have been reshaped. Dorothy, as the white woman present, probably wielded even more power than usual over Susannah and Elizabeth, and she might have communicated to her children that they were more important than their mixed-race half siblings. Her daughters and son were now the most prominent white children on the plantation and could have acted accordingly. What this meant for Elizabeth, Susannah, and their children is impossible to know.

SUSANNAH NAVIGATED A COMPLEX set of intimacies within the Rendezvous household. Not only did she have John's two English wives to appease over at least fifteen years; she also likely had to endure Dorothy ordering her around, especially in the four years between Hester's death and Frances's arrival. Even Elizabeth's presence did not necessarily provide solace or feelings of solidarity. It is possible that each provided the other with comfort and friendship, perhaps even something akin to sisterhood, as they negotiated a life of seemingly unending productive and reproductive labor, although it is equally likely that they had animosity for one other or even felt jealousy because of their forced proximity. Both understood that it was their enslaver and his wives who dictated the outcomes for both them and their children. Just as they could not refuse John's sexual predation, so they could not guarantee a world in which they got to see their children grow up, even if they survived infancy and early childhood. They might even have felt differently about the act of mothering itself.

Giving birth laid bare the stark divisions between the experiences of Susannah and Elizabeth on the one hand, and those of Hester, Frances, and Dorothy on the other. None of the women would have been comfortable during parturition, but the white women got to enjoy the comforts of feather beds, while the enslaved women had little time to recover from the ordeal of childbirth. Susannah and Elizabeth would have had much less privacy, and no doubt a more uncomfortable setting. When it was over, they would have been expected to be back on their feet in the service of Hester or Frances almost immediately. At the same time, the process of giving birth might have offered Susannah or Elizabeth the opportunity to draw on memories or experiences they or the other women had from West Africa. They may have taken ceremonial baths, and relied on African birthing practices to keep themselves, and their newborns, safe.

Motherhood would have affected the women in dramatically different ways. Hester and Frances knew that by becoming mothers, they fulfilled their wifely duty, providing heirs, and spares, to ensure the continuation of the Peers line. In Hester's case, she mothered at a remove of over 4,000 miles from her children. Had she survived, Frances would probably have done the same. Dorothy held her children close and saw them grow up free. They would not be sent away, nor were they considered property to be entered in a ledger book. But they also bore the stain of bastardy and would never be equal to their white half siblings in status or rank. Nonetheless, Dorothy knew that their whiteness provided them protections not afforded Susannah's and Elizabeth's daughters and sons. Susannah's Judith, Richard, and Hester and Elizabeth's Richard, Elizabeth, and Edward all became inheritable chattel at birth. When their father died, there was every chance they would find themselves listed in his will as goods bequeathed to their half siblings, rather than as inheritors of property themselves. When John married Frances in 1682 and when his new bride began producing children of her own, the atmosphere and household hierarchies would have reshuffled once again.

CHAPTER 3

Rites of Passage

FRANCES, GOING INTO LABOR for the third time in as many years in March 1685, was familiar with the risks of bringing a new life into the world. At twenty-five years old, she should have been in her physical prime, but the seemingly unending cycle of pregnancy and childbirth had taken its toll on her body. Since her marriage in 1682 she had barely experienced a few consecutive months in which she was not pregnant. Frances no doubt worried about her physical strength. If she perished, what would become of her (as yet) unborn child? And if she were to survive, would her newborn survive also? Frances's predecessor, Hester, had buried two infant daughters (both named Elizabeth) on the island. Frances's eldest daughter received the same name, and now it appeared to bring good fortune as the third Elizabeth was thriving. So too was Frances's second daughter and namesake. This time around, Frances's labor likely moved more quickly, but it would have been no less exhausting. When Ann arrived, the baby seemed healthy enough. Frances, however, was not. Whether it was puerperal fever or some other childbed complication, weakness enfeebled her exhausted body. Ann was baptized on 22 March 1685; two weeks later, Frances died. Her body was laid to rest in the chancel at St. Michael's Parish church in Bridgetown, as befitting the wife of one of the island's foremost planters and daughter of a former governor.[1]

English elites in Barbados structured colonial society to mimic the one they left behind, importing religious and social practices that marked a child's arrival in the world, the forming of conjugal bonds, and a person's death. Had she given birth in England, Frances would have faced similar risks to those in Barbados, as the death of her own mother in Yorkshire three weeks after Frances was born confirmed.[2] The devastating mortality rates that characterized almost all slave societies dramatically altered the meaning of the universal building blocks of life in Barbados, heightening the importance of life affirming events.[3] The blunted life expectancy of islanders made baptism essential for preparing an infant's soul in the unhappy, but all too likely, event that they perish early. As their counterparts did in England, colonial governing classes ostentatiously displayed their authority and prosperity through lavish christening banquets. So too did couples emphasize their elite status by hosting huge wedding feasts to celebrate their nuptials. Though overshadowed by the specter of death, these occasions also signaled hope for the life that the child might live, and they signified the promise of generations to come. In early Barbados such assertions of largesse took on new importance as the fragile colonial system demanded frequent demonstrations of wealth and legitimacy. When someone of means died, as Frances did in April 1685, the funeral ceremony and place of burial also reinforced the person's rank and eminence.[4]

The enslaved women of Rendezvous had a very different relationship to signal life events. First, the natal alienation, social death, and commodification that undergirded the Middle Passage and enslavement meant that Africans and African-descended people were caught in a seemingly never-ending reassertion of kinship ties that were arbitrarily broken and relentlessly rebroken. Second, in Barbados, custom largely dictated that enslaved people could not marry or be interred in a churchyard, and neither they nor their children could be baptized. By codifying the rituals of birth, marriage, baptism, and death for white English Protestants alone, imperialists underscored the very bedrock on which Englishness, and therefore the colonial regime, stood.[5] In Barbados, as in all English colonies, "kinship could be claimed only in freedom." And as freedom on the island was something available only to white people, Black subjects found themselves in the position of having their kinship ties denied.[6]

And yet African and African-descended people still worked to mark these life events. They welcomed children into the world, forged conjugal relationships, and commemorated their dead through rituals and ceremonies—performed largely in private—that had West African roots. These much less visible practices were important to enslaved people, who used them to claim their own sense of worth and "soul value" in the face of a system of commodification that sought to render them property alone.[7] Often they did so in ways that were unintelligible to the European men who wrote about what they witnessed but who distorted the meaning of significant West African or Caribbean ceremonies through their racist assumptions about African behaviors.[8]

Into this broad frame, Susannah, Elizabeth, and their children emerge as exceptions. Because of the intimacy accorded to them by their proximity to John and his wives, they found themselves among the few enslaved people on the island to undergo initiation into the Church of England. Their baptisms were recorded in Christ Church Parish's register, encouraging a reading of their experiences that emphasizes their adoption of Anglo norms. This fact did not free Susannah or Elizabeth, nor their sons and daughters. Nor were these people now accorded access to marriage rites, or burial in an Anglican churchyard. Like the coerced sex to which the enslaved women were constantly subjected, these acts of baptism reveal much more about John (and perhaps Hester and Frances) than they do about Susannah or Elizabeth. Most importantly, baptism did not preclude the women from engaging in birthing and protection rituals that were West African in origin or prevent them (in Barbados at least) from celebrating enslaved couples or commemorating those who died. Susannah and Elizabeth had more ways than one to work against the disavowal and disruption that characterized enslaved women's lives. These strategies were no less real or important to the women or to the larger enslaved population on Rendezvous.

The initiation rituals, conjugal relationships, and commemorative practices that structured family life on Rendezvous for both English and African people demonstrate how family and kin connections were built and sustained, collectively weaving the fabric of empire.[9] The construction of intimate bonds mirrored colonial hierarchies, as evidenced by the chasm between how Frances (and Hester before her) celebrated marriage and the ways such formal conjugal relationships were denied to Susannah and Elizabeth because of their enslaved status, and to Dorothy by virtue of her birthing children out of wedlock. The reverberations from birth and death, meanwhile, had real-world consequences for all of Barbados's inhabitants.

Inheritance, for white elites, meant the establishment of generational wealth and power. Legitimate offspring had their futures assured. Whatever the loss of a loved one signified emotionally, their bloodlines, and financial heft, survived. For enslaved people, the death of an enslaver connoted the specter of family separation, while the passing of someone from within their own ranks—be it a family member, friend, workmate, or stranger—broke ties and brought community members together in collective acts of commemoration. These familial rites of passage demonstrate the insidious ways that empire was reproduced in Barbados as well as the limitations of that reproduction.

INITIATION AND NAMING

In December 1682 Frances gave birth to her first child, Elizabeth. Marking the event and welcoming Elizabeth into the family required Frances to embrace rituals that had traversed the Atlantic Ocean. English colonists, although generally unenthusiastic about attending church services on Sundays, were fairly scrupulous about baptizing their children. While their willingness may have stemmed from their belief that taking the sacrament was an essential part of becoming a good Christian, or been an expression of a broader set of initiation practices that underscored the arrival of a new community member, the main significance of such events was in underscoring the collective white, free, Protestant community to which English colonists of all ranks belonged.[10]

Although baptisms like Elizabeth's were recorded in Barbados's parish registers, the ceremonies themselves were conducted privately by clergy "always in their houses, never in the Churches." The private nature of the baptism therefore made the public feast for friends and acquaintances that followed especially important. The celebration was such a marker of status that less well-off parents often waited "until the good time comes, and the hog is fat," before arranging it.[11] As one of Barbados's most elite couples, Frances and John did not postpone Elizabeth's baptism feast for financial reasons, nor did the baptism of their second daughter, Frances, a little over a year later cause the family undue economic stress. Repeated displays of wealth were how the Peerses reminded friends, enemies, neighbors, and strangers of the political and social power they wielded on the island.

When Frances married John, and began living in the Rendezvous plantation home, she would not have been surprised that Susannah's and Elizabeth's children were not baptized. For as much as English parents were eager to bring their own children into the Church of England, they balked at the notion that enslaved people should receive the sacrament, worrying that their doing so would provide them a path to freedom.[12] Barbadian baptismal registers make manifest planters' reluctance to convert enslaved people. Although not all island church records have survived, those for Christ Church Parish are fairly complete for the seventeenth century. The first recorded baptism of a person of color in this parish occurred in 1651. In the fifty years that followed, only fifty-six non-whites received the sacrament in Christ Church. One family of six was marked as free, while the other fifty-one African-descended individuals were enslaved. The total recorded baptisms for Christ Church in these same fifty years reached around 4,000, meaning that fewer than 2 percent of those baptized in this period were of African descent.[13]

While the overall numbers of enslaved people baptized in Christ Church Parish were small, ten of the fifty-seven came from the Rendezvous plantation. On 29 May 1670, "John, son of Nocke & Judith, slaves to John Peers," was baptized. Ten days later Susannah and Elizabeth, as well as a third enslaved woman named Hester, experienced the ceremony. Thirteen years following that event, on 13 August 1683, Susannah's and Elizabeth's six mixed-race children were baptized together.[14] For John, one of the island's largest enslavers, these ten baptisms accounted for a very small fraction of his human property, which stood at around 180 men, women, and children in 1680. At the same time, with the exception of the enslaved boy John, and the enslaved woman Hester, all those baptized had a proven personal relationship with their enslaver. Perhaps John felt compelled to baptize the enslaved people to whom he was related, or who performed important roles on his plantation.[15]

When Susannah's and Elizabeth's children were baptized in 1683, English attitudes against baptizing enslaved people in Barbados had recently ossified. Authorities blamed the suspected 1675 slave revolt on Quaker attempts to convert enslaved Africans. In 1676 they endorsed the Quaker Negro Act, which barred Friends from bringing enslaved Africans to meetings in an attempt to quash future rebellious behavior.[16] This act was far from the first time elites expressed anxiety about Christianizing enslaved people. In the late 1640s Richard Ligon noted how enslavers insisted that baptizing enslaved Africans was illegal under English law and a dangerous precedent to set in a slave society.[17] At the beginning of the Restoration of the English monarchy in 1661, the Barbados Assembly and Council refused to pass a bill from England "recommending the christening of Negro children, and the instruction of all adult Negroes, to the several ministers of this place."[18] Twenty years later, in 1681, assembly members again rejected a request from London that they engage in widespread conversion, responding that the "savage Brutishness" of the enslaved "renders them wholly incapable" of becoming Christians. Later statements made by the assembly damned "converted negroes," declaring that they were "more perverse and intractable" (meaning debased and stubborn) than those who remained unsaved.[19]

Unlike their counterparts in England, the governing class of Barbados had a strong desire to draw strict lines between Christian and heathen, free and enslaved, and white and Black. Denying Africans access to the Church of

England helped keep colonial racial and labor hierarchies firmly in place. John, as a member of the Barbados Council in the 1680s, would have been aware of the deliberations in the assembly. Yet he seemingly ignored prohibitions about baptizing enslaved Africans when it came to his own flesh and blood, or to the enslaved women from whom he coerced sex.[20]

Rare as initiation into the Church of England was for enslaved people, when it did occur, it followed formal guidelines. In 1670 Susannah and Elizabeth were probably baptized inside Christ Church Parish church. The recently rebuilt stone building was designed to stand out on the landscape. Positioned around its fifteen-year-old font (the only remnant of the previous structure, which had been destroyed in a hurricane a few years earlier), the women would have orally professed their newfound beliefs. The Church of England liturgy for adult slaves undergoing baptism required individuals to "answer for themselves" when questioned by the minister about the key tenets of the faith.[21] Perhaps John instructed them in the appropriate ways to respond. Or maybe the women asked one of the other enslaved people on the plantation who knew of Christianity to teach them what they knew about the faith. Whether or not they believed in a Christian God was immaterial. Performing the ritual was all that mattered for the minister, who would have finished the ceremony by anointing the women with the water that signified their entrance into Barbados's Christian community.

Whatever Susannah and Elizabeth thought about the spiritual merits of Christianity, there is a good chance that they connected their baptisms, and those of their children, to the possibility of future freedom from bondage. Planters on Barbados insisted that there was no link between becoming a Christian and manumission in an attempt to maintain strict lines of racial division even among the small numbers of enslaved people who did receive the sacrament. Evidence among free persons of color on the island indicates that these former slaves did believe that such an association existed. One of the first steps that many recently manumitted enslaved people took was to claim membership in the Church of England for themselves and their families, using baptism to underscore their new status.[22]

Susannah, Elizabeth, and their children remained enslaved despite their baptisms, but they might have understood the process as predictive of a future beyond enslavement. John treated them differently from the rest of the enslaved population on Rendezvous, an action that both emphasized his control over the women and drew a stark line between them and their counterparts on the estate.[23] The women may well have been forced to acquiesce, but if not, Susannah and Elizabeth might have been expressing their own politics of freedom.

In their bodies they carried out the work of empire, ensuring the reproduction of its bonded class. They may have viewed their baptisms as a counter to this process, creating a "soul value" that would pay off, if not for them, then for their children, at some point in the future.[24]

Regardless of their stance on the ceremony, Susannah and Elizabeth would have been present for their children's baptisms, which (because their sons and daughters ranged in age from eighteen months to eight years) would have fallen under the liturgy guiding the "Ministration of Private Baptism of Children in Houses." Unlike their mothers, the children were too young to account for their understanding of the Christian faith, although the older children (like Judith, who was eight) may have been exposed to some Christian teachings.[25] The record does not indicate whether the women actively engaged in the ceremony or if they were mere bystanders. It is also impossible to tell whether Susannah and Elizabeth instigated the baptism, or if John or Frances decided that it was incumbent on him to acknowledge his progeny to the church.

Whatever brought the children to a baptism ceremony in the "Mancon House," it is probable that Susannah and Elizabeth had already performed rituals that were West African in shape and form that welcomed their children into the enslaved community on Rendezvous. West African parents long celebrated their children's arrival in the world through events that involved extensive kinship networks. When Europeans arrived on their shores, many described these practices, although they often misunderstood their full spiritual or cultural meanings. According to Willem Bosman, a Dutch West India Company official, when a baby was around a week old—"imagining that the Infant is past its greatest Dangers; and in order to prevent the evil Spirits from doing it any Mischief"—West African mothers and fathers held a feast.[26] Wilhelm Johann Müller, a chaplain at the Danish fort of Fredericksburg in the 1660s, suggested that on the thirteenth day of a Fetu newborn's life, the "father gives as large a feast as he can afford, having invited, in particular, the person after whom the child is named."[27] On the Gold Coast, parents allegedly anointed their newborns with palm wine to protect them from both physical and spiritual harms.[28] While food for feasting or the all-important palm wine may have been more difficult to acquire for enslaved families in Barbados, there were numerous people on the plantation who could have pooled their meagre resources to ensure that enslaved newborns got the welcome they deserved. Working inside the Rendezvous plantation house gave Susannah and Elizabeth access to additional food and drink, increasing their ability to hold such a feast.

European observers identified another common tradition among many West Africans: the use of power objects that acted as protection devices. Religious practitioners imbued these small packets of herbs, bones, or materials of other significance (often referred to as "fetishes" by Europeans) that could protect the wearer, combat an illness or disease, provide good luck, or ward off bad spirits.[29] According to Marees, parents were especially likely to hang power objects on the bodies of their children to protect them from various illnesses and accidents, or even to help them sleep.[30] There is reason to believe that, along with other enslaved women on Rendezvous, Susannah and Elizabeth used power objects to shepherd their children through the crucial first years of life long before they participated in the Christian baptism ceremony.[31]

If engaging children in an initiation ritual was one way to signify their membership in a community, then bestowing names was another important indicator of acceptance, belonging, and status. Naming practices in West Africa varied, although some general trends permeated the region. Parents on the Gold Coast described as "above common Rank" gave children three names. Bosman observed that "the first is that of the Day of the Week on which it is born," while the second name was that of a grandparent or other kin relation.[32] Barbot recorded the "customary" names given to girls and boys born in Accra in present-day Ghana, describing the collective process through which friends and family chose names. Sometimes these names included those taken from "white people with whom they have the most commerce and whom they esteem most highly." It is unclear what Barbot made of this practice, but giving a child a European name was the logical extension of West African traditions that honored significant individuals. In this way, contact with Europeans expanded the lexicon of names on the eastern side of the Atlantic Ocean.[33]

Frances was probably unfamiliar with West African naming practices, although customs such as day naming seemingly proliferated among the enslaved population on Rendezvous.[34] She did, however, understand the elite English practice of naming children for significant family members.[35] Hester and John's eldest and youngest sons, Richard and Thomas, were named for their paternal and maternal grandfathers respectively. Their surviving daughter bore the same name as both her grandmothers, Mary, embodying the union of the two families. Meanwhile Hester's middle son, John, was named for his father, and the two deceased Elizabeths were probably named for their paternal aunt.

Frances and John also named their eldest daughter Elizabeth, a necronymic practice that called on her two deceased half sisters, drawing a through thread from Hester's offspring to Frances's children. Frances's middle daughter carried her name, acknowledging the Atkins contribution to John's family status. Only their third daughter, Ann, stands alone. With no Anns in the Atkins or Peers genealogies, it appears that she was named for a nonblood relation, John's sister-in-law through his marriage to Hester. It is possible that her name was chosen to improve his relationship with the Chaplins, which had deteriorated considerably by the time of Ann's birth. Frances may even have encouraged this name as a way to stabilize the family right before she died.

Like John's children with his wives, almost all his "naturall born children" received Peers family first names, even though none of them used "Peers" as their last name. The six enslaved children were named Judith, Richard, Hester, Richard, Elizabeth, and Edward. Dorothy's free daughters and son were called Frances, Ann, and John. Of these names, only two are outliers—Dorothy's elder daughter, Frances (born four years before John married Frances Knights), and Susannah's eldest daughter, Judith. The rest are names that appear with varying degrees of frequency in the Peers family tree. It is therefore easy to assume that John assigned these names to his children. But the women may have been involved in the choices to remind John of his paternity or to tie their daughters and sons more explicitly to their half siblings. Hester or Frances may also have weighed in. And although the children appear to have used these names in their later lives, it is possible that their mothers called them by other names when they were alone, names that perhaps spoke to their West African heritage, like so many parents on Rendezvous appear to have done.

There is no record of how Susannah came to be enslaved on Rendezvous, but the available evidence strongly suggests that she was born in West Africa. In John's will she has a second name, "Mingo," probably the diminutive of the Portuguese word for Sunday, *Domingo*.[36] Given John's proclivity for trading illegally with Portuguese slavers, and the prevalence of day naming in the Gold Coast region of West Africa, the name suggests that Susannah was born in Africa and that her origins can be traced to that region. As "Mingo" was more commonly attributed to men, it is likely that its inclusion was to commemorate one of her important male relatives. Yet "Mingo" was probably not Susannah's last name as Europeans might understand it. Rather, it was likely an additional name that underscored her patrilineal kin connections.[37]

It is not only Susannah's name that offers evidence of West African naming practices: the naming of her first daughter, Judith, also appears to reflect such norms. While using the name of an important male ancestor was common in West Africa, significant women could also be recognized as a way to underscore an existing kinship tie or create a new one. Judith's name does not appear anywhere in the Peers family tree, but it was the name of the mother of the enslaved boy baptized just ten days before Susannah in 1670, the same woman who may well have acted as Susannah's midwife. When Susannah chose Judith as her firstborn's name, she forged a kinship link, a common practice among enslaved women. The name itself might not have been West African, but its meaning was. Moreover, if Susannah named her first daughter after Judith, John would not necessarily have known or understood the full "emotional or social value" of Susannah's choice.[38]

Judith may not have been the only enslaved woman that Susannah recognized when naming her children. Her second daughter, Hester, born in 1681, bore the name of John's first wife. Certainly, John could have insisted on the repeated use of the name in commemorating his recently deceased spouse. Hester was also the name of the third enslaved woman baptized alongside Susannah and Elizabeth in 1670, so it is equally likely that Susannah chose to honor someone with whom she shared a bond.[39] That the name Hester had meaning for both Susannah and John underscores the complex nature of slave naming in the Americas. It also shows how the younger Hester's identity was connected to both sides of her family. She was enmeshed in both her mother's and her father's kinship networks, her name locating her firmly within European and West African traditions of recognizing and celebrating kin.

If the enslaved women did mark the births of their children with a celebration attended by the enslaved population on Rendezvous, there is a good chance that others from within that circle helped to prepare the event. Such a feast, whether to celebrate a Christian baptism or a West African naming ceremony, would not necessarily have demonstrated the women's adaptation to European norms, or indicated a retention of West African practices, but it served both purposes simultaneously. Frances, if she was present at the children's baptisms, might even have encouraged the women to mark the moment, even if she could not have understood, or perhaps been privy to, the other kinds of rituals that Susannah and Elizabeth performed on their newborns. By the time Judith, Richard, Hester, Richard, Elizabeth, and Edward underwent a Church of England initiation ceremony in August 1683, their mothers might have already considered them well protected and prepared for life as a result of adapted West African rites they had performed years before. Equally, Susannah and Elizabeth may have taken comfort in their baptisms, viewing them as a similarly important marker of inclusion in the dangerous world they and their children inhabited.

CONJUGAL RELATIONSHIPS

In February 1679, when she was almost nineteen, Frances wed planter and enslaver Benjamin Knights (her first husband before her marriage to John Peers) in Bridgetown. Whether she had been in Barbados since her father's appointment as governor in 1674, or (more likely) had arrived recently, as the daughter of the island's most prominent person she was a catch. Benjamin, who appears to have lived in Barbados for some years, was already well established, serving as a member of the Barbados Council at the time of their nuptials. Marrying the governor's daughter gave him access to an ever-higher echelon of power in the colony. Thus, their union—like that of so many couples of their class and status—was probably a business transaction first. Desire, romantic love, and affection were not taken into account when elite young Englishwomen married. Just as Hester brought capital and legitimacy to her partnership with John, so too did Frances elevate Benjamin's status when she became his wife. Marriage knitted elite families together and helped ensure colonial stability and success.

Given that her father was the governor, Frances married Benjamin in St. Michael's in Bridgetown rather than in St. James, where Benjamin's Bully Gibbons plantation was located. The ceremony was effectively identical to English weddings. Jonathan Atkins would have "given" his daughter in marriage. Those in attendance would have been asked if they knew of any reason that she and Benjamin should not be wed. Since Frances was a first-time bride, her hands would have been bare, ready to receive her ring. The couple would have exchanged vows, each pledging "to have and to hold from this day forward, for better, for worse, for richer, for poorer, in sickness and in health, to love and to cherish, till death us depart," with Frances adding her promise "to obey" Benjamin.[40] Once these rituals were complete, the minister would summarize the ways that the couple had "pledged their troth" in front of the assembled witnesses, and finish by pronouncing "that they be man and wife together." In the words they spoke, and the promises they made, Benjamin and Frances not only certified their union in the Church of England; they also participated in a centuries-old patriarchal tradition replicated in the colonies.

As in England, the social aspects of weddings were more attractive to Barbados colonists than their religious significance was.[41] The marriage of Benjamin, a prominent planter and council member, and Frances, the daughter of the governor, was politically as well as socially important. To underscore this fact, whether the wedding was attended by only a handful of their closest friends and relatives or a large number of guests, a sumptuous feast accompanied the celebrations. West Indian elites were famous for their hospitality, which one author suggested "exceeded" those in the "Mother Kingdome."[42] Visitors wrote of dinners with over a dozen dishes served as the main event, including (when location permitted) all sorts of seafood and fish, "to wit, *Mullets, Mackerels, Parrot fish, Snappers,* red and gray, *Cavallos, Terbums, Crabs, Lobsters,* and *Cony fish,* with divers sorts more, for which we have no names." Barbados tables overflowed with tropical fruits such as "Plantains, Bananas, Guavas, Melons, prickled Pear, Anchovy Pear, prickled Apple, Custard Apple, water Melons, and Pineapples." And although domestic alcoholic beverages like "Mobbie, Beverage, Brandy, Kill-Devil," and "Drink of the Plantain" were offered, it was the more expensive, imported liquids like "Claret-wine, White-wine, and Rhenish-wine, Sherry, Canary, Red sack, wine of Riall, with all Spirits that come from *England*" that were a real signal of wealth and power.[43] The wedding feast of the daughter of the governor must have been equally extravagant and may have lasted for several days.

It was not only the dishes and libations that separated Barbados from England, but also how these refreshments were prepared. Accounts of elite celebrations in Barbados use a lot of passive voice to describe drinks, rich dishes, and overflowing tables, hiding the labor of the enslaved women and men who procured, cooked, presented, and served the food. Equally, African and African-descended people provided the all-important entertainment, with the "chiefe Musitian" and those who accompanied him mostly likely enslaved. Playing at festivities took musicians away from field work and other tasks, while also placing entertainers under the watchful gaze of whites. They would have altered their musical practices to suit their audience. Fiddlers, lutenists, banjo players, and drummers provided the melodies, but none, as Ligon noted, "that are laborious," as the climate rendered it too dangerous in his estimation for vigorous dancing.[44]

The social effects of marriage rendered white women important helpmeets to their husbands, conferring legitimacy on any children they produced, and establishing a coterie of roles for wives as household managers.[45] This fact meant that a union was most often viewed in England as a business transaction arranged between fathers and would-be husbands; women had little legal standing of their own. Considered their fathers' property before they married, women became covered by their husband's legal personhood when they wed. Frances's marriage to Benjamin bears all the hallmarks of such a financial arrangement as her spouse and father negotiated a marriage contract that stipulated what Frances would receive should Benjamin "depart this life" before her. Rather than leave his widow her share of the acreage and 202 enslaved Africans who labored on Bully Gibbons plantation, his "deare and Loveing wife" would be left money, a substantial £3,000. Half of the payment was that put up by her father as her dowry, and half was money that Benjamin redeemed from his estate. The terms of this arrangement were worked out before Frances and Benjamin were married, and they were codified in his will as a reminder to his brother and executor (who was going to inherit the rest of Benjamin's property "real and personall" in Barbados) to ensure Frances received her due.[46] While Benjamin was alive, the £1,500 that Frances brought to their union could be deployed in shoring up his already substantial plantation.

High rates of widowhood in the colonies changed elite Englishwomen's relationship to property holding, and as a result, arrangements like those between her new husband and her father also provided Frances with some financial and legal independence. Understanding that life was short and could be ripped away at any moment, fathers often sought to protect property that a daughter brought to a marriage from her husband's grasp. For example, enslaved people were often specifically left to a woman "and her heirs forever" to prevent them becoming communal property in marriage. White women enslavers built on this practice, regularly writing wills that privileged a female line of inheritance and bequeathing enslaved property to daughters or nieces to keep property in the hands of their blood descendants.[47] Husbands also sought to protect their estates from the potential suitors who might approach their widows. The marriage contract between Benjamin and Frances contains these elements. When Benjamin died, Frances inherited a large cash sum, but received only "my mollatto Girl Franke" from his enslaved property because he specifically bequeathed this woman to her and her heirs forever. She was not to receive any other enslaved people from the Bully Gibbons estate.

When Frances wed John sometime early in 1682, she most probably did so from her new home, Rendezvous.[48] As with her first wedding, enslaved people prepared the nuptial feast, Susannah and Elizabeth very probably among them. Meanwhile, the "mollatto Girl Franke," who had been bequeathed to Frances specifically "to wait on her" surely assisted her new mistress in dressing and preparing for the ceremony.[49] Almost all brides wore new shoes and specially designed clothing at their weddings in England, a practice that continued in the West Indies, especially among elites. As a second-time bride, Frances would have worn gloves to signify her widowed status.[50] Perhaps Franke helped sew elaborate lace trim to her dress and gloves, as well as helping Frances don her gown and fix her hair. Remarrying meant that Frances was also familiar with the ceremony and understood what to expect when the minister, Thomas Kenny, asked her to recite her vows.

One person who was very likely present at the marriage, though conflicted about its outcome, was Dorothy Spendlove, the Englishwoman with whom John had three children, the youngest of whom was just one year old when Frances wed John. Dorothy was also probably the only white woman on the plantation following John's first wife's death in 1678, and as someone who gave him heirs (albeit ones considered illegitimate by the state), she might have wondered if she could become John's second wife. Dorothy was perhaps aware of the Caribbean's reputation as a place where women of lower status could make a good marriage and advance socially. As one mid-seventeenth-century commentator put it, in Barbados "a bawd brought over puts on a demure comportment, a whore if handsome makes a wife for some rich planter."[51]

If this was Dorothy's hope, she was disappointed.[52] Not only was John unlikely to sully his reputation by marrying a woman who bore children out of wedlock (even if they were his offspring), but by the early 1680s there was no shortage of white women on the island, and so John was able to bide his time and find an appropriate bride. An additional benefit of marrying Frances was the money she brought to the union, and the tantalizing specter of her first husband's property. John waited until he found a bride who could provide not only heirs but also much-needed capital to advance his success.

Weddings were an opportunity for elite classes to celebrate among themselves, and they were also occasions to assert hierarchies closer to home. At Rendezvous, it is likely that the work of the plantation ground to a halt so that John's 180-strong enslaved labor force could witness the arrival of a new mistress and the concurrent assertion of legitimacy and whiteness that Frances's nuptials inaugurated. As Frances and John were probably married in February or March, before the round-the-clock demands of the sugar harvest, permitting the work of the estate to stop for a few hours would have had few financial repercussions. Along with the field workers, Susannah and Elizabeth may well have witnessed the ceremony, even if they were also charged with preparing the feast. There is a chance that Elizabeth may have been less visible—she was either at the very end of her pregnancy with Edward or had recently given birth when the wedding took place.

If elite Barbados society considered John and Frances's marriage to be emblematic of a stable colony, the enslaved people on Rendezvous had the opposite view. Marriage brought uncertainty, and with it, anxiety. What kind of mistress would Frances be? Cruel? Dismissive? Assertive? Aloof? Timid? Attentive? All of the above, according to her caprices? The answers for each enslaved person on any given day would no doubt shift depending on Frances's mood. Enslaved people brought from Bully Gibbons plantation, especially the "mollatto Girl Franke," may have been quizzed by others about her mistress's temperament while at the same time trying to figure out what her own life in John's household or plantation would entail. While preparing for the wedding, Franke might well have come to understand that John was the father of Susannah's and Elizabeth's children, wondered if John would turn his attention to her, and considered how that development would affect her relationship with Frances as well as with the rest of the enslaved population on Rendezvous. The anxiety produced by her unknown future, her curiosity about the people she would meet at her new home, and the pain and trauma of being removed from friends and loved ones at Bully Gibbons no doubt framed Franke's introduction to Rendezvous and to the enslaved people who labored on the plantation.

The enslaved people who witnessed the wedding at Rendezvous might have compared the ceremony to their own rituals surrounding conjugal relationships. If Susannah and Elizabeth helped prepare John and Frances's marriage feast, they may have recognized its importance from comparisons with West African practices where generous displays of hospitality were a way to demonstrate social and political power. Barbot described how, at a wedding in Accra, the groom's relatives gathered at the home of the bride, where music and dancing commenced before she was decorated with gold jewelry. He also noted that on the Gold Coast, when a match was made, "25 or 30 *livres* in gold" were paid as a dowry "to be used for palm wine and other things for the wedding." In addition to the gold, "a slave is also given, to serve the woman the groom marries."[53] When Frances arrived at Rendezvous with Franke in tow, enslaved West Africans, including perhaps Susannah and Elizabeth, might have viewed the girl as a wedding gift and as a sign of Frances's wealth. The parallels between elite practices on both sides of the Atlantic Ocean allowed enslaved people to make sense of colonial hierarchies on their own terms.

But what of conjugal relationships among enslaved people themselves? Recognizing partnerships and marriage-like unions was important to enslaved women and men in Barbados.[54] Legally, they could not wed in a way that English colonists would recognize, although that did not mean that forging conjugal bonds was something they eschewed. Just as with initiation rites and naming, making a marriage commitment served to recreate familial bonds and to rebuild relationships destroyed by the Middle Passage. Captive West Africans were adept at this kind of kin-building work.[55] They may have not had the right to legally marry, but that fact did not mean that enslaved people were bereft of marriage rites.

There are few sources indicating such partnerships in late seventeenth-century Barbados, and those that exist were created by English observers who held racist ideas about African sexuality and who failed to acknowledge the power dynamics of slavery. For example, Ligon claimed that enslaved men could force their enslavers to purchase more women from Africa, complaining that "they cannot live without Wives." Ligon went on to explain how enslaved men chose brides according to how their enslaver perceived the men's strength, fitness, and virility. There was no room in Ligon's assessment for captive women to make partnership choices, or for affection to build over time among enslaved men and women. Rather, in his fantastical imagination, enslaved men held the power to pick their partners, albeit under a system of hierarchy dictated by their enslavers. Ligon also claimed that "planters there deny not a slave, that is a brave fellow, and one that has extraordinary qualities, two or three Wives, and above that number they seldom go: But no woman is allowed above one Husband."[56]

Ligon lays bare the perverse foundations of a system that could self-sustain should enslaved women produce children who survived to adulthood. It was also one in which white Englishmen were unwilling to concede that enslaved women were anything other than objects to be acted on by men, enslaved or otherwise. The prohibition against enslaved women having more than one husband, which Ligon framed as entirely in the power of enslaved men to control, completely obscured the fact that it was Englishmen who dictated access to enslaved women's bodies. An enslaved woman may have or may not have had more than one enslaved man as a partner, but all enslaved women were vulnerable to the white men who enslaved them, who managed them, or who were visitors to the plantations where they lived.[57] When men like Ligon wrote about enslaved women's allegedly "adulterous" behavior, they ignored the reality that it was white men's sexual predation that accounted for many of these accusations. In their world, enslaved women controlled their bodies and their sexual behavior, the precise opposite of reality.

Enslaved couples who formed conjugal relationships are hard to glimpse in the plantation records belonging to Rendezvous. Estate inventories reveal some parent-child relationships and in a few cases hint at multigenerational families. They do not, as a rule, note long-term partnerships between enslaved men and women.[58] Created by plantation managers, these records highlight the kinds of connections that white men found useful and ignore ones that mattered to enslaved people. There is one entry, in Christ Church's baptism register, that hints at a long-term relationship. Judith and Nocke, who appear in their son's May 1670 baptism entry, leave no other trace. This scant record indicated that they were baptized themselves, and that they were a couple whose relationship was recognized by John or Hester.[59] And yet, despite this seeming acknowledgment of a serious attachment between Judith and Nocke, we cannot know how they viewed their relationship, or how they felt about one another. Did they meet at Rendezvous? Was their relationship one they chose? Did they remain together, or did they part ways, either by choice or because one of them died or was sold away? Was this son the only child they had together?[60] Did they engage in a ceremony to share their commitment to one another with the wider enslaved community on Rendezvous?

If Judith and Nocke did seal their relationship in Barbados, then their union was likely marked with the kinds of celebrations that punctuated enslaved life in the colony. We know from English commentaries that days when field work was not carried out—Sundays, as well as a handful of days of significance in the Christian calendar, like Christmas and Easter—were times when enslaved people could gather, play music, dance, and otherwise engage in recreation.[61] Of course, these writers' accounts missed the possible religious, spiritual, or community meanings behind such celebrations, instead often reading them as evidence of lack of civility, or even barbarity. None of these accounts specifically suggests that marriage rituals may have been part of these festivities, or that Sunday might have been a day when enslaved people marked significant life events.

Nonetheless, their "several Ceremonies, as Dances, Playing, &c," and those occasions when they "feast, sing, and dance," might well have included the kind of marriage rites that united couples like Judith and Nocke. At such times, the dancing, which included "mixth men and women together," was accompanied by "their Music, which is of kettle drums, and those of several sizes; upon the smallest the best Musician plays, and the others come in as Choruses."[62] The same enslaved musicians who might have played at Frances's wedding may also have provided the entertainment for enslaved nuptial celebrations on Rendezvous. Playing in this context would have meant something quite different, and no doubt the music and the rhythms reflected enslaved people's choices, not those of their enslavers.

Enslaved women like Susannah and Elizabeth, and the scores of other women who were held hostage at Rendezvous, likely formed affective relationships with other enslaved people for a whole range of reasons including love, lust, loneliness, and boredom. Whether Susannah or Elizabeth were intimate with enslaved men on the plantation, or with enslaved men from estates close by, is unknown, but the records suggest that the children they bore were all fathered by John, although it is possible that Elizabeth had her eldest son and daughter with another man. Not mentioned in the 1683 baptism records, Elizabeth's John and Susanna were born sometime before 1675. Even so, they were provided for in John's will and were described as among his "naturall born" children, a strong indication that they were also his offspring.

Despite their connection to John, it is entirely possible that Susannah and Elizabeth had relationships running the gamut from casual encounters to conjugal partnerships with enslaved men. Then again, other enslaved people on Rendezvous would have known how John treated the women, and this may have prompted potential suitors to keep their distance rather than risk an entanglement that could jeopardize their own well-being. John's claims on Susannah's and Elizabeth's bodies likely curtailed the opportunities and possibilities for intimate connections with other enslaved people on the plantation. And yet both women may have sought comfort and connection elsewhere.

DEATH, MOURNING, AND COMMEMORATION

New lives created through conjugal relationships were important events to mark, but with four burials for every baptism among the white population of Barbados, death was the more ubiquitous experience.[63] English colonizers brought with them a "belief system in which death and the dead stood at the very center." When someone was grievously ill, family and friends came together at the deathbed to bear witness to his or her passage to the other side. Sometimes their actions at the bedside took the form of praying or included outward expressions of sadness such as crying.[64] It is likely that Frances and members of the Bully Gibbons plantation household stood vigil around the bed of her first husband, Benjamin Knights. Benjamin suffered from "a lingering distemper" and was deemed "not likely to recover" when he wrote his last will and testament on 10 December 1681. He died a few weeks later.[65]

Benjamin's prominence in the community demanded that his friends and family members undertake a complex process of grieving upon his death. First, according to long-held Christian practices, his body had to be washed and shrouded in linen cloth. While wives commonly performed this work, Benjamin's status made it more likely that Frances supervised servant or enslaved women in this intimate task, which in her husband's case may well have fallen to the "mollatto Girl Franke." Following the intimate cleaning ritual, Benjamin's body was placed in a simple wooden coffin. The casket was then relocated to a room in the plantation house where friends and family could pay their respects.[66] Although these were solemn affairs, participants often reminisced fondly about the deceased, imbibed alcohol, and even laughed together. Members of the Barbados Council (including John), along with some of the island's other prominent residents, would have come to view Benjamin's body.

Every aspect of Benjamin's funeral would have reflected his high status. A coach and horses likely transported his body to St. James's Parish church. Although records for the island are scarce, his coffin was probably draped with a cloth covering known as a pall, symbolically elevating him above poorer

St. James's Parish Church, Holetown, Barbados, where Frances was married
and her first husband was buried. Author's collection.

whites who could not afford such luxury. Like so many of his counterparts in
St. Michael and Christ Church Parishes, Benjamin was probably laid to rest in
the interior of St. James's church, another signifier of wealth and status, or, as
one historian has termed it, "conspicuous decomposition." Individuals not only
had to pay for the marble stone and for the privilege of a location within the
building's walls; they also had to provide funds for moving the pews to allow the
interment to take place. Interment within church walls reminded future generations of the deceased's social and political power. Benjamin's precise death date
and the location of his grave remain unknown, though his interment inside the
church would permit Frances to be in the presence of her dead husband when
she attended Sunday services.[67]

   As with other important life events, funerals were also marked by a lavish feast at the home of the deceased. For elites, the quantity and quality of
the refreshments underscored the departed's high status, as did the widow's
mourning clothes and loved ones' jewelry and other adornments. Wills often
made specific provision for such outward expressions of grief, bequeathing
money directed to the purchase of "mourning rings." Benjamin's will identified

thirteen people who were to receive "a mourning ring of forty shillings price." Five were current or former council members, two were his "Brother in Law Collonell Thomas Walrond and his Lady," and the rest were prominent judges, merchants, and militia leaders.[68] For these important members of island society, wearing mementos reflected Benjamin's status and the honor due him in death. It also marked their proximity to or membership in the colonial elite and reminded others of their kinship ties to the deceased.

It was at Benjamin's death that Frances, now a widow, found herself in the position of having some momentary power of her own. The monetary inheritance from her first husband was not the only property that Frances would bring into a potential second marriage. She received many personal items from Benjamin's estate including "all the jewells Rings and Gould that I am possest of in this island" and "all my houshold lynnen . . . all my Plate that I have." In addition, she was granted "my Blacke horse with the side saddle and all the furniture for her own Riding And also my Best Bedd and Chamber furniture." Not only did Frances inherit the "mollatto Girl Franke"; she also had the implicit "increase" from Franke—if the enslaved girl was to go to Frances's "heires for ever," so too would any surviving children Franke birthed.[69]

When combined with the £3,000 she got from the estate, this windfall made the twenty-one-year-old France very attractive to single men. Marriage to her brought wealth and connection to an important former governor and a kinship tie to the powerful Walrond family through Frances's sister. Unsurprisingly, "within a very few months" she was married to John Peers "according to the Laws Ecclesiasticall in England."[70] On the first anniversary of Benjamin's death Frances was firmly ensconced at Rendezvous and had given birth to her first child.

When John and Frances wed, John gained access to the finances she brought to the marriage, and he also availed himself of the property of her first husband that was not his (or Frances's) to claim. Frances was allowed to live on the Bully Gibbons plantation only for one year, "provided she shall soe long continue widow." During this year she would have the use of Benjamin's "Coach and Coach horses," and "the service and command of my Negroes for her attendance."[71] Upon her marriage to John these perks were supposed to end. Nonetheless, insisting that she, and therefore he, had a right to one-third of Benjamin's estate, John seized what he considered his, regardless of Benjamin's wishes. It is possible that Frances urged him on in this matter, or at least did not stand in his way. While women in England rarely wielded such power, Frances had already seen one husband perish before his time. She might have hoped to secure an even more lucrative inheritance should John suffer a similar fate.

Benjamin's "lingering distemper" was not uncommon in Barbados. Dysentery and yellow fever, as well as general "agues" tormented Caribbean inhabitants, stalking enslaved and free populations with unremitting persistence. According to a Swiss doctor who visited the island in the 1660s, "Most persons who come here from Europe will have to overcome an illness which the inhabitants call *Contrey Diseas*. Its nature is such that the people turn quite yellow, their stomachs and legs swell, and sometimes their legs burst and remain open." Africans were no less susceptible to infection, frequently suffering from smallpox, yaws, and intestinal distress.[72] While whites may have been infected at higher rates, enslaved populations' harsh working conditions, crowded living arrangements, and poor diets made them especially vulnerable to disease. Because enslaved men, women, and children suffered from malnutrition, illness was often accompanied by death. And given the fact that the enslaved population outnumbered the white population of Barbados over two to one by the final decades of the seventeenth century, even if whites had higher mortality rates, enslaved people's deaths were far more common and more visible.

For the vast majority of enslaved people, death, not birth, was constitutive of life. On the coast of West Africa, as captives waiting to be boarded on cavernous slave ships; during the Middle Passage itself, where an average of 20 percent perished on each voyage; and on plantations, where the demands of sugar production literally and figuratively consumed their bodies: enslaved people died in horrific numbers. Adding complexity to enslaved mourning practices were the high rates of infant mortality and the need to adapt mortuary practices to reflect the new world in which they lived. Thus, for enslaved people on Barbados, deathways (how they said good-bye to deceased friends and loved ones) became an organizing feature of their lives. It was through burial and commemoration that West African beliefs, rituals, and practices sustained connections and emphasized newly formed kinship ties.[73]

The probate and parish records that reveal the deaths of Hester, Frances, Benjamin, and their relations do not have their corollary for enslaved people, and the few extant plantation records for this period rarely include commentary on the deaths of the enslaved. Although we know that Susannah and Elizabeth birthed three children apiece, we do not know whether they bore other children who did not survive. Another question surrounds what happened to the enslaved woman named Hester, who disappears from the parish registers following her own baptism. John singled her out for special treatment alongside Susannah and Elizabeth, and so it is likely that he made claims on her body just as he made claims on theirs.

Perhaps she fell out of favor and was sent away: there is a woman named Hester in the 1705 slave inventory for John's other Barbados plantation, Staple Grove, located three miles away.[74] Given the high rate of mortality in Barbados, it is possible either that the Hester baptized alongside Susannah and Elizabeth in 1670 became ill and died before birthing any of John's children, or that childbirth proved fatal for her. In fact, it is possible her baptism occurred *because* she was sickly and near death. If so, there are no records that mark her passing, nor any that discuss the ceremony that followed her demise.

Although Hester's death might not be visible to us, the practices that surrounded it would have reflected her status within the enslaved community on Rendezvous. When they came together to grieve in Barbados, enslaved people drew on West African deathways encompassing a range of rituals that prepared the deceased for burial, ensured their souls traveled safely to the realm of the ancestors, and kept the newly departed loved one sated and safe in their place of rest. West Africans also fashioned mortuary devices that they hoped would "bring the corpse to the other world."[75] As they mourned their loss, men and women conducted a "spiritual inquest" of the deceased's body to ascertain who, if anyone, had been involved in the individual's death.[76] While Europeans frequently mocked this mortuary ritual, it was an important part of mourning as the bereaved struggled to make sense of their loss. Following the interrogation of the dead, the corpse was washed, wrapped in cloth, and readied for interment as friends and family sprinkled ashes on the shroud.[77]

Unlike the relatively quiet atmosphere that permeated elite European burials, Gold Coast funerals were reportedly noisy affairs. Visceral outpourings of grief were a necessary show of respect for the deceased and often reflected their status in the community. A German pastor who spent several years in the region noted how mourners expressed their sorrow "with much shouting, wailing, and lamenting."[78] Bosman noted that family members "set up such a dismal Crying, Lamentation and Squeaking, that the whole Town is filled with it."[79] Marees described how the corpse was carried, strapped to a board by men while women walked alongside. They sang, wept, and drummed on metal basins throughout the procession to the grave.

Sometimes this journey was short: many individuals were buried inside their homes, a practice known as subfloor burial. Barbot described how "the dead are usually interred in the hut where they died, because they have no cemeteries or special [burial] places."[80] But Barbot missed the point. Keeping loved ones close at hand facilitated communion with ancestors and allowed grievers to furnish burial sites with grave goods that ensured peace in the afterlife. Andreas

Ulshiemer, a German barber-surgeon, asked his West African hosts why a man had been buried in his bedroom and was told that the eldest son "has his bed very close to his father, who lies buried there; and when he eats or drinks something, he gives his father the first mouthful." His doing so ensured both the father's peace and the son's happiness and prosperity.[81] Other Gold Coast residents were laid to rest in community cemeteries, and here too grave goods and offerings were a key part of the ceremony. Clothing and "household stuff" was placed inside the grave, while items like food, drink, and palm oil were laid on top of the burial and replenished over time.[82] The quality of the offerings reflected the standing of the individual who had passed.

The noise that surrounded an interment continued at the postburial feast. French agent Nicolas Villault remarked that following burial, mourners "return weeping and lamenting to their houses, where both men and women do wash themselves forthwith, after which they eat the Beef or Mutton which was bought, passing the rest of the day in feasting and jollity."[83] Another described such events looking "more like a Wedding than a Funeral" because "as soon as the Corps is in the Ground, every one goes where they please, but most to the House of Mourning, to drink and be merry, which lasts for several Days successively."[84]

Many of these practices—shrouding the body, interring it in the ground, feasting, and commemorating the dead—were common in a variety of cultures, but this did not stop Europeans commenting on their supposed unusual qualities in West African settings. Neither were these rituals static. As the seventeenth century progressed, European commodities made their way into grave goods, and European guns became part of the noise-making at funerals.[85] These adaptations continued in the Americas, where the trauma and social death engendered by slavery forced West Africans to modify their deathways to reflect new circumstances.

One of the most commonly observed changes in Caribbean mortuary practices was in enslaved beliefs about the movement of the deceased's soul. Ligon suggested that in Barbados West Africans believed in "a Resurrection, and that they shall go into their own Country again, and have their youth renewed."[86] A German indentured servant who spent time on the island in the early 1650s concurred, describing how "if one among the slaves dies, they say he has returned to his homeland and friends and is doing well."[87] This belief in the soul's transmigration to the homeland upon death was just one of the religious ideologies that shifted as a result of enslavement.

In the Americas, West Africans' theological worldviews had to adapt to allow the deceased to journey across the Atlantic Ocean. Europeans reported that as a result of their belief in this return, West Africans viewed death posi-tively. One early eighteenth-century Jamaican merchant insisted that enslaved people "look on death as a blessing," explaining that "they are quite transported to think their slavery is at an end, and that they shall revisit their happy native shores, and see their old friends and acquaintance."[88] The idea of death as a respite from enslavement was, as Sasha Turner points out, a self-serving way for European observers to mitigate their role in the violence of the institution. Moreover, assuming that enslaved people faced death with confidence reduces or occludes the possibility that they experienced real and sustained grief at the loss of a loved one.[89]

Distress at death may have been especially acute for enslaved parents. Trans-migration for those born in West Africa might have held some comfort, but for saltwater mothers and fathers of children born in the Caribbean, death por-tended a severing of ties. Parents would return to their homeland upon death, whereas their island-born children would remain in the Americas. In this way, "death likely amplified mothers' sense of loss when their creole children died."[90] We do not know if either Susannah or Elizabeth suffered such a loss, but if either of them did, she might well have felt even more removed from her own place of birth as she realized the implications for continued separation from her children in death.[91]

If the enslaved woman Hester did die on Rendezvous, then it is likely that she received a burial at the hands of the enslaved population on the estate. Despite her baptism, her funeral would not have been performed by the Church of England.[92] Hester's resting place would probably have been in an area demar-cated as the slave burial ground close to where the majority of the enslaved population lived. In 1676 Governor Jonathan Atkins described to his superiors in London how "the negroes bury one another in the ground of the plantation where they die, not without ceremonies of their own," although he did not elaborate on what form those ceremonies took.[93] Morgan Godwyn, an English clergyman visiting Barbados, concurred, noting in disgust how rather than per-forming Christian rites, planters instead encouraged funerals to be conducted *"after the Negro fashion."*[94]

"After the Negro fashion" burials were held at the end of the workday and usu-ally included what European writers considered excessive demonstrations of emotion. Ligon noted, "When any of them die, they dig a grave, and at evening they bury him, clapping and wringing their hands, and making a dolefull sound with their voices."[95] Other Englishmen who spent time on Jamaica at the close of the seventeenth century made similar remarks. John Taylor suggested that enslaved people "make a great adoe at their burials for having caryed them to

the grave in a verey mournfull manner, all both men & women which accompany the corpse sing and howle in a sorrowfull manner in their own language 'till being come to the grave."[96] Describing funerals of the enslaved, Hans Sloane remarked how "their country people make great lamentations, mournings, and howlings about them expiring."[97] It is likely that such ceremonies were frequent occurrences on Rendezvous, where the constant influx of West Africans replenished those who succumbed to the brutality and violence of enslavement.

Commentary by English visitors does not offer much information about the precise practices surrounding burial of the enslaved in Barbados, although archaeological work conducted at the Newton plantation does. Located, like Rendezvous, in Christ Church Parish and roughly the same size, Newton has interments in the identified slave burial ground dating to the 1660s. Grave goods were more common for the oldest interments, probably because these individuals were the ones who had come directly from Africa; island-born slaves would not have needed sustenance for a transatlantic journey home.[98]

This physical evidence matches the few extant sources that discuss burials of the enslaved. Sloane explained how attendees at funerals would "throw in rum and victuals into their graves, to serve them in the other world. Sometimes they bury it in gourds, at other times spill it on the graves." Reflective of practices at West African burials, the kinds of materials left at the graveside now had a distinctly American flavor including, as Taylor noted, "casader bread, roasted fowles, sugar, rum, tobacco," all of which were supposed to sustain the deceased "in his journey beyound those plesant hills in their own countrey, whither they say he is now goeing to live at rest."[99] While these grave goods offer insight into how the enslaved population on Rendezvous may have buried a woman like Hester, they do not reveal the specifics of other mourning practices. According to English observers, immediately following interment, again in a practice similar to those observed in West Africa, enslaved people ate and drank around the grave, "singing in their own language verey dolefully, desiering the dead corpse . . . to acquaint their father, mother, husband and other relations of their present condition and slavary, as he passeth thro' their countrey towards the plesant mountains."[100] Giving the grave one last kiss, the mourners then departed for the slave quarters.

Unlike with the case of Benjamin and his mourning rings, there are no records that reveal what enslaved mourners did to commemorate their dead beyond the moment of burial. Perhaps the belongings of the deceased were shared with loved ones in a similar fashion to how Europeans bequeathed property. Or maybe their passing was acknowledged in other ways. The lack of commentary about enslaved people's grief in the late seventeenth century does not confirm the absence of pain, suffering, guilt, and longing that usually accompanies death. Given their connection at their 1670 baptism, it is likely that Susannah and Elizabeth were important mourners when the enslaved woman Hester died. In these ways, we can glimpse kinship ties tethered and broken among enslaved people on Rendezvous.

FRANCES'S DEATH, LIKE HESTER TOMKYNS's before her, was commemorated in a fashion befitting the wife of one of Barbados's most prominent men. Joined in marriage to John in life, the women shared a burial site—both were interred in the chancel of St. Michael's church in the island's capital, Bridgetown.[101] John might have left the island less than one year after his second wife's death, but the marker in St. Michael's church permanently signified his elevated status in Barbados society.[102] The gravestone also provides a pilgrimage site for these women's descendants. From the seventeenth century to the present, the marker reminds the church's visitors of the rank and importance of Hester and Frances because in Barbados as in England, only the most significant people rest inside the church. Departed elites' status is as readable today as it was in the past.

The markers that show us where Frances and Hester were laid to rest have no corollary for the enslaved population of Rendezvous. The men, women, and children who perished on the plantation during John's wives' lifetimes were laid to rest in graves that then, as today, remain unmarked. Viewed as disposable commodities by their enslavers, individuals like the enslaved woman Hester were not deemed worthy of a visible burial site. While their contemporaries well knew where the enslaved burial ground was located and could make return visits to the interments of family and kin, there is no place for their descendants to communally memorialize their ancestors. Just as the written records elide enslaved experiences, so too do the lack of physical markers starkly distinguish between those with the ability and means to commemorate loved ones, and those without. Unlike white plantation owners, the enslaved men and women on Rendezvous had no power to have their feelings about death, or the way they wished to note the significance of their lost kin, remembered.

And yet in the face of devastating mortality and the breaking of familial ties, enslaved people on Rendezvous, and across Barbados, worked to counter the system of hierarchy and oppression that shaped family life by insisting on forging the very kinship ties they were denied by virtue of their status. Making clear the lie that kinship could be claimed only by those who were free and white, they found ways to insist on connection and belonging for themselves and their children. Often, they drew on practices informed by their West African pasts in order to build a Barbados future. Sometimes they took rituals imposed by their enslavers that the English took to have one particular meaning and deployed them in ways opposite to those intended by their captors. When Susannah, Elizabeth, and their children were baptized, they may well have viewed the ceremony as one predictive of a future free from bondage even if none of the white people in attendance—including John—understood their initiation into the Church of England to have any bearing on their enslaved status.

At Rendezvous, Frances's marriage to John changed the course of her life, and so too did it throw into disarray the lives of the enslaved people who labored on her first husband's plantation. Her death, meanwhile, turned John into an absentee owner, creating uncertainty and fear among enslaved laborers on the plantation. Her demise also set the course by which Susannah, Elizabeth, Dorothy, and their children found themselves on a ship bound for England. It was to settle disputes resulting from John's claims to the property of Frances's first spouse that he set sail for London in 1686, taking his "great and numerous family" with him.

Frances's story illuminates the transfer of English practices and values onto colonial spaces, while her death enabled the literal movement of John, the women, and their children to the metropole. Meanwhile, the practices of enslaved people on Rendezvous worked to recreate kin ties and commemorate community members in myriad ways, often unintelligible to English colonists, and always challenging the idea that their worth was only that recorded in a plantation ledger. These were the means through which kin and family were shaped and sustained in Barbados. They were also the manner through which whiteness, legitimacy, and freedom were enshrined.

CHAPTER 4

A Great and Numerous Family in England

STANDING ON DECK as the ship carrying her and her children sailed up the Thames toward London in the early summer of 1686, Dorothy must have found the sheer size of the metropolis almost inconceivable. Although Barbados's Bridgetown was a large and busy port city, nothing could have prepared her for the densely packed streets, hordes of people, and the rooftops and chimneys that stretched almost as far as the eye could see up and down the riverbank.[1] However grand and opulent the Rendezvous "Mancon House" might have seemed, it paled in comparison to the magnificent architecture of Restoration London that hove into view as the ship moved past the imposing medieval architecture of the Tower of London toward London Bridge. Dominating the docks in front of the twenty-one "Legal Quays" was Wren's spectacular neoclassical customhouse, which looked more like a royal palace than a place of commerce. The Thames itself was a hive of activity, with tall ships waiting three deep and more to be offloaded by smaller "lighters" that carried their goods to the docks. Barges and smaller passenger boats vied for space, trying to avoid collisions, as they moved cargo and Londoners up and down the river and to and from the shore.[2]

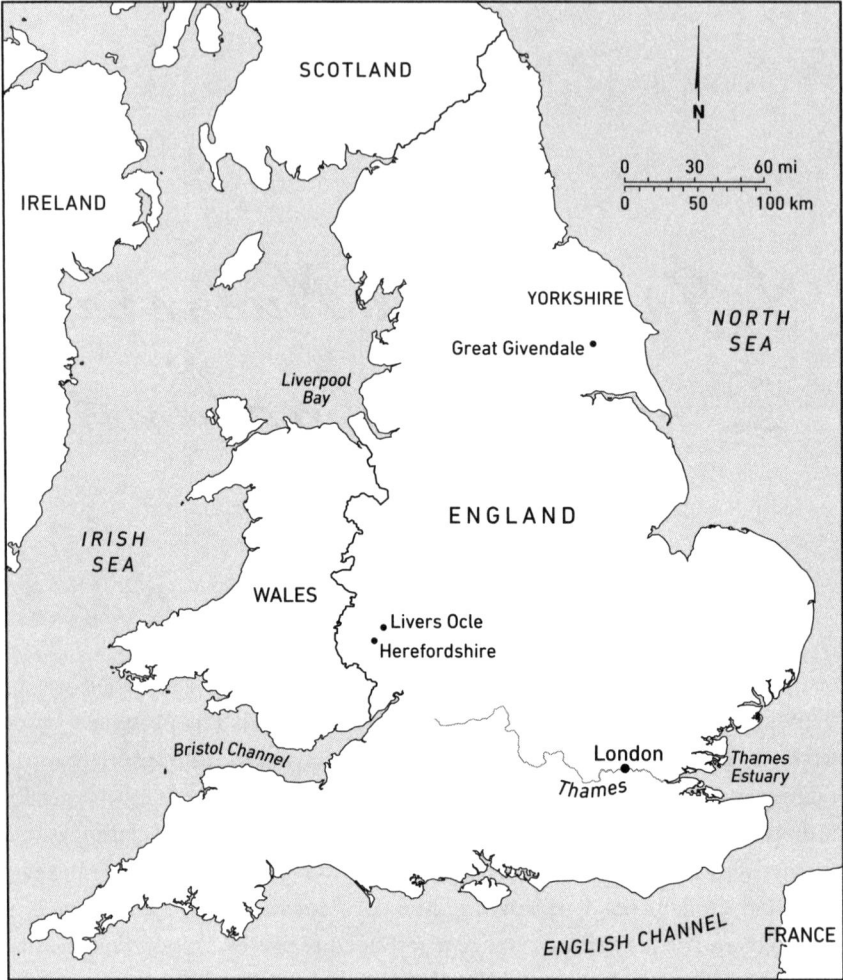

England

Sailing across the Atlantic Ocean was a daunting endeavor in and of itself, but surely Dorothy's relief at finally reaching her destination was tempered by her anxiety about what awaited her and her family now that they were in England. As they waited for a lighter to take them to the quay, Dorothy and the rest of the entourage aboard the ship had plenty of opportunity to steel themselves against the sounds, smells, and sights of the bustling capital. They also had time to note the demographic diversity on display at the docks. In Barbados, Dorothy knew that the fact she was not John's wife left her vulnerable, even as she also understood that her whiteness granted her privileges never accorded to Susannah and Elizabeth. What fate awaited them now they were in London?

The experiences of John's "great and numerous family" in England reveals how the racial, gendered, and class hierarchies of the metropole not only reflected those developed in Caribbean slave societies, but were constituted in the hub of empire itself. Following the women and children east and north across the Atlantic and through the streets of London to the rooms they occupied in Exeter Exchange in the West End demonstrates how the diversity and vibrancy of the city was undergirded by well-established racial hierarchies that were as oppressive as those in Barbados. England had, for at least 150 years, harbored anti-Black sentiment to validate its imperial aspirations, and to justify its participation in the slave trade and slavery. In the late Elizabethan era the Privy Council recommended those they described as "Blackamoors" be removed from England, and despite scholarly debates over whether or not Elizabeth I was anti-Black herself, her government strove to limit the presence of people of African descent in England.[3] Both James I in 1618 and Charles I in 1632 authorized private trading company monopolies to West Africa. The Royal Court also sponsored cultural productions of Blackness. As early as 1605 Ben Jonson's *Masque of Blackness* stressed the exoticization of sub-Saharan and so-called Moorish people.

By the time of the Restoration, James, Duke of York, headed up what would become the Royal African Company, dedicated to supplying African captives to the Americas. His brother Charles II was one of the firm's chief investors. The restored Stuart siblings not only were invested in human capital through the slave trade; they also continued their forebearers' practices of commissioning pageants and presiding over court masques that centered Black actors, or white actors in blackface. These popular artistic representations, created in the empire's seat of power, demonstrated the ways that racism was generated, adapted, and produced in England itself. The colonies were not brought home; their perverse intimacies and racial hierarchies were already in place in the metropole.[4]

When Dorothy, Susannah, and Elizabeth accompanied John to England, Dorothy was the only one whose status as free was assured when they arrived in the metropole. As the only living white woman who had birthed John's children, Dorothy most likely managed John's rooms in London and Streatham. Her whiteness as well as her English origins automatically placed her above the two enslaved women in the social hierarchy. But Dorothy's creole origins may have cast suspicions on her character. Meanwhile, Susannah's and Elizabeth's status might have remained unclear now that they no longer resided on a Barbados sugar estate. That uncertainty did not mean that they would automatically be considered free, or that if they were, they would be seen as Dorothy's equals. Probate and Chancery Court records suggest that Susannah was most likely the "Black Cookmaid" who worked in the kitchen at the Streatham home. Her son, Richard, was probably the enslaved boy who waited on John's oldest white son. Thus, during their time in England, the "great and numerous family" experienced relationships of power that resembled those they endured in Barbados.

Thanks to England's monopoly on the slave trade as well as its imperial ventures, London was a capital city of immense wealth in the last decades of the seventeenth century. Rising out of the ashes of the devastating fire of 1666, the capital expanded beyond its traditional walls. To the west, it encroached into the space between the formerly walled medieval City of London proper and Westminster, creating the West End. Required to attend to imports and exports going to and from England's overseas colonies, and to the West African coast, docks proliferated to the east and along both banks of the Thames. As riches generated by the slave trade increased, so too did the numbers of Black Londoners working in the city. The physical embodiment of white Londoners' capital accumulation, these bonded laborers became emblems of an imperial hierarchy based on race and class. Enslaved pages were adorned in fine livery and wore metal collars of silver, bronze, or brass around their necks as markers of the affluence of those they served and as physical reminders of their bonded status.[5]

It was not only in London where the wealth of empire was on display. Profits gained from sugar plantation investments were being poured into country retreats in villages like Streatham, as merchants and former planters established rural estates whose magnificence and grandeur were undergirded by the labors of enslaved people an ocean away.[6] In the Streatham manor house, furnishings and decor announced John's wealth and bolstered his status. Within its walls, the racialized division of power was not one simply imported. Dorothy, Susannah, and Elizabeth interacted with one another through frameworks developed in England itself.

THE JOURNEY

By the eighteenth century, British Caribbean planters frequently sent the children they fathered with enslaved women to England for an education; they did not, as a rule, change the status of their offspring's mothers, much less take them to the metropole.[7] In this instance, however, not only did John travel with his children, but their mothers made the journey too. Moreover, unlike his counterparts a century later, John does not seem to have been concerned with educating the children he bore with Susannah and Elizabeth, or even with Dorothy. Although his older sons with Hester had long since been sent to England to live with their maternal aunt and her husband to be "maintayned & put to schoole & otherwise educated like the sons of a Gentleman," the only provision he seems to have made for any of his other offspring was to provide money to "bind their apprentice" should they wish.[8]

If education was not the goal in bringing the children, especially his enslaved offspring, to England, then what motivated John? Was it simply that he could not conceive of leaving them behind? Did he not plan to return to the Caribbean? Or was it the women he wanted to keep close, and the children merely an afterthought? If he had left his estates under the management of overseers, John would not have been able to control Dorothy, Susannah, or Elizabeth had they remained in Barbados. If he wanted to dictate their treatment—good or ill—the only way to do so was to have them accompany him to England.

Ships traveling between the Caribbean and the metropole stopped at a variety of ports, though it is likely that John selected one headed directly for London as this is where the "affaires" that demanded "his speedy repairing thither" were being adjudicated in Chancery Court.[9] In 1686, the year John sailed, at least 225 ships entered London from the Caribbean. By the 1680s, most return voyages from Barbados sailed between May and August to maximize profits and reduce the risk of encountering a hurricane. John probably departed shortly after receiving permission to leave the island in April.[10]

At a minimum, John paid for seventeen passengers at perhaps as much as £5 per head; it was more if he, or any of the rest of his entourage, purchased return tickets, or if he wished to travel in a manner befitting his elite status. Just five years later his estate paid out £65 to bring his youngest daughter to England, and for "passage & back againe Provision and Necessaries" for her adult companion, a significantly higher cost than the average.[11] Regardless of what form of passage the family booked, John paid a hefty fee to bring the women, their children, their luggage, and perhaps other significant or sentimental belongings to England.

It is unclear whether Dorothy had ever traversed the Atlantic Ocean. The records of the Spendloves on Barbados point more directly to an island birth for her, which makes it less likely that she had ever sailed on the open sea. Although she might not have known exactly what to expect, she would have understood that this would be a long and uncomfortable voyage. Indeed the average return journey from Barbados lasted somewhere in the region of six weeks, but depending on the weather, the wind, or detours to avoid pirates and privateers, it could take much longer. Dorothy would have traveled on a large and imposing ship, as the English preferred "substantially built, heavy masted, well-armed" vessels for transatlantic voyages, most likely one above eighty tons.[12] She had three children under ten to attend—Frances, John, and Edward—and while Frances might have been expected to mind her younger brothers and keep the siblings out of trouble, the dangers of a tall ship would not have escaped Dorothy's notice.

Having likely experienced a Middle Passage, Susannah and Elizabeth were probably anxious and on edge upon boarding a ship headed for England. All around them at the Bridgetown docks was evidence of the slave trade. Indeed, the ship that took them to England might well have recently swapped out its captive human cargo for hogsheads of muscovado sugar. Over half the ships that left Barbados for London in 1686 had arrived on the island via the west coast of Africa. Or their vessel might have been one specifically designed to carry cash crops not captives. If so, it would have been comparably more comfortable than a ship designed to maximize the number of people who could be crammed aboard.[13] Whether a slaver or not, the two enslaved women were journeying on a tall ship again, sailing into another unknown. Whatever they had been told about their destination, or what would happen upon their arrival, they still had to endure a long and arduous journey on the high seas.

Traveling east and north across the Atlantic was not a comfortable proposition. The environment on board even the largest deep-sea ships was stifling. A man of John's status might well have been given, or shared, the captain's quarters. Dorothy, Elizabeth, and Susannah would have had to find somewhere else to sleep, perhaps in one of the small rooms where dry goods were stored, especially if it was a ship designed for carrying sugar. These spaces lacked ventilation and attracted vermin and insects. Adding to their discomfort was the nausea and discombobulation provoked by the open ocean. Quaker Joan Vokins found herself and her companion, Sarah Lawrence, nauseous and ill on their first transatlantic voyage in 1679; so too did Elizabeth Dean suffer, "the winds being so boisterous, and the foaming Sea in so great a Rage," on a trip in 1681. The women's young children, who had never sailed on the open ocean, would have been especially ill.[14]

If they did eventually find their sea legs, it did not follow that there would be enough food to eat. When captains misjudged the length of time at sea, rations became increasingly meagre, not least because foodstuffs, like "bread, beef, salt-pork, stockfish . . . cheese, peas, and beer" spoiled on the crossing. John might well have paid an additional £1 per passenger for fresh provisions "above the ship's allowances as rice, oatmeal, flower, butter, sugar, and brandy," but there was no guarantee that extra victuals would last.[15] Edward Barlow, who sailed often to the Caribbean in the late 1670s and early 1680s, noted how poor-weather delays resulted in "our provisions growing very short." To remedy the situation, the crew and passengers were put on rations of water and bread "which began to nip us very sore." Barlow described how "boiling all our meat in salt water . . . made us extreme dry" and resigned himself to a "belly half full of victuals."[16] Even on voyages that did not encounter inclement weather, supplies of water and food were always at risk. It is likely that by the time the coast of south-west England came into view that the women and children were desperate for sustenance.

It was not only meager portions that caused difficulty. Passengers also had to navigate the hierarchy aboard ship, and make sure they did not fall afoul of sailors climbing rigging, scrubbing decks, or furling and unfurling sails. On larger vessels there may have been as many as forty seamen aboard ship. The Navigation Acts required at least two-thirds of these men to be English or colonial subjects, although these rules were not necessarily strictly enforced. Crews were usually diverse, resulting in a variety of languages and backgrounds represented on board. Susannah, Elizabeth, and their children would not have been the only non-white individuals on the ship, but whether they found comfort in this fact is impossible to know. Sailors of all backgrounds were notorious for drinking, carousing, and violence, both on leave and on ships at sea.[17] All three of the women who accompanied John might have found themselves targets of harassment and worse.

The dangers posed by crew members were not the only ones that troubled transatlantic voyages. Privateers and pirates alike hoped to pick off ships laden with lucrative goods as they departed the Caribbean. Few points along the trade routes were safe from attack. To increase security, ships often sailed in convoy, which sometimes included vessels of His Majesty's line. The uncertain political situation in England in the 1680s, with rumored popish plots and Monmouth's Rebellion of 1685 stirring up religious antagonisms, meant that war with France was an ever-present threat. Barlow repeatedly noted the consternation aboard the *Guannaboe* or the *Cadiz Merchant* when a ship of undetermined flag hove into view. Sometimes these were friendly vessels, sometimes not, but each time before the crew had identified the flag "we prepared and made our ship in a readiness to fight," a scramble that must have been anxiety producing for all on board, but especially passengers who knew little of what to expect.[18]

Even more threatening than the prospect of conflict was the unpredictability of the weather. While trouble was more likely during hurricane season, storms, even those not as destructive as hurricanes, were constant worries for captains and crew alike. Twenty-foot seas would have been terrifying for all on board and required great leadership from the captain to keep the crew in check.[19] Barlow described "waves breaking into the ship" during one storm on a return voyage in 1680 and noted how "we were forced to keep the pump continually going." The following year he encountered similarly "tempestuous weather" in the north Atlantic, "the seas breaking into our ship and damaging a great deal of goods." The bad weather continued "near a month" until they drew "pretty well near England."[20]

Reaching the eastern side of the Atlantic Ocean did not ensure safety. Strong currents greeted vessels entering the English Channel and, when combined with the sharp rocks that lurked just beneath the waves, took many ships to the bottom of the ocean. One can only imagine the relief that surely washed over the passengers once they had successfully run this perilous gauntlet and come into port along England's south coast. As with most London-bound transatlantic voyages, it is likely that the ship carrying Dorothy and the rest of the women and children dropped anchor at Plymouth to take on fresh water and supplies before making its way eastward along the channel, past the narrow straits that separated England and France at Dover, into the calmer, sheltered waters of the Downs off the coast of Kent, and eventually into the Thames estuary.[21]

It is possible that when they finally arrived in London John's entourage at first encountered much that seemed familiar. Like the docks at the careenage in Bridgetown, where they departed, London's quays were filled with the noise of ships being unloaded. Haulers worked quickly to relieve vessels of precious cargos from across the globe. Huge warehouses, like those along Cheapside and Broad Street in Bridgetown, became the receptacles for sugar, molasses, rum, tea, china, cloth, tobacco, cotton, and indigo. The men who unloaded cargo from the ships moved in unison, their timing impeccable, almost like a ballet. The noise—a cacophony of voices shouting orders, the sound of ballast

A section from Morgan's map of London, 1682, showing the custom house, Tower Hill, and London Bridge. Wikimedia Commons.

shifting, the creaking of timber, and the loud slam of yet another crate landing on the docks—was earsplitting. The same sounds of colonialism characterized the harbor at Bridgetown. Even the workers on the quays may not have looked radically different from those who worked the waterfront in Barbados.

London was a diverse city by the closing decades of the seventeenth century, its docks especially so, with many Black sailors and laborers finding work in the industries linked to the colonial trade. Unlike their Caribbean counterparts, not all these men were enslaved. Some had lived their whole lives in freedom; others had escaped bondage, or challenged their owners' right to their lives and labor in the courts. Among them would have been those who, like Susannah, Elizabeth, and their eight children, were carried to England from the Caribbean, arriving with their enslavers.[22]

Susannah, Elizabeth, and their children would probably have noticed that it was *not only* Black men who were emptying the ships at the quayside, a marked difference from their departure point of Bridgetown, where almost everyone doing manual labor at the docks was of African descent. Moreover, the vast majority of the white people they saw were not in positions of authority or supervision. Rather, they too hauled cargo, worked winches and pulleys, repaired rigging, scrubbed decks, and moved pallets in tandem with Black workers. In Bridgetown, white men on the docks gave the orders, but in London, white and Black men carried orders out.

As much as the docks on the Thames resembled those in Bridgetown, the scale of London must surely have overwhelmed the women. The metropolis teemed with people, and noises, sounds, and smells unfamiliar to the new arrivals.[23] Despite the recently widened and paved streets, part of the postfire rebuilding project, London was still marked mostly by its grime and dirt and the miasma of industrial soot and smoke that filled the air. Coal fires pumped pollution into the skies, tobacco smoke lingered inside and out, and the effluvia of almost half a million people added to the assault on the nostrils. As the women moved through the city, the noises at the docks were replaced by the shouting of street sellers, the clatter of horses' hooves and cartwheels on cobblestones, and the smack of leather shoes on pavements.[24] If the city's soundscape wasn't deafening, it must have been discombobulating to the women and children who traveled with John. He might have remembered the commotion and rush of the streets of London from his adolescence, but they had experienced nothing on this scale.

THE TEEMING METROPOLIS

The Restoration era with its opulence, bawdiness, and anything-goes attitude was in full swing when John arrived in the capital in 1686. Memories of the devastating plague year of 1665 and the ruinous Great Fire of 1666 had faded: London was reborn. While the previously dominant cathedral of St. Paul was slowly rising out of the ashes, the tightly crammed together wooden five- and six-story houses that once overhung Cheapside and the Strand, blocking out the light almost entirely on the smaller lanes and alleys were now replaced with brick and stone residences that were more regular in height and style.[25] The main thoroughfares were wider, allowing light where previously there had been very little, making the City feel less suffocating. Adding to the brighter air were additional open spaces. Churchyards, markets, and increased pavements and street lighting gave the whole metropolis a lift. Those who arrived at the docks alighted onto much broader and more substantial quays, with new steps leading down to the crowded banks of the muddy Thames, and up to the equally hectic hustle and bustle of the city.

Where John and his entourage headed after docking is unclear, although it is likely he made his way to his first residence, "Exeter Exchange in the Strand."[26] No doubt he loaded the women and children into a series of hackney carriages that would carry them into the West End suburbs. These carriages, some with windows, some open to the air, became popular during the second half of the seventeenth century as a way to navigate London's increasingly urban expanse. Located on a street long associated with wealth and power in London, the newly built Exchange was erected on the site of the former home of the Earls of

Exeter.[27] At street level, the new Restoration building housed drapers, hosiers, and milliners, while the rooms above were rented out to men like John—merchants who had business in the city and needed a place to stay when they came to town. Most of these men (and this would soon be true for John as well) had a residence in the country where their families lived.

Reaching John's new city rooms, about two miles from the docks, required a tour through some of London's most arresting sights, sounds, and smells. The Rendezvous party might well have traveled up from the Thames to Cheapside, still a significant shopping thoroughfare and one of the broadest streets in the city, stretching at least sixty feet from pavement to pavement. At its eastern end were textile dealers, while the west was dominated by goldsmiths. Silkmen sold their wares on both sides of Cheapside, and street shops offered fashionable items such as stockings, lace, and bodices for sale. It was not only the shopfronts and crowded streets that were so eye catching and alluring. The streetscape was dominated by the brightly colored signs announcing items for purchase—for example a cow's head suggested leather goods were for sale, while hose might be signified by a hanging leg.[28] If Dorothy, Susannah, and Elizabeth did not fully comprehend all they saw, they would have been able to read the symbolic landscape and understand the significance of this marketplace. After all, the main shopping thoroughfare in Bridgetown went by the same name.

Clothing and furnishings were not the only goods proffered on Cheapside, or in the carriages' destination, the up-and-coming areas of Cornhill and Covent Garden. Food and drink were also readily available, this time the aromas enticing hungry and thirsty customers to the markets, taverns, and coffeehouses every bit as much as the signs outside such establishments. By the 1670s coffeehouses began to dominate the City, Westminster, and the suburbs in between, springing up all over greater London. These premises underscored London's global connections, serving coffee and chocolate and the sugar to sweeten both.[29] As the hackney carriages took the women past the scaffolding surrounding the ruins of St Paul's Cathedral, and the line of new Wren churches on Fleet Street and the Strand with their pleasing lines and soaring spires, they might have wondered about the wealth that financed almost every building they saw. Even areas spared by the Great Fire, like the Strand, were sites of rebirth and reinvention. Older aristocratic homes gave way to new buildings, Exeter Exchange among them.

In addition to rooms at the Exeter Exchange, John also rented "very Good Lodgings" from "Mr. Hart" in Essex Street, an adjacent, recently transformed area of the city.[30] As at his first place of residence, Essex Street was situated on the site of a grand house, this one formerly owned by the Duke of Essex. Just a few years before John departed from Barbados, the house and grounds had been converted into a fine Restoration London residential street, running from the Strand to the Thames, a series of steps leading down to the wharf at the riverside. John's rooms were just minutes away from the Wren-designed church of St. Clement Danes in the parish where his father once worshipped, and conveniently located between the commerce of the City proper, and Westminster, the seat of government.

Essex Street was also situated in the heart of London's entertainment district, where coffee shops, theaters, and taverns abounded, along with less salubrious establishments such as brothels and gaming houses. Residing at the heart of the capital's legal center—surely no coincidence given that legal disputes brought John to London—he might well have been enticed into some of the nearby drinking premises, like the Seven Stars close to Chancery Lane, or Old Man's coffeehouse in Scotland Yard at the end of the Strand.[31] He may also have enjoyed plays staged at the Drury Lane Theatre or tried his luck at the gaming houses in and around Covent Garden. Perhaps some of these establishments were what encouraged John to spend time in London instead of his country estate in Streatham. They could certainly have been seen as a perk of coming to the city to do business.

As the carriages clattered over London's cobblestone streets, the Rendezvous women were no doubt transfixed by the people they observed jostling along the crowded pavements. On Cheapside and the Strand, Dorothy might well have taken note of the latest fashions. Because Englishwomen were said to dress "very elegant, entirely after the French fashion," Dorothy knew she could communicate her social status through her sartorial choices.[32] Long sleeves and low necklines combined with a pointed bodice and a full skirt, pulled up at the front to invite admiration of the wearer's decorated silver-and-lace petticoat, were de rigueur. Those with real wealth to display ensured their garments were made of silk fabrics in bright, alluring (and expensive) colors.[33] While London's skies were often gray, and the city itself was full of soot and dirt, vibrant hues and patterns on women's clothing brightened the landscape considerably.

Presumably used to wearing outfits that were colonial in style, and therefore out of date, Dorothy probably recognized the need to mimic her white English counterparts in order to fit in. Susannah and Elizabeth likely made similar observations, wondering how they would be expected to dress in London, and whether the colors and materials open to white women would be within their reach. They may have made a mental note of the work involved in cleaning and maintaining these fashions, especially in such a dirty and polluted environment—labor that would surely fall to them.[34]

The two enslaved women might also have noticed the diversity of the people around them. Black people had been present in Britain for centuries, but their number began to increase from the middle of the sixteenth century alongside England's engagement with slavery and the slave trade.[35] Most titled property holders in the country counted at least one enslaved Black person among their household staff in the late sixteenth century as a way to underscore their prestige. By the 1660s "having a black slave or two in one household soon became a craze for all who could afford it," a practice that only accelerated with the rise of first the Royal Adventurers into Africa, in 1663, and then again with the establishment of its successor, the Royal African Company, in 1672.[36]

Slavery in England was endorsed at the highest level. Not only did Charles II and his wife invest in slaving firms; in 1682 Charles II paid £50 to the Marquis of Antrim for a Black slave to use as his personal attendant. He also made gifts of Black boys to his many mistresses, helping to cultivate the practice of holding Black people in bondage at the Royal Court. These royal practices soon made their way down the social ladder. In 1669 civil servant Samuel Pepys extoled the culinary virtues of a woman named Doll, whom he described as a "blackmoore cookmaid."[37] Meanwhile, there are myriad examples of runaway advertisements in London newspapers in the second half of the seventeenth century that demonstrate the presence of a sizeable enslaved population in the city.[38] Susannah's and Elizabeth's presentation, and that of their children, was not automatically a curiosity for those who caught a glimpse of them.

The women might also have wondered at the youth of many of the Black figures in London. Perhaps they saw white women who embodied the stereotype of the eponymous "Town Misse" walking along the street in the highest of fashion, accompanied by what one contemporary of the day asserted were "two necessary implements . . . a blackamoor and a little Dog," the author equating the young child with a domesticated pet, and describing both with dehumanizing language more suited to inanimate objects.[39] Dorothy might have noted the woman's clothing, and the other necessary marker of status—the enslaved child who accompanied her, and who by his very association elevated the "Town Misse" from the lower echelons of London's populace.

Susannah and Elizabeth (and also likely their sons, the two Richards, John, and Edward) might instead have fixed their gaze on the Black page trailing behind the white woman. Ever alert to the markers of bondage, the two enslaved mothers probably noted the metal collars around the necks of some of these young Black boys. If they got a closer look, they might well have seen the locks that secured the devices.[40] A discerning eye would quickly pick up subtle markers of class difference—a silver as opposed to a brass collar, for example.

The main effect, however, was to underscore the prestige of the person trailed by the page by emphasizing the child's bonded status.

Collars, in use since the reign of James I, were visible markers of the existence of enslavement in a Britain that wanted to perceive itself as the land of free soil, or at the very least as a place deeply invested in debating the question of whether people of African descent could be held in bondage within its borders.[41] Some enslaved Africans accompanied their owners to the metropole, later returning to the Caribbean with their enslavers, suggesting that there was no change in their status during their stay in England. Legally, enslaved individuals fell under the law of trover in England, a medieval principle that dealt with the recovery of personal property. These were the statutes that determined whether or not enslaved persons might win their freedom in court should they challenge the validity of their enslaved status while on English soil.[42] Some succeeded, at least temporarily; others failed. The very fact that they felt the need to sue for freedom at all demonstrates that for such individuals their presumed status was enslaved rather than free.

If legal proceedings were not always definitive about an African person's status, physical and prominent markers of bondage—like the collars—made clear in truth what was obscured or murky in law: enslavement was a very real experience for people of African descent in England. The collars meant that everyone—old, young, rich, poor, Black, white, women, men—who saw a boy with such a device around his neck knew that this child was not free, nor had the expectation of ever being so. In a country where some African-descended people were free, the collars are evidence that for many enslavement was precisely the norm.

Collars were part of the very elaborate outfits that Black pages wore. Wealthy enslavers often dressed enslaved children in ostentatious liveries of bright-colored fabrics decorated with silver or gold thread.[43] For example, an enslaved boy "called by the name of Othello" ran away from the Navy Office in January 1685 wearing "a Livery of a dark colored cloth, lined with Blue, and so edged in the Seams, the Buttons Pewter, wearing a Cloth Cap," and took with him "a new Blue Livery Suite . . . being laced with Gold Galloom, and lined with Orange Colour, and the Sleeves fringed about with Silk Fringe, and laced upon the Facing with narrow Gold Galloom."[44] In 1678, another Black page aged about twelve, "his name *Africa*," absconded wearing "a gray cloth Livery, the Lace mixed with black, white, and orange colors."[45] An unnamed child described in the advertisement as a "Negro Boy, aged about 14," seized his freedom in October 1689 wearing "a red coloured Cloth Coat, a black Hat, and black Stockings." Meanwhile, in 1703, "Pompey a Black boy of about 15 years of

Portrait including an enslaved child wearing a bright livery and a silver collar around his neck like those worn by runaways in London. Attributed to John Verelst, ca. 1719. Yale Center for British Art, New Haven, CT, gift of Andrew Cavendish, eleventh Duke of Devonshire.

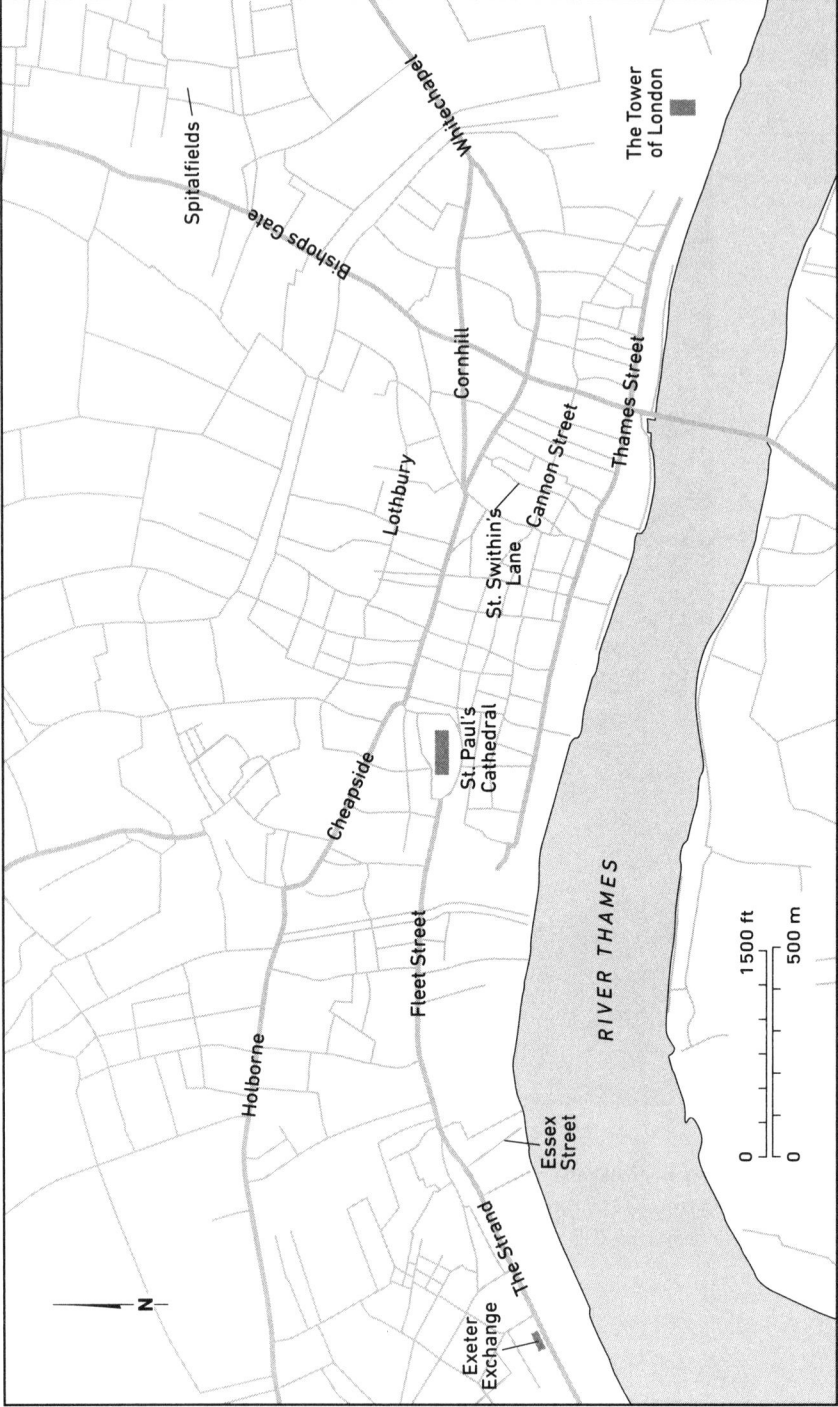

Spitalfields

Whitechapel

Bishops Gate

The Tower
of London

Cornhill

Lothbury

Cannon Street

Thames Street

St. Swithin's
Lane

Cheapside

St. Paul's
Cathedral

RIVER THAMES

Fleet Street

1500 ft

500 m

0

0

Holborne

Essex
Street

The Strand

Exeter
Exchange

N

London

Age" ran off in a "sad colour'd frock, a blue Wastcoat and blue Stocking," with a "brass Collar about his neck."[46]

The metal collars around Black boys' necks not only were visible markers of their enslavement; they also increased the likelihood that a freedom-seeking child would be returned to his enslaver because they normally included identifying information.[47] For example, in March 1686, the same year that the Rendezvous entourage arrived in London, John White, an enslaved boy claimed by Colonel Kirke, ran away from his enslaver with "a Silver Collar about his Neck, upon which is the Colonel's Coat of Arms and Cipher."[48] Two years later a particularly enterprising sixteen-year-old escaped the Tower of London with at least £10 in silver, and "three coloured Coats, two grey, his uppermost Cinamon colour," while the "Silver Collar about his Neck, Engraven, Thomas Dymock at the Lyon Office," told anyone who encountered him that he was not free, and to whom he should be returned.[49] And two years after that, "a Negro Boy, named Toney," who was also about sixteen, ran away with "a Brass Chollar, which directs where he liv'd," around his neck.[50] All three freedom seekers would have had to identify someone willing to break the locks on their collars, or find some way to achieve this themselves, if they hoped to remain free of their enslavers' grasp. One advertisement raised precisely this possibility: Jack Chelsea, described as "a Tall Negro young fellow," absconded from his enslaver in 1703. He allegedly wore "a Collar about his Neck (unless it be lately filed off)," that identified his owner "with these Words; Mr. Moses Goodyeare of Chelsea his Negro."[51]

The prospect of having to remove a padlocked piece of metal from around one's neck raises questions about the experience of wearing such a device. How tight was the fastening? Were the collars replaced with larger models as the child aged, or were enslavers able to adjust them? Either way, a snug fit would prohibit easy or painless removal, no doubt a deliberate feature of the device, as perhaps Jack Chelsea discovered. Did they rub and chaff? If children exerted themselves, did they feel suffocated or have trouble catching their breath? How intolerable did bearing the weight of the collar become as the day wore on? Did it leave marks on the neck, rub sores on the skin, or cause pain across the back and shoulders? In addition to the physical discomfort and pain undoubtedly caused by the collars, they were also a constant reminder to the wearers of their bonded status, an explicit expression of ownership that emphasized to children that their bodies were not their own.

These collars would have been unfamiliar to the women and their children insofar as they were part of the way that English people signified bondage at home: the practice does not appear in Barbados until at least 1708.[52] In that year, an act declared that "all such Negroes and other slaves" who were given permission to sell "Milk, Horse-meat, or Fire-wood" would be identified by "a metaled Collar locked about his, her or their Neck or Necks, Leg or Legs." The collar would have "the name of his or her Master or Mistress engraven thereon, and the name of the Parish wherein they live, and also the name of the person who made such Collar." In other words, these collars were almost exactly the same as those described in runaway advertisements in England in the last decades of the seventeenth century. Moreover, the Barbados act specifically distinguished these collars from the other kinds of "Hooks and Rings, or Collars" that Caribbean enslavers used to punish runaways.

That they had to describe both the form and the function of the identifying collars in a legal statute suggests that white Barbadians were unfamiliar with such devices and that these collars were imported from the metropole, not the other way around. When Susannah, Elizabeth, and their children saw them on Black boys in London, they might have had no prior experience of such devices. But they would have recognized them as markers of ownership. They might also have understood the additional humiliation accorded the boys because the collars were similar to those worn by dogs. Equating enslaved people to animals was not new, and this particular piece of branding intertwined domesticated pets and young Black boys to denigrate the latter as a deferential companion or simply as another plaything.[53]

If Dorothy, Susannah, and Elizabeth observed these displays of status and bondage, the older children in the carriages no doubt were equally transfixed by the cityscape. Frances's daughters, Elizabeth and Frances, were too young (at ages three and two) to comprehend much about their new location, even if they noticed new smells and sounds. Their half siblings—Dorothy's Frances, John, and Ann; Susannah's Judith, Richard, and Hester; and Elizabeth's John, Susanna, Richard, Elizabeth, and Edward—were all older, ranging in age from fifteen to five, likely absorbed as much as their senses would allow.

They might have noticed the large numbers of young people on the streets—small boys trailing the chimney sweeps, who used them to access small flues, or scampering alongside the carpenters, coopers, wheelwrights, and blacksmiths to whom they were apprenticed; girls lugging baskets of laundry, shepherding chickens across the cobblestones, or stumbling under the weight of the groceries they carried; and other young people moving through the crowds. It likely did not surprise them to see children working—after all, they came from a sugar plantation where enslaved girls and boys as young as six were tasked with labor. Like their mothers, they may also have observed the relative diversity of the population. Perhaps they spotted Black boys with collars moving through the city by themselves, some of them flitting in and out of traffic and attempting to keep a low profile. They might even have crossed paths with John White, the boy who had escaped from his enslaver just a few months prior.

The women and children who accompanied John had around six months to get used to the urban environment before they found themselves uprooted to yet another destination. Although he began this visit to England at Exeter Exchange, and later maintained rooms on Essex Street, John quickly worked to find an estate more in keeping in terms of size and scope with the one he had left behind in Barbados. By spring 1687 he had found the perfect site. A mere five miles south of the capital, Streatham was a small village, recently famed for its mineral springs. As such it was fast becoming a popular retreat for London merchants, and increasingly those in the West Indian trade. John leased an established country manor, a large, eight-bedroom residence, with elaborate gardens, stables and coach house, an orchard, and a brewery.[54] This was where Dorothy, Elizabeth, Susannah, and their children would work and reside. It was the household over which Dorothy would become the effective mistress, and where the dynamics of the Rendezvous home an ocean away in Barbados, with all its attendant racial and gendered power relations, would have to adapt to the new circumstances in which the "great and numerous family" found themselves.

A COUNTRY RETREAT

"A small scattering village about a Mile in Length," the Streatham settlement was reportedly "much frequented by the Gentry and Citizens" of London. John Aubrey (the naturalist, philosopher, and antiquary), who surveyed the county of Surrey in the late 1680s, noted that there was a "valuable Rectory, worth about 300l *per Annum*," in Streatham, and among its most illustrious inhabitants was "Mrs. *Howland*, Mother to the present Dutchess Dowager of *Bedford*, who has a fair old Brick Mansion House here."[55] Beyond these remarks, and a detailed accounting of the monuments and inscriptions inside St. Leonard's church, Aubrey spent most of the rest of his discussion of the settlement's charms discussing the "medicinal Virtue" of its "medicated Springs," which had been discovered around 1670.

By the 1680s Streatham was becoming popular with merchants seeking a bucolic escape from the metropolis, as well as those with ailments ranging from intestinal distress to poor eyesight.[56] Perhaps John fell into both categories. His early demise and persistent frequenting of spa towns is suggestive of a chronic illness. He might also have desired to replicate his Barbados home in England. After all, the profits that allowed John to lease and then improve the Streatham

The Thames Valley

estate came from the labors of enslaved Africans in the faraway sugar fields of his Caribbean plantations. John paid "upwards of fifteene hundred pounds" for the manor, which included "the household goods therein," a large sum of money in the late seventeenth century, and comparable to the costs of building a small manor house from scratch.

Despite an expenditure that supposedly covered everything in this fully furnished residence, John set about refurbishing the estate in much the same way that Rendezvous had been improved twenty years earlier. According to testimony given by Dorothy in the early 1690s, John "layd out much money in buying other furniture for the sayd house," no doubt to update the decor in keeping with current fashions. He also paid to remove outbuilding structures that were decaying, and he hired someone to alter "the Court yards & Gardens makeing them more uneforme." By the time he was finished, the home was "as pleasant and delightfull A house, and as well furnished as most Gentlemens houses of . . . Quality about the City of London."[57]

John publicly demonstrated his status and wealth by ensuring his Streatham estate commanded attention for its beauty. He staffed his household with at least some enslaved individuals, an additional marker of hierarchy in the rural setting. The proximity of other merchants from the city increased the likelihood of other people of color close by, working in the homes of those who were involved in England's imperial trading ventures.[58] Relocating to Streatham did not radically alter the experiences of the women and children in the Rendezvous entourage, who found themselves subject to familiar hierarchies in England.

Dorothy was the only woman whose position probably shifted in any significant way. She no doubt entered the manor with the understanding that she would manage those who worked within its walls. Because she and John were not married, Dorothy could not lay claim to an official position as an "English housewife" and therefore was not "the mother and mistress of the family" in the way that Hester or Frances would have been. At the same time, she probably had the power to hire servants as an official mistress would, and she might well have bonded with the "French maid" who would have been the servant most likely to wait on her at close quarters. Although the fashion for hiring foreign domestics ebbed and flowed in concert with declarations of war against European foes, during the Restoration consistent numbers of French and Dutch workers staffed the homes of London and its environs.[59] The "French maid" might well have been among them.

The disbursements in John's will provide an indication of the position Dorothy hoped to attain in the household. He bequeathed Dorothy the same annual remuneration as he allotted for the children born to his wives, and he desired that she and her children remain at Streatham after his death, all signs that she held considerable power in the manor house. Moreover, the only other female relative who could possibly have challenged Dorothy for this role was Hester's Mary, aged around twenty-one, but she was still living with her aunt and uncle in St. Swithin's Lane in London. Meanwhile, Susannah and Elizabeth received less money in John's will and, because of their racial background, would likely not be considered natural supervisors of household staff. In fact, they were more likely to be among those who answered to Dorothy's demands. An inventory taken in May 1689, just two months after John's death, indicates that in addition to the French maid, John hired other (presumably white) servants to tend the house. Who, then, was the "Black Cookmaid" who occupied one of the servant's quarters?[60]

Of the two enslaved women brought from Barbados, Susannah is the more likely candidate. John's will ranked the women of color with whom he had children and placed Elizabeth above Susannah: she was to receive twice as much (£20 per annum for herself, and the same amount for each of her children) as her counterpart. Moreover, as cooking was among the kinds of labor Susannah likely performed at Rendezvous, it would not be too much of a stretch, and well within expectations, for her to act in a similar capacity in England. If the "Picture of the Cook" mentioned in the Streatham inventory was extant, it might identify the sitter and answer the question definitively. It is likely that if she did not work in the kitchen, Susannah performed some other kind of labor. Elizabeth may also have been expected to engage in domestic chores in the Streatham manor house. It is also possible that both women escaped domestic drudgery once they crossed the Atlantic Ocean.

If Susannah was the "Black Cookmaid," she would have had some responsibility for supervising other kitchen maids and servants. Susannah may well have found it unusual to prepare food inside the house, as in the tropics kitchens were generally located in a separate outbuilding. Nonetheless, the smoke, noise, and heat would have been all too familiar. A kitchen was a cacophonous space—multiple people would have worked in it, and it is possible that even Dorothy spent some time there. Despite their suffocating atmospheres, kitchens were "spaces in which elite women and their servants socialized, laughed, and exchanged secrets and gossip," although whether such camaraderie occurred at Streatham is unknown.[61]

The inventory indicates that the kitchen was of substantial size and very well stocked. In addition to the large open fireplace, which held both the "paire of Spitt Racts" and the "Iron crane" for moving the "Brasse Kettle" and other pots and pans on and off the direct heat, it contained a variety of chafing dishes, stew pans, both a granite and a brass mortar and pestle, "sixteene Pewter Dishes," and around fifty plates. Pastries, desserts, and cheeses had their own serving platters, while there were a number of "Box Irons and Heaters" to keep prepared food at the correct temperature. Food was prepared at the large wooden table in the center of the room, and a "spice box" held aromatics for flavoring the dishes.[62] Perhaps the money that funded the kitchen was not the only thing that traveled from Barbados to England; cayenne pepper and sugar might also have made the journey and landed in the "spice box," and in the larder.

Susannah would have slept in a room designated for the person holding her occupation—the "Black Cookmaids Roome" listed in the inventory. Like the "French Maids Roome" that appears to have adjoined it, this room had a feather bed and a "Tester & head piece" with "Printed Curtaines," as well as one rug and two blankets. Thus it was fairly well furnished, and Susannah, if she was its occupant, could rest in relative comfort. Unlike the French maid, however, the Black cook maid had "One little fire grate," perhaps a sign of Susannah's superior position, since the heat from the fire helped alleviate the damp, cool conditions created by the English weather. In close quarters to the French maid, Susannah also slept adjacent to the "Worke Roome," which contained sleeping quarters for at least one more servant. Her chamber was close by the "Maids Roome," where two beds may have accommodated four additional domestics. These arrangements meant the staff had little privacy and were thrust into proximal intimacy with one another whether they desired it or not.

Were there other people of color among the staff at Streatham? One indication that Susannah was not the only Black domestic in the home can be found in a Chancery Court deposition. Hester's Richard, John's oldest son, had what the records describe (using a racial slur) as a Black boy "to waite on him in his Chambre or otherwise as he thought fit." It is possible that this boy was attached to Richard's uncle's house in St. Swithin's Lane in London, as we know that Robert Chaplin had at least one Black woman working in his home, and Richard passed most of his youth under his uncle's care.[63] Given that John's primary inheritor spent time at Streatham, the Black boy might have been Susannah's son—Richard's half brother, also named Richard—who would have been about eight years old when he arrived in England. If Susannah's Richard was the page, he no doubt became intimately familiar with the "young Gentlemans Chamber" in the Streatham home, which seems to have been allocated to his white master. But even if not, this Black page would have to answer to John's heir in every way he desired: "as he thought fit" covered all expectations and eventualities.

The "young Gentlemans Chamber," like most of the family bedrooms at Streatham, was exquisitely and expensively decorated. The inventory notes

The inventory taken at the Streatham manor house in May 1689 following John's death. C6/486/115. Image reproduced by permission of the National Archives, London.

its "Drugget Furniture lined with yellow silke" and "druggett" hangings on the walls, likely a reference to the heavy wool, silk, or linen cloth that added warmth and richness to the room. There were six pictures, perhaps portraits of family members, or scenes from London or Barbados, adorning its walls. Hester's Richard's clothing was stored in the closet, chest, and "hat boxes" that were found in the room. "One case for Books" and three cane chairs allowed Hester's

Richard to spend time reading and relaxing within his chamber. Although the inventory does not specify what books were on these shelves, the list of "Books as followeth" for the manor house included "Two Musick Books," and "One and Twenty Ruled Books for Musick."

Hester's Richard might well have had some of these on his bookcase because "One paire of Virginalls" an early modern kind of harpsicord, was also part of his bedroom's furniture. Popular in the sixteenth century, this highly decorated instrument had two keyboards that could be played individually or together.[64] Hester's Richard, as the son of a gentleman who had, as court documents claimed, been raised in the manner of someone befitting that status, would likely have had musical training. Was Susannah's Richard also taught to play the instrument so he could accompany his half brother? Perhaps this was one of the tasks that his white sibling "thought fit" to have his Black page perform.

If he was the Black page, Susannah's Richard would have known the "young Gentlemans Chamber" as a place to work, not as a space of recreation or repose. His duties undoubtedly included organizing and maintaining the clothing in the closets, ensuring that coats and outerwear like hats were kept clean and in good repair; and while he might not have been personally responsible for cleaning all the furniture and linens in the room, it would have been his keen eyes that ensured that the maids in the house were informed if standards slipped. Perhaps Hester's Richard wanted his page to have some basic skills in literacy and numeracy so he could write notes and deal with correspondence. Certainly the enslaved boy had learned how to read and write by the time he reached maturity. Susannah's Richard also dressed the part—as the Chancery Court depositions note, there were "severall servants in Livryes" in the Streatham house, and the Black page would have been among them.[65] This also made it more likely that Susannah's Richard wore a collar to underscore his status, making it impossible for him or anyone else to forget that he was subservient in every way. If so, was his father's name or coat of arms embellished on the metal, signifying that he was John's property, not just his progeny?

It is possible that Susannah's daughters (Judith, aged eleven in 1686, and Hester, aged five) also waited on John's white children, or at the very least supported their mother in her work. While the French maid was probably white, there was a "Maids Roome" that might have housed Judith and Hester, and perhaps other domestics too. In elite seventeenth-century households, bed sharing was a common occurrence among domestics, and even between mistresses and their maidservants when their husbands traveled, so it likely that the two beds in the room slept four maids. The accommodations in this shared maids' chamber were not quite so generous as in the other domestic quarters in the house, although they were still above the levels of comfort found in the "Servants Roome over the Stables," where the groom, coachman, and postillion stayed, and were an entire step above the "Pallat Bedd" and blankets found in the "Apple Loft," which no doubt marked another place where workers slept. Even in the maid's room, the girls could expect rugs, quilts, and a feather bed. This too was a sign of John's wealth and prestige—keeping one's domestic laborers in decent accommodation was another marker of high social status among the gentry.[66]

At Streatham, the children would have had reinforced a lesson they learned while in London—not everyone who performed manual labor in these spaces was Black. In fact, it is possible that even the sleeping quarters were racially integrated, something that did not happen on Barbados plantations. The sleeping arrangements might, however, have had a terrible familiarity as they were no doubt segregated by sex, a common practice in England by the end of the seventeenth century. In this scenario, women, girls, and personal domestics slept inside the manor house; men and boys not on domestic duty in the outbuildings, where they would have been spared the constant scrutiny of the master or mistress of the house. Such an arrangement probably suited John very well. If his behavior at Rendezvous was any indication, all the women in his home were possible targets of his sexual predation. Servants' quarters did not come with locks, and as in Barbados, in England heads of household assumed access to their domestics' bodies whenever they desired.[67]

However the size of the Streatham manor is assessed, it was large compared to other later seventeenth-century buildings, even if the grounds (which did not appear to include a park) were of more limited scope. With two parlors, a dining room, and a withdrawing room all available for entertaining, in addition to the hall on the first floor, John's home was in keeping with many post-Restoration residences. Moreover, he had a picture gallery on the second floor, where sixteen of the three dozen or so paintings in the house were displayed. These pictures probably included a mixture of family portraits, landscapes, and perhaps even images of the king or queen to go along with *The Kings Arms*, which was positioned in the downstairs passage. All were a sign of wealth.[68]

The sizeable "houses of office" for workers included some rooms—like the laundry and washhouse—not found in smaller homes. Based on the number of rooms designated for "servants," and the commonplace practice of bed sharing, it seems that at least ten people worked in the house, and another four in the stables and the coach house. According to his own estimations, John expected at least £1,000 a year from Rendezvous alone, an amount capable of supporting up to thirty waged servants; the smaller number at Streatham may be due to John following the Restoration fashion for fewer domestics. Then again, he did not have to worry about providing salaries for the enslaved people among his staff. Regardless of the actual number of domestics, running the manor required coordination among and between different workers to ensure that the household functioned smoothly.[69]

Whatever work the women and children did in the Streatham manor house, they were in an atmosphere that emphasized the luxurious decor that John thought befitting a man of his status. The "little Parlour," "First Withdrawing Roome," and "Dining Room" were all lit by "Gilded Sconses" and had expensive "Large looking Glasses," which brightened the spaces as they reflected the flickering light from the candles that illuminated the rooms after dusk.[70] "Fine Tapestry Hangings," among the most costly decoration, adorned the walls of several of the public rooms on the ground floor, while the dining room was lined "with Damaske and Silke fringe," and included a "Walnut Tree Table" around which guests would sit on damask-covered seating. "Six gilded Leather Chaires" added to the luxury of the "Second Withdrawing Roome," while cane chairs provided additional seating, along with the cushioned couch in the parlor.

Meanwhile, all the accoutrements for acting in a gentlemanly fashion were also on display at Streatham. Hester's Richard had a "paire of Virginalls" in his bedchamber, and musical instruments could also be found in the "little Parlour," where "Three Violins and Bowes," as well as "Three base Violls" in a chest, and a flute, were stored. The number and variety of instruments was in keeping with those found in the grander country houses and again signified John's status. As William Higford opined in 1658, "Musick hath been esteemed a quality becoming a noble personage." The parlor also boasted a "Paire of tables," ubiquitous in country houses for playing cards and other board games, including, perhaps, chess. The inventory at Streatham references the tables "and men to play withall," which is likely a reference to the pieces.[71] Whether or not there were people in the manor who genuinely appreciated music and enjoyed gaming, or whether or not the acquisition of the instruments and other forms of entertainment were for show, John laid out a significant amount of money to ensure his home was well stocked to accommodate a range of tastes.

Upstairs, the eight family bedrooms were equally lavish. In addition to the ubiquitous cane chairs and feather bed and bolster, the "Blew Chamber" included "One Japan Table" and "6 Japan Chaires" as well as a "Holland quilt" and "Two peices of Irish Sticht hangings." Similar Irish fabrics lined the walls of "the Canopy Roome," where the bedspread, canopy, and headboard were all covered with rich "brocadella." Green silk curtains framed the windows. The appropriately named "Crimson Roome" was decorated with deep red curtains, silk fringe, and "brocadella"-covered furniture. Meanwhile "the best Chamber" had "Foure peices of Tapestry Hangings," "One Portugall Matt," and "2 Japan Cabinetts," most likely finished in glossy black and gilt, a European imitation of Asian lacquerwork.[72] Was this the space that Dorothy claimed as her domain? As the most senior white woman on the property, she seems likely to have occupied one of the more splendid bedchambers. According to the inventory this room was the most expensively furnished of all.

The elaborate furniture, upholstery, and carpets in the Streatham manor all had to be scrubbed, dusted, and maintained by the household staff, as a home's cleanliness signaled its owner's status. In a 1682 pamphlet extoling the virtues of clean eating and living, Thomas Tryon noted that keeping "a clean Floor to tread on . . . costs many hard days Labour to keep so, and is dirtied in a Moments time." His appraisal of household chores underscored the laborious and never-ending nature of the work that domestics, especially women, undertook. Meanwhile, each of the feather beds in the home (which did not get nearly the same attention as the rest of the furnishings) were magnets for fleas, lice, and other vermin.[73] Tryon advocated deep cleaning of beds and bed linens, but in reality most seventeenth-century gentry preferred to switch into fresh clothing rather than have their furniture aired out or scrubbed.

To keep up with continuous demands for fresh clothing, housemaids spent a good deal of time doing laundry. The Streatham estate was sufficiently large to have its own "Landry" in a "Washhouse," which was most probably located in the yard. As such, it was yet another sign of the size of the estate, and the ways that John's slave-labor-produced wealth provided sufficient funds for dedicated laundresses. Washing clothes and other households linens was probably an almost daily occurrence. In the Caribbean, where the constant changing of linen undergarments to facilitate bodily cleanliness was expected among the elite, John could make demands on enslaved women to keep a fresh supply of clean shirts coming. These expectations likely crossed the ocean with him.[74]

Laundresses at Streatham hauled the water to fill the "five halfe Tubbs," built the fires, added the lye, and scrubbed out any stains or dark marks. Rinsing required yet more fresh water, while wringing out wet linen was hard on the hands and demanded significant strength. Once clean, the garments might have been hung on the wooden "horse for Cloaths" or placed on one of the "Three dryers for Cloaths." In addition to clothing, the laundry maids at Streatham would have had to carefully clean and press the "Four Damaske Table Cloths," "Tenn Draper Table Cloths," and the fine "Holland Sheets" and pillowcases, as well as the "four dozen . . . Draper napkins."[75]

The rich and bright hues—red, green, blue, yellow—that decorated the parlor, dining room, and bedrooms were à la mode; Restoration England's most stylish homes were colorful spaces where clashing goods from around the world sometimes competed for attention. Someone in the house had expensive tastes, as the estimates for the price of the contents of each room in the inventory attest—the "best Chamber" alone ran to nearly £100. Inventories also reflected the cosmopolitan and global nature of high-end goods. "Shipt India Sattin," "Eastern pieces," and "One Russia Leather Close Stoole and Pewter Pan" appeared in the home alongside the furnishings from East Asia, Portugal, and northern Europe.[76] John might well have been the person who ordered the fabrics and furniture, but it seems equally likely that Dorothy had a hand in these purchases as she was the one permanently in residence. In this position, she drew on profits coming from Barbados to ensure the interior at Streatham matched the exterior.

It was not only inside the house that John spent money. In January 1687 he "furnished himself with A very large good Coach . . . and Six or more very good large Coach horses." A private coach was no small investment, and John paid more than the average price of £30 to £60 for his vehicle and between two and four times as much as the going rate for each of his horses. Moreover, in choosing a team of six, as opposed to the more common four horses, either John was being "a little ostentatious" or the weight and heft of his carriage demanded six horses to successfully pull it. His vehicle probably required upgrades and repairs, another outlay that had to be factored into owning transportation. In 1689 John's estate owed "Mr Forrest Coachmaker" £20—no doubt to cover such maintenance.[77]

Further expenses were incurred in supplying the stables and coach house, keeping the horses well fed and tended (which could cost upward of £30 a year), and ensuring that there were a suitable number of hands for grooming, coach maintenance, and driving the carriage. The Streatham manor would have had at least one groom and stable boy to tend the horses and polish the leather saddles and bridles, one postillion (who rode one of two lead horses during excursions), and a coachman, who managed the stables and the servants who worked within its walls. Living quarters for these workers were also available on the estate. The "Three stock Bedds" over the stables probably housed the grooms and under-servants; it was likely that the coachman slept in a room of his own, a practice commensurate with his elevated status. The coachman also probably spent little time at Streatham: John took his coach "once a yeare to Tunbridge and Stayed A greate part of the season there," in addition to traveling to his Essex Street lodgings in London during winter. The coachman's itinerant experiences were fairly common among men with his occupation.[78]

As with the "Stables and Coachhouse," the "Yards, Gardens," and "Orchards" at Streatham required the attention of exterior domestic servants. The yard was the location for the chicken coop and the water cistern, as well as the thirty-six bushels of sea coals that presumably fueled the ten fireplaces inside the house.[79] Fresh eggs no doubt made the cook's job easier, but this also meant that the chickens had to be fed and watered, and their coop cleaned out on a regular basis. The coop's inhabitants also had to be protected from predators like foxes and weasels. Whoever tended the garden and the orchard had "Sheers, Two Sythes," and both stone and wooden rollers to trim and manage the grass. "Three wheele barrows" transported harvested fruits, herbs, and vegetables back to the house, while "19 Earthen flower potts" provided vessels for ornamental plants that might brighten up the exterior of the manor, including roses, daffodils, marigolds, peonies, hyacinths, and primroses.

Reworking gardens for uniformity and pleasing lines was extremely popular among the landed gentry during the Restoration, and John's willingness to pour large sums of money into this enterprise was in keeping with similar investments made by his peers. Manor house gardens were spaces where mistresses of households cultivated plants and herbs, and it was not uncommon for heads of households to become obsessed with fruit trees and bushes. Dorothy, if she did take an interest in gardening, would have struggled to adapt to England's much shorter planting and growing season. Although the fruits grown in England country gardens were expanding in variety during this period (even including some orange groves in nearby locations in the southeast), the Barbadian members of the household did not have access to anywhere near the variety of tropical fruits that they enjoyed in the Caribbean. Sugar and spices for the kitchen might survive a transatlantic voyage, but England's climate was not suitable for growing pineapples, mangos, or plantains. If sweet, juicy fruits continued to be in demand in the Peers household, the garden inventory suggests that the inhabitants had developed a taste for melon. "Twenty Two glasses for melons" are listed among the garden equipment. These clear covers were used to cultivate the fruit by protecting its exterior from the harsh English weather and predators alike.[80]

Whatever role Dorothy played at Streatham, she was not John's wife and therefore would never be more than an unofficial mistress of the estate. Despite lacking a legitimate spouse, John acted the part of the landed gentry through his showy displays of wealth—evidence that he aspired to a status equivalent to the one he held in Barbados. In the colony he had been among the most prominent and wealthy residents, and in England he needed to demonstrate that he was not merely another merchant with Caribbean connections. His estate at Streatham went some way to achieving this goal, but John did not have the pedigree of families like the neighboring Howlands. He would never be their social equals, no matter how much he enriched his estate. A large household staff, including Black domestics, would take him only so far.

AT EVERY TURN IN THE STREATHAM MANOR, family members, domestics, and visitors were reminded of John's wealth. Dorothy (and indeed Susannah and Elizabeth) must have noticed that the grand estate they now occupied was similar in size and scope to the "Mancon House" at Rendezvous. And just as at Rendezvous, the profits from slave-produced sugar provided John the means to flaunt his success through the ways he staffed and decorated his home. Unlike at Rendezvous, however, the labor performed at Streatham was done by a much more diverse group of domestics, including at least one maid from France. That fact, however, did not change the status of Susannah's Richard as he trailed his elder half brother around the estate. Nor did it automatically alter Susannah's or Elizabeth's place in the household.

When the "great and numerous family" arrived in England, the capital's hierarchies made clear that the markers that had dictated the women's status in Barbados—their sex and their race—were just as developed in the metropole. While the identifiers of enslavement might have looked different in each place— for example, elaborate neck collars were not part of the uniform of bondage in Barbados, while coarse osnaburg clothing was not common in England—the idea that Blackness connoted inferiority was active on both sides of the Atlantic Ocean. Although England might have offered the suggestion of a world beyond bondage, on the Streatham estate, at least two of its Black inhabitants likely found themselves in much the same circumstances as they had in Barbados. And all around them were reminders that Black people in England were as likely to be enslaved as to be free.

For all that the relationships at Streatham mirrored those that developed in Barbados, the status of everyone in the household depended on John himself. In the late winter of 1689 John was unwell, probably not for the first time. As February gave way to March, he took to his feather bed in his "Lodgeing Roome." While Susannah no doubt prepared food and drink in the kitchen, Dorothy probably monitored his condition. The water from Streatham's springs did not appear to be having its advertised restorative effect. His health rapidly deteriorating, John dictated his will. If he should not survive he wanted to leave clear instructions for how his children, including those who were "naturall born," and their mothers would be supported when he was gone. Whether his wishes would be followed was something neither he, nor Dorothy, could guarantee. And so, as the patriarch of Rendezvous and Streatham grew increasingly ill, Dorothy must have wondered what the future held.

CHAPTER 5

Courting Legitimacy

TENSIONS IN THE STREATHAM manor house were running high in March 1689. John was gravely ill—fevers and chills wracked his bedridden body—and the specter of death haunted the home's rooms and corridors. As long as he was alive, John's status and wealth provided Dorothy, Susannah, and Elizabeth the security of a place to live, the ability to be with their children, and perhaps even a veneer of respectability. His death would undo this stability. Women like Elizabeth and Susannah who had experienced enslavement knew all too well the turmoil that often resulted when an enslaver died. In the Caribbean the deaths of planters frequently separated enslaved parents from children as estates were broken apart to ensure bequeathals to daughters and sons or to pay off accrued debts. While the circumstances at Streatham were not quite the same, the precarity that serious illness engendered surely permeated the manor house walls.

Whatever complex feelings they might have had about John the man, it is likely that all three women wanted Mr. John Peers Esquire to survive because of the protection his status offered them. As he deteriorated, they might have sought insurance, using the opportunity of nursing him to health to remind

John of all they had done for him over the years, of his responsibilities to them and to their children, and of the financial remuneration they would need once he was gone. Did Dorothy demand to be granted leave to remain in the Streatham home? Might Elizabeth have suggested to John that she and her children deserved a larger annual income than Susannah and hers? Perhaps they used this moment to influence his thinking. Maybe this further strain amplified their friendships or animosities toward each other. John's pending demise surely heightened suspicious feelings and encouraged a lack of trust among the women.

As the household rallied to revive John, the women probably guarded access to his chamber and worked to mitigate his symptoms. In the kitchen, Susannah likely confected medicinal beverages, using the well-stocked "spice box" and pantry, as well as water from the nearby Streatham springs to concoct "possets" and tisanes.[1] It seems that Elizabeth and Dorothy took charge of the "Lodging Room" where the patient lay. They may have followed doctors' orders that the "Brocadella hangings" and "Crimson curtains" be shut to prevent light and air from penetrating the room, leaving only the flames from the "Brasse fire hearth" and the flickering tops of candles to break the suffocating gloom. As maidservants flitted in and out under the women's careful watch—cleaning and replacing the "Close Stoole" and the basin of water used to cleanse John's sweaty brow—so too would the stench of sickness ebb and flow from the room. Candlelight might have reflected from the "Looking glasse" as the women sat in rattan-weave "Cane Chaires," speaking to John in hushed tones.[2] Ultimately, Elizabeth's, Susannah's, and Dorothy's assiduous nursing were for naught. One day after he dictated his new will, John Peers died.

The emotional, financial, and legal fallout of John's death reveals the ways that Caribbean women, and especially women of color, navigated life in England without the protection of a patriarch. John's last days in the Streatham household had all the hallmarks of a modern-day soap opera. First, there were the characters—a fatally ill patriarch, one of his oldest friends, the three women with whom he'd fathered children, a scorned former business partner, and his estranged eldest daughter. Next were the circumstances under which John's final wishes were recorded. At least two of the women—Elizabeth and Dorothy—kept watch at his bedside. If their Chancery Court testimony proved true, they were fully apprised of his financial situation and used their proximity to John to advocate for material support.[3] While an old friend was invited to help him craft his will, John's former factor and brother-in-law Robert Chaplin showed up unannounced to confront John about the eye-popping £22,000 he was allegedly owed. Robert brought reinforcements in the form of Sir William Gregory (a legal and political heavyweight) and John's oldest child,

Mary, presumably present for whatever emotional pressure she could exert on her father.[4]

In the months and years that followed John's death, Elizabeth and Dorothy joined forces to sue Robert Chaplin in Chancery Court for throwing them out of the Streatham manor house and for not paying them their legacies. They did so against a broader cultural milieu that denigrated women from the colonies— Black and white—painting them as lascivious and scandalous. In their careful accounting of John's business practices, finances, and estate management, Elizabeth and Dorothy challenged these characterizations, even as Chaplin cast aspersions on the women's characters, actions, and right to any kind of financial payout. Robert also dragged John's name through the mud despite still supporting John's children with Hester and taking in his daughters with Frances.

Buried deeper still within the drama and scandal of John's death and its aftermath are the choices that Elizabeth made in the decades that followed. Elizabeth refused to accept degraded treatment, insisting on her rights to her inheritance, on the rights of her children to what they were owed, and the right to life in freedom for all of them.[5] Unlike Dorothy (but like her fellow enslaved compatriot Susannah), Elizabeth was not officially permitted to remain in the Streatham home by the terms of John's will. Though resident in England for only three years at John's death, her intimate familiarity with the racial hierarchy of the metropole made her cognizant of the ways she and her children remained at risk of a lifetime in bondage. Nevertheless, she refused to leave the household, and in the 1690s she joined forces with Dorothy to sue for the rights to their legacies in Chancery Court. When the 1690s Chancery suit remained unresolved, Elizabeth continued to fight for her rights. In the following decade she returned to Barbados, further evidence of her continued determination to assert her freedom.[6] Going back to the Caribbean put her status in jeopardy: the risks of reenslavement loomed large. When that strategy did not turn out as she hoped, she came back to England and continued to press for what she was owed, insisting on her rights up to and beyond the grave. Her own will included—to the penny—provision for the inheritance that she and her children were due.

Although she never argued for her right to freedom explicitly, Elizabeth did so implicitly in every action she took. Like other Black mothers, she drew on her kinship ties—to John, and more importantly to her children—to cement her unbonded status. And like so many women of color, her defiance was, ultimately, a solo crusade. Her refusal to accept anything less than what she had been promised is no less radical for that. In Elizabeth we see another example of the ways that individual Black women understood their value in the early modern Atlantic world. She deployed that knowledge over four decades to turn what had once been an assessment of her worth as property into a demand for her right to such property herself.[7]

THE WILL

While John's precise diagnosis is unclear, it seems likely that he suffered from some chronic malady. His choice of Streatham as a home base, and Tunbridge as a place where he spent the summer season, indicates that he found the rejuvenating waters of spa towns especially appealing. Tunbridge, like Streatham, was a popular destination for those in ill health in the middle of the seventeenth century because its nearby wells held waters with a reputation for their restorative powers. Moreover, a series of royal endorsements had recently brought the region to fame.

Although the medicinal properties of the contents of Tunbridge's wells were first discovered during the reign of James I, it was during the 1630s that the waters really came "into fashion," when Charles I's wife, Henrietta Marie, was "sent hither by her physicians . . . for the refreshment of her health." Thirty years later, in 1664, Charles II's wife visited the wells to combat "a dangerous fever." The fact that she was "perfectly cured by these waters" meant that their reputation was "greatly raised" once more. Following the queen's revival, a series of royal visitors including the Duke of York and his daughters came to the area, underscoring its continued popularity.[8] By the time John traveled to Tunbridge in 1687, the wells were among England's premier spa experiences and, unlike the more established Bath, were just thirty miles from London, making them a much more accessible spot for ailing metropolitan elites.

A list of the "cheifest diseases against which *Tunbridge* water may be used with good successe" published in 1670 was long in description. All kinds of obstructions—in the stomach, bowel, liver, or spleen—could allegedly be relieved by drinking from the wells. So too could visitors laid low with various "agues . . . dropsie, the blacke & yeallow jaundice . . . the scurvie, the greene sicknesse" expect to be rejuvenated by daily doses of water. Kidney stones, bladder infections, "bloudy Flixes," vomiting, "Head-ach, Migraine, & Vertigo" all met their match. In addition, venereal diseases like the dreaded "Poxe" or gonorrhea could be cured. And it was not only physical maladies that might be alleviated. The "braine" was strengthened "by the use of this water, and consequently it is good against the palsie, inclination to apoplexy, lethargie, and such like diseases of the head."[9] In 1687 one physician noted that if there was "any such . . . *Universal Remedy*, 'tis here," summing up succinctly the benefits of the waters at Tunbridge Wells. No doubt it was the "great esteem and reputation in Curing many *Chronick* and *Rebellious Diseases*" that encouraged John to spend his summers in the spa town. Whatever illness drove him to seek a cure, the waters failed to remedy it.[10]

The day before John died, the Streatham home was a hive of activity that the women would have observed with interest and perhaps concern. First, Richard Barrow, a merchant from Covent Garden who had known John "from before the late great fire in London," arrived to witness his friend's will.[11] Next, Robert Chaplin, John's brother-in-law and former factor and business partner, showed up unannounced, supposedly to confront John about debts he owed. Although the two men had been related by marriage for over twenty years, and despite the fact that they appeared to have a good working relationship for most of that period, just a few years before John returned to England their relationship had broken down.

Each accused the other of improper practices; John apparently stopped using Robert as a factor in 1684 when Robert refused to pay "A bill of five hundred pounds . . . payable to the Guinea Company for slaves" that John had purchased on credit. As a result, John's reputation allegedly experienced "very greate Damage and dishonour." One year later, in February 1685, Robert retaliated, sending John a letter demanding the £22,000 he claimed he was owed. This sum, the equivalent of around £3.4 million today, was nothing short of a small fortune.[12] John was both insulted and appalled at his brother-in-law's accusation. His arrival in England did not appear to smooth things over between the men. Robert could no longer expect to be made executor of John's will or to be included in its bequeathals.

No doubt anticipating a scene, and presumably wanting to ensure a witness to whatever transpired, Robert arrived at the Streatham manor in March 1689 with Sir William Gregory, a man of unimpeachable integrity who could, if needed, testify to the validity of any conversation that took place between the brothers-in-law. A former member of Parliament (for the seat of Weobley, formerly held by Hester's father), and baron of the Exchequer, Sir William had recently returned to politics following the accession of William and Mary to the throne. A lawyer by training, he would be appointed chief justice of the King's Bench in May 1689.[13] Sir William's reputation bolstered Robert's credibility and the innocent premise for his visit, as well as offering the imprimatur of official legal counsel. Sir William was not the only person accompanying Robert. "Mr Peers Daughter" Mary, now at least twenty-three years old, arrived with her uncle.[14] Her presence might well have been a calculated step by Robert to

The first page of John Peers's will, written the day before he died in March 1689. PROB11/396/91. Image reproduced by permission of the National Archives, London.

pressure John. Having raised Mary in her father's absence, Robert brought her to underscore *all* the ways he had supported John and his family.

Elizabeth, Dorothy, and Susannah must have been aware that Barrow was there to witness John's will. Had they made entreaties to John in advance of Barrow's coming to ensure that the document included provisions favorable to them and their children? According to Barrow, the answer was no. John's friend of over twenty years reported that "noe person did importune or push the said Mr Peers to give decisions for making his said will." Barrow insisted that the document simply recorded John's true wishes. Moreover, he asserted, "the said Mr Peers did very fairly execute the said will & was of sound mind & understanding at the tyme."[15]

Robert, however, believed the women had influenced John. In later court documents, he explained that he had "reason to suspect" that Elizabeth, Dorothy, and the governess attending John's youngest children had been instrumental in shaping the contents of John's will. He described John as "being then much in the power and under the direction of" the women, noting that because of their presence and lobbying, John's final instructions were not given "freely."[16]

Of course, the claims of these two men reveal nothing of what actually occurred inside the Streatham house. If the women did persuade John to make certain allowances in his will, then the fact that Barrow did not recognize their input is simply part and parcel of an early modern mentality where elite white men found it difficult to acknowledge a lower-status woman's ability to sway one of their own. Meanwhile Robert's assertions that they connived to lead John astray was part of an equally insidious set of assumptions about women who birthed children out of wedlock, namely that they were conniving seducers who deployed their feminine wiles to bewitch men and to lay claim to that which was not theirs. Both interpretations erased the women as legitimate influencers or actors, an effacement reflected in the records surrounding the fallout of John's death. While Elizabeth and Dorothy brought a Chancery Court case, neither they nor any other female witnesses were deposed as part of the investigation. The record is silent on what Mary did when she visited Streatham, and neither Susannah, nor any of the other women in the manor house, was asked to give testimony in the legal proceedings.[17]

Given that their futures might well have resided on his deathbed decisions, it would be more surprising if the women had not tried to sway the man who fathered their children.[18] After all, they had been in his households—on both sides of the Atlantic Ocean—for almost twenty years and knew the man, and his foibles, intimately. They could have expressed their wishes and desires subtly: they were all well placed to offer modest daily reminders of their roles, and of the need to provide for their children upon his death. That alone might have been sufficient. Equally, they could have acted more as Robert suggested, deliberately raising questions with John about inheritance and where they and their children would live in the event of his death. That they probably did so is a demonstration of their understandings of their value to John and to his estate.

Women like Elizabeth, Susannah, and Dorothy were all too aware of the hierarchies of race and power at play in their lives. In the slave society of Barbados the women constantly confronted the realities of their relative worth as they witnessed the buying, selling, and birthing of enslaved people. This knowledge of their value informed their deep understanding of the system of racial capitalism that dictated their status. Had John written his will in Barbados, Elizabeth and Susannah might have lobbied for explicit manumission for them and their children. In England, a society with slaves, the women appear to have believed that financial support could ensure a life in de facto freedom.[19] As the later Chancery Court cases make plain, in both locations the women observed or were party to conversations about John's wealth and business arrangements. Rendered invisible through their status as enslaved and servant women, they likely gained some of their knowledge simply by being in rooms where discussions and debates about finances happened. England's society with slaves was predicated on, and financed by, the profits from Caribbean plantations, and no one was better placed than Elizabeth, Susannah, and Dorothy to know the truth of the insidious connections between colony and metropole or to deploy this knowledge to ensure they would be taken care of following John's death.

There is substantial evidence that Elizabeth and Dorothy were at John's bedside when he dictated his will. The Chancery Court case in which they sued Robert for failing to provide their inheritances includes accounts of the conversations between John and Barrow in March 1689. Elizabeth or Dorothy told their lawyers that upon receiving information about the sums and frequency of disbursements to John's legatees, Barrow asked John "how the sayd Annuitys would bee payd"—in other words, did John have the finances to support his many bequeathals? According to the women's bill of complaint, John responded that he could easily cover the annuities because Rendezvous never provided less than "fourteen hundred pounds" yearly. Moreover, he informed Barrow that he also received £1,000 in annual rent from leasing Staple Grove. The conversation then moved to potential debts John owed, and again Elizabeth and Dorothy recalled the words exchanged. They explained how John accounted for the money he had previously owed Robert, and how he had satisfied that debt by signing over his Herefordshire property to him in 1666. The women went so far as to assert that "on his sayd deathbed" John raised his concern that Robert "not

Intermeddle with or have any thing to Doe in the management or disposal of his estate," because John was "not well sattisfyed in the Integrity or Justice of the said Robert Chaplyn."[20]

Because Elizabeth and Dorothy were present when Barrow asked for specific assurances about the contents of John's will, it seems impossible that they were not also present when John discussed the clauses that enumerated what they and their children would receive. The will's contents reveal how the women—either overtly or covertly—shaped these decisions. Both Dorothy and the woman charged with "the education" of his youngest daughters with Frances were granted "the use of my house and grounds with the appurtenances and all the goods and furniture of the House wherein I dwell at Stretham," so long as neither woman married.[21] Such a guarantee was no small victory, especially for Dorothy, who had young children. It seems plausible that her English background and whiteness were part of what propelled John to make this provision, or to acquiesce to her request if she made it, because neither Elizabeth nor Susannah received the same benefit.

It was not only this stipulation that drew lines between the women with whom John fathered children. Dorothy and her younger son and daughter received £100 per annum. In addition, Dorothy's older daughter, Frances, aged eleven, was left "the sum of five and twenty pounds per annum" as well as "forty pounds to bind her apprentice." Elizabeth and her children, however, only received £20 per year, while Susannah and her daughters and son were to be paid half as much again: £10 each annually.[22] Even if they had been asked to leave the room while their inheritances were discussed, the women might have used John's frailty as an excuse to come and go, catching snippets of conversation and gleaning information about the decisions he dictated as they moved to and from his bedside.

With the will written and witnessed, and the business part of the day concluded successfully, it must have been something of an unpleasant surprise for everyone when Robert Chaplin arrived unannounced. Elizabeth and Dorothy knew he had raised John's daughter and three sons with Hester, and that he had acted as a factor for John in the metropole, receiving and selling "greate quantityes . . . of sugar with goods, Commodityes and Merchandizes" from his Barbados estates to the tune of "some thousands of pounds in every yeare," and extending credit to John whenever necessary. They also knew that the relationship had broken down.[23] According to a deposition given by Barrow in 1695, he and Robert crossed paths at the door of the Streatham manor, and Robert asked Barrow "if he had been with Mr Peers and if he had made any settlement"—meaning had John written his will? Given the ways the women moved around the house, it is possible that they witnessed this conversation or overheard Robert challenge Barrow about the "great debt due from Mr Peers to him." One of them might have observed Barrow's attempt to deflect Robert's ire by suggesting that he "goe up & discourse with Mr Peers about the said debt."[24]

When he came back downstairs Robert reported that he found John "better than he Expected" and "apprehended him in a way of Recovery." Somewhat unintuitively, but allegedly "out of due respect to him," Robert claimed he had *not* spoken to John about the large debt he was owed. While in the bedchamber, Robert apparently decided he "would not disturbe" John "with busenesse of soe great importance." According to Robert, physical improvements aside, John was still in "noe way fitt to discourse about" the subject of his debts. Robert ended his account of their interactions with yet another dramatic flourish, suggesting that he could not be so ungentlemanly as to berate an ill man about his unpaid accounts. He believed that raising the issue would have sent John into a tailspin or even into his grave, for which Robert would rightly, in his estimation, have "drawne a censure of Inhumanity" from both family and friends.[25]

By not raising, or not admitting to raising, the question of the money he believed he was due, Robert avoided reporting John's response. If John had rejected Robert's version of events, as he would surely have done, and denied that he was in debt for such a vast sum of money, Robert would have had to account for the discrepancies between the two men's accounts while they were both alive. Once John died, Robert could push his version of events and stake his claim on John's estates in Streatham and Barbados.

Robert claimed that he entered the Streatham manor house to determine whether or not he, or the debts he was owed, were accounted for in John's will. By his own admission, he did not discover that he was omitted from the will until after John's death. His fury at not being made executor of the estate led Robert to bully and berate the three business acquaintances given the role, Richard Barrow, Richard Guy, and Richard Howell, all "merchants of Covent Garden." Guy and Howell were in their sixties, and Robert used both their ages and the complexity of John's affairs to pressure both men into signing over the executorship to him. They both agreed to do so in short order. Not long afterward, Robert persuaded Barrow to do the same. He was successful, in part, because he had the full support of his nephew, and John's oldest son, Hester's Richard. Once Robert took charge as executor he moved swiftly to recover the financial losses he claimed he was due.

By mid-May 1689, just two months after John's death, Robert evicted Elizabeth, Dorothy, their children, and the governess from the Streatham manor house. Robert insisted that he did so "in respect to the friendshipp and Relation" between him and John and "out of a true compassion to the said wedlocke borne Children." Elaborating on his reasoning, Robert explained that he removed the three women "from the said house and from the Children of the said Mr Peers (as not fit to be Trusted with their Education)" because they had "notoriously Signalized their unfittnesse by their former Cohabitation with the said Mr Peers."[26] Thus the relationships that had ensured they were included in John's will were the very ones that Robert cited as justification for ignoring John's wishes and turning the women out of their home. In addition to ignoring John's wish that they be allowed to remain at Streatham as long as they did not marry, Robert also allegedly refused to pay the women their promised legacies. As the financial and practical support that they enjoyed while John was alive evaporated, Elizabeth and Dorothy had to find new ways to sustain themselves and their children. Homeless, and with no money coming to them, the women turned to the "Compassion and Charyty of their friends," without whom they "must have starved."

Who were these friends who ensured that they had food on the table and a roof over their heads? Might Susannah (who was allegedly receiving her inheritance) have helped her former housemates? It seems unlikely, given that both women placed her firmly on the other side of the court case, listing her (and her children) as among the "confederates" who conspired to cheat them out of what they were rightfully owed. Perhaps Elizabeth or Dorothy built networks in their first months in London back in 1686 that they could turn to for assistance. Or there may have been people closer to the Streatham estate who intervened. While it is possible that the women exaggerated their financial distress in order to heighten the stakes of their claims, and perhaps elicit sympathy from those standing in judgment, it is equally likely that they were in dire straits without the income provided by John's Barbados sugar estates. Without their legacies, they turned to the one place where they could receive a hearing, and possibly justice: England's Chancery Court.

THE COURT CASE

Bringing a suit in Chancery Court could be a lengthy, costly, and time-consuming process. Essentially a civil court in place since the fourteenth century, at the time Elizabeth and Dorothy brought their case against Robert (*Spendlove and Ashcroft v. Chaplin*) in the 1690s, the Lord Chancellor presided over suits. Inheritance claims, property trusts, debts, marriage settlements, bankruptcy, and apprenticeships were all disputes that came before the court. One of its attractions was the ability of anyone (in theory) to bring a claim. Another was that the court could adjudicate quite complicated matters.[27]

Those bringing a case—the plaintiffs (in this case Elizabeth and Dorothy)—first took their bill of complaint to the court in writing. This action required the services of a lawyer, whom the women had to pay. They also were responsible for the costs of the ink and vellum on which the bill would be written. Finding a lawyer in London might not have been especially difficult. In fact, John's second son with Hester (also named John) was trained in the law. Moreover, when they resided in the Essex Street rooms that John rented in London, Elizabeth and Dorothy were just a short distance from the Old Bailey and the Inns of Court, where barristers and solicitors had their chambers.[28] Identifying someone willing to represent their case would have been well within their grasp even if paying their fees proved a challenge.

Once the plaintiffs entered their bill of complaint into the record (spoken activity in Chancery Court was not recorded), Robert Chaplin could provide his bill of answer. Answers usually responded point by point to accusations about improper actions or behavior in the bill; unlike the plaintiffs, Robert would have given his response under oath. As a case wound its way through the court, plaintiffs sometimes responded to bills of answer with new information or allegations, and defendants regularly did the same. Robert, for example, submitted three separate answers to the complaint brought by Elizabeth and Dorothy in an effort to persuade the court to rule for him and against them.[29] In turn, the women could respond to each answer and include new claims of their own.

For these reasons suits generally dragged on for years, and many were abandoned before a verdict was rendered. Sometimes a plaintiff died in the middle of a case, throwing the process into turmoil. The parties could also settle out of court, and such agreements did not always make it into the record. Most commonly, plaintiffs ran out of funds to continue their pursuit of the defendant, which is what seems to have happened in this instance.[30]

The materials gathered during the four years that Elizabeth and Dorothy fought Robert in Chancery Court reveal a lot about their relationship to John's former factor. These sources also lay bare his opinion of them. Insisting that the women had lived with John "in a very scandalous manner," Robert referred to their sons and daughters as "Bastard children."[31] The fact that they bore John's children out of wedlock was not the only factor that infuriated him. Robert deemed Elizabeth and Dorothy insufficiently grateful for what he perceived as his generosity toward them following John's death. Avoiding the circumstances of their eviction from the Streatham manor house altogether, Robert instead insisted that he "did take care alsoe of the Complainants by making payments to them . . . of such Annuities as were intended them." Not only did he claim he paid the women their due; he asserted that he had also placed "Two of the Children to Trades," fulfilling the stipulation in John's will that guaranteed apprenticeships for his "naturall born" children. This largesse, according to Robert, was not met with appropriate appreciation on the part of Dorothy and Elizabeth. He noted that he would have continued to pay them annuities "had they behaved themselves with such gratitude and respect as this Defendant Conceives was due unto his care and kindnesse."[32]

If insufficient gratitude aggrieved Robert, his real frustration with Dorothy and Elizabeth emerged from their refusal to accept their fate and acquiesce to his decisions about their futures. Instead "the mothers" chose a different tack, "carrying themselves very ungratefully and rudely towards this Defendant," according to Robert. He found their "Clamouring at his House in London" while he was at his country estate in Herefordshire most upsetting. At his St. Swithin's Lane residence they allegedly made "threats" toward Robert "to compell him by force" to pay them their annuities.

St. Swithin's Lane was in the heart of the City of London, a stone's throw from the Royal Exchange, the center of business, and about half a mile from St. Paul's Cathedral. Like those famous locations, it had been burned to the ground during the Great Fire of 1666, and although the rebuild did not widen the street much beyond its narrow medieval path, the house that Robert occupied was of the newest Restoration style. His neighbors were also among the area's merchant elites: the Salter's Company, one of the twelve most prominent guilds in London, had its location on the same street.[33] For Elizabeth and Dorothy to arrive at his front door and allegedly create a scene was further proof of their uncouth and unladylike behavior.

The women not only appeared at Robert's residence to complain verbally about his treatment of them but also brought legal ammunition in the form of "a Subpena." This document informed Robert of the Chancery suit and commanded his presence in court. That Elizabeth and Dorothy made public their grievances toward him was embarrassing enough. Now they were supporting their accusations with paperwork in the form of an order for his appearance before the Lord Chancellor. Moreover, their arrival at his door strongly suggested that he had previously ignored their bill of complaint: subpoenas were normally issued only when there was no response to a plaintiff's case. Perhaps nothing incensed Robert more than what he described as "their Arrogancies" in making such official demands.[34] How could women of their rank and status—creoles from the colonies, mothers of children English society considered illegitimate, a servant and even an enslaved woman he viewed as "kept" by a man to whom they were not married—dare challenge his authority?

By characterizing their actions in this way, Robert placed Elizabeth and Dorothy firmly within existing discourses surrounding women who had spent time in the Caribbean. Such women's sexuality and pruriency were understood to have been influenced by the tropical climate and their ambiguous racial presentation.[35] Prejudiced attitudes toward women with Caribbean experience, such as those espoused by Robert, were popularly expressed in literature and other forms of entertainment in the late seventeenth and early eighteenth centuries, and stereotypes and pejorative depictions of creole women had been building since the days of Shakespeare and Ben Johnson. These works initially mocked and demeaned white Englishwomen, but authors soon began raising questions about racial purity, writing into their novels and plays women of allegedly suspect parentage, and leaning into other bigotries about the wanton sexuality of women who spent time in the Caribbean.

Robert even went as far as to call into question the paternity of Elizabeth's and Dorothy's children, archly noting that they were only John's "in reputation." Thus, the women were doubly problematic—their children were "bastards" and possibly not even the progeny of the man who had claimed them as his "naturall born" offspring, adding another layer of insinuated scheming. The women's subterfuge with regards to their erstwhile "benefactor" and their conniving natures clearly knew no bounds as far as Robert was concerned. Through his portrayal of the women as debauched wenches, he created scandal to sway judgment in his favor.[36]

A common story line for novels and plays set in the Caribbean mocked Englishwomen who traveled to the tropics in search of husbands, assuming that they did so because their efforts to secure a good match in England had failed. For example, Thomas Southerne's, *Oroonoko: A Tragedy* (his 1696 spin on Aphra Behn's 1688 antislavery novella *Oroonoko; or The Royal Slave*) centers on the tragic story of the love between Imoinda (an African woman in Behn's original, but a white Englishwoman in Southerne's adaptation) and Oroonoko, an enslaved man owned by the governor of Suriname. However, the subplot that opens the play features a caricature of the frustrated English huntress prowling for a marriage partner. In the play's first scene, the Welldon sisters, Charlotte and Lucia, go "Husband-hunting into *America*," the older Charlotte in disguise as the younger Lucia's brother.[37] This subterfuge allowed the siblings to present themselves as the inheritors of the recently deceased "Richest Planter" in Suriname, and to parlay their supposed inheritance into making good marriages.

In short order Charlotte's gamble pays off: Lucia marries the recalcitrant son of a wealthy widow. By the end of the play Charlotte has abandoned her breeches to wed a man she befriended while impersonating Lucia's brother. By dressing in men's clothes and assuming masculine privilege Charlotte embodied the European conceit that in the colonies individuals could pretend to be anyone they wished, transgressing norms of class and gender impenetrable back home.[38] In this case the two sisters not only engaged in a confidence game rooted in successful cross dressing; they also usurped male authority and challenged class hierarchy by portraying themselves, falsely, as wealthy beneficiaries of a large sugar estate.

To Robert, then, might Dorothy have been playing out a version of this "husband hunting" herself? She appears to have been born in Barbados, although in the Caribbean—where high death rates made blended families, remarriages, and stepparents and stepsiblings a common enough occurrence—her status did not necessarily bar her from stepping up the social ladder despite not being John's social equal. Her father may have been a small planter on Barbados, while her brother was probably an acquaintance or neighbor of John's, as he witnessed several business transactions relating to Rendezvous.[39]

Dorothy could have found herself in the Rendezvous household because she crossed paths with John as a result of her family connections and found herself coerced into a sexual relationship that she did not seek. Perhaps her father or brother positioned her to take advantage of the death of John's first wife, Hester. She may even have desired a place as the second Mrs. Peers herself, thus fulfilling the stereotype of a social climbing "husband hunter," although she gave birth to her first child with John one year before his first wife's death.[40] As with Southerne's Welldon sisters, Caribbean social mores allowed Dorothy to behave in what Robert considered a dissolute, immoral, and shameless way without suffering the consequences of social ostracization that generally accompanied such actions in England.

Satirist Ned Ward's *A Trip to Jamaica* (1698) also presents the West Indies as a place of dissimulation, where middle- and upper-order English norms were transgressed and even abandoned. The protagonist (likely a loosely veiled version of Ward himself) leaves England for the Caribbean aboard a ship with "Three of the *Troublesome Sex*," including "one *Unfortunate Lady*" who was in "pursute of a *Stray'd Husband*," who had taken up with a *"Lacker-Fac'd Creolean."* According to Ward, the woman would not have been "vex'd" if her bigamist spouse had "Marri'd another Handsomer than her self," but "to be Rival'd by a *Gipsy*, a Tawny Fac'd *Moletto* Strumpet, a Pumpkin colour'd Whore, no, her Honour would not suffer to bear with patience so coroding an Indignity."[41] Here Ward elaborates common English (mis)conceptions of creole women in the Caribbean, depicting them as sexually voracious ("Strumpet," "Whore"), and rooting their moral degeneracy as well as their lack of beauty in their non-whiteness.

By using a range of descriptors—"*Gipsy*," "Tawny," "*Moletto*," and "Pumpkin colour'd"—to describe the woman's physical appearance, Ward ensured that his broadsheet's readers had multiple opportunities to associate skin color and ethnicity with vice. These stereotypes built on much older sixteenth-century ideas that made "white" a synonym for "good" or "fair," and that connected "black" with "evil" or "ugly."[42] Elizabeth's African descent meant that she could easily be painted as one of the women about whom Ward warned his readers—exactly the kind of person who would instigate infidelity and seduce a prominent white man—a woman whose skin color and background rendered her incapable of restraint and conditioned her to give in to her base desires.

If Elizabeth wore the markers of her ancestry on her body, Dorothy also found it hard to hide her colonial upbringing. Although she may have worked hard to shield her pale complexion from the Barbados sun, thereby keeping herself as "white as possible" in the context of a colonial population, it is probable that in London her skin appeared more weathered and bronzed than most Englishwomen of elite status. She might well have utilized makeup to "produce the desired 'whiter than white' complexion" that would prove she belonged among them. Perhaps Dorothy applied ceruse, a lead compound sold by apothecaries as a white paste, which was then diluted with water or egg white and hid a host of blemishes and imperfections. Or she may have relied on the less dangerous ground alabaster or starch to lighten her skin and hide her origins.[43]

Dorothy also suffered by association in her relationship with Elizabeth. In Barbados, she might have used her proximity to women of African descent to emphasize her own whiteness.[44] Reverend Francis Crow, a minister in Port Royal, Jamaica, noted how even middling white creole women, like the wife of a cooper, could "go forth in the best flowered silk and the richest silver and gold lace . . . with a couple of Negroes at her tail," as a way to underscore her English heritage and her whiteness.[45] Whereas being seen with Elizabeth in Barbados would have underscored Dorothy's superiority by virtue of her skin color alone, in England, where her time in the colonies had already rendered her racially suspect, any association with Elizabeth only raised questions about Dorothy's own racial heritage. Elizabeth, of course, could not avoid her racial status. Proximity to Dorothy did nothing to improve her chances of being seen as English in London.

Londoners who heard either woman speak would have their suspicions of their otherness confirmed. In the 1720 novel *The Jamaica Lady*, which recounts the experiences of several women who traveled to Restoration England from Jamaica, the mixed-race protagonist, Holmesia, is described as especially unbecoming because of how she sounds. When she spoke, according to the narrator, "her Language was a sort of Jargon, being a Dialect peculiar to the Natives of that Island, it being partly *English*, and partly *Negroish*; so that unless a Man had been some time in the Country, he could not well understand their Meaning."[46] This suggestion that she mixed "English" and "Negroish" into a form of speech that was allegedly unintelligible to white island visitors signaled Holmesia's racial ambiguity as well as her depravity. Equally, Elizabeth's and Dorothy's speech patterns and accents would have marked their colonial backgrounds. Elizabeth was probably also speaking a second language, rendering her communication even more obviously foreign to English people. No doubt part of what was so disturbing about the women's "clamouring" at Robert's St. Swithin's Lane home were the precise sounds their voices made as they spoke their unhappy truths.

There were other ways, too, that Elizabeth's appearance betrayed her foreign status. In 1710 a German visitor to London, Zacharias Conrad Von Uffenbach, commented on the city's Black population, especially the women. Noting that "there are, in fact, such a quantity of Moors of both sexes in England that I have never seen so many before," he went on to juxtapose Black women's bodies against the "European dress" that they wore. Uffenbach declared that "there is nothing more diverting than to see them in mobs or caps of white stuff and with their black bosoms uncovered, as we often saw them."[47]

The exoticization of Black women's bodies was nothing new, and Uffenbach's descriptions offer insight into how many white European men, like Robert, perceived women of African descent, and especially how they tied their bodies to their character and their supposed sexual perversion. When they first came to England, Elizabeth and Dorothy would have worn clothing that marked them apart from the local female population. The seven years that had passed since the women's arrival in London might have allowed them to update their wardrobes, but the financial distress that John's death imposed could equally have meant that they had to wear attire that bore the marks of wear, tear, and repair.[48] This too may have caused consternation for Robert, as their clothing would have stood as visible reminders of their penury, a financial circumstance caused by his refusal to pay them their due.

For all of Robert's anger at Elizabeth's and Dorothy's behavior, from their perspective, their actions were entirely reasonable. By his own admission Robert had left "their Annuity in Arreares": he clearly stated that he did not think he was required to make good on the promises left in John's will.[49] Perhaps the biggest indication of his attitude toward them was in how swiftly he moved to evict the women from the Streatham house: within two months of John's death Elizabeth and Dorothy were effectively homeless. What choice did Robert leave them but to challenge his actions in court by insisting on the rights granted to them by John's will?

The women's expert knowledge of John's finances underwrote their conviction that the money owed them was readily available. Stating that everything they were due was worth no more than "the vallue of five hundred pounds per Anno or thereabouts," the women explained that the "lesser Plantation in Barbadoes" was "lett" for "above one thousand pounds" annually, while a much smaller seaside dwelling brought in £100 per year. Rendezvous itself, they asserted, had never produced annual profits of less than "fourteene hundred pounds."[50] Armed with these figures, the women insisted that Robert was doing some creative bookkeeping when he claimed he could not afford to pay them: at minimum he should have been receiving £2,500 a year from Barbados, a sum that would easily have allowed him to make the good on the quarterly payments the women, and their children, were supposed to receive.

Elizabeth and Dorothy fought for their rights in England's Chancery Court for at least four years. Where they lived during this period is unclear, but given that they were able to "clamour" in person at Robert Chaplin's home in St. Swithin's Lane in London, it seems probable that they moved to the city following their eviction from the Streatham manor house. They were also supporting relatively young children. Frances Spendlove may have been apprenticed, but Dorothy was still raising Ann and John, aged ten and eight respectively at the time of their father's death. Meanwhile, although her eldest children, John and Susanna, were of age by the time Elizabeth took her suit to Chancery, Richard, Elizabeth, and Edward Ashcroft were all under the age of sixteen.

Perhaps supporting their children resulted in their Chancery Court case petering out, like so many others did. The expense of continuing to pursue civil justice, especially if they were not receiving their legacies, would have put a real strain on Elizabeth's and Dorothy's abilities to secure housing, food, clothing, and other necessities. Neither had another obvious steady income that would finance her actions in court, or help to support her family. The mothers might well have had their time and attention drawn elsewhere and eventually found the pressure, financial and emotional, of pursuing their case too much to endure. After 1696 there appears to have been no further activity in the long-running battle of *Spendlove and Ashcroft v. Chaplin*.[51]

THE AFTERMATH

The decades following the end of the women's suit against Robert are silent on the whereabouts or activities of Dorothy and Susannah. Elizabeth, however, appears in the most unexpected place—back in Barbados—sometime between 1707 and 1714. A solitary phrase, tucked away in a deed discussing the assets of the Rendezvous and Staple Grove plantations dated 1714, recorded the presence of "Eliza Ashcroft . . . a mullato woman" on the island in the previous few years.[52] This short reference is the only evidence placing Elizabeth back in the Caribbean.

Elizabeth's return suggests either her full confidence in maintaining her assumed free status in a slave society, or her belief that the perils of returning to Barbados (which included reenslavement) were overridden by the possible benefits of finally inheriting what she insisted she was due. This potentially risky return demonstrates how Elizabeth pursued her right to her inheritance by a variety of means, and in more than one jurisdiction. It also offers a remarkable opportunity to explore how a woman of color staked her claim to a Caribbean legacy.

By sailing back to England's most developed slave society in the first decades of the eighteenth century, Elizabeth's decision invites us to reassess what we know about taking such a gamble. Our familiarity with people returned to the colonies, or with the rate of reenslavement, comes from two different groups, neither of which Elizabeth squarely fell into. First, there are the contemporaneous examples of women of African descent sent from England back to the West Indies, deported precisely to place them back in chattel slavery in the colonies. Dinah, a woman of color who lived in Bristol in the 1650s, was one such woman. She tried to establish her free status in English courts after being brought to the metropole by her enslaver. Put on a ship departing for Barbados, where she would return to the hardships of plantation labor, she was saved only by a last-minute appeal that saw the courts rule that she could remain in England.[53]

A similar case appeared in 1690, when Katherine Auker tried to gain her freedom from Richard Rich, a Barbados planter who brought her to England just a few years before John traveled to the metropole with Elizabeth and Susannah. Rich had returned to Barbados and ordered Katherine arrested and imprisoned in his absence. The court ruled that Katherine could stay in England and serve anyone she wished until Rich next arrived in the country. Unlike Elizabeth, however, Dinah's and Katherine's enslavers were still alive, and it was at their instigation that these women were slated to be returned to the Caribbean.[54] There is no direct comparison for someone like Elizabeth, who was living in de facto freedom without her enslaver.

Second, most examples of the reenslavement of free people of color in the Caribbean come from the late eighteenth century and are usually framed in the context of legal statutes restricting the rights of free people of color on the island that made reenslavement more likely. But Barbados did not pass its first act of this kind until 1721.[55] It does not follow that the same risks were present in the 1700s or 1710s. In fact, Elizabeth may well have crossed the ocean more worried about the dangers of undertaking another transatlantic voyage than about what arriving in the Caribbean would mean for her status. After all, she knew at least one formerly enslaved person who had sailed back into Caribbean waters and safely returned to England.

Susannah's son, Richard, became a mariner on a British naval ship of the line in the 1700s, and in 1705 and 1706 he sailed on HMS *Montague* to the West Indies, with Barbados listed as one of his ports of call.[56] Elizabeth's years in London no doubt placed her in proximity to other Black sailors who might have been enslaved, as she was, in Barbados, and who now lived in freedom. Noting this flexibility for some freed people does not change the fact that Elizabeth was intimately acquainted with the horrors and violence of enslavement, having lived that life herself for around two decades. It also does not remove her cognizance of the color line that connected whiteness with freedom and African ancestry with bondage in Barbados. This knowledge certainly informed her decision-making process as she weighed the odds of sailing across the Atlantic once more.

When Elizabeth arrived in Barbados she was far from the only formerly enslaved person on the island, and she was familiar with this freed population from her time in Barbados twenty years earlier. Since at least 1652 island laws had attested to the presence of free people of color. Evidence from baptism records shows that some Black inhabitants who began their lives in slavery had later been manumitted or purchased their freedom.[57] Close to Rendezvous, there appear to have been very few free individuals of African descent. The baptism records for Christ Church Parish indicate that in July 1683, just one month before Elizabeth's and Susannah's children were baptized, "John aged 38 & Margaret aged 25 free negroes" were christened in the parish along with their four young children.[58] Apart from this family of six, there was only one other person of color marked as "free" in the Christ Church baptism records between 1651 and 1701. While these numbers surely underestimate the real size of the free population in Christ Church, it is probably not by much.

However, if Christ Church was not a locus for free people of color, Elizabeth was familiar with the demographics of Bridgetown, where the numbers of people either born free or manumitted were much higher.[59] She would have traveled to the island's capital to attend the market, or to accompany Hester, Frances, or Dorothy on an errand to town, and had plenty of opportunity to observe that not everyone of African descent in the city was enslaved. Of the

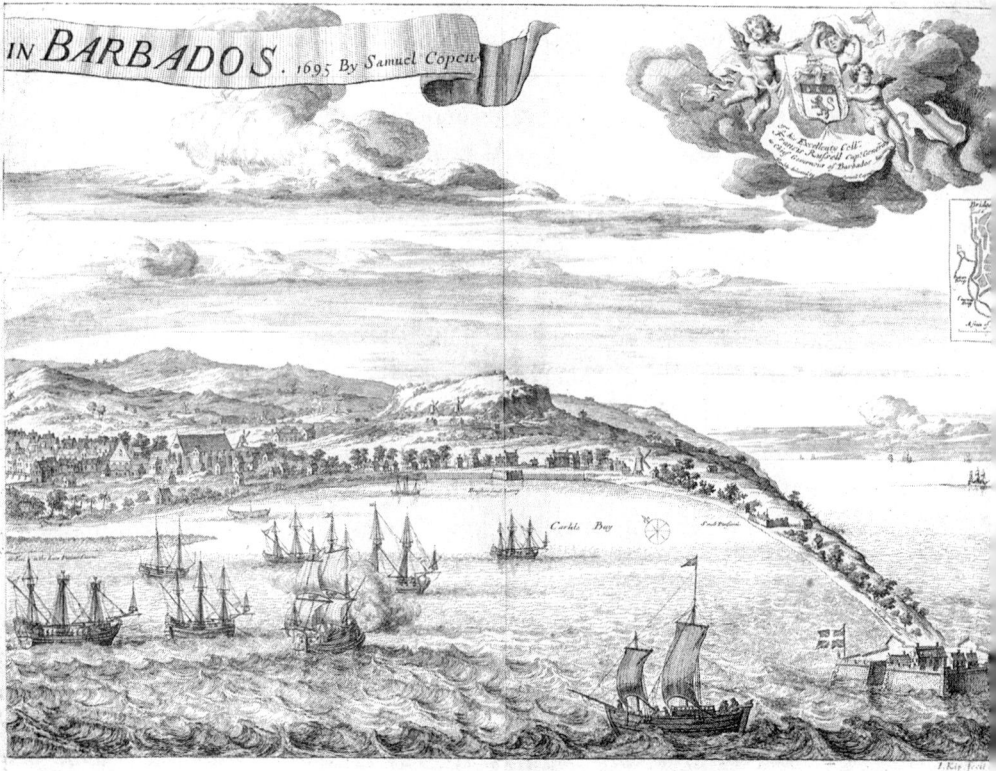

A Prospect of Bridgetown in Barbados by Samuel Copen, 1695.
Courtesy of the John Carter Brown Library, Providence, RI.

seventy-eight people of color baptized in St. Michaels (the parish where Bridge-town was located) between 1665 and 1715, almost half were marked as "free." At least twenty-three of those baptized were explicitly listed alongside their parents, underscoring the preponderance of free families of color in Bridgetown.

For example, "Thomas Ravell & Mary Ravell, free negroes," were married in St. Michael's, Bridgetown, in 1688. Thomas, at least, had been manumitted eight years after his enslaver's death according to a stipulation in his will. Charles Cuffee, "a negro freed by his master" in 1677, went on to marry Mary Jones, described as a "free negro" in 1694. Both couples baptized their children in the Church of England, creating a new generation of free people of color on the island. That they resided in Bridgetown is probably no accident: urban areas like the port city tended to be where free communities of colored concentrated.[60]

Although there had always been free women of color living singly or with children in Bridgetown, by the time of Elizabeth's return their numbers appears to have increased. Mary Jacks, Mary Edy, Elizabeth Richards, Mary Jones, "Katherine . . . old woman," "Sarah a Madagascar woman," and Judith were all adult women of African descent living free in Bridgetown in the 1690s and 1700s. Meanwhile Hannah, aged twenty-one, and her four-month-old son, John, and "Frank Hollard a free negro woman . . . aged 40 years" and "Robert Hollard her son aged 7 years" were also residing in the city in this period.[61]

Most of these women either had worked, like Elizabeth, as enslaved domestics, or had taken their wares from the plantation to Sunday markets. Both groups were more likely to be manumitted than those who did field work; domestics might be freed upon the death of their enslaver, while peddlers sometimes made enough money to purchase their freedom. Elizabeth fell into the former category, although she was never officially freed. By the 1750s many such women (whether formerly enslaved or born free) ran taverns, boardinghouses, or brothels in Bridgetown, and while there is not much evidence to show what freed women did for work in the first decades of the eighteenth century, it is likely that they, like so many other free women of color in port cities across the Caribbean, were engaged in similar practices.[62]

Why did Elizabeth return to Barbados at all? It appears that the reasons center on her desire to ensure her inheritance. In 1705 Robert Chaplin, whom she had fought so hard in the 1690s, died. Immediately following his uncle's death, Hester's Richard, the eldest of John's sons, reasserted his extended family's claims to the profits from Rendezvous and Staple Grove. He appointed a business acquaintance, Samuel Barwick, as manager of the Barbados plantations. Samuel had previous experience in the Caribbean and took up his new role in 1706. Fewer than twelve months later, Samuel sued Richard's younger brother, John, and Richard's attorney, Conrade Adams, in Barbados's Chancery Court.[63]

The following year, Samuel traveled to Barbados to inspect the plantations and to pursue his case, which seemed to be languishing. Appalled at the condition in which he found the plantations, he described them as "run very much to decay as well as in respect of the buildings thereon as of the negroes and other stock necessary for the well manageing thereof."[64] According to his account, Samuel invested large quantities of his own money into improving Rendezvous and Staple Grove. Given this outlay, he later argued that he was under no obligation to pay annuities to John's inheritors, insisting that any profits from the Barbados plantations were his alone until he recovered his initial investment. Elizabeth was among the legatees who could expect nothing from the estate until Samuel's accounts were settled.

By 1711 Richard's younger brother, John, was in Barbados. Presumably the brothers realized that trying to assert their rights from 4,000 miles away was a fool's errand. It may have taken four full years, but by August 1711 the siblings provided "their answer on oath to the Bill of Complaint" brought by Samuel. John was "in the Island aforesaid," living as a "merchant in Bridge Town." Conrade Adams represented Richard's interests. None of the paperwork from the case survives, but other suits reveal that Samuel was victorious. Claiming that he had invested his own money in "repairing all and singular the buildings remaining on the said plantations" as well as in erecting new structures "for the better management of the estate," Samuel explained that he had spent energy "recruiting and Keeping up a sufficient stock of negroes and cattle" and money "discharging severall considerable debts." The court agreed that he should be compensated, and in October 1711 it granted him £2,728 15s 7½ d.[65]

Richard, furious that the court had not recognized the brothers' claims, and deeply suspicious that Samuel had used personal relationships to sway the judge's ruling, sailed for Barbados in 1713, determined to seize control of the plantations. He died, according to Samuel, "about six weeks" after his arrival "of a feaver happening to Europeans at their first coming to the . . . Island." At this point, apparently, "the said suite in the said Court of Chancery in Barbadoes abated."[66]

The court case brought in Barbados required John's sons to respond to Samuel's complaint. The strength of the sibling's case rested on the condition of their father's estate when Samuel took charge and on how the plantations were run in the years immediately following their father's move to England in 1686. Elizabeth had already proved her intimate knowledge of the finances of the Peers estate when she and Dorothy sued Robert Chaplin in the 1690s. She would have made an excellent witness on questions of the value and condition of Rendezvous and Staple Grove in this legal proceeding too. Moreover, Elizabeth was deeply invested in the brothers' claims because she and her children were also owed legacies. If Samuel was forced to pay out money, she would finally receive her due. This circumstantial evidence, along with the fact that the two were listed as present in Barbados in the same 1714 deed, suggests that Elizabeth traveled to Barbados with Hester's John.[67]

Elizabeth's and John's presence back in Barbados in 1714 had its roots in the intimate connections they had forged thirty years earlier. She had known him, and his older brother, Richard, as children on Rendezvous and was herself baptized as an adult within days of John's birth and baptism.[68] While Hester's Richard and John were sent to England for their educations early in life, Elizabeth no doubt made their reacquaintance as young men in London and Streatham. The brothers also kept tabs on Elizabeth, Susannah, and Dorothy over the decades as later court proceedings reveal.[69] These connections indicate that there might

CHAPTER 5

have been some mutual obligations between the brothers and Elizabeth. Perhaps they persuaded Elizabeth to travel to the Caribbean to aid in their case against Samuel. Or maybe Elizabeth desired to return for other reasons and took advantage of the opportunity to travel with a prominent white man who might offer her protection.

There is another interpretation of Elizabeth's actions, one that does not contradict a decision to travel to Barbados at the behest of John's sons, but that may suggest that she did not work entirely in concert with them. In yet another Chancery Court case brought in England in 1719, Samuel claimed that he had paid Elizabeth at least some of what she was due. The deal he made with her coincided with her time in Barbados. Describing her among the "necessitous persons" who received at least part of what they were owed, Samuel stated that he had paid Elizabeth around £255 by "Lady Day," 25 March 1718. In the same suit, Samuel indicated that she had willingly signed over her inheritance to him with the promise of earning 10 percent interest. None of the documentation or supposed "receipts" that would support his assertions survive.[70]

Importantly, both sides of *this* case agreed: the 1719 suit was brought by John's grandson, and namesake, and he also alleged that as early as 1712 Elizabeth received some payment from Samuel, even if it was not a full accounting of her inheritance.[71] Whether or not Elizabeth struck a deal with Samuel or was merely caught in the fight between two men over the profits from Rendezvous and Staple Grove, it would be in keeping with her consistent demands to have acquired her inheritance by any means necessary. This might have included accepting a less-than-perfect deal from Samuel if doing so resulted in a payout of at least some of the money she was owed.

When Elizabeth returned to Barbados she probably stayed in accommodations in Bridgetown run by a free woman of color involved in the hospitality trades. Access to a boardinghouse or tavern notwithstanding, the city was home to Barbados's Chancery Court, and proximity to the institution was necessary if Elizabeth's purpose was to give a deposition or provide testimony in the case brought by Samuel.[72] She would have blended into the free population of color, and also had access to John at his residence in the city. Is it possible that Elizabeth made time to visit Rendezvous? Two decades was a long time to be away, and there were probably few left on the estate who would have remembered her. In the 1705 inventory for the plantation, an "Old Judith Parry" is listed, who might well have been the Judith who witnessed the baptism of her son, John, back in 1670. If so, she could have faint memories of Elizabeth as one of her contemporaries. It is equally likely that Elizabeth avoided the estate and stayed in Bridgetown, where she was less likely to encounter anyone she knew. Even if she did see enslaved market women from Rendezvous who journeyed to the port city to sell their wares on Sundays, the chances of her knowing any of them were small.[73]

We do not know how long Elizabeth remained in Barbados. At some point between the 1714 deed that placed her on the island and the 1719 Chancery Court case brought in London, Elizabeth returned to the metropole. Perhaps Richard's death precipitated her return, as this supposedly ended the Barbados lawsuit against Samuel. Or, if Samuel did pay her some of what she was owed, this money might have supported a return and a new life in London. By 1719 three of her five children were dead, but her oldest daughter and middle son were still alive and forging lives of their own in the capital. The 1719 case does not specify their precise location or Elizabeth's. An uninked space was left on the line for that information to be added, and it remained blank, emblematic of all we do not know about Elizabeth from this era.[74] Given that Dorothy was in Covent Garden and Susannah was in St. Clement Danes—both places they had familiarity with from the months spent in London in 1686—it seems likely that Elizabeth too resided somewhere close to the heart of the capital. Where, precisely, remains unknown.

Elizabeth did not stay in London for long. By 1722, when she dictated her own will, she had moved to Sunbury, a village on the Thames about fifteen miles southwest of the city, probably to be close to the daughter she later lived with. In the boilerplate of the day she noted "I command my soul unto the hands of God that gave it and for my body I command to the Earth to be buried in a Christian like manner at the Discretion of my Executors." However Elizabeth viewed her 1670 baptism, half a century later she appears to have embraced the Church of England. Her will is less revealing about what work she might have done to support herself toward the end of her life. If she did receive some money from the Barbados plantations (as Samuel asserted she did), she believed she was still owed a significant payout. As she made bequeathals to her daughter, son, and four grandchildren, she noted that she was still due "the sume of five hundred thirty eight pounds . . . from the accounts of Balance and notes payable to me from the Plantations of Barbados," no small sum of money. In fact, had she received this payment in a lump sum, she would have been able to purchase a very fine house—small manors cost around £1,000 at this time.[75]

Elizabeth's will was settled in 1729, the very same year of England's infamous *Yorke-Talbot* ruling. That judgment declared unambiguously that enslaved people's status did not change when they stepped foot on English soil, that enslaved people could be forcibly returned to the West Indies, and that baptism did not guarantee an enslaved person's freedom.[76] Elizabeth's life was a direct counter to all three propositions. Her status did appear to change, if not immediately upon her arrival in England, then certainly after John's death. She was not forcibly sent back to Barbados as an enslaved person but instead traveled to the Caribbean freely. The baptism that was not supposed to connote freedom appears to have been important enough for Elizabeth to emphasize her Christian faith when she dictated her will. *Yorke-Talbot*, decided just after her death, closed down the possibilities open to a woman who spent her early life enslaved on a Barbados sugar plantation; but Elizabeth was able to end her own in de facto freedom in a small southern English village on the banks of the Thames.

JOHN'S DEATH THREW the world that Elizabeth, Susannah, and Dorothy knew into turmoil. Although the implications for their lives, particularly those of Elizabeth and Susannah, were not as great as they might have been had they all still been living in Barbados, the security, stability, and protection offered by the Streatham home and John's wealth was swept away by his untimely demise. Since he was only forty-four when he succumbed to illness, the women might have expected him to be around for another two decades. Longevity in the early modern era, especially for elites, was not unusual once a person had made it past the risky childhood years and through adolescence.

Suddenly the women found themselves legatees of his estate, yet forced to rely on another elite man, someone who did not hold them in high esteem, to receive what they were due. Perhaps Susannah, marked in the will as "a Black" and in a court document provided by Robert Chaplin as "Black Susan," was viewed as sufficiently deferential and unimportant and so received at least some of what she was due as a result. Elizabeth and Dorothy, however, were clearly not behaving in an appropriately grateful manner as far as Robert was concerned. They needed to be put in their places, and refusing them their inheritance was one means of doing so.

That neither woman was willing to take Robert's ill treatment without putting up a fight reveals much about their strong sense of themselves and the confidence they held about their rights and inheritance. For his part, Robert's insistence on portraying both Elizabeth and Dorothy as debauched creole women who were unfit mothers in addition to all their other deficiencies underscores the ways he deployed stereotypes to discredit them. Equally, their refusal to accept this damning characterization and to challenge Robert in Chancery Court shows that both Elizabeth and Dorothy were determined to assert their rights as Englishwomen making claims on a Caribbean estate. They deployed their deep knowledge of John's finances and their role in the management of the plantations to advance their claims on John's will. It may not have ended as either woman hoped, but keeping a suit active for over four years and forcing Robert to respond to their claims was no small achievement in and of itself.

Elizabeth's bold assertion of her rights over a period of forty years is astonishing. As a formerly enslaved woman, she would have been intimately aware of the fact that at one time she would have been construed as property, not propertied, and thus included in a planter's probate record as property to be bequeathed, not as a legatee herself.[77] And yet she persisted in claiming what she was due as a legitimate heir to a Barbados plantation. Elizabeth kept her focus squarely on the recompense to which she was entitled. Refusing to acquiesce meant that she also, perhaps unwittingly, forced into the record an account of what happened on Rendezvous half a century earlier, and what transpired in England in the decades that followed.

Like John, Elizabeth projected her desires beyond her mortality. After forty years, she no doubt had little faith that the money from Barbados would ever be paid. Her tenacity exposes more than a simple demand of rights to her inheritance. By pursuing her claim, and her children's claims, Elizabeth insisted that her family had a right to "meaningful freedom."[78] She asserted that they deserved a life in England lived on their terms and not one dictated to them by the patriarch who brought them to the metropole in the first place.

CHAPTER 6

Bloodlines and Birthrights

IN 1716 JUDITH MINGO, AGED FORTY-ONE, resided in St. Clement Danes Parish, close to the area where she lived thirty years earlier on her arrival in London at age eleven. Near the Inns of Court and bridging the fashionable shopping district of the Strand, the neighborhood was now an established site of entertainment and business. Judith had moved from the heart of the capital to Streatham on the outskirts of London and then, following her father's death, back to the metropole, first to Spitalfields, then to Lothbury, where St. Paul's newly finished dome rose just to the west. This economically diverse part of the city was a short walk from where Elizabeth Ashcroft and Dorothy Spendlove "clamoured" for redress at Robert Chaplin's house in St. Swithin's Lane. Famed for its copperworks and foundries, Lothbury's streets were lined with warehouses holding goods brought from Britain's colonies and with the opulent homes of merchants, like Robert, who facilitated the trade.[1]

The rest of Judith's branch of the "great and numerous family" had suffered in the intervening years. In 1700, her younger sister Hester died and was buried in the nearby churchyard of St. Christopher Le Stocks. Before the decade was

Susannah Mingo
b. ?
Baptized June 1670
(Barbados)
Resided in St. Clement Danes, London, 1718
d. 1726
(St. Christopher Le Stocks, London)

Judith Mingo/e
b. ca. 1675
(Barbados)
Spinster in Lothbury, London, ca. 1700
m. Thomas Elliott, April 1718
(St. Clement Danes, London)
d. ?

Susannah
b. August 1718
(St. Clement Danes, London)
d. ?

Richard De/Mingo
b. ca. 1678
(Barbados)
Mariner on the *Montague*, living
in Lothbury, London, ca. 1700
d. 1709
(Lothbury, London)

Hester Mingo
b. ca. 1681
(Barbados)
d. 1700
(St. Christopher Le Stocks,
London)

b. born
ca. circa
d. died
m. married

———

The Mingo and Ruslin lineages.

Hester Tomkyns
b. ?
(Weobly, Herefordshire)
m. John Peers, ca. 1664–65
d. 1678
(Christ Church, Barbados)

Richard Peers ———— **Hannah Ruslin**
b. 1668   b. ?
(Barbados)   m. 4 July 1695
m. 4 July 1695   (St. Mary's Lambeth)
(St. Mary's Lambeth)   d. after 1718
d. 1713
(Barbados)

- **John**
  b. 1696
  (Weybourne, Surrey)
  d. 1761
  (buried in St. Leonard's)

- **Richard**
  b. 1700
  (Weyborne, Surrey)
  d. ?

- **Mary**
  b. 1703
  (Bagshot, Surrey)
  d. ?

- **Robert**
  b. 1706
  (Surrey)
  d. ?

- **Thomas**
  b. 1709
  (Bagshot, Surrey)
  d. ?

- **Elizabeth**
  b. 1712
  (Surrey)
  d. ?

out, her younger brother, Richard, had also passed away, leaving Judith executrix of his small estate.[2] Despite being heir to a Barbados plantation's profits, she could not rely on her inheritance being paid by the ever-changing managers of her father's estate. A "spinster" by status, Judith was unmarried and likely spinning thread to make ends meet, a common occupation for a woman of her age and status. With her siblings gone, and only her elderly mother left, it seemed as though the Mingo name would die with them.

Just outside London another woman wondered about her legacy. Hannah Ruslin had been a servant at Streatham, working alongside Judith, when both were engaged in domestic service in the manor house. Unlike Judith, Hannah had married, and married very well. Her recently deceased husband was Richard Peers, the oldest of John's sons, and the primary inheritor of the Rendezvous and Staple Grove plantations. As she was a lowly servant, Hannah's nuptials with Richard caused a scandal: they married without his family's approval.[3] Unsurprisingly, becoming Mrs. Peers transformed Hannah's fortunes. The name she took provided her and her progeny with considerable social power and hitched her to a legacy that stretched back to the earliest foundations of colonial Barbados. Three years a widow in 1716, Hannah was trying to ensure that her oldest son, who had not quite reached the age of maturity, receive the inheritance he was due. With her husband dead, the grandson and namesake of the wealthy Barbados enslaver he never met was now the primary Peers heir. Mother and son took their case to Chancery Court, fighting the latest in a long line of plantation managers for the money they were owed.[4]

Contemporaries in age and in service, Judith and Hannah both had labored in John Peers's home. Both stood to benefit from Barbados sugar estates and the enslaved labor that ran them. They both also found themselves at the whims of a succession of men who managed those estates. While Hannah had married the chief inheritor of Rendezvous and Staple Grove, Judith was one of the non-white "naturall born" children of the Peers patriarch. Hannah's marriage legitimated her children and washed away her unsuitable class origins; meanwhile Judith, defined by her enslaved mother's name and station, could not escape the threat of bondage.

In England Judith did not look to a "Peers" surname to improve her outlook or to consolidate her freedom. Like the Ashcroft and Spendlove children, she chose her mother's name, in effect bringing the de facto practice of *partus sequitur ventrem* across the Atlantic Ocean to England. Now the association was no longer one of bondage or illegitimacy. Instead, the children's second names linked them to an ancestral line that promised independence. By consciously taking their mothers' names the children enacted a strategy that indicates a different understanding of inheritance and generational continuity in a country where legitimacy was still understood as a function of paternity.[5]

Examining the lives of the children born to John Peers reveals the different pathways open to his sons and daughters, legitimate and "naturall born." For the Mingos and Ashcrofts who began their lives in slavery in Barbados, an existence in England's society with slaves remained precarious. It appears that they learned how to survive from their mothers: Susannah's children earned livings in the metropole while Elizabeth's used the court system to pursue their inheritance. Perhaps these are among the reasons that they insisted on using their mothers' last names, and not "Peers," as they moved through the city. Dorothy's children made the same choice. Forging lives in London appears to have been difficult for the white Spendlove children too, but they did not abandon their mother's name. Meanwhile, John's children with Hester and Frances also had to navigate a rapidly changing London, whose population was exploding as Britain's imperial ambitions became ever more fervent. Cleaving closely to the birthright left them by their father, his legitimate children persistently laid claim to their inheritance from Rendezvous and Staple Grove to cement their status in the imperial metropole.

The bloodlines and birthrights of John's children did not play out quite as their father might have anticipated. As much as early modern England was a place of seemingly rigid hierarchy and patriarchal control, in reality there was room for negotiation within those systems of oppression. Not only was primogeniture no guarantee of continued wealth and success for Hester's Richard (John's eldest son), but John's daughters—especially those who were born to Susannah, Elizabeth, and Dorothy—were not as hampered by their sex and status as we might suppose. Their kinship ties and the lessons they learned from their mothers provided them with strategies for asserting autonomy and for surviving in London and its suburbs. Less reliant on whatever inheritance they could expect to receive than John's children with Hester and Frances (perhaps because they had fewer expectations that the money would be forthcoming), the Mingos, Ashcrofts, and Spendloves managed to build lives that were not contingent on profits from a Barbados plantation. Their stories, in parallel with the lives of their white Peers half sisters and half brothers, reveal the contradictory nature of the legacies of slavery in early modern London.

IN THE NAME OF THE MOTHER

When John died, Susannah's children were young—fourteen, eleven, and seven or eight—so their mother would have decided where they should live next.

Moving back to London made sense: the greatest possibility for work for Susannah and her children was in the capital, which had a sizeable Black population. Although the majority of this population was male (in part because of the many Black sailors who counted London as their home port), significant numbers of Black women lived in the city, many doing the kinds of domestic work that had shaped Susannah's life. Shortly after Elizabeth and Dorothy began their court case in 1692, Susannah and her children were living in the Spitalfields area of the city on George Street in St. Dunstan Stepney Parish, an area famed for its weaving, especially silk produced by French Huguenot refugees who settled the region from the mid-1680s. These immigrant weavers taught local residents how to produce "lustrings, velvets, brocades, satins, very strong silks known as paduasoys, watered silks, black and coloured mantuas, ducapes, watered tabies, and stuffs of mingled silk and cotton—all of the highest excellence."[6]

Might Judith or one of her siblings have learned a skilled trade? Her father's will made specific allowances that any of his "naturall born" children be apprenticed at either their own or their mother's request. This meant that the siblings and half siblings had the opportunity to earn money sufficient to have a relatively high quality of living. Dorothy's eldest daughter, Frances, was singled out by John to receive "twenty-five pounds" to secure her apprenticeship, although the specifics of her traineeship went unrecorded.[7] Elizabeth's sons, John, Richard, and Edward, also took advantage of this clause. James Maydwell of "Ludgate Hill London, Glasseseller," claimed John Ashcroft as an apprentice in 1690. In April that year, when he was fourteen, "Richard Ashcrofte" of "Streetham, Surrey," was bonded for seven years as a "new apprentice" to William Cozens, a master goldsmith. And in December 1697 Edward Ashcroft became a "Tallow-Chandler" when he was apprenticed to Daniel Wane.[8]

These professions would have served the brothers well. The last decades of the seventeenth century saw a revolution in glass technology, making the industry more profitable and creating new markets. As a glass seller, Elizabeth's John was responsible for not only procuring glass and producing drinking vessels but also acting as an agent of quality control, ensuring fair prices, and maintaining a high standard of production among glaziers. By 1697 someone bearing John's name was a member of the Worshipful Company of Glass Sellers and had taken on an apprentice himself, suggesting that John had some success in his new trade.[9]

Training as a goldsmith required that Elizabeth's Richard have an even higher skill set. Goldsmith apprentices had to be literate, and, as he trained, Richard would have become expert in filing, soldering, sawing, forging, and casting metal. If he also added jeweler to his talents, then he needed to be practiced in dexterity and fine work. The records are silent on when, exactly, Richard completed his training. Later Chancery Court cases from the 1730s describe him as a "Citizen & Goldsmith of London," indicating that he practiced the trade for four decades.[10] Far less salubrious was Elizabeth's Edward's status as a tallow chandler, or candlemaker, a job that was smelly, hot, and dirty. Although candles were in high demand in early modern London, many people made their own at home, and by the first decades of the eighteenth century new technologies were beginning to render animal wax candles obsolete. Still, it was a living, and one that could have supported Edward, albeit perhaps not as richly as his goldsmith or glass-seller brothers.[11]

Susannah's Judith may have exercised her right to an apprenticeship too. References to Judith as a "spinster" in her brother's 1704 will and as a "former spinster" in the 1718 Chancery suit are indicative of more than her marital status. In the seventeenth century *spinster* referred to a person's status as a "never-married woman," but it also suggested a woman's profession as a spinner of wool, or perhaps silk. Adjudicating between the definitions is made more difficult because so many single women supported themselves by working as spinners. In her late teens, when she resided in Spitalfields, Judith was perfectly primed for an education in spinning. She may have learned her trade at the hands of the Huguenot silk-weaving experts.[12]

Perhaps this proximity to recent Huguenot arrivals allowed Judith to consider herself less of an immigrant and more of a Londoner, or at least someone who could lay claim to an English ancestry and English as her mother tongue. Anti-French sentiment was prevalent in the capital throughout the late seventeenth century despite the Crown's official welcome to Huguenot refugees. Then again, being among foreigners might equally have had the effect of reminding her of her own outsider status. Judith may have spoken English, but her African heritage was a visual marker of her own presumed alien roots.[13]

Living among refugee Huguenot silk makers was far from the first time that Judith experienced proximity to luxury items. Friends and acquaintances of the Peers children noted that John and his household lived "very splendidly & in good Fealty at Streatham."[14] In the dining room, parlors, and great hall, silver utensils and serving dishes and damask tablecloths adorned rooms that were lit by gilded sconces. Fine tapestries, paintings, and mirrors decorated all the public rooms, and many of the private ones. Not only was the house filled with sumptuous decor, but according to the merchant John Thrayle, the "Brothers & Sisters" were raised "very Gentily & handsomely" and kept "in all things suitable & fit for Gentlemans Children."[15] Of course the "Brothers & Sisters" who received this good treatment did not include any of the Mingo, Ashcroft, or

Spendlove children, even though the sons and daughters of Susannah, Elizabeth, and Dorothy would have observed the expense outlaid for their father's other children and may have benefitted, unintentionally, from his lavish tastes. Living in a luxurious home where rich food, heated rooms, and the latest fashions were de rigueur meant that even those who served generally got to experience warmth, more calories than they might otherwise have consumed, and clothing suitable to those waiting on a gentry family.[16]

Their living quarters and consumables were not the only connections that Susannah's, Elizabeth's and Dorothy's children had to luxury. Hester's sons and daughter were "maintained" by Robert Chaplin before and after their father's death, and this included fitting out their wardrobes with clothes suitable for a gentleman's children. According to John Ward, the boys' tailor, he made garments "fitting for persons of their quality to wear," perhaps including the expensive "haire Camlett Cloake," the "Two paire of Breeches, Two Silke wastcoats," and the "silke night gowne" listed in the "Boys Roome" in the Streatham inventory.[17]

While it is likely that Richard Mingo encountered Richard Peers's clothing largely as a result of dressing his older half brother, we know servants wore fine liveries in the Streatham household, and as these outfits were designed, in part, to showcase the wealth and status of the head of household, they were made of vibrant, good-quality fabrics. Even if Richard was not serving in a capacity that would have caused him to wear a livery, it is likely that he received hand-me-downs from his older brother when his clothes no longer fit or were in less-than-ideal shape. Elite households dressed non-livery-wearing servants in this manner to emphasize their own high status and good fortune.[18]

From a very young age, therefore, Judith and her other servant and enslaved half siblings learned a great deal about luxury. This was an important bit of cultural literacy—it is likely not only that she could discern different qualities of fabric and furniture, for example, but also that she could carry this knowledge out of the house, onto the streets of Streatham (and later London) and use this information to read the status and position of people around her. Whether or not she ever learned to write her name, read a text, or keep an account book, Judith had gained a useful skill set, one honed from her earliest years. When she, her mother, and her siblings found themselves homeless following her father's death in 1689, this was precisely the kind of knowledge that she could parlay into earning a living. If she continued in domestic service as her mother had done, then Judith knew about the quality of goods, their prices, and their use and upkeep that would have served her employer very well. And if spinning was the way she made a living, she would have known which fabrics and finishes would earn her the highest prices.

The earliest description of Judith as a "spinster" is from her brother's 1704 will, at which time the siblings were no longer living among Huguenots, but residing in Lothbury, closer to the Thames. Perhaps Judith was a spinner of wool rather than silk. In either case she would likely have earned sufficient money to support herself and her mother. Whether she used a spinning wheel or a distaff (the preferred tool for spinning the finest yarn), by the time she reached her forties, Judith's ability to produce quality thread, and to earn a comfortable living doing so, would have been assured. Judith might well have made up to £25 per year from spinning alone, especially if she was turning out high-quality product. Even if she spun an inferior yarn used for worsted clothing, Judith could still earn as much as £15 per annum.[19] These sums placed her earnings in the same range as that of men who wove garments, and they significantly exceeded the supposed annual bequests from her father's will. In the early eighteenth century, when the demand for yarn skyrocketed, her earning ability would have increased accordingly, allowing her a comfortable income.

If the people who identified Judith as a "spinster" understood this term to mean that she was merely "never-married" at this stage in her life, her single status placed her among the majority of women living in London in the late seventeenth century. Many women either married late or did not marry at all and therefore retained a measured degree of independence. Indeed her half sisters—Dorothy's and Elizabeth's daughters—were also described in the 1718 case as "spinsters."[20] At the same time, Judith's African ancestry marked her apart. There were, of course, women of color in England in this period, but they were not as numerous as the men. Although she would have seen Black faces on London's busy streets, most of them would have belonged to the young boys with collars around their necks, or men working at the docks. And yet Judith managed to carve out a space for herself in the metropole, ensuring that regardless of whether she received her inheritance, she would survive.

Judith's younger brother, Richard, no doubt had many more opportunities to encounter people of color than his sister did. In 1701 (when he was twenty-three) Richard entered a profession where he worked alongside other Black men, some from sub-Saharan Africa, some from the West Indies, some born and bred in London itself. That year he sailed as a mariner on "her Majesty's ship *Montague*," making him one of the many men of color in London who found employment on the high seas. While most of these sailors served in merchant vessels, he chose to enlist in the British Navy. Unlike at least some of the

Black sailors aboard HMS *Montague*, Richard was not of full African descent. It is unclear whether this caused white superiors to view him differently. Certainly, in the later eighteenth century his racial presentation would have resulted in unequal treatment. His tenure aboard the small fourth-rate two-decker sixty-gun warship coincided with the War of the Spanish Succession and would see him sail to destinations around the Atlantic basin.[21]

By 1704, Richard attained the rank of midshipman, which made him an inferior officer among the enlisted elite. In the 1702 and 1703 HMS *Montague* muster rolls Richard was listed as an "able seaman," and it seems likely that he had been a sailor before joining the navy. Maybe he had spent time at the docks and worked on merchant vessels prior to his enlistment. Experience alone would not have been sufficient for Richard to reach his new rank of midshipman: it is most likely that he also needed an elite white sponsor to recommend him for the role.[22] Did Richard rely on one of his white half siblings as a reference? Might Hester's Richard, the man he most likely served as a boy, have fulfilled this role? Or had Richard made other connections since leaving Streatham and returning to the city? Whatever the reasons behind the promotion, he clearly impressed his superiors because midshipmen were groomed to become ship's officers. The vast majority, like Richard, were in their early to mid-twenties when they earned this rank. On board HMS *Montague* Richard would have been one of ten men serving in this position.

Given that he would also have been barred from the rank of midshipman unless he had clothes "to appear properly as a quarter deck officer," Richard must have dressed appropriately. Perhaps Judith assisted him in this area—if she was spinning, her earnings, or the very fruits of her labor, might have helped clothe her brother. Their arrangement was probably similar to that of many single women with bachelor brothers: Judith living as Richard's dependent in their Lothbury home while taking responsibility for his housekeeping. Richard was also literate, as his full signature on his 1704 will attests. Perhaps he learned to read and write, a requirement for midshipmen, as a young boy in his father's Streatham household.[23]

Richard also appears to have been a quick study. His rise up the ranks indicates that he could both follow directions and take initiative and knew the difference between the two. Over four years Richard made almost a third as much again as he was supposed to receive from his father's will, and so even without receiving any of the disbursements that were his due, Richard could support himself with what he earned aboard ship.[24] Between his earning power and the mobility made possible by his occupation, Richard was not waiting for a Chancery Court case to make him financially stable.

Unlike his mother and his sister, whose movement was limited to London's streets, Richard's profession provided an opportunity to travel. He sailed to the Mediterranean, the coast of North Africa, and across the Atlantic, spending a good deal of his last two years on board HMS *Montague* in the Caribbean. Richard was therefore enlisted on a British vessel at a time when the Royal African Company was still a major player in the international slave trade.[25] Like the vast majority of Africans forcibly transported on RAC slave ships, Richard's voyage also took him to the West Indies. He could not have failed to notice the slavers at anchor in the harbors of the western Atlantic as HMS *Montague* came into port.

Might Richard have disembarked in Barbados? His ship docked there in 1705, and perhaps he set foot on the island of his birth during that visit. If so, he must have seen captives being driven along the docks toward the warehouses that were designed to hold them until sale. An observant man, Richard surely noticed the "RAC" branding seared into the flesh of the women, men, and children. He might have been familiar with such branding from his childhood, when saltwater slaves arrived at Rendezvous. Equally, Richard may have contrived to remain on board HMS *Montague*, not wishing to kindle memories from his youth in Barbados. That Richard sailed to the West Indies and was not reenslaved demonstrates that for him, at least, a life beyond bondage was real.[26]

By 1709 Richard was dead. Because he was a sailor, his will allowed for his body to be committed to "the earth or sea as it shall please God," suggesting that he was only too aware of the mortality rates for members of the navy, particularly during war. Sailors frequently made wills before they went to sea, understanding that they might not return. Recording final wishes cost money, and so Richard had to expend some of what he earned to secure the services of a clerk. The document further ensured his sister's future: Richard named Judith as executrix and inheritor of his estate. Thanks to his will's provisions, Judith was set to receive "all such payments and wages, sume and sume of Money, Goods, Chattells, and Estate whatsoever" owed to her brother when he died.[27] In trying to guarantee some additional support for his sister, Richard might well have been thinking of his navy wages—he was surely aware that she stood little chance of receiving his share of the money they were still owed from their father's estate.

Susannah's Richard was not the only "naturall born" sibling to write a will. Elizabeth Ashcroft's second daughter, also named Elizabeth, composed a succinct testament in September 1693, when she was just fourteen.[28] Unlike Richard, she does not state her occupation nor note a location of residence more specific than "London." Elizabeth described herself as a "Legatory" of "John Peirce late of Streatham." Apart from committing her soul to God, Elizabeth

Will of Elizabeth's Elizabeth, 1693. London Metropolitan Archives with the permission of the bishop of London and the London Diocesan Fund.

left her "wordly Goods" to her older "loving sister" Susanna Ashcroft, whom she also made her executrix. Among her witnesses were two women who were also legatees of her father's will, including the governess who joined forces with her mother and Dorothy Spendlove in their court case against Robert Chaplin.

What prompted Elizabeth's Elizabeth to make a will is unclear. The date coincides with the Chancery Court litigation—perhaps the uncertainty engendered by the case prompted Elizabeth to ensure that "all the Goods I have and arreares of mony due to me" would be secure. Or it could have been her own health that prompted her actions. There is no boilerplate in the document about being sound of mind and body, so it is possible that she was ill and feared she was not long for this world. When she signed the document, she did so with "the marke of Elizabeth Ashcroft," a shakily and spindly constructed letter "E," which may indicate she was too ill to write with a strong hand.[29] Or maybe the letter is suggestive of someone who did not have the opportunity to often practice her letters, contrasting her skill set with that of her half brother.

If Elizabeth was unwell, she appears to have recovered, in the short term at least. Her will was not proved until January 1699, so it seems likely that she lived for around another five years. Like Richard Mingo, Elizabeth bequeathed her small estate to her older sister, perhaps believing that it would help Susanna, who was a single woman at the time, more than either of her brothers. This action placed in her in good company—women, including free women of color, most often made other women their primary inheritors.[30]

Elizabeth's Susanna did not remain single for long. Although she was described as a spinster in 1694, during her mother's Chancery Court case, Susanna Ashcroft became Susanna Tomlinson just one year later, when she married a sailor named Henry on 17 October 1695 at St. Bride's Fleet Street, close to the neighborhood where she first lived in London. The couple went on to have at least three children before Henry's death sometime in early 1710, when they were living in St. Mary's Southwark, an area on the south side of the Thames whose proximity to the docks made it a popular location for sailors.[31] Henry's will made clear that he was often at sea. Both the neighborhood in which they lived and his work as a mariner meant that he, as well as Susanna, came into contact frequently with men of African descent. Perhaps their life in Southwark among a diverse population provided Susanna access to friendships and interactions with other Black women that she would have found harder to forge in the whiter city suburbs.

Following Henry's death Susanna married a second time. Her new spouse, whom she wed in a clandestine ceremony in October 1715, was John Aldridge: the man named as her husband in the 1718 Chancery Court case. No longer living in diverse Southwark, she now resided in the western suburbs of London. It is unlikely that this marriage elevated Susanna's status given that the records describe John as a "higler," someone who peddled goods, usually door to door.[32] These peddlers were often itinerant and illiterate and usually had little in the way of stable income.

In this way, Susanna's match was similar to her half sister Judith's. Although she married much later in life, Judith also wed a man of fairly low status, a comb maker called Thomas Elliott. The nuptials took place in Aldersgate, east of the City in St. Anne and St. Agnes Parish church on 29 April 1718, when Judith was forty-three years old.[33] By the time she married Thomas, Judith was living in St. Clement Danes, in the same neighborhood where she and the rest of the Mingos had spent their first months in England. Her mother was living either with her, or close by, as both were mentioned in the same section of the 1718 Chancery Court case that noted Judith's marriage and recounted the locations of the living beneficiaries of John's will. The same bill of complaint that referenced her residence also marked Judith as a "former spinster." Whether this meant she had abandoned a profession or referred only to her recent marriage is unclear.

Not all of John's "naturall born" children are as visible in the records as the Mingos. Information about the Ashcrofts remains incomplete, and there is virtually nothing about the Spendlove siblings in the London parish registers, probate records, or even Chancery Court proceedings. Death came early for many of John's children. Hester Mingo was buried in a decent spot in St. Christopher Le Stocks churchyard in 1700. By 1718 Edward Ashcroft was dead. He had married and had at least one child (named Sophia) in 1704, although when he wed and where he was laid to rest are unknown.[34] If not for his mother's will, we would not have even these brief biographical snippets.

Dorothy's children are the least accounted for. It seems likely that Frances married—a Frances Martin is mentioned as a beneficiary of John's will in the later Chancery Court cases—but other than her apprenticeship, little else of her life comes into view. Ann Spendlove was still alive and living in Covent Garden in 1718. Described as a "spinster," she might well have been earning a living through spinning wool like her half sisters Judith Mingo and Susanna Ashcroft. Her older brother, John, is a phantom. Other than the fact that he was dead by 1718, the records are stubbornly silent on any other aspect of his life.

That John's "naturall born" children all took their mothers names when they left the Streatham household is important. They did not trade on the Peers name to secure their inheritances or to ensure success. Perhaps they understood that their father was not someone worthy of emulation or that leaning on their paternity would not go far in London or its suburbs. After all, John Peers was a big fish in Barbados's relatively small pond, but in England he was merely a middling member of the elite. They may have assumed that there was much to gain by *not* being associated with their father. Their mothers had raised and protected them in both Barbados and Streatham. Watching them survive might have been lesson enough for the Mingo, Ashcroft, and Spendlove offspring.

PATERNAL LINES

As the daughters and sons of a prominent landowner, enslaver, and Barbados politician, John's children with Hester and Frances never questioned whether they would be considered legitimate in the eyes of the English state: their father's marriages to their mothers made it so. John drew on his status as patriarch to set the children up in life, and to provide for them after his death. Hester's daughter and sons were around twenty-three, twenty, eighteen, and twelve when their father died. Frances's daughters were orphans by the time they were seven, five, and four respectively.

None of these children spent much time with their father. Mary, the eldest sibling, who had been left behind when her parents departed for Barbados in 1666, knew her parents least. Ann and Robert Chaplin became, in effect, her surrogate mother and father. Her younger brothers had a similar experience. Although they were born in Barbados, as soon as they were old enough to travel—around four or five years old—Hester and John sent them to England. Family friend Sir Edward Turnor remembered how in the early 1670s Richard "& his Brother John Peers came very young" to the Chaplin's "house in St Swythins Lane." Thomas, the youngest son, would have made the journey a few years later. Joining Mary in the city, the siblings had plenty of opportunity to get to know one another even if memories of their parents were dim at best. As the eldest child, and the one who had never left London, Mary knew the city, its streets, and the immediate neighborhood around the home well, and she would likely have introduced her siblings to the metropole.[35]

Life in London was, by all accounts, good for the older Peers children. Sir Edward recounted how the brothers lived with Robert and were "maintyned & educated together . . . in Clothes, dyet, Lodging, & Schooling" until their father returned in 1686. His recollections extended to their sister, Mary, and he noted that all four children "comonly & usually" called Robert "father." He believed that they had "good reason . . . soe to doe for he provided for them as a father their own father not being in England." Another business associate noted that Robert "did take as much care of & was as kind to Richard & his Brothers & Sisters as if they had been his own Children." Robert allegedly promised that if they considered him their father "they should have all he had when he dyed." Friends of the siblings agreed; Ralph Hutchinson, who lived in the same house as Richard as a boy, confirmed that John's son was "educated at schoole & main-tyned in all things fit for a Gentleman of his Quality," at Robert's expense.[36]

In many ways, there was nothing unusual about the Peers siblings' upbringing. Richard was groomed to step into his father's shoes, perhaps to return to Barbados and manage the plantations. Treated by his uncle, his acquaintances, and his friends like a gentleman-in-waiting only exposed him to the privileges accorded firstborn English sons. Society in England still centered on primogeniture in the late Stuart era. Unlike his younger brothers, Richard grew up believing that he would be the future patriarch of the Peers estates. His uncle might have ensured his good upbringing, but it was his father's name and prestige that cemented his place in the hierarchy. As someone with claims to land and people in the Caribbean, moreover, Richard was trained to be an effective member of a large and ever-growing imperial machine.[37]

For boys like Richard, John, and Thomas, being "educated at schoole" could mean a number of things. They may have attended one of the many grammar schools in the London area. These institutions educated the sons of gentlemen as well as the most promising boys from the lower ranks who secured scholarships or who gained the sponsorship of wealthy benefactors. At such institutions young boys usually received a classical education, and they were introduced to a stringent disciplinary regime that supposedly instilled leadership traits necessary for a more public life. They probably also benefitted from a curriculum that taught them much about slavery and bondage using literature and philosophy from the ancient world.[38] It is possible that Robert instead hired a tutor to teach the boys French and Latin rather than send them out of his house, or that the boys experienced both forms of education. Perhaps Ann took the lead in thinking through the best options for her nephews and niece. The women and men who stood in as parental figures to nieces, nephews, or godchildren took this responsibility very seriously, and given that these were her sister's children, Ann would likely have been the person to persuade Robert that they take up the charge.[39] With no children of their own, the Chaplins had plenty of time and money to devote to their younger relations.

Richard was groomed to be John's primary inheritor, so it was imperative that his younger brothers find professions to support themselves. A 1698 Chancery Court record reveals that John was "of the Inner Temple, London," meaning that he was trained in the law, a common occupation for second sons. His legal education began in November 1690, when he was twenty years old, and he was admitted to the bar in June 1697. Throughout his apprenticeship he would have required financial support from Robert to maintain his lifestyle as well as to support the costs of living and studying at the Inns. John was close to St. Swithin's Lane—the Inner Temple was about a mile west of his uncle's home—but staying on site was a necessary part of becoming a barrister. Despite his training, John might not have had the explicit goal of practicing law. Becoming a member of the Inner Temple was as much a way to engage in society as it was to gain a profession. Students admitted to the Inns of Court made important connections, forged lucrative friendships, and cultivated a wide circle of acquaintances on whom they could draw in the future, in addition to completing their legal training.[40]

Thomas, the youngest of the Peers boys, also gained an education beyond early childhood. In 1694, at around the age of eighteen, he was sent "to the University" at Oxford, where he attended Christ Church, one of the institution's oldest and most prestigious colleges. It is likely that he followed in his older brother's footsteps. Most men who attended the Inner Temple spent around two years taking classes in rhetoric and logic at either Oxford or Cambridge before beginning their legal training, so John had likely studied at Oxford too.[41] According to Chancery Court depositions, Thomas was "maintained . . . as a Gentleman" by his uncle while at university, underscoring the many ways that Robert provided for his nephews long after their father's death. Even after the boys reached the age of twenty-one, their uncle continued to manage their lives. Four years after Thomas left Christ Church, Robert continued to pay for his upkeep "at a French boarding house in Oxford," perhaps an indication that Thomas had not yet settled on a profession of his own.

The boys' sisters also appear to have been educated in a manner befitting young ladies in this era. Hester's Mary spent her life under the supervision of her aunt and uncle, until her aunt's death in 1683.[42] Probably eight or nine when Richard arrived from the Caribbean, she might well have been deployed initially in caring for her younger brother, a common role for young girls in elite families. Over a decade separated Mary from her youngest brother, and twenty years lapsed between her birth and that of her youngest half sister, so Richard may not have been the only sibling she supervised. In this role she would have learned much about raising a family and running a household.

It is also likely that Mary received a formal education. Robert insisted that he "maintained and educated the rest of the legittimate Children of the said Mr. Peers" following his brother-in-law's death. True to his word, within two months of John's passing, Robert placed Mary's younger half sisters, Elizabeth and Frances, at "a Boarding school at Kensington." In 1692 her youngest half sister, Ann, joined them. Given that the school was run by Elizabeth and Charles

Seward, acquaintances of the Chaplins for over twenty years, Mary might well have attended the institution herself. By the second half of the seventeenth century such establishments were effectively finishing schools, concerned less with giving girls a classical education than with priming them for making good marriages. Pupils might learn French (the language of the court and diplomacy), but generally music, dancing, and needlework were the prominent lessons.[43]

Because her parents moved to Barbados before she was two years old, Mary would have had her first proper introduction to her father in her early twenties, the prime age for marriage for women in England. Was this why she accompanied her uncle to her father's house when he was ill and on his deathbed? Given her estrangement from her biological parents, Mary might have felt loyal to the Chaplins rather than to her ailing father. At the same time, her future rested on what he bequeathed her, so she may have hoped to gain his good favor and ensure her inheritance. Upon John's passing, she received the same annuity as her other siblings, £100 per year. This was a fine income, if it was paid, although hardly sufficient to land a good husband, and when she died in her early thirties in 1696 she had not wed.

Mary was not the only Peers child to die unmarried. Of the six children who survived to adulthood, only her half sister Ann and her oldest brother, Richard, made a match. It was not unusual for second and third sons to find it difficult to build a living that would have resulted in a marriage, so the lack of partner for either John or Thomas is unsurprising. Daughters too depended on a dowry or marriage portion to attract men of an appropriate rank.[44]

Ann married "William Hall of London, Esquire," in July 1707 in St. Martin-in-the-Fields church in the capital. Other than his name and the date of their marriage (which occurred when she was twenty-two) very little is known about her husband. A later reference in the 1718 Chancery Court case describes him as "Captain Hall," suggesting that he might have been a military man. Perhaps Ann brought enough to the match to secure a husband with a similar social standing to her father.[45] Her annual inheritance of £100 was not a princely sum by any means, but if the claims in the Chancery Court case are to be believed, by Christmas 1717 William received the arrears Ann was owed from the Barbados estates, a substantial £1,200. Whether this money came in the form of a lump sum or was doled out over time, it might have made Ann an attractive prospect as a bride. Although both Ann and William were alive in 1719, whether they had children, where they lived, and when they died remains a mystery.[46]

If not much is known about Ann's marriage, then Richard's nuptials more than make up for an absence of information. We might assume that his rich record is a result of his position as John's eldest son and chief inheritor. But most of the detail we have about Richard's life is thanks to the fact that in the summer of 1695 he decided to marry against his uncle's wishes. This action had no small consequence because he and Robert were extremely close at the time of the wedding. In the years following his father's 1689 death, Richard had supported Robert in his quest to wrest control of John's estate from its original executors. And he remained in Streatham after Robert turned Dorothy Spendlove, Elizabeth Ashcroft, and their children out of the house. Following his marriage, however, Richard sued his uncle in Chancery Court for sole control of his Barbados inheritance. Robert claimed, with some good evidence, that he had treated Richard "as tho he was his owne sonne" both when he first came to London "and ever since his fathers death." Richard did not disagree, noting that "having been brought up and liveing the greatest part of his lifetime" with his uncle, he once had "a great Trust and confidence in him."[47]

All that changed on 4 July 1695, when Hannah Ruslin, domestic servant and daughter of a metalworker, married Richard at St. Mary's in Lambeth on the south side of the Thames River.[48] The newlyweds had likely known each other for some time, because Hannah had grown up on the same street in London where Richard lived with his uncle. Robert's objections to the match were rooted in Hannah's background and no doubt were augmented by his familiarity with her family and her status. London merchant John Thrayle described Hannah's father, John Ruslin, as "a Painstaking Man & in pritty good Cercumstances," but while Ruslin might have been honest, and while silversmithing might have been a reputable occupation, it placed him outside the social circle to which Robert believed Richard should aspire.[49]

Various witnesses noted that they did not consider Hannah "a good match," raising both her father's occupation and the lack of sizeable dowry as reasons that they, and Robert, disapproved. Richard's friend Ralph Hutchinson speculated that there might not be more than "[£]700" for a dowry. But "being not acquainted with the said Hannahs said fathers circumstances in the world," Hutchinson could not be more specific.[50] Hannah's father provided testimony in Richard's case. Describing himself as "of the parish of St Swythyn, London, Goldsmith," he elevated his precious metal work to the more valuable medium. He admitted that he was not present at his daughter's wedding though claimed that he had advance warning "that the said Match was goeing forward." Even Ruslin knew that Robert was displeased and noted that he had been quite willing "to match his Daughter to A Tradesman" instead. Ultimately, however, Richard had insisted that he did not want the "30l a yeare" that Ruslin might supply and was instead marrying for love.[51]

Robert's real issue with Hannah was probably not what her father did for a living, or what kind of dowry she would bring, but rather the fact that she worked as a domestic—and was employed in John's Streatham home. While she might have begun life in St. Swithin's Lane, she had later, and probably as a consequence of her familiarity with the Chaplins, taken up a position in the Streatham manor house. Sir Edward testified he clearly remembered that "the young woman to whom Richard is married did live in the house . . . at Streatham for some considerable tyme before the said Marriage." He noted that he was unsure "whether she lived as a servant" or was "paid wages." In trying to deduce her status, Sir Edward observed that he "doth not remember that she ever satt at the Table" when he visited the manor house, which he claimed he did "some tymes for 2 or 3 dayes at a tyme." Emphasizing her unequal position in the household—had she merely been a visitor or ward of John, then she would have had a place to eat with the family—Sir Edward explained how he ferreted out her low rank. Together with her father's occupation this made him "judge & believe she was by noe meanes a suitable match" for Richard.[52] Like his father before him, Richard entered into a relationship with a subordinate woman, who, like Dorothy, was a white servant. Unlike his father, however, Richard married the object of his affection.

Richard's younger brother, John, was more equivocal than his uncle about his brother's choice of bride, noting that he "doth by one means look on her to be a suitable match . . . because she hath been well spoken of." At the same time, John acknowledged that Hannah's father was "not . . . able to give her a fortune." John's unwillingness to declare Hannah completely unsuitable may be indicative of the nature of his relationship with his older brother. Both he and Thomas understood that Richard was under no legal obligation to support them beyond ensuring that they received the annuities due them from their father's will. For his part, Richard might well have recognized that an income of £100 per year would not allow the kind of lifestyle to which his siblings had become accustomed. He could also have believed himself responsible for John and Thomas precisely because of his status as primary heir, perhaps understanding that their well-being and future success rested, at least in part, on his support.[53]

<hr/>

Facing: The front page of the deposition folder with the names of men deposed in the 1699 Chancery Court case *Peers v. Chaplin.* Hester's John (the eighth person listed) answered questions about his father, his older brother Richard, and his uncle, Robert Chaplin, who was also deposed. C24/1211 *Peers v. Chaplin* cover page. Image reproduced by permission of the National Archives, London.

Robert Chaplin ⎯⎯⎯⎯
Ralph Hutchinson ⎯⎯⎯
Christopher Howlder ⎯⎯
William Sordy ⎯⎯⎯⎯
John Ruslin ⎯⎯⎯⎯⎯
John Ward ⎯⎯⎯⎯⎯
Richard Barron ⎯⎯⎯
John Leay ⎯⎯⎯⎯⎯
John Thrale ⎯⎯⎯⎯
Samuel Barwick ⎯⎯⎯
William Rumbold ⎯⎯
Michael Glyde ⎯⎯⎯⎯
John Gray ⎯⎯⎯⎯⎯
Sr Edward Evander ⎯⎯
John Adams ⎯⎯⎯⎯⎯

Hill. 1698.

10th Septr 1723 Copied for the Dft by Mr. Reynolds....

By not raising explicit concerns about Hannah, John may have succeeded in gaining his older brother's trust, perhaps even benefitting financially as a result. The 1719 Chancery Court case suggests that Richard was more generous than necessary with his two younger brothers, allowing them both an equal share in the Staple Grove plantation in Barbados, which they in theory had no right to inherit. Working in concert, the siblings agreed to take a small amount out of the estate every year—£150 in total—using the rest of the profits for the "improvement & repaire" of the plantation. They estimated that after ten years in a plantation manager's hands that they could sell Staple Grove and divide the anticipated handsome profit.[54] This deal, and the fact that they had to cooperate with one another to make it work, suggests a closeness among the brothers.

For all that he walked the line on Hannah, John was privy to conversations about the wedding and reported that Robert had offered to "furnish" Richard "with money to maintayne himselfe & More" if he married someone more "suitable to his Quality." Describing the same conversation, Sir Edward did not mince words, noting that Robert was "Extreamly consearned and Disgusted" at the marriage because the debts on the Rendezvous and Staple Grove estates could only be discharged if Richard "marryed a wife with a good fortune." According to Sir Edward, Robert pressured his nephew, promising that if he "marryed well and to his liking," Robert would "send him over to the Barbadoes to live upon the Estate there."[55] Richard rebuked the emotional blackmail and the threat of his "utter Ruine" and married Hannah.

Whether uncle and nephew were able to repair their relationship is unclear. John noted that "notwithstanding his matching against his consent," Robert had offered to visit Hannah and Richard if they would "goe into the Country."[56] Richard did live with Hannah in Surrey, although there is no evidence that his choice of location for his family home improved relations between uncle and nephew. However, there is an indication, in the name of one of their children, that the frostiness had begun to thaw. Richard and Hannah had at least six children between 1696 and 1712. They gave their fourth child, born the year after Robert Chaplin died, the name of his recently deceased great uncle, suggesting, perhaps, that Richard had been on good terms with Robert at the end of his life. Further evidence of a rapprochement can be found in Robert's will. Although he left the bulk of his estate to a nephew on the other side of the family, Robert acknowledged that he owed Richard £1,300 and John and Thomas the remainder of what was due from the sale of Staple Grove, guaranteeing them this payout "within two years of my decease."[57] This bequeathal coincided with Richard employing Samuel Barwick to manage the Barbados plantations in 1706 and may have been what precipitated John's move back to the Caribbean sometime that decade.

The constant chasing of their inheritance necessitated the Peers children's attachment to their paternity. With an estate mired in alleged debt and their annual legacies at best irregularly paid, however, they may have felt ambivalent about their connection to their father. The older children could well have considered themselves closer to their surrogate father, and uncle, Robert Chaplin, and (while she was alive) their maternal aunt Ann. Frances's daughters had only the vaguest memory of their father, and probably none of their mother. Holding tight to the money that was owed them and making ties with their legitimate half siblings seemed the best possibility for any kind of life reflecting the one of excess they enjoyed while their father was alive. Despite the difficulties surrounding the estate and its disbursement, the interconnective tissue of such relationships was the last name that bound them all: Peers.

GENERATIONAL WEALTH

For all that the Peers children should have benefitted from their father's standing, there is not much evidence that his name ensured the kinds of prestige that John might have expected for his progeny. As the primary heir, Hester's Richard spent the best part of the decade after his uncle's death trying to gain access to the money due him from Rendezvous and Staple Grove. This was why, in 1713, he traveled back to Barbados. Unfortunately for him and his heirs, he fulfilled another Barbados stereotype, dying just a few weeks after his arrival, intestate, and without achieving his goal. Richard's wife, Hannah, and their oldest son, named for his paternal grandfather and only seventeen at the time of his father's death, now had to repeat what by now must have seemed a familiar family pattern. They sued the manager of Rendezvous and Staple Grove—Samuel Barwick—in Chancery Court. The case did not appear to go very far. Records show that Barwick strongly contested the suggestion that he acted without Richard's full approval and denied that he owed the Peers siblings or their descendants any money.

John was no more successful than his older brother in ensuring that he received money due him from the estate. Journeying back to Barbados sometime in the 1700s, he appears to have lived out the rest of his life on the island. On 26 September 1745 John was buried "in the Chancel" of St. Michael's Church in Bridgetown, just as his mother, Hester, had been almost seven decades earlier. Claiming in his will that he was still owed upward of £3,000 over half a century after his father's death, John seems not to have received much, if anything, from his father's estates, despite the earlier deal done with Richard for his share of Staple Grove.[58] Considering that his will described him as a "Councilor in Law," he most likely made money through that profession. Unmarried and childless, John left his estate to one of his business acquaintances.

Having gone from second son of one of Barbados's largest landowners and enslavers to a lawyer in Bridgetown was quite the tumble down the social scale. Living back on Barbados for around four decades and *not* being able to draw on the prestige and status afforded someone who could claim 1,000 acres and hundreds of enslaved people among their property as his father had done when John was a boy must have been jarring. With only "a negro man named Cuffy" among the "real estate" he could bequeath, John's small estate stood in stark contrast to his father's. The shifting reputation of the Caribbean as a place for "second sons" to make their fortunes in the early colonial period to somewhere where such transformations were not guaranteed took place during John's lifetime, and to his detriment.[59]

Given that John did not mention his younger brother, Thomas, in his will, and had reached the age of seventy-five at the time of his death, it is likely that the youngest Peers brother was dead by 1745. John might have slipped down the social scale, but at least he had a profession and a small estate to bequeath. Thomas appears not to have achieved even this limited success. First, although he too was supposed to receive money from the sale of Staple Grove, his cut was not forthcoming. Second, while the 1718 Chancery Court case indicates that he was granted a portion of his inheritance through an arrangement with Samuel Barwick, it only resulted in "payment of some part" of his legacy "in sattisfaccon of the whole."[60]

It seems, desperate for money, Thomas made a very bad deal. Indebted to five people—including two family friends, one Barbados planter, and his older brother's father-in-law—Thomas, the man his nephew described as "of London, Gentleman," had accrued debts totaling almost £1,000, all of which appear to have stacked up in just the previous few years. Using his annuity (of £100) and his share in Staple Grove as collateral, Thomas slowly signed his inheritance away. Eventually he ended up accepting around £150 from Barwick for his share of Staple Grove, a mere fraction of what he was owed. Resident "at or in the South Porch of the Royal Exchange" since 1715, he was probably trading in stocks or acting as a merchant. His finances suggest he made a poor fist of this work.[61] He does not appear to have married, nor to have had children, and so another branch of the Peers line ended with him.

If John and Thomas lived into middle or old age, death came early for most of John's daughters. Two, born to Hester, died as infants in Barbados. Elizabeth, the oldest of Frances's daughters, made it to London, where, following her father's death, she was "maintayned & Educated . . . at Kensington Schoole until she dyed" sometime in the mid 1690s. She could not have been more than thirteen years old. She was laid to rest during a funeral costing "a great deal of money" that Robert Chaplin financed, although the date and location of her burial are unknown. John's oldest daughter, Hester's Mary, "a very sensible Judicious Gentlewoman," was dead by her early thirties. She too received an ostentatious funeral. Friend of the family Ralph Hutchinson described the event as "very splendid she lying in state & being buryed accordingly." Her younger brother, John, concurred, noting that Mary was buried "very diesireably & at great expense."[62] Her body, along with that of her aunt, was disinterred from St. Swithin's Stone in London and moved to Shobdon in Herefordshire when Robert returned to his place of birth in the early 1700s. Her uncle commemorated their new resting place with an ornate marble wall marker, another sign of the deep respect, and perhaps love, he felt for the woman who was, in all but blood, his daughter.

Of all John's children with Hester and Frances, only one, Frances's middle daughter and namesake, ended her life with anything approaching the wealth that John might have hoped for his children. Frances remained a single woman all her life, dying at the age of seventy-six in 1760. Her will reveals that despite the fact (or perhaps because) she never married she had managed to accrue something of a fortune. She left £500 each to four of the children fathered by her half brother, Hester's Richard, as well as another £500 to her godson. In addition to leaving such fine sums of money to her nieces and nephews, Frances made Richard's two oldest sons her executors, and they inherited the remainder of her considerable estate.[63] Although there is no direct commentary from Frances on her half brother's marriage to Hannah, she remained close enough to him and to his children to leave her estate to them, suggesting that if she had a problem with his choice of bride it did not extend to his offspring.

Some of Frances's wealth had, indeed, come from the Barbados plantations. Like many of the beneficiaries listed in the 1718 Chancery Court case, Barwick claimed he had paid the money she was due from her father, noting that he gave "Ms Frances Peers for 12 years to Christmas 1717" some £1,200. Five years later she received an additional £336 as part of the deal that saw the Rendezvous and Staple Grove plantations sold out of the Peers family altogether.[64] But the bulk of Frances's fortune came from elsewhere, and a clue to its origins comes

Monument to Hester's Mary and Ann Chaplin in Shobdon Church following their removal from St. Swithin's Church in London to Herefordshire in 1700. The oval beneath marks Robert Chaplin's death in 1705. Author's collection.

in one of the physical bequeathals she made to her godson. In addition to the money he was to receive upon reaching the age of majority, she left him "my own picture and the two pictures of Lady Milman." Lady Elizabeth Milman was the third wife and widow of Sir William Milman, a very wealthy London barrister and stock trader. Lady Elizabeth inherited her husband's estate in 1714 and maintained control over it until her death in 1733, when she left "all such money plate jewells goods chattels and reall and personal Estate whatsoever" to the woman she described as "my Cousin Frances Peers." She also made Frances executrix of her will.[65]

Who were the Milmans, and why did Lady Elizabeth leave everything she had to Frances? It is possible the couple was involved in Frances's upbringing. Depositions taken in 1698 (when Frances was fourteen) reveal that after she and her sister, Ann, were finished at the Kensington boarding school, they were taken by Robert Chaplin to "his houses in Herefordshire and London" and "after that placed out to board with a Relacon."[66] Although there is no extant evidence of a kin connection among the Chaplins, the Milmans, and the Peers, Lady Elizabeth's use of the term "cousin" to describe her relationship to Frances suggests that they could have been related. Whatever their connection, Sir William had an extensive property portfolio in St Andrews Holborn, including a grand townhouse in Ormond Street. He was also landlord to a large number of Londoners: Frances was among the people who paid him rent. Likely her contemporary, Frances perhaps moved into the Ormond Street house as a lady's companion when Lady Elizabeth became a widow. Sir William left a small fortune to his wife, who in turn passed it onto Frances.[67] No wonder she could be so generous to her nieces and nephews when she died.

Names, if not monies, passed down the generations of John Peers's descendants. Hester's Richard (named for his own grandfather) had six children, whom he and Hannah named John, Richard, Mary, Robert, Thomas, and Elizabeth. All family names. Their third child, Mary, was perhaps even more enterprising when it came to her own offspring. Naming her daughter (John's great-granddaughter) Frances Ann Elizabeth, Mary linked Hester's descendants to those of Frances because these three names were the ones given to her stepgrandmother's daughters. Together with Frances's Frances bequeathing almost all her property to her half brother's progeny, these actions suggest that the surviving children of John's two wives were close. The repetition of names across the generations—John, Richard, Elizabeth, Mary, Ann, Frances, Thomas—emphasizes the certainty with which those who bore the name Peers understood their birthright. The names linked them back to the earliest Peers in Barbados and forward into a future that continued to connect kin, mark important relations, and provide continuity across generations. If it did not work out as expected for all of them, then it was surely not as a result of the failings of the patriarch who had built his fortune in Barbados while sugar boomed and the slave trade accelerated.

The Mingos, like the Peers, passed on names. Five months after her marriage to Thomas Elliott, Judith Mingo gave birth to a daughter whom she named Susannah, no doubt in honor of her mother, who may well have been living with her and her husband at the time of her granddaughter's birth. Susannah Elliott was baptized on 10 August 1718 in St. Clement Danes church. That Judith was pregnant when she married was not especially unusual; around a third of women gave birth before their first wedding anniversary, and some of those women did so at the fifth or sixth month past their nuptials.[68] Susannah was Judith's only child, or at least the only child records show she bore. By giving her child her mother's first name, Judith ensured the same kind of generational continuity the Peers side of her family practiced. Elizabeth's Susanna also named her daughter after her grandmother. Doing so demonstrates again the ways that names, first and last, secured maternal bonds across generations. Susanna may have made this decision because Elizabeth Ashcroft "lived for many years & till the Time of her Death" with her, probably in Sunbury in Middlesex. When Elizabeth passed away in 1729, Susanna's younger brother, Richard Ashcroft, became the executor of their mother's estate.

Just as her mother had sued Robert Chaplin in the 1690s for her rightful inheritance, so did Susanna Ashcroft take her brother to court to secure her own. Between 1734, when she brought the case, and 1740, when her son took over following her death, Susanna insisted that her brother, who was living "near Aldersgate Street" in London, was "intending to defraud & injure" her, her children, and her grandchildren by refusing them the legacy left by Elizabeth. For his part, Richard countered that following their mother's death, Susanna had "possest herself" of all her "Goods moneys notes writings & other Effects." Further, he claimed that he had never received any money from Barbados, despite repeated attempts to avail himself of the £538 their mother left her children in her will.[69]

So determined was Richard Ashcroft to recoup his inheritance that he followed in his mother's footsteps, returning to Barbados just as she had done a quarter century earlier. According to depositions taken as part of his sister's Chancery case, Richard "stayed & resided at Barbados for the tyme of five months or thereabouts," in 1730. His attempts at securing redress failed. Determined to purse his inheritance, "in the month of January 1736 he again went from England to that Island of Barbados," this time remaining in the colony for two years.[70] Once again, Richard left empty-handed.

Making a journey to the Caribbean was no small matter, and paying for it required a substantial outlay. The ship's surgeon estimated that Richard's voyages alone "did not cost him less than sixty four pounds," and this sum did not include the expense of living on Barbados, which the surgeon placed at around £60 per year. Richard's profession as a goldsmith evidently provided him with the resources to support these transatlantic voyages. Risking multiple trips to the island of his birth suggests that there was some imperative—financial or otherwise—that drove Richard's decisions. And yet he must have known that as a man with African ancestry his freedom was not ensured. Like his mother before him, he returned to England, a further indication that spending time on the island as a formerly enslaved man of color continued to be possible in the 1730s.

Elizabeth's Susanna may well have needed the inheritance her mother bequeathed her far more than her brother. When she died, in March 1736, she did so "from the workhouse" in Richmond-upon-Thames. At some point between her mother's demise and her own, she had moved up the river from Sunbury, but she clearly no longer had the ability to support herself. Susanna named her younger daughter, Elizabeth, executrix, leaving her the £150 she claimed she was promised by "my mother Elizabeth Ashcroft," and which she insisted her brother had been withholding. While Elizabeth was left the bulk of her estate, her son, Joseph received only "one shilling." Meanwhile her two grandsons, born to her daughter Frances, were to received £20 each, and "Ann Bagshott," whom she described as "brought up by me," was to gain £30.[71] She left no personal or household items to any of her children, probably an indication that without the money promised her from her own mother, she was without any property worth bequeathing.

IN THE END, very little of what might have been expected came to pass for the children who bore the last name "Peers." While Judith Mingo named her daughter for her mother, and while Susanna Ashcroft tried to ensure her own children's legacies by going to court as her mother had before her, the Peers siblings had less success in emulating their father's actions. By 1724 Richard's heir had sold off his family's claims to Rendezvous and Staple Grove in exchange for a £5,000 cash sum and additional smaller annuities of around £200 for the rest of his life.[72] None of the rest of John's inheritors, save Frances Peers, gained anything in this sale. The plantations and the enslaved laborers who had supported the family for almost 100 years were now in the hands of Barbados merchants, who would sell them off again in years to come.

The birthrights that the children of Hester Tomkyns and Frances Knights carried with them should, in theory, have set them up for life. The sons and daughters of a prominent Barbados planter would have expected their lives to be ones of luxury and opulence. Educated at the best institutions and trained in the ways of being gentlemen or ladies, John's legitimately recognized children had no reason to expect that they would not go on to marry well (for the daughters) or to achieve even greater wealth and political success than their father (for the sons). Richard in particular, groomed from a young age as a patriarch-in-waiting, must have anticipated that the labor of the enslaved women, men, and children who toiled on Rendezvous and Staple Grove would support him throughout his life. He might even have aspired to return to Barbados and, like his father, become one of the island's most prominent political actors. He could not have expected to die just two weeks after his return to the colony.

The bloodlines of John's children with Susannah Mingo, Elizabeth Ashcroft, and Dorothy Spendlove manifested in both the status the children held in Barbados and the ways they took the names of their mothers following John's death. Although so many of his sons and daughters disappear from the records and prove almost untraceable by the 1720s, the evidence for those who remain demonstrates the ways that they each forged paths of survival. The daughters spun thread; the sons became sailors, glass sellers, candlemakers, and goldsmiths. Some even took up the broader family tradition of using the Chancery Court system to try to recoup their inheritance.

The rippling effect of the bequeathals the children expected to see from their father's estate may never have been fully realized, but this reality did not condemn the children (or indeed their mothers) to a life of penury and poverty. Resourceful and entrepreneurial, they took the knowledge they had gained in the house that colonial slavery built and transformed what they learned into skills that served them well in early modern London's society with slaves.[73] For the children who began their lives in bondage this was no small achievement. For their mothers it was a powerful legacy to leave.

Conclusion

THE LEGACIES OF RENDEZVOUS

BY 1760 ALL OF JOHN PEERS'S children were dead. Frances's middle daughter and namesake was the last one to die. Perhaps, as the child who ended her life with a fortune more in keeping with the one her father might have imagined for her, it makes sense that the younger Frances took time in her will to make specific instructions about her place of burial. She asked to be laid to rest "under the marble stone" where her father's body rested in St. Leonard's, and that "an Inscription be put upon that same stone" reminding the world that "Frances Peers Daughter of the said John Peers" was also entombed in the Streatham church.[1] The vast sums of money she had inherited meant that Frances achieved what the other Peers children had not—burial with her father, at great expense. And yet the implications contained within the story of the women and children of Rendezvous stretch far beyond the simple financial legacies that John's will was supposed to bestow.

England's imperial vision and dominance of the transatlantic slave trade soared as the seventeenth century gave way to the eighteenth. At the same time Susannah and Elizabeth traveled east across the Atlantic and into lives

HERE LYETH THE BODY OF THE HONORA[BL]
IOHN PEERS ESQ; WHO WAS ONE OF THIER
MAJESTIES COUNCELL IN THE ISLAND OF
BARBADOS WHO DEPARTED THIS LIFE THE
17 MARCH 1688 IN THE 44 YEAR OF HIS
AGE.

ALSO HIS DAUGHTER
FRANCES PEERS
WHO DIED IUNE 16
1760

LIKEWISE IOHN PIERS ESQ[r]
GRANDSON OF THE ABOVE
IOHN PIERS ESQ[r]
WHO DIED THE 7th APRIL 1761
AGED 62 YEARS

Grave marker for John Peers, his daughter Frances's Frances, and his grandson
Hannah's John in St. Leonard's Parish Church, Streatham, England.
Author's Collection.

of eventual freedom in England. Their very presence in the metropole underscores what scholars have been showing for decades: Black people were part of English society centuries before the Windrush generation of the twentieth century.[2] Like that later, more famous, migration, Susannah, Elizabeth, and their children helped build modern England. First, they were part of the enslaved workforce that made Barbados more profitable than all of England's mainland American colonies combined. The vast wealth generated from sugar plantations ignited the English economy, making it a world leader in finance and industrialization by the mid-eighteenth century.[3] Then, when they arrived in London, they made livings in what had previously been important trades but now were some of the capital's key industries—spinning, goldsmithing, and sailing. In both large and small ways their efforts shaped England's empire at home and abroad.

The generational fallout for the children of Rendezvous show that a prominent father's legacy was no guarantee of future wealth. When John died, the fortunes of Hester's and Frances's children took a severe knock. His primary heir (Hester's Richard) and Richard's primary heir (Hannah's John) were the only descendants who stood any chance of inherited success. And yet neither found it. The security and stability supposedly granted by being the son and grandson of one of Barbados's most prominent enslavers and landowners never fully manifested following John's death. Instead, his direct line spent decades trying to wrest their due in Chancery Court. Only Frances's Frances reached the kinds of prominence her father might have imagined, and she did so by remaining unmarried and inheriting huge sums of money from a wealthy white widow.

Despite his demise shortly after arriving in England, John was the sinew that tethered the lives of the women and children long after his death. Thirty years later, his grandson was still able to explain the whereabouts of his father's half siblings, who they married, how they made their livings, whether they were still alive, and if they had received any of their promised payments from the Rendezvous estate. But his knowledge was not deep. These were not people he knew intimately. Rather, he was aware of their marital and financial status, sometimes their professions, often where they lived, and in a few cases when they died. Who they were as people clearly escaped him, and the full ways they lived their lives remained obscured from his vision.

It would be a mistake, however, to think that once the mixed-race children arrived in England they no longer were subject to the coercion of enslavement. England, after all, was a society with slaves, and so anti-Black racism and the hierarchies and power dynamics of bondage shaped the lives of anyone who did not appear to be English born. John (at least by the time of his death) treated Susannah, Elizabeth, and their children as free—his will did not mention their manumission or discuss their bonded status. Had their freedom been challenged, forcing them to sue in court, it is unclear whether they would have succeeded. Many of their contemporaries did not. London, Bristol, Glasgow, and other larger British cities whose ports were important sites of imperial trade had significant Black populations in this period, many among them were enslaved. Runaway advertisements in newspapers, freedom suits in the courts, and the attitudes of everyone from Charles II to colonial merchants who held people in bondage all speak to the existence and persistence of slavery *as one of* the forms of labor operating in England.[4]

This is why the women at the heart of this story matter, and the enslaved women especially so. When they came to England their very existence remained precarious precisely because even if they believed themselves to be free, the chance of being returned to a life in bondage was always present. Their children also walked that thin line. The *Yorke-Talbot* ruling of 1729 was clear that enslaved Africans brought from the West Indies to Britain did not become free by virtue of being on British soil. Judith Mingo, Richard Ashcroft, and Susanna Ashcroft were, as far as records show, all alive and living in London in 1729. Each of them could have been returned to Barbados in chains because they arrived in the metropole as enslaved children in 1686. The risks for those who began their lives in bondage were present in England's society with slaves before 1729, but they were all the more acute in the decades after.

The women's lives are important for other reasons too. Hester and Frances brought wealth to their marriages and additional prestige to John and their children because of who they were. As elite Englishwomen in seventeenth-century Barbados, they were responsible for replicating the whiteness and freedom that should have guaranteed their sons' and daughters' status. Both daughters of prominent politicians and both from prestigious English families, they possessed the *bodies* that ensured John's children's futures. By giving John multiple sons, Hester confirmed that the primogeniture and patriarchal systems of inheritance functioned as they did in England. Frances, by birthing only daughters, arguably created the next generation of legitimacy and whiteness. If everything went according to plan, her girls would marry elite Englishmen, keeping the wealth and property of empire—whether in Barbados or England—a legacy for white families alone.

Dorothy's presence allowed a hierarchy of labor to emerge within the Rendezvous household. In Barbados her whiteness elevated her class position, ensuring she would never be expected to labor in perpetuity. Moreover, her children would also be spared the ignominy of plantation service even if they were unlikely to reach the dizzy heights of land ownership themselves. In England Dorothy's connection to the colonies and her association with Elizabeth rendered her whiteness more suspect, complicating her racial status. Her children were free, but their illegitimacy meant that they could never expect to gain access to the kinds of education or positions of power that were open to the Peers siblings. As part of the rapidly growing London population of people with experience in the colonies, they may have been able to use the lessons they learned in Barbados to further their lives in the metropole. Whatever measure of success Dorothy and her children were able to find was not due to their connection to John.

Susannah and Elizabeth were intimately aware of the power dynamics of the places where they lived and worked. They knew, arguably better than Hester, Frances, or Dorothy, how racial capitalism operated in the colonies. At base level, they understood their own productive and reproductive value, and the price placed on their children's heads. As Elizabeth and Dorothy's Chancery suit makes clear, they had a firm grasp on the finances of the Peers estate. With the knowledge that the freedom they enjoyed in England was contingent and could be swept away at any moment, each formerly enslaved woman approached her new life in a different way.

Susannah left Streatham and headed first for Spitalfields, where she and her daughters could gain skills in spinning, making enough money to support themselves if they never received legacies from John's estate. Elizabeth advocated for her and her children's inheritance using England's profligate civil legal system. She also ensured that her sons were apprenticed in decent trades, providing pathways for sufficient financial independence so that they too could continue the fight in Chancery long after Elizabeth was dead. Savvy at reading the political, social, and economic landscape of early modern England, Susannah and Elizabeth forged lives in the metropole in spite of their tenuous freedom, not because of it.

THERE IS LITTLE MORE POWERFUL than the stories countries tell about themselves. Refusing to acknowledge the existence of racial slavery right in the very heart of London results in a form of amnesia in the present about the legacies of slavery in the British Empire. While historic homes and institutions ranging from museums to the Bank of England have begun grappling with the ways that racial capital built the infrastructure of the metropole, the belief that

England itself was "a society epitomized by its commitment to ideas of liberty and freedom" persists.[5]

The very public tearing down of Edward Colston's statue in Bristol in June 2020 centered on his leadership of the Royal African Company and the wealth he built by trading in human beings. The profits Colston returned to England are a key part of that story, of course, but the ways that fortune was amassed is still viewed as something that happened "over there," not in England itself. Thus, England became one of the wealthiest and most dominant empires the world has ever seen through the labor of women, men, and children from Africa, and yet there is virtually no acknowledgment at the state level that some of those women, men, and children were enslaved in England itself.[6]

On the other side of the Atlantic Ocean, slavery and colonialism are remembered in very different ways. The island that was the most prosperous colony in England's empire in the seventeenth and early eighteenth centuries finally rejected the British monarch as head of state and declared itself a republic in November 2021. Independent since 1966, this most recent act—prompted by Prime Minister Mia Mottley—replaced Queen Elizabeth II with Barbados's first president, Sandra Mason, a Black woman whose enslaved ancestors labored on the island. Announced at the same time as Barbados threw off its final constitutional ties to Britain, a new heritage site dedicated to the history of the transatlantic slave trade will be erected in Barbados on the grounds of another of Christ Church's infamous plantations, just a few miles east of where Rendezvous stood.[7] In a country that historically has also shied away from directly engaging the intertwined histories of enslavement and colonialism in its tourism, school curriculum, or built landscape, this move is a significant shift for the world's newest republic.

Rendezvous ceased to exist as a plantation sometime after 1724, when John's grandson sold the Barbados estates out of the Peers family. Unlike Staple Grove, it does not appear in University College London's Legacies of British Slavery database, a project that reveals the reparations paid to enslavers for their loss of property when Britain finally abolished slavery in 1834. No future owner received compensation for the estate on which Susannah and Elizabeth had labored in the last quarter of the seventeenth century. In 1836 John Pollard Mayers, who inherited Staple Grove, received £5441 6s 3d (over £550,000 today) from the British government as restitution for 239 enslaved people who still worked its sugar fields. The debt created by the reparations paid out to enslavers stayed on England's books until 2015.[8] British tax payers—many from the Windrush Generation and their descendants—were paying for what amounted to a bailout of an elite class all the way into the twenty-first century.

There was no such similar payout for Rendezvous, which might well have been broken up and absorbed by other plantations in Christ Church. Of course, this does not mean that descendants of the enslaved people Susannah and Elizabeth worked alongside were not laboring in slavery in Barbados, perhaps even on the same land, in 1834. Unlike the Englishmen and women who built their fortunes in the Caribbean, recently freed people received nothing from the British government. Instead, they were coerced into six more years of hard labor called "apprenticeship" that was supposed to mitigate white colonists' distress at losing their workforce. When newly freed people pushed back against this new repressive system of labor, they were released two years early into a begrudged freedom.[9] Like formerly enslaved men and women across the Atlantic world, free people in Barbados worked hard to build lives for themselves that looked very different from those they experienced in bondage. They did so in a continued atmosphere of anti-Black racism and white supremacy.[10]

Rendezvous itself might have disappeared, but 300 years later its legacy remains in the name of a neighborhood in Christ Church Parish that perches on a hill overlooking Bridgetown to the west and the Caribbean Sea to the south. Located in roughly the same territory as the Peers plantation, the Rendezvous neighborhood bears no signs of the "Mancon House" or the sugar mills that were seventeenth-century emblems of its owner's status. In the place of the 600 acres of sugar fields are single-family homes and a retirement village. Further down the hillside, supermarkets, restaurants, and resort hotels hug the shoreline just a short distance from St. Lawrence Gap, a popular nightlife spot for visitors to the island. Tourism has long since replaced sugar as the driving economic force in Barbados. Those making a pilgrimage to John Peers's estate will be unable to find any evidence of the hundreds of enslaved people who lived, labored, and died in this area for over two centuries.

The women and children of Rendezvous have long afterlives. The experiences of Susannah, Elizabeth, Dorothy, Hester, and Frances help us understand the complicated and brutal nature of imperialism that knitted England and its overseas colonies together for almost 400 years. The intimate ties—between the women and John, among the women, and between the white and mixed-race children—were the threads that wove England's early modern empire. Moving vast distances between continents and across oceans, they all experienced the myriad ways that whiteness and freedom were juxtaposed against Blackness and enslavement. The women also came to understand the ways that patriarchy and power reinscribed themselves on and through their bodies. Together they built a household where reckoning with the very building blocks of colonialism was a daily occurrence. Their interactions with one another forced a recognition of the ways their children—white, Black, free, enslaved, legitimate, "naturall born,"—were the bedrock on which England's imperial ambitions would be realized and sustained. The experiences of the women of this one family reproduced across the centuries in ways large and small. This is the legacy left by the women of Rendezvous.

Notes

ABBREVIATIONS USED IN THE NOTES

ADM   High Court of Admiralty Records, National Archives, London, Kew, UK

BNA   Barbados National Archives, Black Rock, Bridgetown, Barbados

C   Chancery Court Records, National Archives, London, Kew, UK

CO   Colonial Office Records, National Archives, London, Kew, UK

PROB   Probate Records, National Archives, London, Kew, UK

RB   Registers of Wills or Register of Deeds, Barbados National Archives, Black Rock, Bridgetown, Barbados

RL   Parish Registers, Barbados National Archives, Black Rock, Bridgetown, Barbados

T   Treasury Records, National Archives, London, Kew, UK

TNA   The National Archives, London, Kew, UK

INTRODUCTION

1. Smallwood, *Saltwater Slavery*, 135.

2. TNA, C24/1211 *Peers v. Chaplin, Hilary*, box 1, bundle unnumbered, Deposition of John Peers II, 20 February 1698.

3. Zahedieh studies transatlantic voyages between the Caribbean and London in 1686 in *Capital and the Colonies*.

4. BNA, RL1/17; Shaw, *Everyday Life*, 110–14.

5. BNA, RL1/17, p. 123. Susannah and Elizabeth also appear in the Christ Church baptism records, alongside another enslaved woman. On 8 June 1670 "Hester, Susanna, & Elizabeth negro women slaves to John Peers" were baptized. BNA, RL1/17, p. 91.

6. Gerbner, *Christian Slavery*, 67–68; Gerbner, "Ultimate Sin," 59–61, 65–68.

7. TNA, CO1/44 no. 47 VII; Dunn, *Sugar and Slaves*, 90, 99, 232; BNA, RB3/1, p. 13, August 1640. "Mancon House" here means "Mansion House," indicating the main plantation dwelling.

8. BNA, RL1/17, pp. 82, 86, 97, 106, 121, 124, 126.

9. Hester's burial can be found at TNA, CO1/44 no. 47 IV, 15 September 1678. Frances's burial is recorded as 5 April 1685 also in the chancel in St. Michaels. "Frances Peers," Barbados, Church Records, 1637–1849, ancestry.com, www.ancestry.com/search/collections/9788/.

10. Dunn, *Sugar and Slaves*, 232–33.

11. Dorothy is listed as "Mistress Dorothy Spendlove," which, as Erickson points out, is not an indication of marital status, but rather her age, in "Mistresses," 39–40.

12. Dunn, *Sugar and Slaves*, 43–86; Menard, *Sweet Negotiations*.

13. V. Brown, "Eating the Dead."

14. See Dunn, *Sugar and Slaves*; Fuentes, *Dispossessed Lives*, 1; J. Morgan, *Laboring Women*; and Beckles, *White Servitude*. On the ways that racial capitalism shaped the early modern world, see J. Morgan, *Reckoning with Slavery*.

15. On the customary nature of *partus sequitur ventrem* in the Caribbean, see M. Newton, "Returns to a Native Land," 115; Handler, "Custom and Law," 241–42. For an exploration of 1662 Virginia law, see J. Morgan, "*Partus Sequitur Ventrem.*"

16. On the English Caribbean, see, for example, S. Smith, *Slavery, Family, and Gentry Capitalism*; Rothschild, *Inner Life of Empires*; Pearsall, *Atlantic Families*; Livesay, *Children of Uncertain Fortune*; Hancock, *Citizens of the World*; Clancy-Smith and Gouda, *Domesticating the Empire*; J. Palmer, *Intimate Bonds*; and Mangan, *Transatlantic Obligations*. For a call to interrogate family as a category of analysis, see Hardwick, Pearsall, and Wulf, "Centering Families in Atlantic History"; Wulf, "Women and Families"; Hardwick, "Family Matters."

17. Spillers, "Mama's Baby," 67–68. In *Black Family*, Gutman argues that despite the debilitating trauma of slavery, enslaved people were often able to form households with two parents. For the West Indies context, see Higman, "Slave Family." For scholarship that centers women's roles in family, see D. G. White, *Ar'n't I A Woman?*; J. Jones, *Labor of Love*; and J. Morgan, *Laboring Women*. On the trauma and dislocation of the Middle Passage, see Patterson, *Slavery and Social Death*, 5; Smallwood, *Saltwater Slavery*; Turner, *Contested Bodies*; J. Morgan, *Laboring Women*; and V. Brown, *Reaper's Garden*. For the idea that maternal inheritance codified kinlessness among slaves, see Spillers, "Mama's Baby," 74; Hartman, "Belly of the World," 168; J. Morgan, "*Partus Sequitur Ventrem,*" 14–17; Kennedy, *Between Fitness and Death*, 54–60, esp. 58. For a discussion of the ways that "fictions of blood ancestry" justified enslavement in British contexts, see B. Newman, *Dark Inheritance*.

18. Fuentes, *Dispossessed Lives*, 1. The island's slight female majority meant that sex-ratio imbalances like those in Virginia, Maryland, or Jamaica never materialized; Sackett, "'Greater Numbers.'"

19. J. Morgan, *Reckoning with Slavery*, 5.

20. On the significance of matrifocal households in slavery and freedom, see K. Brown, *Good Wives*, 229; D. G. White, *Ar'n't I A Woman*; and Stevenson, *What Sorrows*, 25–26.

21. Stoler, *Carnal Knowledge*, chap. 1; Stoler, "Intimidations," 4; Forde-Jones, "Mapping," 18.

22. On early English settler colonial failures, see Kupperman, *Jamestown Project*.

23. Harkness and Howard, "Introduction," 1; Finlay and Shearer, "Population Growth," 38; Field, *London, Londoners and the Great Fire*, 7.

24. The field of premodern critical race studies has long established the existence of "Race Before Race" in the medieval and early modern periods. Foundational works in the field include Hendricks and Parker, *Women, "Race," and Writing*; Hendricks, "Race," 535–44; K. Hall, "Reading What Isn't There"; K. Hall, *Things of Darkness*; Habib, *Black Lives*. See also Edwards, "Early African Presence," 15–16, 20.

25. On enslaved people in Britain, see Habib, *Black Lives*; Lorimer, "Black Slaves"; K. Hall, "Reading What Isn't There"; Lynch, "Whatever Happened to Dinah the Black"; Shyllon, "Black Presence," 202–4; Fryer, *Staying Power*, 113–14; Gerzina, *Black London*; Chater, *Untold Histories*, 1, 77–101; C. Smith, *Black Africans*; Guasco, *Slaves and Englishmen*; and S. Newman, *Freedom Seekers*. Molineux differentiates between the "chattel status of African slaves in colonial settings" and "the involuntary servitude or near slavery of blacks living in the metropole," in *Faces of Perfect Ebony*, 11. In *Black Tudors*, Kaufman emphasizes Black people who were not enslaved. There is a vast historiography that situates slavery in the English world as a colonial invention. Classics include E. Morgan, *American Slavery, American Freedom*; and Dunn, *Sugar and Slaves*. For the Continental comparison, see Otele, *African Europeans*.

26. I employ Berlin's famous formulation to emphasize that England, as much as colonies like seventeenth-century Virginia and New England, was a society with slaves. Berlin describes such societies as places where "slavery was just one form of labor among many." This fact, however, did not affect the treatment of enslaved people. In societies with slaves, "slaveowners treated their slaves with extreme callousness and cruelty at times because this was the way they treated all subordinates, whether indentured servants, debtors, prisoners-of-war, pawns, peasants, or simply poor folks"; see *Many Thousands Gone*, 8. For a discussion of how ideas about England being a place free of slavery bleed from the past into the present, see Guasco, *Slaves and Englishmen*, introduction, esp. 9.

27. Chakravarty has most recently made this case in *Fictions of Consent* when she describes how "the fictions of slavery and those of race are coarticulated and coextensive in this period," 8n20. In *Freedom Seekers*, S. Newman notes that "enslavers in London were . . . engaged in making slavery real," xxvi–xxvii, quotation on xxvii; Brewer also argues that "real slavery did exist" in England prior to the 1772 Somerset case, in "Creating a Common Law," 765–834, quotation on 771.

28. See, for example, S. White, *Voices*, 10. See also J. Johnson, *Wicked Flesh*, 230; and Inniss, "Freed Women and Unequal Inheritance."

29. In part, I read sources along what Fuentes calls "the bias grain," a method that stretches sources while maintaining their "historical integrity"; see *Dispossessed Lives*, 7, 78. This has also been a project that demands "slow archival work" and deep contextualization of "place and culture"; see E. Owens, *Consent in the Presence of Force*, 6–7. Trouillot's *Silencing* has long been foundational to my methodological approaches. For a superb example

of how to use "communal biography" to decenter white men, see S. Johnson's exceptional *Encyclopédie noire*.

30. Dunn, *Sugar and Slaves*; Gragg, *Englishmen Transplanted*; S. Smith, *Slavery, Family, and Gentry Capitalism*; S. Newman, *New World*; Burnard, *Mastery*, 209–40; P. Morgan, *Slave Counterpoint*, 398–411. Important exceptions include J. Morgan, *Laboring Women*; Fuentes, *Dispossessed Lives*; and Beckles, *Centering Women*.

CHAPTER 1

1. TNA, C6/478/3 *Spendlove v. Chaplin*, Bill and Answer, 10 April 1695. John's first wife is listed only by her married name in the Barbados records; her family name (Tomkyns) and connections can be found in Charles Robinson, *History of the Mansions*, 293.

2. Fryer, *Staying Power*; Habib, *Black Lives*; Chater, *Untold Histories*.

3. Dunn, *Sugar and Slaves*, 54–55, 75–76, 87–89.

4. Mintz, *Sweetness and Power*. For the connections between slavery, colonialism, and the rise of capitalism in Europe, see Williams, *Capitalism and Slavery*; and Cedric Robinson, *Black Marxism*.

5. BNA, RB3/1, pp. 10–14, August 1640.

6. "Marie Payce," England Marriages, 1538–1973, findmypast.com, https://search.findmypast.co.uk/search-world-records/england-marriages-1538-1973. For Richard's 1661 will, see BNA, RB6/15, p. 199, 2 April 1661.

7. Dunn, *Sugar and Slaves*, 51–52.

8. Ligon, *True and Exact History*, 24. For an excellent annotated edition of Ligon, see Kupperman, *True and Exact History*.

9. For Hay's correspondence, see Dunn, *Sugar and Slaves*, 53–54. On Ligon's opinion of tobacco, see *True and Exact History*, 24.

10. Higman summarizes the historiography in "Sugar Revolution." See also Dunn, *Sugar and Slaves*, 43–86; Beckles, *White Servitude*; and Menard, *Sweet Negotiations*.

11. Dunn, *Sugar and Slaves*.

12. BNA, RB6/15, p. 199, 2 April 1661. Richard had a second sugar plantation, Staple Grove, that was close to Rendezvous, although about half its size.

13. For the family tree, see Neal, *Ashcraft Family*, 3. On early Barbados history, see Amussen, *Caribbean Exchanges*, 25–27; Dunn, *Sugar and Slaves*, 49–51; Gragg, *Englishmen Transplanted*, 29–31. For Richard's time as lieutenant governor, see Duke, *Memoirs*, 80. The same account discusses the factional infighting that led to the Earl of Carlisle winning the patent; see Duke, *Memoirs*, 4–13.

14. Amussen, *Caribbean Exchanges*, 30, 32, 109–10; Duke, *Memoirs*, 19–20.

15. BNA, RB3/1, pp. 10–14, August 1640; BNA, RB6/13, p. 116, 15 October 1647. There are few extant records from 1630s and 1640s Barbados, so evidence that might reveal links among and between Lancelot, Marie, and Richard is not available.

16. Norton, *Founding Mothers*, 57, 95. On women as "good wives," see K. Brown, *Good Wives*, 86–87. See also Zacek, *Settler Society*, 169–73.

17. "Peirce Ashcroft," Barbados, Church Records, 1637–1849, ancestry.com, www .ancestry.com/search/collections/9788/.

18. Amussen, *Caribbean Exchanges*, 177–78.

19. Dunn, *Sugar and Slaves*, 79–80; Amussen, *Caribbean Exchanges*, 31–32. For Richard's role in peace negotiations, see "America and West Indies: January 1652," in *Calendar of State Papers Colonial, America and West Indies*, vol. 1, *1574–1660*, 370–73, *British History Online*. On his time in the assembly, see "State Papers, 1656: March (7 of 8)," in *A Collection of the State Papers of John Thurloe*, vol. 4, *Sep. 1655–May 1656*, 639–52, *British History Online*. On being reappointed to the Council, see "America and West Indies: December 1660," in *Calendar of State Papers Colonial, America and West Indies*, vol. 1, *1574–1660*, 492–98, *British History Online*.

20. BNA, RB6/15, pp. 199–202, 13 March 1661. For Edward Peers burial record, see "Edward Peers," Barbados, Church Records, 1637–1849, ancestry.com, www.ancestry .com/search/collections/9788.

21. TNA, C24/1211 *Peers v. Chaplin, Hilary*, 1698–99, box 1, bundle unnumbered, Deposition of Sir Edward Turnor, 25 February 1698, answer to Q.7.

22. For the Barbados census, see TNA, CO1/44, fols. 142–379. There were eight "white servants" on Peers's estate in 1680, in addition to John, Hester, and their youngest child. See also Dunn, *Sugar and Slaves*, 87–89. On how John stocked his estate, see TNA, C/6/478/3 *Spendlove v. Chaplin*, Bill and Answer, 1695.

23. Ligon, *True and Exact History*, 46–47; Dunn, *Sugar and Slaves*, 316. On Barbados's enslaved population, see Handler and Lange, *Plantation Slavery*, 67–68; and Beckles, *Natural Rebels*, 7–9. J. Morgan notes a similar demographic on Brey's plantation in St. Michaels, although the total number of enslaved people on the estate was much smaller; see *Laboring Women*, 122.

24. Although the numbers produced through the Transatlantic Slave Trade database (slavevoyages.org) are imperfect, a search reveals that 318,483 captives disembarked in Barbados between 1650 and 1725. A full 81.8 percent embarked from the Gold Coast, Bight of Benin, or Bight of Biafra in this period. See also Eltis, "Volume and African Origins," 617–27; and J. Morgan, *Laboring Women*, 57, 119. On the geography of West Africa, see J. Thornton, *Africa and Africans*, xii, xiv, xxi; and Law, *Slave Coast*, 13. For more on demography, see Curtin, *Atlantic Slave Trade*, 55; and Eltis and Richardson, "West Africa," 16–35. The Gold Coast was a major departure point for the majority of slaves shipped to the British West Indies in the second half of the seventeenth century; see J. Thornton, *Africa and Africans*, 119; J. Morgan, *Laboring Women*, 57. For slave ports, see Chambers, "Ethnicity in the Diaspora," 25; Eltis and Richardson, "West Africa," 17, 22–23; J. Thornton, *Africa and Africans*, 192–94.

25. Ligon, *True and Exact History*, 46.

26. Eltis, "Diaspora," 18–19. Many of the names that Europeans associated with Africans were either imposed by slave traders or developed in diaspora by Africans. See Chambers, "Ethnicity in the Diaspora," 25–39; Miller, "Historical Appreciation," 42; Lovejoy, "African Diaspora," 7–8; C. Palmer, "From Africa to the Americas," 224–25; and G. Hall, *Slavery and African Ethnicities*. See also Smallwood, *Saltwater Slavery*.

27. Dunn, *Sugar and Slaves*, 232–33.

28. TNA, T 70/939. I thank Marisa Fuentes for seeing John's name and sharing these records with me. Smallwood also notes the preponderance of slave ships departing for the Americas from 1672 to 1725 from the Gold Coast, in *Saltwater Slavery*, chap. 1.

29. Bodleian Library, C/WIN/BAR 1–4, Inventories of Rendezvous Plantation and Garden, October 1705; J. Thornton, *Africa and Africans*, map 5, xiv; Handler and Jacoby, "Slave Names," 698–99; S. Block, *Colonial Complexions*.

30. Transatlantic Slave Trade database, slavevoyages.org.

31. Browne and Sweet, "Florence Hall," 206–21, narrative on 216.

32. Equiano, *Interesting Narrative*, 48–58.

33. V. Smith, *Narrative of the Life*, 9–13.

34. Bodleian Library, "Two Narratives of Slave Women, 1799, Written Down by John Ford, Barbados," MS. Eng. Misc. b. 4, fols. 50–50v. Smallwood has a wonderful analysis of this account in *Saltwater Slavery*, 202–7. See also Handler, "Life Histories," 129–41.

35. V. Smith, *Narrative of the Life*, 13. See also Lovejoy, *Transformations in Slavery*; Shumway, *Fante*; T. Green, *Rise of the Transatlantic Slave Trade*; Sparks, *Where the Negroes Are Masters*; Candido, *African Slaving Port*.

36. Smallwood, *Saltwater Slavery*; Hartman, *Lose Your Mother*.

37. Hair, Jones, and Law, *Barbot on Guinea*, 2:392.

38. Bodleian Library, "Two Narratives."

39. Hair, Jones, and Law, *Barbot on Guinea*, 1:170–71.

40. Hair, Jones, and Law, *Barbot on Guinea*, 1:292, 302.

41. Browne and Sweet, "Florence Hall," 216. H. Bennett, *African Kings*, chap. 4; S. Newman, *New World*, 139–65.

42. Smallwood, *Saltwater Slavery*; Rediker, *Slave Ship*; Mustakeem, *Slavery at Sea*; Hartman, *Lose Your Mother*.

43. Browne and Sweet, "Florence Hall," 216.

44. Equiano, *Interesting Narrative*, 73–74.

45. Bodleian Library, "Two Narratives"; Smallwood, *Saltwater Slavery*, 202–7.

46. Equiano, *Interesting Narrative*, 73.

47. A search of the Trans-Atlantic Slave Trade database for the years 1650–1700 shows a total of 204,064 captives left West Africa, while only 156,100 arrived in Barbados, a mortality rate of 23.5 percent (slavevoyages.org). The database cannot account for records lost, enslaved people smuggled as contraband into the Americas, or inaccuracies in the records it relies on.

48. On the enduring trauma evident in 'Sibell's account, see Smallwood, *Saltwater Slavery*, 205–6.

49. Dunn, *Sugar and Slaves*, 106–8, 232; Welch, *Slave Society in the City*, xiv.

50. Smallwood, *Saltwater Slavery*, 160–65. Fuentes notes how by the eighteenth century most enslaved people were taken into Bridgetown and sold at warehouses on the wharves, in *Dispossessed Lives*, 26–27.

51. Bodleian Library, "Two Narratives."

52. Fuentes expertly lays out the geography and visceral experiences of Bridgetown from the perspective of an enslaved woman named Jane in *Dispossessed Lives*, 21–30, quotation on 25. See also S. Newman, *New World*, 166–87; and H. Bennett, *African Kings*.

53. Ligon, *True and Exact History*, 109; Dunn, *Sugar and Slaves*, 282–84.

54. Beckles, *Centering Women*, 60–72; Bush, *Slave Women*, 61–62; Bush, "White 'Ladies.'" For a contemporary view of seasoning, see Littleton, *Groans*, 19. See also Johnston, "Endangered Plantations."

55. Anonymous, *Great Newes from the Barbadoes*.

56. TNA, CO1/35 no. 29, Atkins to Secretary Joseph Williamson, Barbados, 3–13 October 1675. On contemporary views of "Cormantee" people, see K. Wilson, "Performance of Freedom," 67.

57. For more on the revolt, see Shaw, *Everyday Life*, 132–40; and K. Block, *Ordinary Lives*, 175–79.

58. Ligon, *True and Exact History*, 88. For an overview of sugar production practices in the Caribbean, see Dunn, *Sugar and Slaves*, 192–201; Amussen, *Caribbean Exchanges*, 75–82; Menard, *Sweet Negotiations*, 17–19, 29–30; Beckles, *White Servitude*, 128–29; and Shaw, *Everyday Life*, 74–82.

59. Ligon, *True and Exact History*, 48.

60. Littleton, *Groans*, 18.

61. Tryon, *Friendly Advice*, pt. 2, 88. See also Ligon, *True and Exact History*, 85–86.

62. Ligon, *True and Exact History*, 89.

63. Ligon, *True and Exact History*, 89; Mintz, *Sweetness and Power*, 21.

64. Tryon, *Friendly Advice*, 301.

65. Ligon, *True and Exact History*, 90.

66. Tryon, *Friendly Advice*, 89; Mintz notes that there was an axe on hand in most sugar mills specifically to amputate injured limbs caught in the grinder, in *Sweetness and Power*, 50. See also Littleton *Groans*, 20.

67. Bodleian Library, C/WIN/BAR 1–4, Inventories of Rendezvous Plantation and Garden, October 1705; see also Robert Ford's map of Barbados, 1674, which demonstrates the double windmills at Rendezvous.

68. J. Morgan, *Laboring Women*, 148–49.

69. Bodleian Library, C/WIN/BAR 1–4, Inventories of Rendezvous Plantation and Garden, October 1705.

70. Ligon, *True and Exact History*, 91.

71. Tryon, *Friendly Advice*, 89. See also Littleton, *Groans*, 20; and Amussen, *Caribbean Exchanges*, 98–99.

72. Ligon, *True and Exact History*, 90. Rendezvous had three coolers. Bodleian Library, C/WIN/BAR 1–4, Inventories of Rendezvous Plantation and Garden, October 1705.

73. BDA, RB3/12, pp. 163–65, 31 October 1682.

74. Ligon, *True and Exact History*, 92–93; Bodleian Library, C/WIN/BAR 1–4, Inventories of Rendezvous Plantation and Garden, October 1705.

75. Littleton, *Groans*, 19. See also Ligon, *True and Exact History*, 92–93.

76. TNA, CO1/44 no. 47; Bodleian Library, C/WIN/BAR 1–4, Inventories of Rendezvous Plantation and Garden, October 1705. There is a vast literature on the transition from servitude to enslavement, and the relative positions in which this placed white servants on plantations. See, for example, Newman, *New World of Labor.*

77. Ligon, *True and Exact History*, 45, 47.

78. Biet, *Voyage*, 290. For an excellent translation of Biet's account of his time in Barbados, see Handler, "Father Antoine Biet," 56–76.

79. Ligon, *True and Exact History*,

80. Sloane, *Voyage*, 1:57.

81. Tryon, *Friendly Advice*, 85.

82. On English perceptions of West Africans, see K. Hall, *Things of Darkness*; J. Morgan, *Laboring Women*; Guasco, *Slaves and Englishmen*; Beckles, *White Servitude*; and D. Davis, "Constructing Race." Scholarship seriously engaging the question of religious influences on the development of racism includes Kidd, *Forging of Races*; Goetz, *Baptism of Early Virginia*; Kopelson, *Faithful Bodies*; and Gerbner, *Christian Slavery.*

83. Ligon, *True and Exact History*, 96.

84. On labor organization on plantations, see Dunn, *Sugar and Slaves*, 189–95; and S. Newman, *New World*, 203–14. For time away from whites, see Gordon-Reed, *Hemingses*, 30.

85. Bodleian Library, C/WIN/BAR 1–4, Inventories of Rendezvous Plantation and Garden, October 1705.

86. Dunn, *Sugar and Slaves.*

87. Bodleian Library, C/WIN/BAR 1–4, Inventories of Rendezvous Plantation and Garden, October 1705; Dunn, *Sugar and Slaves*, 66–67, 273–74.

88. Anonymous, *Great Newes from the Barbadoes*, 8.

89. TNA, C6/478/3 *Spendlove v. Chaplin*, Bill and Answer, 10 April 1695; Bodleian Library, C/WIN/BAR 1–4, Inventories of Rendezvous Plantation and Garden, October 1705.

90. Ligon, *True and Exact History*, 39. Ligon was describing Colonel Humphrey Walrond's estate; John would later become an in-law to the Walronds when he married Frances Knights, née Atkins.

91. Beckles, *Natural Rebels*, 57–62; K. Brown, *Foul Bodies*, 30–31, 110; J. Morgan, *Laboring Women*, 159; Fischer, *Suspect Relations*, 150. For the English comparison, see Richardson, *Household Servants*, 165–67. On the lack of risk for elite men fathering illegitimate children, see Hubbard, *City Women*, 110.

92. Beckles, *Natural Rebels*, 58, 60.

93. TNA, CO1/44 no. 47 ii. One of the "Inhabitants of Barbados in the Year 1638 who then possess'd more than ten Acres of Land" was John Spendlove; see Duke, *Memoirs*, 82. For deeds pertaining to Spendlove/Speedlove, see BNA, RB3/3, p. 528, April 1649; RB3/3, pp. 595–97, April 1649; RB3/3, pp. 630–31, 1649. I thank Lorena Walsh for sharing these records with me.

94. K. Brown, *Good Wives*, 102–3.

95. K. Brown, *Foul Bodies*, 66.

96. For more on Anna, see J. Morgan, *Laboring Women*, 175–76; K. Block, *Ordinary Lives*, 176; and Shaw, *Everyday Life*, 137–39.

97. Prince, *History of Mary Prince*, 6.

98. Bodleian Library, C/WIN/BAR 1–4, Inventories of Rendezvous Plantation and Garden, October 1705.

99. C. Jones, *Engendering Whiteness*, 3, 161. The role of the mistress has been explored in the context of the plantations of the United States south in the nineteenth century. See, for example, Glymph, *Out of the House of Bondage*; and Jones-Rogers, *They Were Her Property*.

100. Prince, *History of Mary Prince*, 10.

101. J. Morgan, *Laboring Women*.

CHAPTER 2

1. Crawford, *Blood*, 91.

2. J. Morgan, *"Partus Sequitur Ventrem,"* 14; Spiller, "Mama's Baby," 74, 78. See also J. Morgan, *Reckoning with Slavery*; Hartman; "Belly of the World," 166–68; and Kennedy, *Between Fitness and Death*, 54–55.

3. On Black women's bodies "as economic rather than domestic spaces," and on enslaved women as "outside the protective cover of domestic life," see J. Morgan, *"Partus Sequitur Ventrem,"* 14. Susannah's first two children were born before Barbados's 1680 census. They, along with Susannah and Elizabeth and Elizabeth's eldest children, were among the 180 "negroes" accounted on John's estate, TNA, CO1/44 no. 47 VII, 1680.

4. J. Morgan, *"Partus Sequitur Ventrem,"* 17. Morgan develops this argument and stresses enslaved women's cognizance of their value in J. Morgan, *Reckoning with Slavery*.

5. Pearsall, *Polygamy*. Neville's *Isle of Pines* uses the literary device of a "true account" to examine the fortunes of five English people (one man, four women) shipwrecked on an uninhabited island somewhere in the Pacific Ocean in the 1560s. George Pines, the protagonist, fathers children with each of the women—two servants, one enslaved women, and his boss's daughter—to populate the place they now inhabit. Often read as a commentary on the sexual politics of Charles II's Restoration court, Hendricks suggests that the "white supremacist ideology at the core of the text" bears more scrutiny; see *Race and Romance*, 42. I thank Margo Hendricks for introducing me to Neville's work.

6. On enslaved women birthing enslavers' offspring, see, among others, D. G. White, *Ar'n't I A Woman?*; Gordon-Reed, *Hemingses*; S. Green, *"Remember Me to Miss Louisa*; and Burnard, *Mastery*. On consent in slavery, see Bush, "White 'Ladies'"; Hartman, *Scenes*; Beckles, *Centering Women*, 25–27; Snyder, "Sexual Consent," 46–60; Fischer, *Suspect Relations*; Miles, *Ties That Bind*, esp. chap. 3; J. Morgan, *Laboring Women*; S. Block, *Rape and Sexual Power*, 65–74; and E. Owens, "Promises." On sexual violence against enslaved persons perpetrated by white women, see Jones-Rogers, "Rethinking Sexual Violence"; and Foster, "Sexual Abuse." On servants and consent in the Americas, see Fischer, *Suspect Relations*, 150. On the same attitude in England, see Richardson, *Household Servants*, 165–67. On marital rape, see C. Jones, *Engendering Whiteness*, 86–92; and S. Block, *Rape and Sexual Power*, 74. See also Vigarello, *History of Rape*, 149–50.

7. For more on the idea that "neither could claim her body and its various productions—for quite different reasons, albeit—as her own," see Spillers, "Mama's Baby," 77. On coverture in England, see Erickson, *Women and Property*; and Bailey, "Favoured or Oppressed." For coverture in the British colonies, see Salmon, *Women and the Law*; Sturtz, *Within Her Power*; and Walker, *Jamaica Ladies*, 44–45, 89, 174–75. On the inequities of maternal inheritance, see J. Morgan, "*Partus Sequitur Ventrem*," 12. On women enslavers' power, see Fuentes, *Dispossessed Lives*, 88; Glymph, *Out of the House of Bondage*, 3–4; and Walker, *Jamaica Ladies*, 10. See also K. Brown, *Good Wives*, 30–33; D. G. White, *Ar'n't I A Woman?*; and Jones-Rogers, *They Were Her Property*.

8. As Fuentes articulates, "white women made free humans and enslaved women birthed other slaves"; see *Dispossessed Lives*, 76. See also Paton, "Gender History."

9. J. Morgan, "*Partus Sequitur Ventrem*," 14. For more on enslaved women's "capitalized wombs," see Paton, "Maternal Struggles," 252.

10. Habakkuk, *Marriage*, 214. Charles II's lack of male heir caused his son, the Duke of Monmouth, to lay claim to the English throne; see McClure, *Coram's Children*, 173n14. Charles II's brother, the Duke of York, behaved in similar fashion. For issues surrounding the acknowledgment of mixed-race children from Jamaica who were sent to England, see Livesay, *Children of Uncertain Fortune*.

11. Pearsall notes that there was "no singular tradition" among West Africans. *Polygamy*, 117. See also Osborn, *Our New Husbands*, 27–31; J. Thornton, *Africa and Africans*, 86; and J. Thornton, "Sexual Demography," 43–44.

12. Whyte, "Mothering Solidarity," 62.

13. I thank Sharon Block for suggesting the phrase "practical polygyny."

14. Fischer, *Suspect Relations*, 150; Painter, "Soul Murder," 15–39; Jennings, "'Us Colored Women,'" 45–74; Oldmixon, *British Empire*, 2:129. See also Bush, *Slave Women*, 12–13, 17–18, 94–95; and Beckles, *Centering Women*, 26.

15. J. Morgan, *Laboring Women*, 13, 14–15.

16. Vermeulen has written powerfully about this problem in "Thomas Thistlewood," 18–38. See also Shaw, "In The Name of the Mother," 186n23.

17. J. Morgan reminds us of the dangers of the "vacuum of perpetual resistance," in *Laboring Women*, 167.

18. Scholars working on women enslavers and their property often make the same interpretive move. For example, Walker suggests that Lucy was able to manipulate her mistress into getting what she wanted, although the source material reveals only Callender's desires and actions, in *Jamaica Ladies*, 109–13. For critical engagement with the concept of agency, see Hartman, *Scenes*, 11–12; and W. Johnson, "On Agency." J. Morgan develops a critique of gendered agency in *Laboring Women*, 6–7, 167. Fuentes builds on this work and questions the utility of agency altogether in "Power and Historical Figuring." Beckles articulates the problem, noting that enslaved women were placed in a position of "accepting offers they could not possibly reject," in *Centering Women*, 22–37, esp. 37.

19. I thank Marisa Fuentes for stating this problem so succinctly.

20. E. Owens, *Consent in the Presence of Force*, 157. If either Susannah or Elizabeth had a reputation as a "good breeder," this may have contributed to John's sexual exploitation. Barclay, "Bad Breeders," 289–90.

21. Writing about the nineteenth century, D. Owens explains the problem with language used to discuss the scientific tradition as it pertains to enslaved men and women, in *Medical Bondage*.

22. S. Block, *Rape and Sexual Power*, 3–4, 54, 65–75. See also Paton, "Mary Williamson's Letter."

23. E. Owens, *Consent in the Presence of Force*, 14.

24. Richardson, *Household Servants*, 98, 165–67; S. Block, *Rape and Sexual Power*, 66; Reinke-Williams, *Women, Work*, 77; K. Brown, *Good Wives*, 101–10; Wood, "Servant Women," 95–117. On "serial servitude" among Native women, see Newell, *Brethren by Nature*, 15, 57.

25. Amussen, *Caribbean Exchanges*, 135. For examples from seventeenth-century England, see Gowing, *Domestic Dangers*, 165–66, 252–53. Hodes discusses the abilities of white women both to testify in court and to bring their own actions, in *White Women*, 5, 25–26. Fischer notes that white servants could name masters as fathers of their children in bastardy cases but were generally unsuccessful when bringing charges of rape against white men. Of course, they could still bring the charge, something unavailable to Black women. *Suspect Relations*, 108–9.

26. Cressy, "Purification," 115–16, 141–42.

27. Mary's birth date comes from Hester's brother-in-law, Robert Chaplin, in TNA, C6/478/3 *Spendlove v. Chaplin*, Bill and Answer, 1695. The children born in Barbados were Richard (March 1668, BDA, RB1/17, p. 82), Elizabeth (March–April 1669, BDA, RB1/17, p. 86), John (May 1670, BDA, RB1/17, p. 91), Elizabeth (March–September 1672, BDA, RB1/17, p. 97), and Thomas (January 1676, RB1/17, p. 106). On Hester fulfilling her wifely duty by providing suitable heirs, see Norton, *Founding Mothers*, 57.

28. The birth dates for Frances, Elizabeth, and Ann can be found in V. Oliver, *Caribbeana*, vol. 2. Frances's death so soon after the birth of her daughter raises questions about who nursed Ann. Doyle, *Maternal Bodies*, 129–31. Pearsall notes how repeated childbearing can kill and how a man's sexual desires usually won out against a woman's health in *Polygamy*, 13–14.

29. Crawford, *Blood*, 56, 82; Cressy, *Birth, Marriage, and Death*, 17; Perry, "Colonizing the Breast," 216. On sexual pleasure for white women, see Crawford, *Blood*, 58–59; L. Cody, *Birthing the Nation*, 32. Fuentes, *Dispossessed Lives*, 76. See also Bush, *Slave Women*, 112; and Amussen, *Caribbean Exchanges*, 232. Sexual pleasure (and how it was measured in the early modern era) looked very different for enslaved women. See E. Owens, *Consent in the Presence of Force*, 23–24; and LaFleur, "Whither Rape." Lindsey and Johnson give a different reading of the possibilities in "Searching for Climax."

30. See Cressy, *Birth, Marriage, and Death*, 74, on the average age of women in England who had "bastards."

31. S. Block, *Rape and Sexual Power*, 63–68.

32. Vermeulen argues that Thistlewood took great pleasure in noting the precise location of his assaults, so it is not impossible that the same was true for John. See "Thomas Thistlewood's," 33–34.

33. S. Block, *Rape and Sexual Power*, 69–71.

34. S. Block, *Rape and Sexual Power*, 72–74.

35. For European averages, see Klepp, *Revolutionary Conceptions*, 51. For West African spacing, see Klein and Engerman, "Fertility Differentials," 371; and Bush, *Slave Women*, 126–27.

36. Ogilby, *Africa*, 466; Marees, *Description*, 38. For birth rates and infant mortality rates in early modern England, see Cressy, *Birth, Marriage, and Death*, 28–30; and L. Cody, *Birthing the Nation*, 40–41. For the English Caribbean, see J. Morgan, *Laboring Women*, 110; Turner, *Contested Bodies*, 14; and Paton, "Maternal Struggles," 255–56. On West African abstinence practices, see Klein and Engerman, "Fertility Differentials," 371; Bush, *Slave Women*, 126–27; and Handler and Corruccini, "Weaning," 111–17.

37. J. Morgan, *Laboring Women*, 66; Bush, *Slave Women*, 126. In *Contested Bodies*, Turner describes how late eighteenth-century Jamaica planters believed that enslaved women were deliberately spacing their children, using what to them appeared to be extended lactation to regulate their fertility (189–90). For the Brazilian comparison, see Soares and Hora, "African Mothers," 879.

38. J. Morgan notes the transportation of reproductive practices across the Atlantic Ocean in *Laboring Women*, 66. See also Soares and Hora, "African Mothers," 879.

39. J. Morgan, *Laboring Women*, 111.

40. Roth, "From Free Womb," 273; West and Shearer, "Fertility Control," 1010; Schiebinger, "Agnotology and Exotic Abortifacients"; Schiebinger, *Plants and Empire*, chap. 4; Bush, *Slave Women*, 141–42; J. Morgan, *Laboring Women*, 113–14; Cressy, *Birth, Marriage, and Death*, 47–50.

41. Klein and Engerman, "Fertility Differentials," 369. On European misunderstandings of polygyny, see C. Palmer, "From African to the Americas," 227; and Bush, *Slave Women*, 20, 124–25.

42. Marees, *Description*, 23.

43. Jones, *Brandenburg Sources*, 89, 191.

44. Hair, Jones, and Law, *Barbot on Guinea*, 2:505. For the potential problems with Barbot's writings, see Law, "Jean Barbot," 155–73.

45. Law notes there is little evidence that polygynous practices transferred across the Atlantic Ocean, in *Slave Coast*, 65–66. See also Sweet, *Domingo Álvares*, 33; J. Morgan, *Laboring Women*, 60–61; and Sparks, *Where the Negroes Are Masters*. The slave trade itself was shaped by polygyny; see Klein, "African Women," 29–32; Whyte, "Mothering Solidarity," 62.

46. Tryon, *Friendly Advice*, 127.

47. TNA, PROB 11/370/288, proved 4 July 1682.

48. Clark, "'Their Negro Nanny Was with Child,'" 533–62, quotation on 537.

49. For the baptisms of Susannah and of the sons, see BNA, RL1/17, p. 91.

50. Bodleian Library, Codrington Plantation Records, C/WIN/BAR 1–4, 17 February and 17 October 1705.

51. Crawford, "Construction and Experience"; C. Wilson, "Ceremony of Childbirth." For Hester's family tree, see Charles Robinson, *History of the Mansions*, 293. Only married sisters were allowed to be present at childbirth. Crawford, *Blood*, 67. For a contemporary account written by a midwife, see Sharp, *Midwives Book*. For more on midwives' control of the delivery room, see L. Cody, *Birthing the Nation*, 34–36.

52. Sowerby, *Ladies Dispensatory*, 164, 157, 81; Pollock, "Embarking on a Rough Passage," 52.

53. Pechey, *General Treatise*, 126; K. Brown, *Foul Bodies*, 88. On the atmosphere in the birthing room, see Cressy, *Birth, Marriage, and Death*, 53–54.

54. Barret, *Companion for Midwives*, 8. Similar descriptions can be found in Pechey, *Compleat Midwife's Practice*, 109; Anonymous, *English Midwife Enlarged*, 36; Sermon, *Ladies Companion*, 94–95; and Wolveridge, *Speculum Matricis*, 27. See also C. Wilson, "Ceremony of Childbirth," 74, for the variety of birthing techniques.

55. Cressy, *Birth, Marriage, and Death*, 61–62, 80–81.

56. For elite women who "did not bother with breastfeeding at all," see L. Cody, *Birthing the Nation*, 37. On the widespread nature of wet-nursing in seventeenth-century England, see Perry, "Colonizing the Breast," 218; and Fildes, *Breasts, Bottles, and Babies*, 288–92. On pressure put on new English mothers to breastfeed, see Cressy, *Birth, Marriage, and Death*, 87–88. Wet nurses were employed for at least the first day or two because colostrum was viewed as indigestible and possibly harmful to newborns.

57. L. Cody, *Birthing the Nation*, 37, 39; K. Brown, *Foul Bodies*, 17; Cressy, "Purification," 140; Cressy, *Birth, Marriage, and Death*, 83, 84, 197–229.

58. TNA, PROB 11/370/288, proved 4 July 1682; Cressy, *Birth, Marriage, and Death*, 51.

59. Bodleian Library, C/WIN/BAR 1–4, Inventories of Rendezvous Plantation and Garden, October 1705; Cressy, *Birth, Marriage, and Death*, 52.

60. Paugh, *Politics of Reproduction*, 96–97.

61. Sloane, *Voyage*, 1:cxlvii.

62. Sharp, *Midwives Book*.

63. Turner, *Contested Bodies*, 140–41; Cressy, *Birth, Marriage, and Death*, 84–88. For more on the role of gossips, see L. Cody, *Birthing the Nation*, 36–39.

64. Gouge, *Of Domesticall Duties*, 506; L. Cody, *Birthing the Nation*, 33. See also Pollock, "Childbearing," 286–304.

65. Knight, "Mothering," 145.

66. J. Oliver, *Present for Teeming Women*, 41; Cressy, *Birth, Marriage, and Death*, 54.

67. Tryon, *Friendly Advice*, 103.

68. Whyte, "Mothering Solidarity," 69.

69. Turner, *Contested Bodies*, 243; Naylor, *Unsilencing*, 55–57.

70. Ligon, *True and Exact History*, 28.

71. Ligon, *True and Exact History*, 47–48.

72. Paton, "Maternal Struggles," 257.

73. Ligon, *True and Exact History*, 48.

74. Schwartz, *Birthing a Slave*, 51, 65, 150.

75. J. Morgan, *Laboring Women*, chap. 1.

76. Ligon, *True and Exact History*, 48.

77. Tryon, *Friendly Advice*, 103.

78. J. Morgan "*Partus Sequitur Ventrem*," 14. For the definitive analysis of enslaved motherhood in Barbados, see J. Morgan, *Laboring Women*, 113–23.

79. Kennedy, *Between Fitness and Death*, chap. 2. The classic work on slavery and family is Gutman, *Black Family*, which argues that despite the debilitating trauma of slavery, enslaved people were often able to form households with two parents. For the West Indies

context, see Higman, "Slave Family," 261–87. For scholarship that centers women's roles in family, see D. G. White, *Ar'n't I A Woman?*; J. Jones, *Labor of Love*; and J. Morgan, *Laboring Women*.

80. J. Morgan, *Laboring Women*, 111. See also Steckel, "Birth Weights," 172, 177. Fertility rates in the colonies were higher for both white *and* Black women than they were in England; see Klepp, "Revolutionary Bodies," 918.

81. J. Morgan, *"Partus Sequitur Ventrem,"* 12; J. Morgan, *Laboring Women*, 115; Amussen, *Caribbean Exchanges*, 83; Turner, *Contested Bodies*, 11. On the lack of sources on enslaved women's attitudes to motherhood, see Turner, *Contested Bodies*, 190.

82. Fuentes discusses the urban enslaved auction scene in Barbados in *Dispossessed Lives*, 26–27. For the conflicting emotions generated by mothering in slavery, see J. Morgan, *Laboring Women*, 122 and Turner, *Contested Bodies*, 190. Roth notes the tension through which enslaved women might simultaneously desire to mother and also not to conceive in "From Free Womb," 274.

83. Camp argues that motherhood could bring joy and camaraderie among peers, in *Closer to Freedom*. See also West and Shearer, "Fertility Control," 1007–9. On the challenges for African mothers birthing creole children, see J. Morgan, *Laboring Women*, 119–21; and Turner, *Contested Bodies*, 190.

84. Bodleian Library, C/WIN/BAR 1–4, Inventories of Rendezvous Plantation and Garden, October 1705, Staplegrove Plantation, October 1705; BDA, RB3/26, fols. 397–401, 3 February 1714.

85. J. Morgan, *Laboring Women*, 123; TNA, C6/277/67 *Knights v. Atkins*, Bill and Answer, John Knights's Bill, 6 February 1685; John Peers's answer, 2 June 1686.

86. Prince, *History of Mary Prince*, 9. See also J. Morgan, *Laboring Women*, 122–23; Turner, *Contested Bodies*, 236–43; Glymph, *Out of the House of Bondage*, 26–30; and Jones-Rogers, *They Were Her Property*, 7–13.

87. Knight, "Mothering," 150.

88. On ideas about mixed-race children and their propensity for skilled domestic work, see Turner, *Contested Bodies*, 233–34. On children of domestics being schooled in the same work that their parents performed, see Dunn, *Tale of Two Plantations*, 187–88. The young children of enslaved field workers also began work early. See Ligon, *True and Exact History*, 110.

89. Turner, *Contested Bodes*, 121; Perry, "Colonizing the Breast," 219; Fildes, *Wet Nursing*, 99. Although talking about enslaved Tartar women in Barcelona in the fourteenth century, Winer notes how "masters actively profited from the byproduct of the sexual exploitation of their slaves: breastmilk"; see "Enslaved Wet Nurse," 305.

90. Roesslin, *Birth of Mankind*, 157.

91. Perry, "Colonizing the Breast," 219.

92. Machado is talking about Brazil, but the stereotype appears to have pervaded the Caribbean too; see "Between Two Beneditos," 321. Turner notes how racist ideas about enslaved wet nurses changed over time in Jamaica, in *Contested Bodies*, 121–23.

93. J. Morgan, *Laboring Women*, chap. 1.

94. Sloane, *Voyage*, cxlviii.

95. Schwartz, *Birthing a Slave*, 94–95. Knight discusses the possibility of white women in the US South timing births to match those of enslaved women, who could then act as wet nurses for white children, in "Mistresses," 994.

96. For "delegated mothering," see Knott, "Theorizing and Historicizing Mothering's Many Labours," 11. See also Machado, "Between Two Beneditos," 323; and West and Shearer, "Fertility Control," 1015.

97. West and Shearer, "Fertility Control," 1013; Handler and Corruccini, "Weaning," 115. On the "tension and negotiation" brought on by wet nurses' own children, see Machado, "Between Two Beneditos," 324. On "othermothering," see Collins, *Black Feminist*, 131–32. On cross-feeding, see Whyte, "Mothering Solidarity," 69.

98. Turner, *Contested Bodies*, 125; West and Knight, "Mothers' Milk," 41; Glymph, *Out of the House of Bondage*, 139; Jones-Rogers, *They Were Her Property*, chap. 5. For the Brazilian comparison, see Cowling, *Conceiving Freedom*, 86–87. See also Cowling, Machado, West, and Paton, "Mothering Slaves."

99. Machado, "Between Two Beneditos," 330–31. For more on the plantation dynamics of child care, see Paton, "Driveress."

100. TNA, C24/1211 *Peers v. Chaplin, Hilary*, 1698–99, box 1, bundle unnumbered, Deposition of John Peers II, Inner Temple, London, 20 February 1698, response to query 1. Knott discusses how "rarely was a single maternal caregiver the historical norm." In many ways Ann was performing "delegated mothering" for her sister; see "Theorizing and Historicizing Mothering's Many Labours," 9.

101. Glymph, *Out of the House of Bondage*; Knight, "Mistresses," 991–92, 996–97.

102. Martha Jefferson and Sally Hemings were half sisters. Gordon-Reed discusses contemporary reports of their resemblance in *Hemingses*, 284–85.

103. Berry, *Price*, 36–41; Jones-Rogers, *They Were Her Property*, 16–17.

CHAPTER 3

1. For the baptisms of Hester's Elizabeth I and Elizabeth II, see BNA, RL1/17, Christ Church Parish Baptism Registers, p. 76, March 1669; p. 97, 10 March 1672. For their deaths, see "Elizabeth Peers," Barbados, Church Records, 1637–1849, ancestry.com, www.ancestry.com/search/collections/9788. For the baptisms of Frances's first two children, Elizabeth III and Frances, see BNA, RL1/17, Christ Church Parish Baptism Registers, p. 121, 18 December 1682; p. 124, 16 January 1684. For Ann's baptism, see BNA, RL1/17, Christ Church Parish Baptism Registers, p. 126. For Frances's burial, see "Frances Peers," Barbados, Church Records, 1637–1849, ancestry.com, www.ancestry.com/search/collections/9788. See also Langford, *Monumental Inscriptions*, 7.

2. Frances's mother, Mary Atkins (née Howard), died on 9 April 1660. Her burial is memorialized in a monument inside St. Ethelburga's Church, Great Givendale, Yorkshire. Frances was born on 20 March 1660.

3. Dunn, *Sugar and Slaves*, 314–15, 330–32; Turner, *Contested Bodies*, chap. 5, esp. 172–73.

4. Beasley, *Christian Ritual*, 4–5; Gragg, *Englishmen Transplanted*, chap. 4; Seeman, *Death in the New World*, 43.

5. Patterson, *Slavery and Social Death*, 5. See also Smallwood, *Saltwater Slavery*; Turner, *Contested Bodies*; and Kennedy, *Between Fitness and Death*, chap. 2. Antigua (1644) and Virginia (1691) both passed laws on interracial sex, and Virginia famously passed the *partus sequitur ventrem* law in 1662. See Shaw, *Everyday Life*, 35–37; and J. Morgan, *Reckoning with Slavery*, 3–6. On marriage as connoting inclusion and exclusion, see McDougall and Pearsall, "Introduction," 509; Stoler, *Carnal Knowledge*. In French colonies the *Code Noir* made provision for enslaved women and men to marry. It also, in theory at least, allowed white men to marry enslaved women. Similar practices pervaded the Spanish Caribbean. Baptism into the Catholic faith was common for enslaved and free people of color in both the French and the Spanish worlds.

6. J. Morgan, *Reckoning with Slavery*, 1.

7. Young, *Rituals*; Berry, *Price*, 61–63; Berry, "Soul Values."

8. C. Palmer, "From Africa to the Americas," 224. Tracing connections between ceremonies that took place on the eastern and western sides of the Atlantic Ocean is fraught. Not only are there many fewer sources that record the birth, marriage, and death celebrations and commemorations of those enslaved in Barbados, but none that have survived provide the direct perspective of African or African-descended people. This fact stands in stark contrast to the voluminous parish registers that scrupulously record the many births, marriages, and deaths of English people in Barbados.

9. Stoler, "Intimidations," 4; Jones, "Mapping," 18; Naylor, *Unsilencing*, 43–44.

10. Glasson, *Mastering Christianity*, 18; Gragg, *Englishmen Transplanted*, 70–72; Gerbner, *Christian Slavery*, 36.

11. Thomas Waldruck to James Petiver, 12 November 1710; reprinted in *Journal of the Barbados Museum and Historical Society* 15 (1947): 27–51; Gerbner, *Christian Slavery*, 36.

12. Gerbner, "Ultimate Sin," 59–61, 65–68; Goetz, *Baptism of Early Virginia*, 98. For the New England comparison, see Kopelson, *Faithful Bodies*, 103–4 and chap. 4, esp. 121–24. Enslaved people in Spanish settings often used conversion to argue for their release from slavery. See, for example, H. Bennett, *Africans in Colonial Mexico*; and K. Block, *Ordinary Lives*, part 1.

13. The Christ Church Baptism Registers for the last half of the seventeenth century can be found at BNA, RL1/17. The records begin in 1637; the first marked person of color appears in 1651. Gerbner has also examined these records, although she includes the years 1650–1725 in her analysis, in *Christian Slavery*, 76–79.

14. BNA, RL1/17, Christ Church Parish Baptism Registers, p. 91; BNA, RL1/17, Christ Church Parish Baptism Registers, p. 123. In 1678 a similar series of baptisms occurred on 24 December: "Susanna a Negro woman of John Osburn"; "William son of the above written Susanna"; and "Martha a mulatto daughter of John Osburn and Susanna." BNA, RL1/17, Christ Church Parish Baptism Registers, p. 111. For "baptism parties," see Barnett-Woods, "Bequeathed," 477.

15. Gerbner, *Christian Slavery*, 76; Beasley, *Christian Ritual*, 70, 77.

16. Gerbner, "Ultimate Sin," 66–70. For more on Quakers and their complicated relationship with enslaved people in this period, see Gerber, *Christian Slavery*, chap. 3; and K. Block, *Ordinary Lives*, part 4. See also Beasley, *Christian Ritual*, 66–67.

17. Ligon, *True and Exact History*, 50. Other scholars who have given Ligon's work a similar read include Goetz, *Baptism of Early Virginia*, 97; Beasley, *Christian Ritual*, 80; and Gerbner, "Ultimate Sin," 59–60.

18. Gerbner, *Christian Slavery*, 2.

19. TNA, CO31/1, fol. 366, Assembly to Governor Dutton, 30 March 1681; Gerbner, "Ultimate Sin," 69–70. The quotation comes from Sainsbury and Fortescue, *Calendar of State Papers, Colonial Series*, 611, cited in Gerbner, "Ultimate Sin," 70.

20. For Dunn, baptism in the Church of England was one way for a planter to express his "love and responsibility towards his illicit black family"; see *Sugar and Slaves*, 254.

21. Beasley, *Christian Ritual*, 68–69, 74. Thomas Lewis donated the font to the church in 1654. On adult baptism in church, see Gerbner, *Christian Slavery*, 37.

22. Shaw, *Everyday Life*, 110–14; Beckles, *Centering Women*, 23. For a similar trend in Virginia, see J. Morgan, "*Partus Sequitur Ventrem*," 9; and Goetz, *Baptism of Early Virginia*, 100–101. Sweet notes that in the Portuguese Atlantic World, "acculturated slaves, especially women and children, were the most likely to benefit from institutional mechanisms like manumission"; see *Domingo Álvares*, 94. J. Johnson explains how in the French world, enslaved women "secured manumission for themselves despite the slave-owning and non-slaveholding whites around them." *Wicked Flesh*, 133.

23. On the ways that enslavers used religion to exert control on the women and men they owned, see Gerbner, *Christian Slavery*, 76–80.

24. Ball, Seijas, and Snyder, "Introduction," 8; Berry, "Soul Values."

25. Beasley, *Christian Ritual*, 74. In New England children were baptized in church. Whiting, "Power," 597.

26. Bosman, *New and Accurate Description*, 444.

27. Jones, *German Sources*, 218.

28. Marees, *Description*, 69–70; Jones, *German Sources*, 88. See also Sweet, *Recreating Africa*, 186; and V. Brown, *Reaper's Garden*, 65–66.

29. Young, *Rituals*, chap. 3; Sweet, *Recreating Africa*, 104–5; Sweet, *Domingo Álvares*, 13–14; Law, *Slave Coast*, 13, 21–25. Sweet discusses the similarities between *bolsas de Mandinga* and what Europeans called "fetishes," in *Recreating Africa*, 181–83; and Sweet, *Domingo Álvares*, 128–29.

30. Marees, *Description*, 69. See also Sweet, *Domingo Álvares*, 76; and Seeman, *Death in the New World*, 18.

31. J. Morgan, *Laboring Women*, 67.

32. Bosman, *New and Accurate Description*, 209.

33. Hair, Jones, and Law, *Barbot on Guinea*, 2:506 (notes on origins of the names can be found on 2:510n22); Naylor, *Unsilencing*, 71–73.

34. See, for example, the 1714 slave registers for Rendezvous, which note the prevalence of names connected to West Africa, even for creole children born in Barbados to parents with ostensibly European names. BNA, RB3/26, fol. 397–401. On multiple names, see Price and Price, "Saramaka Onomastics," 342, 349–52. C. Cody suggests that slaves might use African names among themselves but that these would not appear on slave inventories, in "There Was No 'Absolom,'" 573. Handler and Jacoby concur; see "Slave Names," 689–90. See also Whiting, "Power," 599–600.

35. Amussen, *Ordered Society*, 1. See also K. Brown, *Good Wives*, 15–17; and J. Morgan, "*Partus Sequitur Ventrem*," 12.

36. Handler and Jacoby, "Slave Names," 707. Older work indicates a West African provenance, noting that Mingo might have been of Hausa or Wolof origins; see Puckett, "Names," 158–74, esp. 165. See also Whiting, "Power," 600.

37. Dunn, *Sugar and Slaves*, 232–33. The only source to raise some ambiguity about Susannah's origins is the 1683 baptism record of her children, wherein she is marked as "mulatto," a designation that was commonly attributed to mixed-race, island-born enslaved people but that does not preclude the possibility that she was born in Africa to a Portuguese father. Her own 1670 baptism record defines her as a "negro," suggesting African parents. BNA, RL1/17, p. 123, 13 August 1683; RL1/17, p. 91, 8 June 1670. Barbot notes that among the population in Elmina in present-day Ghana there were many "mulattoes" who had been "born from the union of Portuguese men with indigenous black women"; see Hair, Jones, and Law, *Barbot on Guinea*, 2:381. On naming patterns, see J. Thornton, "Central African Names," 736–37, 741. See also Burnard, "Slave Naming Patterns," 336.

38. For Judith in the baptism records, see BNA, RL1/17, p. 91, 29 May 1670. On naming, see Handler and Jacoby, "Slave Names," 691, 694; quotation on 694. Price and Price note the emphasis on reputation and identity when naming, in "Saramaka Onomastics," 354. See also C. Cody, "There Was No 'Absolom,'" 573. Some scholars assert that patterns of naming can reflect African influences even when the names given to children were of European origin; see Gutman, *Black Family*, 186; and Price and Price, "Saramaka Onomastics." Higman claims it is too difficult to determine whether slaves chose their own names or were given them by enslavers, in "Terms for Kin," 61.

39. BNA, RL1/17, p. 91, 8 June 1670. For a similar example from New England, see Whiting, "Power," 595.

40. Clay, *Liturgical Services*, quotation on 219; Warren, *Sarum Missal*, 145–46; Cressy, *Birth, Marriage, and Death*, 339-40.

41. Cressy, *Birth, Marriage, and Death*, 350.

42. Anonymous, *Great Newes from the Barbadoes*, 7.

43. Ligon, *True and Exact History*, 38–39. See also Anonymous, *Great Newes from the Barbadoes*.

44. Rath, "African Music;" Ligon, *True and Exact History*, 105–6. See also Kupperman, *True and Exact History*, 1–3n246. Sloane collected African instruments in Jamaica and included music from his visit to a sugar plantation transcribed by a "Mr. Baptiste" in his *Voyage*. To see the scores and to listen to modern interpretations of the music, see *Musical Passage*, by Laurent Dubois, David Garner, and Mary Caton Lingold, www.musicalpassage.org. The creators posit that "Mr. Baptiste" was a free man of color from Saint-Domingue.

45. Amussen, *Ordered Society*; McDougall and Pearsall, "Introduction," 510.

46. TNA, C6/277/67 *Knights v. Atkins*, Bill and Answer, John Knights's Bill, 6 February 1685; John Peers's answer, 2 June 1686. See also Benjamin's will, TNA, PROB 11/370/288, 4 July 1682.

47. C. Jones, *Engendering Whiteness*, 161–62, 165–68; Fuentes, *Dispossessed Lives*, 73–74, 87–88.

48. Weddings in the English colonies were usually conducted privately, but over time the excessive costs of marrying at home made such privilege the purview of the elite. By 1705 having a private wedding was four times as expensive as marrying in church. Beasley, *Christian Ritual*, 57–60; Gerbner, *Christian Slavery*, 36.

49. TNA, PROB 11/370/288, Will of Benjamin Knights.

50. Cressy, *Birth, Marriage, and Death*, 362.

51. Whistler, *Journal*, 145–47.

52. Servant women, like Dorothy, found their options limited, particularly if they were indentured: custom, if not statutory law, dictated that women could not marry until their contract was complete. K. Brown, *Good Wives*, 192–93.

53. Hair, Jones, and Law, *Barbot on Guinea*, 2:502.

54. Hunter calls these "committed conjugal relationships," in *Bound in Wedlock*, 7.

55. Sweet, "Defying Social Death," 251–72.

56. Ligon, *True and Exact History*, 47. "Brave" in this context connoted the positive and valuable qualities of the enslaved: *Oxford English Dictionary Online*, s.v. "brave, adj., n., and int.," www.oed.com. See also Bush, *Slave Women*, 124–25. Higman notes the significance of polygynous households in Jamaica and Trinidad in the nineteenth century, in "Slave Family," 275–79.

57. Burnard, *Mastery*, 232.

58. Bodleian Library, C/WIN/BAR 1–4, 17 October 1705; BNA, RB3/26, fols. 401–17, 3 February 1714; RB3/33, fols. 140–47, 2 April 1724.

59. Beasley, *Christian Ritual*, 74.

60. On whether conjugal relationships between enslaved men and women can be consensual when enslavers enforce "breeding," see Berry, "Swing the Sickle," 77–88. See also Foster, "Sexual Abuse," 124–44; and Foster, *Rethinking Rufus*. Nocke does not appear in the estate inventories for Rendezvous, but a "Judith Parry, past labour" is included on the October 1705 list. If this is the Judith from the 1670 baptism record, she would probably have been in her sixties. Bodleian Library, Codrington Plantation Records, C/WIN/BAR 1–4, 17 October 1705.

61. See, for example, Ligon, *True and Exact History*; Sloane, *Voyage*; and Taylor, *Second Part of the Historie*.

62. Sloane, *Voyage*, 1:lvi; Taylor, *Second Part of the Historie*, 542; Ligon, *True and Exact History*, 48.

63. The 4:1 ratio comes from St. Michael's Parish on Barbados between 1648 and 1694 and was calculated by Beasley, *Christian Ritual*, 110.

64. Seeman, *Death in the New World*, 39, 41.

65. Parish records for St. James in Barbados are not extant, so Benjamin's burial date remains unknown.

66. Seeman, *Death in the New World*, 41–42. Litten, *English Way*, 12; Gittings, *Death*, 114–15, 240; Cressy, *Birth, Marriage, and Death*, 433–35; Houlbrooke, *Death, Religion, and the Family*, 339–41.

67. Beasley, *Christian Ritual*, 119-20, 121–22, 125–27; Seeman, *Death in the New World*, 43; "Records of the Vestry," 100, 4 November 1665.

68. TNA, PROB 11/37/288, proved 4 July 1682. The one woman among the group was Frances's sister, Elizabeth Walrond, married to Thomas, a member of the politically powerful Walrond family. See also Cressy, *Birth, Marriage, and Death*, 438; and Houlbrooke, *Death, Religion, and the Family*, 297–98.

69. On the significance of "increase" as part of English understandings of the value of enslaved women, see J. Morgan, *Laboring Women*, 79–86.

70. TNA, C6/277/67 *Knights v. Atkins*, Bill and Answer, John Knights's Bill, 6 February 1685; John Peers's answer, 2 June 1686. I have been unable to locate a marriage record for John Peers and Frances Knights (née Atkins).

71. TNA, PROB 11/370/288, proved 4 July 1682.

72. Gunkel and Handler, "Swiss Medical Doctor," 5–6; E. Mitchell, "Morbid Crossings."

73. V. Brown, *Reaper's Garden*; V. Brown, "Eating the Dead;" Turner, "Nameless," 232–50; For more on the use of "deathways," see Seeman, *Death in the New World*, introduction.

74. Bodleian Library, Codrington Plantation Records, C/WIN/BAR 1–4, 17 October 1705.

75. Marees, *Description*, 69–70.

76. This practice traversed the Atlantic Ocean as V. Brown has shown in *Reaper's Garden*, 66–69.

77. Seeman, *Death in the New World*, 19. See also Bosman, *New and Accurate Description*, 448; Jones, *German Sources*, 123, 257; and Marees, *Description*, 180.

78. Jones, *German Sources*, 257.

79. Bosman, *New and Accurate Description*, 228.

80. Hair, Jones, and Law, *Barbot on Guinea*, 2:640.

81. Jones, *German Sources*, 42.

82. Seeman, *Death in the New World*, 21; Villault, *Relation*, 195; Bosman, *New and Accurate Description*, 156, 232; Jones, *German Sources*, 31, 42, 258; Jones, *Brandenburg Sources*, 88; Hair, Jones, and Law, *Barbot on Guinea*, 2:591.

83. Villault, *Relation*, 194–95.

84. Bosman, *New and Accurate Description*, 230.

85. Seeman, *Death in the New World*, 22.

86. Ligon, *True and Exact History*, 50–51.

87. Gunkel and Hander, "German Indentured Servant," 94.

88. Leslie, *New and Exact Account*, 323–24; see also V. Brown, *Reaper's Garden*, 132–35; Seeman, *Death in the New World*, 188.

89. Turner, "Nameless and Forgotten," 237–38.

90. Turner, "Nameless and Forgotten," 238.

91. It is possible that young children or infants were memorialized differently from adults. Lange and Handler, *Plantation Slavery*, 181.

92. Lange and Handler, *Plantation Slavery*, 175–76. Only eight enslaved people were buried in a Church of England ceremony before 1780, according to extant parish registers. By 1800 that number rose to twenty-five.

93. CSPC, 4 July 1676, Governor Sir Jonathan Atkins to the Lords and Trade of Plantations, 417–35.

94. Godwyn, *Negro and Indian's Advocate*, 135–37, quotation on 136, emphasis in original.

95. Ligon, *True and Exact History*, 50.

96. Taylor, *Second Part of the Historie*, 544.

97. Sloane, *Voyage*, 1:xlviii.

98. Lange and Handler, *Plantation Slavery*, 200.

99. Sloane, *Voyage*, 1:xlviii; Taylor, *Second Part of the Historie*, 544.

100. Taylor, *Second Part of the Historie*, 544.

101. V. Oliver, *Monumental Inscriptions*, 7.

102. Hester's Richard was also buried in this grave. His burial record can be found in St. Michael's Parish, 2 September 1713, "in the Chancell." See chapter 6 for his return to Barbados.

CHAPTER 4

1. Bridgetown was the busiest port in the English Americas in 1686. The level of traffic it received was surpassed only by that in London. Zahedieh, *Capital and the Colonies*, 144.

2. Jordan, *King's City*, 254–55; Ward, "Taming of the Thames," 55–75; Zahedieh, *Capital and the Colonies*, 167, 170.

3. "Family" in this period usually referred to children, wives, stepchildren, full-time servants, and others like governesses or tutors who made the household function. Cliffe, *World of the Country House*, 82. For more on the ways that English anti-Blackness developed in the early modern era through cultural productions, see K. Hall, *Things of Darkness*, esp. 14, 128–38, 211–12. On Elizabethan policy, see Shyllon, "Black Presence," 202; Habib, *Black Lives*, chap. 2. For a contrary view, see Weissbourd, "'Those in Their Possession,'" 1–19.

4. On Jonson's masque, see K. Hall, "'I Rather Would Wish'"; and K. Hall, *Things of Darkness*, 128–38. On trading companies, royals, and slavery, see Habib, *Black Lives*, 124–27; Pettigrew, *Freedom's Debt*; Fryer, *Staying Power*, 21; and Swingen, *Competing Visions*, 8 and chaps. 3, 4, and 5. Brewer examines the connections between the Restoration Stuarts and slavery in "Slavery, Sovereignty, and 'Inheritable Blood.'" See also Fryer, *Staying Power*, 29–30; Brewer, "Creating a Fashion"; and Molineux, *Faces of Perfect Ebony*, 5.

5. Shyllon, "Black Presence," 202. Molineux argues that "the black presence in Britain was both broader and more important to the development of metropolitan culture than a head count would necessarily suggest"; see *Faces of Perfect Ebony*, 7. Numerous scholars have commented on the use of collars on enslaved boys in London. See Fryer, *Staying Power*; S. Newman, *Freedom Seekers*; and Brewer, "Creating a Fashion."

6. Author's conversation with John Brown, church archivist, St. Leonard's Parish Church, Streatham, July 2014.

7. See, among others, Livesay, *Children of Uncertain Fortune*.

8. TNA, C24/1211, Deposition of Robert Chaplin, 20 February 1698; BNA, RB6/41, p. 328, 23 July 1690.

9. TNA, CO31/1, fol. 395, Barbados Council Minutes, 11–12 April 1686.

10. Zahedieh, *Capital and the Colonies*, 138–30, 142; R. Davis, *Rise of English Shipping*, 7, 298–99, 395; Kelley, *Voyage of the Slave Ship Hare*, 52.

11. TNA, C6/483/115 *Spendlove v. Chaplin*, 1693. On variations in costs, see Cressy, *Coming Over*, 193; and Zahedieh, *Capital and the Colonies*, 171.

12. Zahedieh, *Capital and the Colonies*, 140, 152; Rediker, *Slave Ship*, 124–27; Mossiker, *Pocahontas*, 216.

13. For the number of hogsheads expected to be shipped from Rendezvous to London in the years 1712–16, see TNA, C11/2286/12 *Peers v. Barwick*, Bill, 1719. On the routes taken, see Zahedieh, *Capital and the Colonies*, 144. Rediker discusses Equiano's experiences on the *Industrious Bee*, the ship that took him from Virginia to England, in *Slave Ship*, 125.

14. Vokins, *God's Mighty Power*, 70–71, 36–37. *See also,* Townsend, *Pocahontas*, 136–38; Mossiker, *Pocahontas*, 211–18; and Herbert, *Female Alliances*, 150.

15. Budd, *Good Order Established*, 24, as cited in Zahedieh, *Capital and the Colonies*. See also Townsend, *Pocahontas*, 137; and Rediker, *Slave Ship*, 126.

16. Barlow, *Barlow's Journal*, 339.

17. Zahedieh, *Capital and the Colonies*, 159–61; Linebaugh and Rediker, *Many-Headed Hydra*, 132, 150, 151–52; Christopher, *Slave Ship Sailors*, 56–57; R. Davis, *Rise of English Shipping*, 121.

18. Barlow, *Barlow's Journal*, 311–19, 324–28, quotations on 319; Zahedieh, *Capital and the Colonies*, 152, 161.

19. Zahedieh, *Capital and the Colonies*, 141, 161.

20. Barlow, *Barlow's Journal*, 338, 348–49.

21. Cressy, *Coming Over*, 196; Townsend, *Pocahontas*, 138. On the Downs, see Barlow, *Barlow's Journal*, 309, 311, 317, 326, 331, 340.

22. Fryer, *Staying Power*, chap. 3; Molineux, *Faces of Perfect Ebony*, 10; Christopher, *Slave Ship Sailors*, introduction; Linebaugh and Rediker, *Many Headed Hydra*, chap. 5; Foy, "Britain's Black Tars;" Picard, *Restoration London*, 179.

23. Townsend notes London's likely impact on Pocahontas seventy years earlier, in *Pocahontas*, 139. For an overview of London in this era, see Cockayne, *Hubbub*. On foul smells, see Cockayne, *Hubbub*, 210–14. See also Finlay and Shearer, "Population Growth," 38; and Field, *London, Londoners and the Great Fire*, 7.

24. Cockayne, *Hubbub*, chap. 5, esp. 121–12, 169–73, 181–83; Earle, *City Full of People*, 6; Picard, *Restoration London*, 15–16; Mulry, *Empire Transformed*; Harkness and Howard, "Introduction," 1; Beier, "Engine of Manufacture," 149.

25. The date of John's departure is unclear. He filed a Chancery Court case in May 1666. TNA, C10/79/77 *Peers v. Hawley*, 12 May 1666. Barrow witnessed John sign papers in London in May 1666. TNA, C24/1211 *Peers v. Chaplin*, Hilary, Deposition of Richard Barrow, 23 February 1698. See also Earle, *City Full of People*, 3–6, 10; Jordan, *King's City*, 439; and Zahedieh, *Capital and the Colonies*, 23–25.

26. TNA, C24/1211 *Peers v. Chaplin*, Hilary, Deposition of John Peers II, 20 February 1698.

27. Picard, *Restoration London*, 16; Cockayne, *Hubbub*, 169–70; Whyman, *Sociability and Power*, 100–102; Power, "Social Topography," 202.

28. Harding, "Cheapside," 78, 80, 84–84; Picard, *Restoration London*, 8.

29. Earle, *City Full of People*, 14; Cockayne, *Hubbub*, 85–105; Zahedieh, *Capital and the Colonies*, 26.

30. TNA, C6/478/3 *Spendlove v. Chaplin*, 1695, Bill.

31. Earle, *City Full of People*, 14; Field, *London, Londoners and the Great Fire*, 8; Ward, *London Spy*.

32. Magolotti, *Travels of Cosmo*; Cockayne, *Hubbub*, 157–62, 169–73.

33. Bendall, "Queen's Dressmakers;" Picard, *Restoration London*, 107–11.

34. Taylor, *Establishing Dress History*; Cockayne, *Hubbub*; K. Brown, *Foul Bodies*, 30–31.

35. For a strong articulation of this argument, see Habib, *Black Lives*, chap. 3.

36. Fryer, *Staying Power*, 9, 14, 20–21.

37. Pepys, *Diary of Samuel Pepys*, 9:510, 5 April 1669; Fryer, *Staying Power*, 21, 24; Molineux, *Faces of Perfect Ebony*, 31.

38. Fryer, *Staying Power*, 22–23; Shyllon, "Black Presence," 203–4.

39. Anonymous, *Character of a Town Misse*; K. Hall, *Things of Darkness*, 247. The "Town Misse" purported to be a middle-class woman but was, in this telling, a prostitute. The enslaved boy accompanying her underscored her attempt to present herself as a high-status person. Amussen, *Caribbean Exchanges*, 178, 193; Gerzina, *Black London*, 17. For more on the way the "writer's description reflects an actual social practice that in this case connects the commodification of white women in prostitution and blacks in slavery," see K. Hall, *Things of Darkness*, 240.

40. William III, who reigned from 1689 to 1702, supposedly commissioned a marble bust of an enslaved man who served him that included the collar and padlock around the man's neck; see Fryer, *Staying Power*, 22–23.

41. K. Hall, *Things of Darkness*, 247; Fryer, *Staying Power*, 32, 113–14. Molineux argues that the free-soil principle was able to persist despite the presence of enslaved people in England because of what she describes as "the legal uncertainty of black slavery" in the late seventeenth century; see *Faces of Perfect Ebony*, 12.

42. Trover is "an action at law to recover the value of personal property illegally converted by another to his own use" but not the recovery of the property itself; *Oxford English Dictionary Online*, s.v. "trover, n.," www.oed.com/. See also Fryer, *Staying Power*, 113; Gerzina, *Black London*, 22–24; and Chater, *Untold Histories*, 82–92.

43. Fryer, *Staying Power*, 25; Gerzina, *Black London*, 15–16; Molineux, *Faces of Perfect Ebony*, 23–24. Chakravarty notes that liveries were part of the clothing "given to members of livery companies . . . when they became freemen" and thus could also be evidence of "*release* from service"; see *Fictions of Consent*, 21.

44. *London Gazette*, issue 1996, 1–5 January 1685. Chakravarty suggests that blue coats were increasingly associated with service in the seventeenth century; see *Fictions of Consent*, 28–29.

45. *London Gazette*, issue 1338, 12–16 September 1678.

46. *Daily Courant*, 22 May 1703, r0671, Runaway Slaves in Britain database, www.runaways .gla.ac.uk.

47. Here I borrow S. Newman's phrasing from *Freedom Seekers*.

48. *London Gazette*, issue 2122, 18–22 March 1686.

49. *London Gazette*, issue 2309, 2–5 January 1688.

50. *London Gazette*, issue 2605, 27–30 October 1690.

51. *Post Man and the Historical Account*, 24 June 1704, r0674, Runaway Slaves in Britain database, www.runaways.gla.ac.uk.

52. See the 1708 act "to prohibit the Inhabitants of this Island from employing, their Negroes or other Slaves, in selling or bartering." I thank Stefanie Hunt-Kennedy for alerting me to the existence of this law, and for sharing the text with me. See also Hunt-Kennedy, *Between Fitness and Death*, 47.

53. At the Rijksmuseum in the Netherlands, collars long assumed to have been used for dogs are now understood to have been collars for enslaved pages. Daniel Boffey, "Rijksmuseum Slavery Exhibition Confronts Cruelty of Dutch Trade," *Guardian*, 18 May 2021, https://www.theguardian.com/world/2021/may/18/rijksmuseum-slavery-exhibition -confronts-cruelty-of-dutch-trade. See also S. Newman, *Freedom Seekers*, 120–22.

54. TNA, C6/478/3 *Spendlove v. Chaplin*, 1695, Bill; TNA, C6/483/115 *Spendlove v. Chaplin*, 1693, Estate Inventory.

55. Aubrey, *Natural History*, 1:199.

56. Aubrey, *Natural History*, 1:215–17.

57. TNA, C6/478/3 *Spendlove v. Chaplin*, 1695, Bill; Cliffe, *World of the Country House*, 11.

58. Amussen, *Caribbean Exchanges*, 217–25; Cliffe, *World of the Country House*, 87. See also Browning, Geiter, and Speck, *Memoirs of Sir John Reresby*, 108.

59. Markham, *English Housewife*, 1–2; Meldrum, *Domestic Service*, 41–42, 56, 84. On the increasing fashion for foreign servants in the eighteenth century, see Richardson, *Household Servants*, 66–67.

60. TNA, C6/483/115 *Spendlove v. Chaplin*, 1693. Herbert uses estate inventories to explore "the difficult material conditions of women's domestic labor"; see *Female Alliances*, 79–84, quotation on 79.

61. Richardson differentiates between cooks and "cook-maid[s]," in *Household Servants*, 83–84. On kitchen arrangements, see Crowley, *Invention of Comfort*. For camaraderie among domestic workers, see Herbert, *Female Alliances*, 82.

62. TNA, C6/483/115 *Spendlove v. Chaplin*, 1693, Estate Inventory.

63. Fryer, *Staying Power*, 72; Amussen, *Caribbean Exchanges*, 192, 217. "Elizabeth Picket, a black, servant to Mr. Robert Chaplin," was laid to rest in the churchyard of St. Swithin's Church in London on 25 June 1683. See "Elizabeth Pickett," London, England, Church of England Baptisms, Marriages and Burials, 1538–1812, ancestry.com, www.ancestry.com /search/collections/1624/.

64. Kottick, *History of the Harpsicord*; O'Brien, *Ruckers*. Vermeer produced a series of paintings of women playing virginals.

65. TNA, C24/1187, fol. 96, Deposition of Richard Barrow of Covent Garden, 29 January 1695. On dressing male servants as gentlemen, see Meldrum, *Domestic Service*, 56–57; and Chakravarty, *Fictions of Consent*, 40. For liveries as markers of servitude but also of "social affiliation," see Chakravarty, *Fictions of Consent*, 16–17.

66. TNA, C6/483/115 *Spendlove v. Chaplin*, 1693. For more on Black servants in English households, see Richardson, *Household Servants*, 67–69. On bed sharing, see Herbert, *Female Alliances*, 83. On inventories indicating servant hierarchy, see Vickery, "Englishman's

Home,", 147–73. On the relative luxury of servants' quarters as a marker of status, see Richardson, *Household Servants*, 100–101.

67. On sex-segregated servant quarters and servants' lack of privacy, see Richardson, *Household Servants*, 97–98. On masters assuming access to female servants' bodies, see Reinke-Williams, *Women, Work*, 77. See also Meldrum, *Domestic Service*.

68. TNA, C6/483/115 *Spendlove v. Chaplin*, 1693, Estate Inventory; Cliffe, *World of the Country House*, 28–30, 42–45.

69. On the reduction of domestics, see Cliffe, *World of the Country House*, 82–83. On the variety and coordination of service, see Herbert, *Female Alliances*, 78.

70. Mirror glass was very expensive; see Picard, *Restoration London*, 45.

71. Higford, *Institutions or Advice*, 77–78; Cliffe, *World of the Country House*, 160–61.

72. TNA, C6/483/115 *Spendlove v. Chaplin*, 1693, Estate Inventory.

73. Tryon, *Treatise of Cleanness*, 6. Meldrum, *Domestic Service*; Richardson, *Household Servants*.

74. Meldrum, *Domestic Service*, 147–48; Cliffe, *World of the Country House*, 35; K. Brown, *Foul Bodies*, 26–28, 110.

75. TNA, C6/483/115 *Spendlove v. Chaplin*, 1693, Estate Inventory; K. Brown, *Foul Bodies*, 30–31.

76. TNA, C6/483/115 *Spendlove v. Chaplin*, 1693, Estate Inventory. On costs of upholstery, see P. Thornton, *Seventeenth-Century Interior Decoration*; and Picard, *Restoration London*, 41–45.

77. C6/478/3 *Spendlove v. Chaplin*, 1695, Bill; TNA, C6/483/115 *Spendlove v. Chaplin*, 1693, Estate Inventory. Whyman, *Sociability and Power*, 100; Meldrum, *Domestic Service*, 174–75. On the average costs of coaches and horses, see Cliffe, *World of the Country House*, 124–25.

78. TNA, C6/478/3 *Spendlove v. Chaplin*, 1695, Bill; Meldrum, *Domestic Service*; Cliffe, *World of the Country House*, 126–28.

79. TNA, C6/483/115 *Spendlove v. Chaplin*, 1693, Estate Inventory; Cliffe, *World of the Country House*, 36, 59.

80. TNA, C6/483/115 *Spendlove v. Chaplin*, 1693, Estate Inventory. See also Cliffe, *World of the Country House*, 57.

CHAPTER 5

1. Leong, *Recipes and Everyday Knowledge*. On Streatham's springs, see Aubrey, *Natural History* 1:215–17.

2. Information from the estate inventory has been used to describe the John's bedchamber. For details, see TNA, C6/483/115 *Spendlove v. Chaplin*, 1693, Estate Inventory. Cane chairs became very popular in London among elites during the Restoration. Dewing, "Cane Chairs," 53–82. On sickness and nursing, see Beier, "In Sickness and in Health," 101–28.

3. TNA, C8/438/47 *Spendlove v. Chaplin*, Bill and Answer, 3 December 1692; C6/486/115 *Spendlove v. Chaplin*, Answer and Two Schedules, 17 May 1693; C9/261/46 *Spendlove v.*

Chaplin, Bill and Answer, 21 November 1694; C6/478/3 *Spendlove v. Chaplin*, Answer, 10 April 1695.

4. TNA, C24/1187, fol. 96, *Spendlove v. Chaplin*, Deposition of Richard Guy, 29 January 1696; Deposition of Richard Howell, 29 January 1696; Deposition of Richard Barrow, 5 February 1696.

5. Elizabeth's use of the courts is reminiscent of that of Elizabeth Keye, who used a similar venue in 1640s Virginia to assert her right to freedom. There are significant differences in these cases: Keye argued her right to freedom following the end of her indenture and advocated for the free status of her daughter; Elizabeth Ashcroft was not arguing the point of freedom explicitly, but she also reckoned with the questions of race and kinship, and her status as a free woman of color who bore children by a white man is similar to that which Keye also confronted. See J. Morgan, *Reckoning with Slavery*, 1–4.

6. For more on the politics of freedom, see Snyder, "Trafficking," 217.

7. J. Morgan, *Reckoning with Slavery*, 4, 208–11; Ball, Seijas, and Snyder, "Introduction," 14–15; J. Johnson, *Wicked Flesh*, 2–3; Marquez, "Witnesses"; Browne, Lindsay, and Sweet, "Rebecca's Ordeal." On enslaved people understanding their monetary value but also their *soul* value, see Berry, *Price*, 6–8, 61–66. Fuentes points out that Rachel Pringle Polgreen, a free(d) woman of color in late eighteenth-century Barbados, also placed a large amount of value on property; see *Dispossessed Lives*, 48.

8. Hasted, "Parishes: Speldhurst," 275–300.

9. Rowzee, *Queens Wells*, 40–45.

10. Madan, *Phylosophical and Medicinal Essay*, 2–3.

11. TNA, C24/1187, fol. 96, *Spendlove v. Chaplin*, Deposition of Richard Barrow, 29 January 1695.

12. TNA, C6/478/3 *Spendlove v. Chaplin*, Bill, 10 April 1695; TNA, C9/261/46 *Spendlove v. Chaplin*, Answer, 21 November 1694. "Five Ways to Compute the Relative Value of a UK Pound Amount, 1270 to Present," MeasuringWorth, 2021, www.measuringworth.com/ukcompare/. The National Archives Currency Converter, 1270–2017, places the worth of John's debt at £26.4 million in 2017 value, www.nationalarchives.gov.uk/currency-converter/#currency-result.

13. Key, "Gregory, Sir William (1625–1696)." Sir William was distantly related to Robert Chaplin and John Peers by marriage. His wife was Katherine Tomkyns, great-aunt to Robert's wife, Ann, and John's first wife, Hester.

14. TNA, C24/1187, fol. 96, *Spendlove v. Chaplin*, Deposition of Richard Barrow, 29 January 1695.

15. TNA, C24/1187, fol. 96, *Spendlove v. Chaplin*, Deposition of Richard Barrow, 29 January 1695.

16. TNA, C8/438/47 *Spendlove v. Chaplin*, Bill and Answer, 3 December 1692, Chaplin's answer.

17. Amussen, *Ordered Society*; Erickson, *Women and Property*. Elizabeth Seward (who ran a boarding school in Kensington with her husband) was the only woman deposed in a Peers Chancery Court case. In May 1702 she was asked about her knowledge of John's daughters' schooling. TNA, C24/1240, unnumbered depositions. At least twenty-two individuals were deposed over three separate Peers family cases.

18. It is possible that John altered his wishes based on his current circumstances, including as a result of influence from the women. See Morales, *Happy Dreams of Liberty*. For the New England comparison, see Whiting, "Race," 438.

19. J. Morgan, *Reckoning with Slavery*, 15–17, chaps. 4 and 5. On explicit manumission in Barbados wills, see Inniss, "Freed Women and Unequal Inheritance," 133–36.

20. TNA, C6/478/3 *Spendlove v. Chaplin*, Bill, 10 April 1695.

21. BDA, RB 6/41, p. 328. Elizabeth Hill, the governess, was also a co-plaintiff in the case against Chaplin. For "her paines" and "in toaken of my love," John left Hill £40 per annum.

22. BDA, RB 6/41, p. 328.

23. TNA, C6/478/3 *Spendlove v. Chaplin*, Bill, 10 April 1695; TNA, C8/438/47 *Spendlove v. Chaplin*, Bill and Answer, 3 December 1692.

24. TNA, C24/1187, fol. 96, *Spendlove v. Chaplin*, Deposition of Richard Barrow, 29 January 1695.

25. TNA, C9/261/46 *Spendlove v. Chaplin*, 21 November 1694, Chaplin's answer.

26. According to the women's account, Robert had the "Sheriffe of Surrey" take an inventory of the Streatham estate on 14 May 1689, and the women were evicted shortly thereafter. See TNA, C6/428/3 *Spendlove v. Chaplin*, Bill, 10 April 1695; and TNA, C6/483/115 *Spendlove v. Chaplin*, 1693. TNA, C8/438/47 *Spendlove v. Chaplin*, Bill and Answer, 3 December 1692, Chaplin's answer.

27. On the numbers of women bringing suits in Chancery Court, see Horwitz, *Chancery Equity Records*, 36. See also Hunt, "Wives," 110. Hunt finds that by the early eighteenth century, suits could be brought by those with little money if they claimed in forma pauperis status; see "Wives," 112. For a thorough description of Chancery Court proceedings, see Horwitz, *Chancery Equity Records*.

28. Horwitz, *Chancery Equity Records*, 11; TNA, C24/1211 unnumbered folder, *Chaplin v. Peers*, Deposition of Ralph Hutchinson, 24 February 1698; Deposition of John Peers, 20 February 1698; Deposition of John Thayle, 24 February 1698. For London geography, see Morgan, *Morgan's Map of the Whole of London in 1682*.

29. Horwitz notes that in theory defendants had eight days to produce an answer but that this rule was not enforced and it was not unusual for cases to lie dormant for two or three years. In addition to Bills and Answers witnesses were deposed and evidence, where applicable, collected. In Elizabeth and Dorothy's case, seven different witness depositions were taken; in a later case between Robert and John's oldest son, fifteen men gave sworn testimonies. Answering the same set of questions, witnesses shared what they knew under oath. For more on witness depositions, see Horwitz, *Chancery Equity Records*, 3–4, 18–19.

30. Horwitz, *Chancery Equity Records*, 25; Hunt, "Wives," 112.

31. TNA, C8/438/47 *Spendlove v. Chaplin*, Bill and Answer, 3 December 1692, Chaplin's answer.

32. TNA, C9/261/46 *Spendlove v. Chaplin*, Bill and Answer, 21 November 1694, Chaplin's answer.

33. Jordan, *King's City*, 439; Field, *London, Londoners and the Great Fire*, 31, 33; Lincoln, *London and the 17th Century*, 35–44. See also Chakravarty, *Fictions of Consent*, chap. 1.

34. TNA, C8/438/47 *Spendlove v. Chaplin*, Bill and Answer, 3 December 1692, Chaplin's answer; Horwitz, *Chancery Equity Records*, 14–15. Horwitz notes that the court could put pressure on defendants to produce an answer by either confiscating property or putting them in prison. See also Hunt, "Wives," 112.

35. K. Wilson, *Island Race*, 144–45; Walker, *Jamaica Ladies*, 10.

36. Hunt, "Wives," 113.

37. Southerne, *Oronooko*, act 1, scene 1. For more on the popularity of the play, see Gerzina, *Black London*, 7–8. For an excellent analysis of why Imoinda is white in Southerne's version, see Nussbaum, *Limits of the Human*, 161–72.

38. *Oronooko*, act 5, scene 1. For other examples of early moderns who transgressed supposed norms of gender or sexuality (or both), see Erauso, *Lieutenant Nun*; Velasco, *Lieutenant Nun*; and K. Brown, "'Changed into the Fashion of a Man.'"

39. A 1643 Barbados deed records John Spendlove as owner of Frenches plantation in St. George's Parish (next door to Christ Church). However, an estate with this name does not appear on either Richard Ligon's 1657 map or Richard Ford's 1674 map, indicating that Dorothy's family's financial stability might well have been fleeting. A second John Spenlowe married Laura Pickett in Christ Church in 1675; see "Laura Pickett," Barbados, Church Records, 1637–1849, ancestry.com, www.ancestry.com/search/collections/9788/. This marriage suggests that he and Dorothy were siblings, rather than father and daughter. He then appears in two deeds, first witnessing a 1679 real estate purchase in Jamaica by John Peers (BNA, RB3/11 fols. 109–11, 1679) and second witnessing a 1682 deal between John and his sugar boiler (RB3/12 fols. 163–65, 1682).

40. Dorothy's oldest daughter is listed at six years old in August 1683, placing her birth in 1677. BNA, RL1/17, p. 123, 13 August 1683. Hester was buried on 15 September 1678. TNA, CO1/44 no. 47 IV and IX.

41. Ward, *Trip to Jamaica*, 9–10.

42. K. Hall, "Reading What Isn't There"; K. Hall, *Things of Darkness*; Lynch, "Whatever Happened to Dinah the Black."

43. Bush, "White 'Ladies,'" 250; K. Brown *Good Wives*, 300; C. Jones, *Engendering Whiteness*, 5, 25-26. For an examination of discourses and ideologies of race based on complexions, see S. Block, *Colonial Complexions*. On cosmetics, see Picard, *Restoration London*, 124.

44. Bush, "White 'Ladies,'" 248.

45. Dunn, *Sugar and Slaves*, 285n31.

46. Anonymous, *Jamaica Lady*, 9. Not only was Holmesia described in racial terms that marked her as not white, but her perceived dishonesty also made her an untrustworthy woman. Eventually, it is revealed that her mother was either English or Irish, and her father a mixed-race sailor whom her mother encountered on a voyage to Jamaica in the late seventeenth century. This reveal serves to affirm the narrator's (and the audience's) prejudice toward Holmesia: her African heritage dictated her uncouth behavior from the very beginning. The authorship is sometimes attributed to William Pittis, a Tory political writer. Englishmen and Englishwomen in eighteenth-century Jamaica commented disparagingly about white creole women's accents; see Nugent, *Lady Nugent's Jamaica Journal*, 9; and Long, *History of Jamaica*, 278–79.

47. Uffenbach, *London in 1710*, 88. While "moor" could be used to describe Muslim North Africans in the early modern era, it was a more general term for people of African descent, including sub-Saharan Africans. Habib, *Black Lives*, 13. Here, Uffenbach was clearly referring to Black women.

48. Taylor, *Establishing Dress History*; K. Brown, *Foul Bodies*, 148–49.

49. TNA, C9/261/46 *Spendlove v. Chaplin*, Answer, 21 November 1694.

50. TNA, C6/428/3 *Spendlove v. Chaplin*, Bill, 10 April 1695.

51. Horwitz notes that between two-thirds and three-quarters of all cases never made it beyond the initial complaint, or the pleadings. Horwitz, *Chancery Equity Records*, 23–24. That depositions were taken in this case places it in the minority.

52. BDA, RB3/26 fols. 401–17, 3 February 1713/14.

53. Lynch, "Whatever Happened to Dinah the Black?," 258–80.

54. Fryer, *Staying Power*, 23–24.

55. Handler, *Unappropriated People*, 67–69. Scholarship on free people of color in Barbados tends to concentrate on the mid-eighteenth century forward. See Handler, *Unappropriated People*; Welch, *Slave Society in the City*; and M. Newton, *Children of Africa*; Fuentes, *Dispossessed Lives*, chap. 2.

56. TNA, ADM33/250, Pay Books for HMS *Montague*, 1704–6; TNA, ADM33/260, Pay Books for HMS *Montague*, 1706–7.

57. M. Newton, *Children of Africa*, 24, 41; Handler, *Unappropriated People*, 13; Shaw, *Everyday Life*, 111–14. Neither the 1680 census nor the 1715 assessment of Bridgetown's population counts free people of color. A 1692 law codified manumission for those who informed on anyone prepared "to commit or abet any insurrection or rebellion"; see Handler, *Unappropriated People*, 30.

58. BDA, RL/17, p. 122, 3 July 1683.

59. While Handler is probably right to suggest that there were very few free people of color in Barbados at any time in the seventeenth century, baptism entries reveal a concentration of this population in Bridgetown; see *Unappropriated People*, 14.

60. BDA, RL1/1, p. 378, 11 October 1688; BDA, RL1/1, p. 485, 25 June 1694; Welch, *Slave Society in the City*, xv, 47–48.

61. BNA, RL1/1, pp. 393, 406, 434, 485, 505, 529; BNA, RL1/2, p. 51; BNA, RL1/2, pp. 34, 67. See also M. Newton, *Children of Africa*, 38.

62. Welch, *Slave Society in the City*, 18–19; Handler, *Unappropriated People*, 53–54. Wheat discusses how formerly enslaved women in port cities in the Spanish Caribbean in the sixteenth century held these occupations, in *Atlantic Africa*, 146–56.

63. BNA, RB3/26 fol. 406, 3 February 1714.

64. BNA, RB3/26 fols. 401–17, 3 February 1713/14.

65. BNA, RB3/26 fols. 401–17, 3 February 1713/14; TNA, C11/2286/12 *Peers v. Barwick*, Bill, 1719. See also TNA, C11/741/28 *Peers v. Barwick*, Answer, 1719.

66. TNA, C11/741/28 *Peers v. Barwick*, Barwick Plea, November 1718.

67. In the same deed Samuel notes that the other living legatees are in England.

68. For both baptisms, see BNA, RL1/17, p. 91, 29 May 1670 and 8 June 1670.

69. TNA, C11/2286/12 *Peers v. Barwick*, Bill, 1719.

70. TNA, C11/741/28 *Peers v. Barwick*, Barwick Plea, November 1718.

71. TNA, C11/2286/12 *Peers v. Barwick*, Bill and Answer, 1719.

72. Scott has discussed the necessity of proximity to courts for freed people who wanted to assert their claims, in *Degrees of Freedom*.

73. Bodleian Library, C/WIN/BAR 1–4, Inventories of Rendezvous Plantation and Garden and Staple Grove Plantation, February and October 1705; Welch, *Slave Society in the City*, 18–19.

74. TNA, C11/2286/12 *Peers v. Barwick*, Bill and Answer, 1719.

75. Cliffe, *World of the Country House*, 11.

76. Glasson, "'Baptism,'" 279–318; Gerbner, *Christian Slavery*.

77. Berry, *Price*.

78. Dantas, "Anna Maria Lopes de Brito," 206.

CHAPTER 6

1. "Lothbury," in Thornbury, *Old and New London*, 1:513–15; Fryer, *Staying Power*, 72; Guasco, *Slaves and Englishmen*, 115–18. For more on opportunities open to Londoners, see Schwarz, *London*.

2. "Hester Peers," London, England, Church of England Baptisms, Marriages and Burials, 1538–1812, ancestry.com, www.ancestry.com/search/collections/1624/; TNA, PROB 11/512/116, 8 March 1704, proved 17 October 1709.

3. TNA, C9/383/1 *Peers v. Chaplin*, Hilary, Bill and Answer, January 1696.

4. TNA, C11/2286/12 *Peers v. Barwick*, Bill, 1719.

5. J. Morgan, *"Partus Sequitur Ventrem."* We could view the children's actions as their creation of what Marquez calls a "counterarchive," in "Witnesses," 253. For a Cuban example of formerly enslaved women trying to free their children, see Díaz and Fuentes, "African Women."

6. "Susanna Mingoe," in Tim Hitchcock, Robert Shoemaker, Sharon Howard, Jamie McLaughlin et al., *London Lives, 1690–1800* (www.londonlives.org, version 1.1, 24 April 2012). On the Huguenots in Spitalfields, see Page, "Industries: Silk-Weaving," in *History of the County of Middlesex: Volume 2*, 132–37, British History Online, www.british-history.ac.uk/.

7. Gowing, "Girls on Forms," 447–73. See also Birt, "Women, Guilds," 146–64. Bendall argues that not all women's skill sets and training are visible in guild records that emphasize male apprenticeships, in "Queen's Dressmakers."

8. TNA, C24/1187, fol. 96, *Spendlove v. Chaplin*, Deposition of James Maydwell, 29 January 1695; "Richard Ashcrofte," Apprentices and Freemen, 1400–1900, Records of London's Livery Companies Online, www.londonroll.org; "Edward Ashcroft," London Apprenticeship Abstracts, 1442–1850, findmypast.co.uk, https://search.findmypast.co.uk/search-world-records/london-apprenticeship-abstracts-1442-1850.

9. Dungworth, "Value of Historic Window Glass," 21–48; Ramsey, *Worshipful Company of Glass Sellers*; "John Ashcroft," London Apprenticeship Abstracts, 1442–1850, findmypast.co.uk, https://search.findmypast.co.uk/search-world-records/london-apprenticeship-abstracts-1442-1850.

10. D. Mitchell, *Goldsmiths, Silversmiths and Bankers*; TNA, C11/2466/32 *Tomlinson v. Ashcroft*, Bill, 1734; Answer, 1740.

11. Huang, *Franklin's Father Josiah*, 29; Rothenberg, "'Diligent Hand Maketh Rich,'" 219.

12. TNA, PROB 11/521/116, Will of Richard Mingo, 8 March 1704, proved 17 October 1709; TNA, C11/741/28 *Peers v. Barwick*, Plea and Answer, November 1718. See also Trahey, "Among Her Kinswomen," 268; J. Bennett and Froide, "Singular Past," 1–37, esp. 2. Huguenots arrived in Spitalfields to escape persecution following the 1685 Edict of Nantes creating a "little France" in the area; see Gwynn, *Huguenots*, 2:209–11, 251. According to Plummer there were so many Huguenot weavers in the eastern part of London that the Weavers' Company appointed a French-speaking clerk; see *London Weavers' Company*, 33.

13. Gwynn, *Huguenots*, 212, 234–36, 256.

14. TNA, C24/1211 *Peers v. Chaplin*, Hilary, Deposition of Ralph Hutchinson, 24 February 1698.

15. TNA, C24/1211 *Peers v. Chaplin*, Hilary, Deposition of John Thrayle, 24 February 1698.

16. Tomalin, *Pepys*, 16–17.

17. TNA, C24/1211 *Peers v. Chaplin*, Hilary, Deposition of John Ward, 23 February 1698; TNA, C6/483/115 *Spendlove v. Chaplin*, 1693, Estate Inventory.

18. Hecht, *Domestic Servant Class*, 119–21; Meldrum, *Domestic Service*, 56. For an excellent discussion of the role of liveries and hand-me-down clothing in marking race and class in early modern England, see Chakravarty, *Fictions of Consent*, 14–44.

19. Coleman, "Innovation," 417–29; Muldrew, "'Th'Ancient Distaff,'" 498–526, esp. 499–500, 503–4, 520; Styles, "Spinners and the Law," 145–70, esp. 148, 152–53.

20. Women outnumbered men in London by 1690. See Reinke-Williams, *Women, Work*, 7. On domestic labor in the metropole, see Earle, "Female Labour Market," 339–40; Amussen, *Caribbean Exchanges*, 219; and Hubbard, *City Women*. For the definitive work on unmarried women in early modern England, see Froide, *Never Married*. Froide notes that 54.5 percent of women in London were single at this time, in *Never Married*, 3, 16–17, 27–28, 32, 60. The 1718 case incorrectly accounted for Elizabeth's Susanna, who had married twice by 1718, first to Henry Tomlinson in 1695 and then to John Aldridge twenty years later; see TNA, C11/2286/12 *Peers v. Barwick*, 1719.

21. Richard first appears in the HMS *Montague* Pay Books in 1700–1702; see TNA, ADM33/212. On the supposed lack of racism in the Royal Navy, see Carretta, "Naval Records," 143–58, esp. 145. For an alternative view, see Foy, "Royal Navy's Employment."; and Foy, "Britain's Black Tars," 67, 72. For more on Royal Navy warships, see Rodger, *Command of the Ocean*. On HMS *Montague*, see Lavery, *Ship of the Line*, 167–68.

22. TNA, ADM 22/212, Pay Books for HMS *Montague*, 1700–1702; TNA, ADM 33/328, Muster Rolls for HMS *Montague*, 1702–4. On elite sponsors, see author's personal correspondence with Charles Foy, 31 January 2020. See also Chater, *Untold Histories*, 236–37.

23. Rodger, *Wooden World*, 24–25, 56, appendixes 1, 7. We know that Olaudah Equiano's enslavers encouraged his literacy and numeracy because it was helpful to them; see *Interesting Narrative*. On literacy and numeracy in early modern England, see Cressy, "Literacy," 141–50; and Earle, "Female Labour Market," 328–53, esp. 336.

24. The extant Pay Books for HMS *Montague* reveal that Richard netted £35, 15s, and 5d for the years 1704 and 1705, and £19, 10s, and 5d for the years 1706 and 1707. The difference in pay might be owing to his discharge in August 1707; see TNA, ADM 33/250, Pay Books for HMS *Montague*, 1704–6; and TNA, ADM 33/260, Pay Books for HMS *Montague*, 1706–7. For more on wages earned at sea, see Shaw, "In the Name of the Mother," 204n63.

25. TNA, ADM52/233, Ship's Log, HMS *Montague*, 1702–7; Smallwood, *Saltwater Slavery*. See also Pettigrew, *Freedom's Debt*.

26. Hubbard, "Sailors," 348–58.

27. TNA, PROB 11/521/116, 8 March 1704, proved 17 October 1709; Rodger, *Wooden World*, 53. Judith needed the means to prove the will. Probate fees (the cost of proving a will in court) in the seventeenth century came to around £1 15s; see Erickson, "Using Probate Accounts," 103–19, esp. 112. See also Marsh, "Attitudes to Will-Making," 158–75.

28. Her age is based on her Barbados baptism record.

29. "Elizabeth Ashcroft," Will no. 7, London, England, Church of England Baptisms, Marriages and Burials, 1538–1812, ancestry.com, www.ancestry.com/search/collections/1624/.

30. Walker, *Jamaica Ladies*, 170; Trahey, "Among Her Kinswoman," 265–66.

31. "Susanna Ashcroft," London, England, Church of England Baptisms, Marriages and Burials, 1538–1812, ancestry.com, www.ancestry.com/search/collections/1624/. Henry wrote his will on 23 April 1707, and it was proved three years later, on 14 April 1710. TNA, PROB 11/515/78. In it he leaves all his property to Susanna and also makes her his executor. He does not mention their children, but in Elizabeth Ashcroft's will she notes two grandchildren with the last name Tomlinson—Joseph and Elizabeth—and another with the last name Clark. TNA, PROB 11/634/66, 22 March 1722, proved 5 December 1729.

32. "Susanna Tomlinson," London, England, Clandestine Marriage and Baptism Registers, 1667–1754, www.ancestry.com/search/collections/5344/. Clandestine marriages were extremely common in the London suburbs in the seventeenth and early eighteenth centuries. See G. Newton, "Clandestine Marriage," 151. In 1718 the couple were living in Chiswick close to the Thames. For John's profession, see *Oxford English Dictionary Online*, s.v. "Higgler, n.," www.oed.com.

33. "Judith Mingoe," London, England, Church of England Baptisms, Marriages and Burials, 1538–1812, ancestry.com, www.ancestry.com/search/collections/1624/. Neither the court records nor the marriage register commented on Judith or Susanna Ashcroft's racial status, or that of their husbands. It is probable that Thomas Elliott, Henry Tomlinson, and John Aldridge were white, although given Henry's occupation as a mariner, and the low social status of all three men, it is possible that they were not. In any case, none of the men appear to have found their wives' African ancestry any bar to marriage. On the likelihood that Thomas was white, see Walvin, *Black and White*, 52. On courtship, see Hubbard, *City Women*, 63–64.

34. "Sofia Ashcroft," Westminster, London, England, Church of England Baptisms, Marriages and Burials, 1558–1812, ancestry.com, www.ancestry.com/search/collections/61865/.

35. See Berry and Foyster, "Childless Men," 158–83; Capp, *Ties That Bind*, 15–17. Peck, *Women of Fortune*, 49. On sibling relationships, see Capp, *Ties That Bind*, esp. chap. 4. On children sent to England from Jamaica for their educations in the eighteenth and nineteenth centuries, see Livesay, *Children of Uncertain Fortune*, 96–104, 374.

36. TNA, C24/1211 *Peers v. Chaplin, Hilary*, Deposition of John Thrayle, 24 February 1698; TNA, C24/1211 *Peers v. Chaplin, Hilary*, Deposition of Ralph Hutchinson, 24 February 1698.

37. Capp, *Ties That Bind*, 2; Livesay, *Children of Uncertain Fortune*, 213–15.

38. Tomalin, *Pepys*, 20; Capp, *Ties That Bind*, 14, 32; Fletcher, *Growing Up*, chaps. 11–13; Chakravarty, *Fictions of Consent*, chap. 2.

39. Benzaquén, "Educational Designs," 464–66; Capp, *Ties That Bind*, 79.

40. TNA, C24/1211 *Peers v. Chaplin, Hilary*, Deposition of John Peers, 20 February 1698. John's Inner Temple admission records can be found in the admissions database hosted on the Inner Temple website, www.archives.innertemple.org.uk; O'Day, *Professions*, 136, 141–43. Thirsk points out that men like John who had not been raised to think they would have to work hard at a profession often found it hard to dedicate themselves to making money; see "Younger Sons," 358–77.

41. O'Day, *Professions*, 129.

42. Burial marker in Shobdon Parish Church, Herefordshire, photograph in author's collection.

43. TNA, C9/383/1 *Peers v. Chaplin, Hilary*, Bill and Answer, 1695; TNA, C24/1240 *Peers v. Chaplin, Hilary*, Deposition of Elizabeth Seward, May 1702; Capp, *Ties That Bind*, 14; Fletcher, *Growing Up*, chaps. 15–17; Peck, *Women of Fortune*, 88–90.

44. Capp, *Ties That Bind*, 51–53; Peck, *Women of Fortune*, chap. 3.

45. "Ann Peers," Westminster, London, England, Church of England Baptisms, Marriages and Burials, 1558–1812, ancestry.com, www.ancestry.com/search/collections/61865/; TNA, C11/2286/12 *Peers v. Barwick*, 1719. For more on matches for love or affection in the seventeenth century, see Peck, *Women of Fortune*, 8, 13, 122.

46. TNA, C11/741/28 *Peers v. Barwick*, Barwick's Answer, November 1718. A search of the probate records held at the National Archives reveals dozens of wills for individuals named William Hall or Ann/e Hall in the eighteenth century, but none correlate to Ann Peers or her spouse. In 1758 Ann's sister, Frances Peers, made her last will and testament and did not mention her sister or her sister's husband.

47. TNA, C9/383/1 *Peers v. Chaplin, Hilary*, Bill and Answer, 1695.

48. "Richard Peers," London, England, Church of England Baptisms, Marriages and Burials, 1538–1812, ancestry.com, www.ancestry.com/search/collections/1624/.

49. TNA, C24/1211 *Peers v. Chaplin, Hilary*, Deposition of John Thrayle, 24 February 1698.

50. TNA, C24/1211 *Peers v. Chaplin, Hilary*, Deposition of Ralph Hutchinson, 24 February 1698.

51. TNA, C24/1211 *Peers v. Chaplin, Hilary*, Deposition of John Ruslin, 23 February 1698. Peck, *Women of Fortune*, discusses fears of clandestine marriage in this period, although she concentrates on wealthy girls and women being seduced by feckless men (123–24). In this

period it was not unusual for weddings to be quiet and relatively small affairs, as Samuel Pepys noted in his diary. Tomalin, *Pepys*, 51–52.

52. TNA, C24/1211 *Peers v. Chaplin*, Hilary, Deposition of Sir Edward Turnor, 25 February 1698.

53. Perhaps the early death of their mother and father made Richard feel responsibility toward his younger siblings. Capp, *Ties That Bind*, 7, 30, 32–33, 35.

54. TNA, C11/741/28 *Peers v. Barwick*, Barwick's Answer, November 1718.

55. TNA, C24/1211 *Peers v. Chaplin*, Hilary, Deposition of John Peers, 23 February 1698; Deposition of Sir Edward Turnor, 25 February 1698.

56. TNA, C24/1211 *Peers v. Chaplin*, Hilary, Deposition of John Peers, 23 February 1698.

57. TNA, PROB 11/480/42, proved 8 January 1705. He did not divide the remainder of the money equally: John was to receive "nine parts . . . of the said purchase money" while Thomas would receive one-tenth of this amount. A Chancery Court case from 1702 shows that John and Thomas joined forces to sue Robert Chaplin. They accused Chaplin of taking control of the house at Streatham, after which he "possessed himself of all the papers writings and accounts." The brothers suggested that Chaplin had done a deal with their older brother Richard for Rendezvous, and that they were owed money from Staple Grove; see TNA, C9/454/1 *Peers v. Chaplin*, Hilary, Bill only, 1702.

58. When Susanna Tomlinson (née Ashcroft) sued Robert Chaplin in 1699, Chaplin suggested that he had been paying out legacies to John's children up to December 1697; see TNA, C10/455/42 *Tomlinson v. Chaplin*, Answer, 19 May 1699.

59. BNA, RB6/36, fol. 5, written 9 September 1740, proved 27 September 1745; Hancock, *Citizens of the World*. On the white hierarchy that placed lawyers below planters but above those who performed manual labor, see C. Jones, *Engendering Whiteness*, 25.

60. TNA, C11/2286/12 *Peers v. Barwick*, 1719.

61. TNA, C11/741/28 *Peers v. Barwick*, Barwick's Answer, November 1718; BDA, RB3/27 fols. 201–13, 14 July 1715.

62. TNA, C24/1211 *Peers v. Chaplin*, Hilary, Deposition of John Peers of the Inner Temple, 23 February 1698; Deposition of Ralph Hutchinson, 24 February 1698.

63. TNA, PROB 11/857/138, proved 17 June 1760. Frances wrote her will with the kind of detail and attention common to women in this era; see Erickson, "Possession," 372–74.

64. TNA, C11/741/28 *Peers v. Barwick*, Barwick's Answer, November 1718; BNA, RB3/33 fol. 300, 11 March 1724/4.

65. They married on 21 March 1703 at St. Mary Magdalene Parish Church, where Elizabeth was described as being "Elizabeth Horner of St. Margaret's Westminster" and William (who was knighted in 1706) as "William Milman Esqr of the Inner Temple." "William Milman," London, England, Church of England Baptisms, Marriages and Burials, 1538–1812, ancestry.com, www.ancestry.com/search/collections/1624/; TNA, PROB 11/663/181, 24 March 1714, proved 2 June 1733.

66. TNA, C24/1211 *Peers v. Chaplin*, Hilary, Deposition of John Peers, 23 February 1698; Deposition of Ralph Hutchinson, 24 February 1698.

67. TNA, C108/2 *Buckle v. Milman*, Receivers Accounts, 1705–66. The Milman's had no children; Sir William's nieces sued first Lady Elizabeth and then Frances in Chancery.

See TNA, C11/2337/37 *Buckle v. Milman*, Bill, 1714; C11/1833/8 *Buckle v. Peers*, Bill and Answer, 1734. Deponents in the 1715 case argued that Milman was not of sound mind when he wrote his will and was under the influence of Lady Elizabeth. Frances Peers is also described as present for several business transactions that appeared unfavorable to Sir William. C24/1344 *Buckle v. Milman*, Depositions, 1715. For a similar case, see Barnett-Woods, "Bequeathed," 479–80.

68. Baptism of Susannah Elliot, August 1718, St. Clement Danes, Westminster Baptisms, City of Westminster Archives Centre, London. For the Black presence in St. Clement Danes, see Habib, *Black Lives*, 174. See also Hubbard, *City Women*, 25. For births within six months of marriage, see O'Gorman, *Long Eighteenth Century*, 11.

69. TNA, C11/2677/1 *Aldridge v. Ashcroft*, Bill, 19 December 1734; TNA, C11/2466/32 *Tomlinson v. Ashcroft*, Bill and Answer, 18 October 1740.

70. TNA, C24/1552 no. 4, *Ashcroft v. Tomlinson*, Deposition of John Parkhurst, 9 February 1740; Deposition of John Blair, 9 February 1740.

71. "Susanna Ashcroft," London, Selected Church of England Parish Registers, ancestry. com, www.ancestry.com/search/collections/3067/; Trahey, "Among Her Kinswomen," 278; J. Johnson, *Wicked Flesh*, 189.

72. BDA, RB3/33, fols. 140–47, Sale of Rendezvous and Staple Grove, 2 April 1724; RB3/33, fols. 148–62, 15 February 1724; RB3/33, fol. 178, 2 April 1724; RB3/33, fols. 299–302, 11 March 1725.

73. Thanks to Elena Schneider for the conversation around "the house that colonial slavery built."

CONCLUSION

1. TNA, PROB 11/857/138, proved 17 June 1760. See also Gittings, *Death, Burial, and the Individual*.

2. See, among others, Habib, *Black Lives*; Gerzina, *Black London*; Shyllon, *Black People*; Fryer, *Staying Power*; Chater, *Untold Histories*; and Olusoga, *Black Britain*.

3. Williams, *Capitalism and Slavery*; Mintz, *Sweetness and Power*; Blackburn, *Making of New World Slavery*.

4. Chakravarty, *Fictions of Consent*; S. Newman, *Freedom Seekers*; Brewer, "Creating a Common Law of Slavery."

5. Guasco, *Slaves and Englishmen*, 9.

6. Scholars have long noted this connection. See Habib, *Black Lives*; Chakravarty, *Fictions of Consent*; S. Newman, *Freedom Seekers*; and Brewer, "Creating a Common Law of Slavery."

7. The announcement came following Barbados's transition to a republic on 30 November 2021. See Public Relations, "Prime Minister Announces Creation of Barbados Heritage District," Barbados Government Information Service, December 3, 2021, https://gisbarbados .gov.bb/blog/prime-minister-announces-creation-of-barbados-heritage-district/.

8. For the Staple Grove entry, see University College London's Center for the Study of the Legacies of British Slavery, www.ucl.ac.uk/lbs. For the relative worth of the payout, see "Five Ways to Compute the Relative Value of a UK Pound Amount, 1270 to Present,"

MeasuringWorth, 2021, www.measuringworth.com/ukcompare/. On the broader pay-out to enslavers, see University College London's Study of the Legacies of British Slavery, www.ucl.ac.uk/lbs.

9. Although apprenticeship was to last until 1840, protests against the policy from recently freed people in the West Indies ended the policy in 1838.

10. See, among others, Lightfoot, *Troubling Freedom*.

Bibliography

ARCHIVES

Ancestry, ancestry.com
Barbados National Archives, Black Rock, Bridgetown, Barbados
    Parish Registers
    Registers of Deeds
    Registers of Wills
Bodleian Library, Oxford University, UK
    Codrington Family Papers
British History Online, www.british-history.ac.uk
East Riding Archives, Beverly, Yorkshire, UK
Find My Past, findmypast.co.uk
Herefordshire Archive and Records Centre, Hereford, Herefordshire, UK
London Metropolitan Archive, London, UK
The National Archives, London, Kew, UK
    Chancery Court Records
    Colonial Office Records
    High Court of Admiralty Records
    Probate Records
    Treasury Records
Runaway Slaves in Britain Database, www.runaways.gla.ac.uk
Transatlantic Slave Trade Database, slavevoyages.org
Westminster Archives, London, UK

PRINTED PRIMARY SOURCES

Akerman, John Yonge. *Moneys Received and Paid for Secret Services of Charles II and James II from 30th March 1679 to 25th December 1688*. London: Camden Society, 1851.
Anonymous. *The Character of a Town Misse*. London, 1680.
———. *The English Midwife Enlarged*. London, 1682.

————. *Great Newes from the Barbadoes, or A True and Faithful Account of the Grand Conspiracy of the Negroes against the English and the Happy Discovery of the Same.* London, 1676.

————. *The Jamaica Lady, or The Life of Bavia. Containing an Account of Her Intrigues, Cheats, Armours in England, Jamaica, and the Royal Navy [. . .] with the Diverting Humours of Capt. Fustian.* London, 1720.

————. *Proceedings of the Huguenot Society of Great Britain and Ireland,* vol. 5.

Aubrey, John. *The Natural History and Antiquities of Surrey Begun in the Year 1673 by John Aubrey and Continued to the Present Time.* London, 1718–19.

Barlow, Edward. *Barlow's Journal of His Life at Sea in King's Ships, East and West Indiamen and Other Merchantmen from 1659 to 1703.* Edited by Basil Lubbock. Vol. 2. London: Hurst and Blackett, 1934.

Barret, Robert. *A Companion for Midwives, Child-Bearing Women, and Nurses Directing Them How to Perform Their Respective Offices.* London, 1699.

Biet, Antoine. *Voyage de la France Equinoxiale en L'Isle de Cayenne, entrerpis par les François en l'anné'e M.DC.LII [. . .].* Paris, 1656.

Birch, Thomas ed. *A Collection of the State Papers of John Thurloe.* Vol. 4, Sept 1655–May 1656. London: Fletcher Gyles, 1742.

Blome, Richard. *A Description of the Island of Jamaica with the Other Isles and Territories in America to Which the English Are Related.* London, 1672.

Bosman, Willem. *A New and Accurate Description of the Coast of Guinea.* London, 1705.

Budd, Thomas. *Good Order Established in Pennsylvania and New Jersey in America.* Philadelphia, 1685.

Duke, William. *Memoirs of the First Settlement of the Island of Barbados and Other the Carribbee Islands: With the Succession of the Governors and Commanders in Chief of Barbados to the Year 1742.* London, 1743.

Equiano, Olaudah. *The Interesting Narrative of Olaudah Equiano or Gustavus Vassa a Slave.* London, 1789.

Erauso, Catalina de. *Lieutenant Nun: Memoir of a Basque Transvestite in the New World.* Boston: Beacon, 1996.

Godwyn, Morgan. *The Negro and Indian's Advocate, Suing for Their Admission to the Church, or, A Persuasive to the Instructing and Baptizing of the Negro's and Indians in Our Plantations.* London, 1680.

Gouge, William. *Of Domesticall Duties Eight Treatises.* London, 1622.

Hair, P. E. H., Adam Jones, and Robin Law, eds. *Barbot on Guinea: The Writings of Jean Barbot on West Africa, 1678–1712.* 2 vols. London: Hakluyt Society, 1992.

Hasted, Edward. "Parishes: Speldhurst." In *The History and Topographical Survey of the County of Kent.* Vol. 3. Canterbury: W Bristow, 1797.

Higford, *Institutions or Advice to His Grandson.* London, 1658.

Jones, Adam. *Brandenburg Sources for West African History, 1680–1700.* Stuttgart: Franz Steiner Verlag Wiesbaden GMBH, 1985.

————. *German Sources for West Africa History, 1599–1669.* Wiesbaden: Franz Steiner Verlag GMBH, 1983.

King, Gregory. "Natural and Political Observations and Conclusions." In George Chalmers, *An Estimate of the Comparative Strength of Great-Britain, During the Present and Four Preceding Reigns*. London: Stockdale, 1974.

Kupperman, Karen Ordahl, ed. *A True and Exact History of the Island of Barbados*, by Richard Ligon. Indianapolis: Hackett, 2011.

Leslie, Charles. *A New and Exact Account of Jamaica*. 3rd ed. London, 1740.

Ligon, Richard. *A True and Exact History of the Island of Barbadoes*. London, 1657.

Littleton, Edward. *Groans of the Plantations*. London, 1689.

Long, Edward. *The History of Jamaica or, A Genera Survey of the Antient and Modern State of That Island with Reflections on Its Situation, Settlements, Inhabitants, Climate, Products, Commerce, Laws, and Government, in Three Volumes*. London, 1774.

Madan, Patrick. *A Phylosophical and Medicinal Essay of the Waters of Tunbridge Written to a Person of Honour*. London, 1687.

Magolotti, Lorenzo. *Travels of Cosmo the Third Grand Duke of Tuscany through England during the Reign of Charles II in 1669*. London: J. Mawman, 1821.

Marees, Pieter de. *Description and Historical Account of the Gold Kingdom of Guinea (1602)*. Translated and edited by Albert van Danzig and Adam Jones. Oxford: Oxford University Press, 1987.

Markham, Gervais. *The English Housewife, Containing the Inward and Outward Virtues Which Ought to Be a Complete Woman*. 9th ed. London, 1683.

Morgan, William. *Morgan's Map of the Whole of London in 1682*. London, 1682.

Neville, Henry. *Isle of Pines*. London, 1668.

Nugent, Maria. *Lady Nugent's Jamaica Journal*. Edited by P. Wright. Kingston, 1966.

Ogilby, John. *Africa*. London, 1670.

Oldmixon, J. *The British Empire in America [. . .]*. London, 1708.

Oliver, John. *A Present for Teeming Women, or, Scripture-Directions for Women with Child How to Prepare for the Houre of Travel*. London, 1663.

Oliver, Vere Langford, ed. *Caribbeana: Being Miscellaneous Papers Relating to the History, Genealogy, Topography, and Antiquities of the British West Indies*. Vol. 2. London, 1912.

———. *Monumental Inscriptions: Tombstones of the Island of Barbados*. Wildside, 1995.

Pechey, John. *The Compleat Midwife's Practice Enlarged*. London, 1698.

———. *General Treatise of the Diseases of Maids Bigbellied Women, Child-Bed-Women, and Widows Together with the Best Methods of Preventing or Curing the Same*. London, 1696.

Pepys, Samuel. *Diary of Samuel Pepys*. 11 volumes. Edited by R. C. Latham and W. Mathews. London: HarperCollins, 1974.

Prince, Mary. *The History of Mary Prince: A West Indian Slave Narrative*. New York: Dover, 2004.

"Records of the Vestry." *Journal of the Barbados Museum and Historical Society* 15 (1948): 98–104, 119–27.

Rochefort, Charles de. *The History of the Caribby-Islands, viz Barbados, St Christophers, St Vincent, Martinico, Dominico, Barbouthos, Montserrat, Mevis, Antego &c in Two Books*. London, 1666.

Roesslin, Eucharius. *Birth of Mankind, Otherwise Cal[l]ed, The Womans Book*. London: J. L., Henry Hood, Abel Roper, and Richard Tomlins, 1654.

Rowzee, Lodwick. *The Queens Wells, That Is, a Treatise of the Nature and Vertues of Tunbridge Water. Together, with an Enumeration of the Chiefest Diseases, Which It Is Good for, and against Which It May Be Used, and the Manner and Order of Taking It.* Robert Boulter at the Turks Head in Bishop-gate-street, 1670.

Sainsbury, W. Noel, ed. *Calendar of State Papers Colonial, America and West Indies.* Vol. 1, *1574–1660.* London: Her Majesty's Stationery Office, 1860.

———. *Calendar of State Papers Colonial, America and West Indies.* Vol. 9, *1675–1676 and Addenda 1574–1674.* London: Her Majesty's Stationery Office, 1893.

Sainsbury, W. Noel, and John William Fortescue. *Calendar of State Papers, Colonial Series, America and West Indies, 1677–1680.* London: Her Majesty's Stationery Office, 1896.

Sermon, William. *The Ladies Companion, or, The English Midwife Wherein Is Demonstrated the Manner and Order How Women Ought to Govern Themselves during the Whole Time of Their Breeding Children and of Their Difficult Labour, Hard Travail and Lying In, Etc.* London, 1671.

Sharp, Jane. *The Midwives Book. Or the Whole Art of Midwifry Discovered: Directing Childbearing Women How to Behave Themselves in the Conception, Breeding, Bearing, and Nursing of Children.* London, 1671.

Sloane, Hans. *A Voyage to the Islands Madera, Barbados, Nieves, S. Christophers and Jamaica: In Two Volumes.* London, 1707.

Smith, Venture. *A Narrative of the Life and Adventures of Venture, a Native of Africa: But Resident above Sixty Years in the United States of America. Related by Himself.* New London, 1798.

Southerne, Thomas. *Oronooko: A Tragedy.* London, 1696.

Sowerby, Leonard. *The Ladies Dispensatory.* London, 1652.

Taylor, John. *Second Part of the Historie of His Life and Travels in America.* London, 1688.

Tryon, Thomas. *Friendly Advice to the Gentlemen-Planters of the East and West Indies in Three Parts.* London, 1684.

———. *A Treatise of Cleanness in Meats and Drinks of the Preparation of Food, the Excellency of Good Airs and the Benefits of Clean Sweet Beds Also of the Generation of Bugs and Their Cure: To Which Is Added, a Short Discourse of the Pain in the Teeth Shewing from What Cause It Does Chiefly Proceed, and Also How to Prevent It.* London, 1682.

Uffenbach, Zacharias Conrad Von. *London in 1710 from the Travels of Zacharias Conrad Von Uffenbach.* Translated and edited by W. H. Quarrell and Margaret Mare. London: Faber and Faber, 1934.

Villault, Nicolas sieur de Bellefond. *A Relation of the Coasts of Afrik Called Guinee.* London, 1670.

Vokins, Joan. *God's Mighty Power Magnified as Manifested and Revealed in His Faithful Handmaid Joan Vokins, Who Departed This Life the 22d of the 5th Month, 1690, Having Finished Her Course, and Kept the Faith: Also Some Account of Her Exercises, Works of Faith, Labour of Love, and Great Travels in the Work of the Ministry, for the Good of Souls.* London, 1691.

Ward, Ned. *The London Spy.* London, 1703.

———. *A Trip to Jamaica, with a True Character of the People and the Island.* London, 1698.

Whistler, Henry. *Journal of the West Indies Expedition.* Edited by C. H. Firth. London: Longmans, 1900.

Wolveridge, James. *Speculum matricis hybernicum, or, The Irish Midwives Handmaid Catechistically.* London: E. Okes, 1670.

SECONDARY SOURCES

Amussen, Susan Dwyer. *Caribbean Exchanges: Slavery and the Transformation of English Society, 1640–1700.* Chapel Hill: University of North Carolina Press, 2007.

———. *An Ordered Society: Gender and Class in Early Modern England.* New York: Columbia University Press, 1994.

Bailey, Joanne. "Favoured or Oppressed? Married Women, Property, and 'Coverture' in England, 1660–1800." *Continuity and Change* 17 (2002): 351–72.

Ball, Erica L., Tatiana Seijas, and Terri L. Snyder. *As If She Were Free: A Collective Biography of Women and Emancipation in the Americas.* New York: Cambridge University Press, 2020.

Barclay, Jenifer L. "Bad Breeders and Monstrosities: Racializing Childlessness and Congenital Disabilities in Slavery and Freedom." *Slavery and Abolition* 38 (2017): 287–302.

Barnett-Woods, Victoria. "'Bequeathed unto My Daughter [. . .] Slaves': Women, Slavery and Property in the Eighteenth-Century Atlantic World." *Journal for Eighteenth-Century Studies* 44 (2021): 469–86.

Beasley, Nicholas. *Christian Ritual and the Creation of British Slave Societies, 1650–1780.* Athens: University of Georgia Press, 2009.

Beckles, Hilary McD. *Centering Women: Gender Discourses in Caribbean Slave Society.* Jamaica: James Randle, 1999.

———. *Natural Rebels: A Social History of Enslaved Women in Barbados.* New Brunswick, NJ: Rutgers University Press, 1989.

———. *White Servitude and Black Slavery in Barbados, 1627–1715.* Knoxville: University of Tennessee Press, 1989.

Beier, A. L. "Engine of Manufacture: The Trades of London." In *London 1500–1700: The Making of a Metropolis,* edited by A. L. Beier and Roger Finlay, 141–67. London: Longman, 1986.

———. "In Sickness and in Health: A Seventeenth Century Family's Experience." In *Patients and Practitioners: Lay Perceptions of Medicine in Pre-industrial Society,* edited by Roy Porter, 101–28. Cambridge: Cambridge University Press, 1986.

Bendall, Sarah A. "The Queen's Dressmakers: Women's Work and the Clothing Trades in Late Seventeenth-Century London." *Women's History Review* 32, no. 3 (2023): 389–414.

Bennett, Herman L. *African Kings and Black Slaves: Sovereignty and Dispossession in the Early Modern Atlantic.* Philadelphia: University of Pennsylvania Press, 2018.

———. *Africans in Colonial Mexico: Absolutism, Christianity and Afro-Creole Consciousness, 1570–1640.* Bloomington: Indiana University Press, 2003.

Bennett, Judith M., and Amy M. Froide. "A Singular Past." In *Singlewomen in the European Past, 1250–1800,* edited by Judith M. Bennett and Amy M. Froide, 1–37. Philadelphia: University of Pennsylvania Press, 1999.

Benzaquén, Adriana. "Educational Designs: The Education and Training of Younger Sons at the Turn of the Eighteenth Century." *Journal of Family History* 40 (2015): 464–66.

Berlin, Ira. *Many Thousands Gone: The First Two Centuries of Slavery in North America*. Cambridge, MA: Harvard University Press, 2000.

Berry, Daina Ramey. *The Price for Their Pound of Flesh: The Value of the Enslaved from Womb to Grave in the Building of a Nation*. New York: Beacon, 2017.

———. "Soul Values and American Slavery." *Slavery and Abolition* 42 (2021): 201–18.

———. *"Swing the Sickle for the Harvest Is Ripe": Gender and Slavery in Antebellum Georgia*. Urbana-Champaign: University of Illinois Press, 2007.

Berry, Helen, and Elizabeth Foyster. "Childless Men in Early Modern England." In *The Family in Early Modern England*, edited by Helen Berry and Elizabeth Foyster, 158–83. Cambridge: Cambridge University Press, 2009.

Birt, Sarah. "Women, Guilds and the Tailoring Trades: The Occupational Training of Merchant Taylors' Company Apprentices in Early Modern London." *London Journal* 46 (2021): 146–64.

Blackburn, Robin. *The Making of New World Slavery: From the Baroque to the Modern, 1492–1800*. New York: Verso, 1997.

Block, Kristen, *Ordinary Lives in the Early Caribbean: Religion, Colonial Competition, and the Politics of Profit*. Athens: University of Georgia Press, 2012.

Block, Sharon. *Colonial Complexions: Race and Bodies in Eighteenth-Century America*. Philadelphia: University of Pennsylvania Press, 2018.

———. *Rape and Sexual Power in Early America*. Chapel Hill: Omohundro Institute of Early American History and Culture and the University of North Carolina Press, 2006.

Boose, Lynda E. "'The Getting of a Lawful Race': Racial Discourse in Early Modern England and the Unrepresentable Black Woman." In *Women, "Race," and Writing in the Early Modern Period*, edited by Margo Hendricks and Patricia Parker, 35–54. London: Routledge, 1994.

Brewer, Holly. "Creating a Common Law of Slavery for England and Its New World Empire." *Law and History Review* 39 (2021): 765–834.

———. "Creating a Fashion for Slavery in the Stuart Court(s)." Paper presented at the Columbia Seminar on Early American History and Culture, 9 March 2021.

———. "Slavery, Sovereignty, and 'Inheritable Blood': Reconsidering John Locke and the Origins of American Slavery." *American Historical Review* 122 (2017): 1038–78.

Brown, Kathleen M. "'Changed into the Fashion of a Man': The Politics of Sexual Difference in a Seventeenth Century Anglo-American Settlement." *Journal of the History of Sexuality* 6 (1995): 171–93.

———. *Foul Bodies: Cleanliness in Early America*. New Haven, CT: Yale University Press, 2009.

———. *Good Wives, Nasty Wenches, and Anxious Patriarchs: Gender, Race, and Power in Colonial Virginia*. Chapel Hill: Omohundro Institute of Early American History and Culture and the University of North Carolina Press, 1996.

Brown, Vincent. "Eating the Dead: Consumption and Regeneration in the History of Sugar." *Food and Foodways* 16 (2008): 117–26.

———. *The Reaper's Garden: Death and Power in the World of Atlantic Slavery*. Cambridge, MA: Harvard University Press, 2008.

Browne, Randy M., Lisa Lindsay, and John Wood Sweet. "Rebecca's Ordeal, from Africa to the Caribbean: Sexual Exploitation, Freedom Struggles, and Black Atlantic Biography." *Slavery and Abolition* 43 (2022): 40–67.

Browne, Randy M., and John Wood Sweet. "Florence Hall's 'Memoirs': Finding African Women in the Transatlantic Slave Trade." *Slavery and Abolition* 37 (2016): 206–21.

Browning, A., Mary K. Geiter, and W. A. Speck, eds. *Memoirs of Sir John Reresby.* London: Offices of the Royal Historical Society, 1991.

Burnard, Trevor. *Mastery, Tyranny, and Desire: Thomas Thistlewood and His Slaves in the Anglo-Jamaican World.* Chapel Hill: University of North Carolina Press, 2004.

———. "Slave Naming Patterns: Onomastics and the Taxonomy of Race in Eighteenth-Century Jamaica." *Journal of Interdisciplinary History* 31 (2001): 325–46.

Bush, Barbara. *Slave Women in Caribbean Society, 1650–1838.* Bloomington: Indiana University Press, 1990.

———. "White 'Ladies,' Coloured 'Favourites,' and Black 'Wenches': Some Considerations on Sex, Race and Class in Social Relations in White Creole Society in the British Caribbean." *Slavery and Abolition* 2 (1981): 245–62.

Camp, Stephanie. *Closer to Freedom: Enslaved Women and Everyday Resistance in the Plantation South.* Chapel Hill: University of North Carolina Press, 2004.

Candido, Mariana P. *An African Slaving Port and the Atlantic World.* Cambridge: Cambridge University Press, 2013.

Capp, Bernard. *The Ties That Bind: Siblings, Family, and Society in Early Modern England.* Oxford: Oxford University Press, 2018.

Carretta, Vincent. "Naval Records and Eighteenth-Century Black Biography." *Journal for Maritime Research* 5 (2003): 143–58.

Chakravarty, Urvashi. *Fictions of Consent: Slavery, Servitude, and Free Service in Early Modern England.* Philadelphia: University of Pennsylvania Press, 2022.

Chambers, D. B. "Ethnicity in the Diaspora: The Slave Trade and the Creation of African 'Nations' in the Americas." *Slavery and Abolition* 22 (2001): 25–39.

Chater, Kathleen. *Untold Histories: Black People in England and Wales during the Period of the British Slave Trade, c. 1660–1807.* Manchester: Manchester University Press, 2009.

Christopher, Emma. *Slave Ship Sailors and Their Captive Cargoes, 1730–1807.* Cambridge: Cambridge University Press, 2006.

Clancy-Smith, Julia, and Frances Gouda, eds. *Domesticating the Empire: Race, Gender, and Family Life in French and Dutch Colonialism.* Charlottesville: University of Virginia Press, 1998.

Clark, Emily Jeannine. "'Their Negro Nanny Was with Child by a White Man': Gossip, Sex, and Slavery in an Eighteenth-Century New England Town." *William and Mary Quarterly* 79 (2022): 533–62.

Clay, William Keatinge, ed. *Liturgical Services: Liturgies and Occasional Forms of Prayer Set Forth in the Reign of Queen Elizabeth.* Cambridge: Cambridge University Press, 1847.

Cliffe, J. T. *The World of the Country House in Seventeenth-Century England.* New Haven, CT: Yale University Press, 1999.

Cockayne, Emily. *Hubbub: Filth, Noise and Stench in England, 1600–1770.* New Haven, CT: Yale University Press, 2007.

Cody, Cheryll Ann. "There Was No 'Absolom' on the Ball Plantations: Slave-Naming Practices in the South Carolina Low Country, 1720–1865." *American Historical Review* 92 (1987): 563–96.

Cody, Lisa Forman. *Birthing the Nation: Sex, Science, and the Conception of Eighteenth-Century Britons*. Oxford: Oxford University Press, 2008.

Coleman, Donald C. "An Innovation and Its Diffusion: The 'New Draperies.'" *Economic History Review* 22 (1969): 417–29.

Collins, Patricia Hill. *Black Feminist Thought: Knowledge, Consciousness, and the Politics of Empowerment*. London: Hyman, 1990.

Cowling, Camillia. *Conceiving Freedom: Women of Color, Gender, and the Abolition of Slavery in Havana and Rio de Janeiro*. Chapel Hill: University of North Carolina Press, 2013.

Cowling, Camillia, Maria Helena, P. T. Machado, Diana Paton, and Emily West. "Introduction—Mothering Slaves: Comparative Perspectives on Motherhood, Childlessness and the Care of Children in Atlantic Slave Societies." *Slavery and Abolition* 38 (2017): 223–31.

———. "Special Issue of *Women's History Review*—Mothering Slaves: Motherhood, Childlessness and the Care of Children in Atlantic Slave Societies." *Women's History Review* 27 (2018): 867–74.

Crawford, Patricia. *Blood, Bodies, and Families in Early Modern England*. London: Routledge, 2014.

———. "The Construction and Experience of Maternity in Seventeenth Century England." In *Women as Mothers in Pre-industrial England*, edited by Valerie Fildes, 3–38. London: Routledge, 1990.

Cressy, David. *Birth, Marriage, and Death: Ritual, Religion, and the Life Cycle in Tudor and Stuart England*. Oxford: Oxford University Press, 1997.

———. *Coming Over: Migration and Communication between England and New England in the Seventeenth Century*. Cambridge: Cambridge University Press, 1987.

———. "Literacy in Seventeenth-Century England: More Evidence." *Journal of Interdisciplinary History* 8 (1977): 141–50.

———. "Purification, Thanksgiving, and the Churching of Women in Post-Reformation England." *Past and Present* 141 (1993): 106–46.

Crowley, John E. *The Invention of Comfort: Sensibilities and Design in Early Modern Britain and Early America*. Baltimore: Johns Hopkins University Press, 2003.

Curtin, Philip D. *The Atlantic Slave Trade: A Census*. Madison: University of Wisconsin Press, 1969.

Dantas, Mariana L. R. "Anna Maria Lopes de Brito, Eighteenth-Century Minas Gerais (Brazil)." In *As If She Were Free: A Collective Biography of Women and Emancipation in the Americas*, edited by Erica L. Ball, Tatiana Seijas, and Terri L. Snyder, 190–206. New York: Cambridge University Press, 2020.

Davis, David Brion. "Constructing Race: A Reflection." In "Constructing Race." Special issue, *William and Mary Quarterly* 54 (1997): 7–18.

Davis, Ralph. *The Rise of the English Shipping Industry in the Seventeenth and Eighteenth Centuries*. London: Macmillan, 1962.

Dewing, David. "Cane Chairs, Their Manufacture, and Use in London, 1670–1730." *Regional Furniture* 22 (2008): 53–82.

Díaz, Aisnara Perera, and María de Los Ángeles Meriño Fuentes. "The African Women of the *Dos Hermanos* Slave Ship in Cuba: Slaves First, Mothers Second." *Women's History Review* 27 (2018): 892–909.

Doyle, Nora. *Maternal Bodies: Redefining Motherhood in Early America*. Chapel Hill: University of North Carolina Press, 2018.

Dungworth, David. "The Value of Historic Window Glass." *Historic Environment: Policy and Practice* 2 (2011): 21–48.

Dunn, Richard S. *Sugar and Slaves: The Rise of the Planter Class in the English West Indies, 1624–1713*. 1972. 2nd ed. Chapel Hill: Omohundro Institute of Early American History and Culture and the University of North Carolina Press, 2000.

———. *A Tale of Two Plantations: Slave Life and Labor in Jamaica and Virginia*. Cambridge, MA: Harvard University Press, 2014.

Earle, Peter. *A City Full of People: Men and Women of London, 1650–1750*. London: Methuen, 1994.

———. "The Female Labour Market in London in the Late Seventeenth and Early Eighteenth Centuries." *Economic History Review* 42 (1989): 328–53.

Edwards, Paul. "The Early African Presence in the British Isles." In *Essays on the History of Blacks in Britain: From Roman Times to the Mid-twentieth Century*, edited by Jagdish S. Gundara and Ian Duffield, 9–29. Aldershot: Avebury, 1992.

Eltis, David. "The Diaspora of Yoruba Speakers, 1650–1865: Dimensions and Implications." In *The Yoruba Diaspora in the Atlantic World*, edited by Toyin Falola and Matt D. Childs, 17–39. Bloomington: Indiana University Press, 2004.

———. "The Volume and African Origins of the British Slave Trade before 1714." *Cahiers de'Études Africaines* 35 (1995): 617–27.

Eltis David, and David Richardson. "West Africa and the Transatlantic Slave Trade: New Evidence of Long-Run Trends." In *Routes to Slavery: Direction, Ethnicity and Mortality in the Transatlantic Slave Trade*, edited by David Eltis and David Richardson, 16–35. London: Frank Cass, 1997.

Erickson, Amy Louise. "Mistresses and Marriage: or, A Short History of the Mrs." *History Workshop Journal* 78 (2014): 39–57.

———. "Possession—and the Other One-Tenth of the Law: Assessing Women's Ownership and Economic Roles in Early Modern England." *Women's History Review* 16 (2007): 369–85.

———. "Using Probate Accounts." In *When Death Do Us Part: Understanding and Interpreting the Probate Records of Early Modern England*, edited by Tom Arkell, Nesta Evans, and Nigel Goose, 103–19. Oxford: Oxford University Press, 2000.

———. *Women and Property in Early Modern England*. London: Routledge, 1993.

Field, Jacob F. *London, Londoners and the Great Fire of 1666: Disaster and Recovery*. London: Routledge, 2018.

Fildes, Valerie A. *Breasts, Bottles, and Babies: A History of Infant Feeding*. Edinburgh: Edinburgh University Press, 1986.

———. *Wet Nursing: A History from Antiquity to the Present.* Oxford: Blackwell, 1988.

Finlay, Roger, and Beatrice Shearer. "Population Growth and Suburban Expansion." In *London 1500–1700: The Making of a Metropolis,* edited by A. L. Beier and Roger Finlay, 37–59. London: Longman, 1986.

Fischer, Kirsten. *Suspect Relations: Sex, Race, and Resistance in Colonial North Carolina.* Ithaca, NY: Cornell University Press, 2002.

Fletcher, Anthony. *Growing Up in England: The Experience of Childhood, 1600–1914.* New Haven, CT: Yale University Press, 2008.

Forde-Jones, Cecily. "Mapping Racial Boundaries: Gender, Race, and Poor Relief in Barbadian Plantation Society." *Journal of Women's History* 10 (1998): 9–30.

Foster, Thomas A. *Rethinking Rufus: Sexual Violations of Enslaved Men.* Athens: University of Georgia Press, 2019.

———. "The Sexual Abuse of Black Men under American Slavery." In *Sexuality and Slavery: Reclaiming Intimate Histories in the Americas,* edited by Daina Ramey Berry and Leslie M. Harris, 123–44. Athens: University of Georgia Press, 2018.

Foy, Charles R. "Britain's Black Tars." In *Britain's Black Past,* edited by Gretchen H. Gerzina, 63–80. Liverpool: Liverpool University Press, 2020.

———. "The Royal Navy's Employment of Black Mariners and Maritime Workers, 1754–1783." *International Journal of Maritime History* 28 (2016): 6–35.

Froide, Amy M. *Never Married: Singlewomen in Early Modern England.* Oxford: Oxford University Press, 2005.

Fryer, Peter. *Staying Power: The History of Black People in Britain.* London: Pluto, 1984.

Fuentes, Marisa J. *Dispossessed Lives: Enslaved Women, Violence, and the Archive.* Philadelphia: University of Pennsylvania Press, 2016.

———. "Power and Historical Figuring: Rachael Pringle Polgreen's Troubled Archive." *Gender and History* 22 (2010): 564–84.

Gerbner, Katharine. *Christian Slavery: Conversion and Race in the Protestant Atlantic World.* Philadelphia: University of Pennsylvania Press, 2018.

———. "The Ultimate Sin: Christianising Slaves in Barbados in the Seventeenth Century." *Slavery and Abolition* 31 (2010): 57–73.

Gerzina, Gretchen H. *Black London: Life before Emancipation.* New Brunswick, NJ: Rutgers University Press, 1995.

Gittings, Clare. *Death, Burial, and the Individual in Early Modern England.* London: Routledge, 1984.

Glasson, Travis. "'Baptism Doth Not Bestow Freedom': Missionary Anglicanism, Slavery, and the Yorke-Talbot Opinion, 1701–30." *William and Mary Quarterly* 67 (2010): 279–318.

———. *Mastering Christianity: Missionary Anglicanism and Slavery in the Atlantic World.* New York: Oxford University Press, 2012.

Glymph, Thavolia. *Out of the House of Bondage: The Transformation of the Plantation Household.* Cambridge: Cambridge University Press, 2008.

Goetz, Rebecca Anne. *The Baptism of Early Virginia: How Christianity Created Race.* Baltimore: Johns Hopkins University Press, 2012.

Gordon-Reed, Annette. *The Hemingses of Monticello: An American Family.* New York: W. W. Norton, 2008.

Gowing, Laura. *Domestic Dangers: Women, Words, and Sex in Early Modern London*. Oxford: Oxford University Press, 1999.

———. "Girls on Forms: Apprenticing Young Women in Seventeenth-Century London." *Journal of British Studies* 55 (2016): 447–73.

Gragg, Larry. *Englishmen Transplanted: The English Colonization of Barbados, 1627–1660*. Oxford: Oxford University Press, 2003.

Green, Sharony. *"Remember Me to Miss Louisa": Hidden Black-White Intimacies in Antebellum America*. Dekalb: University of Northern Illinois Press, 2015.

Green, Toby. *The Rise of the Transatlantic Slave Trade in Western Africa, 1300–1589*. Cambridge: Cambridge University Press, 2012.

Guasco, Michael. *Slaves and Englishmen: Human Bondage in the Early Modern Atlantic World*. Philadelphia: University of Pennsylvania Press, 2014.

Gunkel, Alexander, and Jerome S. Handler. "A German Indentured Servant in Barbados in 1652: The Account of Henrich von Uchteritz." *Journal of the Barbados Museum and Historical Society* 33 (1970): 91–100.

———. "A Swiss Medical Doctor's Description of Barbados in 1661: The Account of Felix Christian Spoeri." *Journal of the Barbados Museum and Historical Society* 33 (1969): 3–13.

Gutman, Herbert G. *The Black Family in Slavery and Freedom, 1750–1925*. New York: Vintage, 1975.

Gwynn, Robert. *Huguenots in Later Stuart Britain*. Vol. 2, *Settlement, Churches, and the Role of London*. Oxford: Oxford University Press, 2018.

Habakkuk, John. *Marriage, Debt, and the Estates System: English Landownership 1650–1950*. Oxford: Clarendon, 1994.

Habib, Imtiaz. *Black Lives in the English Archives, 1500–1677: Imprints of the Invisible*. Aldershot: Ashgate, 2008.

Hall, Gwendolyn Midlo. *Slavery and African Ethnicities in the Americas: Restoring the Links*. Chapel Hill: University of North Carolina Press, 2005.

Hall, Kim F. "'I Rather Would Wish to Be a Black-Moor': Beauty, Race, and Rank in Lady Mary Wroth's *Urania*." In *Women "Race," and Writing in the Early Modern Period*, edited by Margo Hendricks and Patricia Parker, 178–94. London: Routledge, 1994.

———. "Reading What Isn't There: 'Black' Studies in Early Modern England." *Stanford Humanities Review* 3 (1993): 23–33.

———. *Things of Darkness: Economies of Race and Gender in Early Modern England*. Ithaca, NY: Cornell University Press, 1995.

Hancock, David. *Citizens of the World: London Merchants and the Integration of the British Atlantic Community, 1735–1785*. Cambridge: Cambridge University Press, 1995.

Handler, Jerome S. "Custom and Law: The Status of Enslaved Africans in Seventeenth-Century Barbados." *Slavery and Abolition* 37 (2016): 233–55.

———. "Father Antoine Biet's Visit to Barbados in 1654." *Journal of the Barbados Museum and Historical Society* 32 (1967): 56–76.

———. "Life Histories of Enslaved Africans in Barbados." *Slavery and Abolition* 19 (1998): 129–14.

———. *The Unappropriated People: Freedmen in the Slave Society of Barbados*. Baltimore: Johns Hopkins University Press, 1974.

Handler, Jerome S., and Robert S. Corruccini. "Weaning among West Indian Slaves: Historical and Bioanthropological Evidence from Barbados." *William and Mary Quarterly* 43 (1986): 111–17.

Handler, Jerome S., and JoAnn Jacoby. "Slave Names and Naming in Barbados, 1650–1830." *William and Mary Quarterly* 53 (1996): 685–728.

Handler, Jerome S., and Frederick W. Lange. *Plantation Slavery in Barbados: An Archaeological and Historical Investigation*. Cambridge, MA: Harvard University Press, 1978.

Harding, Vanessa. "Cheapside: Commerce and Commemoration." *Huntington Library Quarterly* 71 (2008): 77–96.

Hardwick, Julie. "Family Matters: The Early Modern Atlantic from the European Side." *History Compass* 8 (2010): 248–57.

Hardwick, Julie, Sarah M. S. Pearsall, and Karin Wulf, eds. "Centering Families in Atlantic History." Special Edition, *William and Mary Quarterly* 70 (2013): 205–424.

Harkness, Deborah, and Jean E. Howard. "Introduction: The Great World of Early Modern London." *Huntington Library Quarterly* 71 (2008): 1–9.

Hartman, Saidiya V. "The Belly of the World: A Note on Black Women's Labors." *Souls: A Critical Journal of Black Politics, Culture, and Society* 18 (2016): 166–73.

———. *Lose Your Mother: A Journey along the Atlantic Slave Route*. New York: Macmillan, 2008.

———. *Scenes of Subjection: Terror, Slavery, and Self-Making in Nineteenth-Century America*. New York: Oxford University Press, 1997.

———. "Venus in Two Acts." *Small Axe* 12 (2008): 1–14.

Hecht, J. Jean. *The Domestic Servant Class in Eighteenth-Century England*. London: Routledge & Paul, 1956.

Hendricks, Margo. "Civility, Barbarism, and Aphra Behn's *The Widow Ranter*." In *Women "Race," and Writing in the Early Modern Period*, edited by Margo Hendricks and Patricia Parker, 225–41. London: Routledge, 1994.

———. *Race and Romance: Coloring the Past*. Tempe: Arizona Center for Medieval and Renaissance Studies, 2022.

———. "Race: A Renaissance Category?" In *A New Companion to English Renaissance Literature and Culture*, edited by Michael Hattaway, 535–44. Malden, MA: Blackwell, 2010.

Hendricks, Margo, and Patricia Parker, eds. *Women, "Race," and Writing in the Early Modern Period*. London: Routledge, 1994.

Herbert, Amanda. *Female Alliances: Gender, Identity, and Friendship in Early Modern Britain*. New Haven, CT: Yale University Press, 2014.

Higman, B. W. "The Slave Family and Household in the British West Indies, 1800–1834." *Journal of Interdisciplinary History* 6 (1975): 261–87.

———. "The Sugar Revolution." *Economic History Review* 53 (2000): 213–36.

———. "Terms for Kin in the British West Indian Slave Community: Differing Perceptions of Masters and Slaves." In *Kinship Ideology and Practice in Latin America*, edited by Raymond T. Smith, 59–84. Chapel Hill: University of North Carolina Press, 1984.

Hodes, Martha. *White Women, Black Men: Illicit Sex in the 19th-Century South*. New Haven, CT: Yale University Press, 1997.

Horwitz, Henry. *Chancery Equity Records and Proceedings, 1600–1800: A Guide to Documents in the Public Record Office*. London: H.M.S.O., 1995.

Houlbrooke, Ralph. *Death, Religion, and the Family in England, 1480–1750*. Oxford: Oxford University Press, 2000.

Howard, Jean E. "'An English Lass amid the Moors: Gender, Race, Sexuality, and National Identity in Heywood's *The Fair Maid of the West*." In *Women "Race," and Writing in the Early Modern Period*, edited by Margo Hendricks and Patricia Parker, 101–17. London: Routledge, 1994.

Huang, Nian-Sheng. *Franklin's Father Josiah: Life of a Colonial Boston Tallow Chandler, 1657–1745*. Boston: American Philosophical Society, 2000.

Hubbard, Eleanor. *City Women: Money, Sex, and the Social Order in Early Modern London*. Oxford: Oxford University Press, 2012.

———. "Sailors and the Early Modern British Empire: Labor, Nation, and Identity at Sea." *History Compass* 14 (2016): 348–58.

Hunt, Margaret. "Wives and Marital 'Rights' in the Court of Exchequer in the Early Eighteenth Century." In *Londonopolis: Essays in the Social and Cultural History of Early Modern London*, edited by Paul Griffiths and Mark S. R. Jenner, 107–29. Manchester: Manchester University Press, 2000.

Hunter, Tera W. *Bound in Wedlock: Slave and Free Black Marriage in the Nineteenth Century*. Cambridge, MA: Harvard University Press, 2017.

Hunt-Kennedy, Stefanie Dawn. *Between Fitness and Death: Disability and Slavery in the Caribbean*. Urbana: University of Illinois Press, 2020.

Inniss, Tara. "Freed Women and Unequal Inheritance in Barbados (Early Eighteenth Century): Evidence from the Archive." *Clio: Women, Gender, History* 50 (2019): 129–42.

Jennings, Thelma. "'Us Colored Women Had to Go through a Plenty': Sexual Exploitation of African-American Slave Women." *Journal of Women's History* 1 (1990): 45–74.

Johnson, Jessica Marie. *Wicked Flesh: Black Women, Intimacy, and Freedom in the Atlantic World*. Philadelphia: University of Pennsylvania Press, 2020.

Johnson, Sara E. *Encyclopédie noire: The Making of Moreau de Saint-Méry's Intellectual World*. Chapel Hill: Omohundro Institute of Early American History and Culture and the University of North Carolina Press, 2023.

Johnson, Walter. "On Agency." *Journal of Social History* 37 (2003): 113–24.

Johnston, Katherine M. "Endangered Plantations: Environmental Change and Slavery in the British Caribbean, 1631–1807." *Early American Studies* 18 (2020): 259–86.

Jones, Cecily. *Engendering Whiteness: White Women and Colonialism in Barbados and North Carolina*. Manchester: Manchester University Press, 2007.

Jones, Jacqueline. *Labor of Love, Labor of Sorrow: Black Women, Work, and the Family from Slavery to the Present*. New York: Basic Books, 1985.

Jones-Rogers, Stephanie. "Rethinking Sexual Violence and the Marketplace of Slavery: White Women, the Slave Market, and Enslaved People's Sexualized Bodies in the Nineteenth-Century South." In *Sexuality and Slavery: Reclaiming Intimate Histories in the Americas*, edited by Daina Ramey Berry and Leslie M. Harris, 109–23. Athens: University of Georgia Press, 2018.

———. *They Were Her Property: White Women as Slave Owners in the American South*. New Haven, CT: Yale University Press, 2020.

Jordan, Don. *The King's City: A History of London during the Restoration: The City That Transformed a Nation*. New York: Pegasus, 2018.

Kaufman, Miranda. *Black Tudors: The Untold Story*. London: Oneworld, 2017.

Kelley, Sean M. *The Voyage of the Slave Ship* Hare: *A Journey into Captivity from Sierra Leone to South Carolina*. Chapel Hill: University of North Carolina Press, 2016.

Key, Newton E. "Gregory, Sir William (1625–1696), Judge and Speaker of the House of Commons." *Oxford Dictionary of National Biography*, 23 September 2004. www .oxforddnb.com.

Kidd, Colin. *The Forging of Races: Race and Scripture in the Protestant Atlantic World, 1600–2000*. Cambridge: Cambridge University Press, 2006.

Klein, Herbert S., and Stanley L. Engerman. "Fertility Differentials between Slaves in the United States and the British West Indies: A Note on Lactation Practices and Their Possible Implications." *William and Mary Quarterly* 35 (1978): 357–74.

Klepp, Susan. "Revolutionary Bodies: Women and the Fertility Transition in the Mid-Atlantic Region, 1760–1820." *Journal of American History* 85 (1998): 910–45.

———. *Revolutionary Conceptions: Women, Fertility, and Family Limitation in America, 1760–1820*. Chapel Hill: Omohundro Institute of Early American History and Culture and the University of North Carolina Press. 2009.

Knight, R. J. "Mistresses, Motherhood, and Maternal Exploitation in the Antebellum South." *Women's History Review* 27 (2018): 990–1005.

———. "Mothering and Labour in the Slaveholding Households of the Antebellum American South." *Past and Present* 246, no. S15 (2020): S145–66.

Knott, Sarah. "Theorizing and Historicizing Mothering's Many Labours." *Past and Present* 246, no. S15 (2020): S1–23.

Kopelson, Heather M. *Faithful Bodies: Performing Religion and Race in the Puritan Atlantic*. New York: New York University Press, 2014.

Kottick, Edward. *A History of the Harpsicord*. Bloomington: Indiana University Press, 2003.

Kupperman, Karen Ordahl. *The Jamestown Project*. Cambridge, MA: Harvard University Press, 2007.

LaFleur, Greta. "Whither Rape in the History of Sexuality? Thinking Sex alongside Slavery's Normative Violence." *Journal of the History of Sexuality* 33 (2024): 153–87.

Lavery, Brian. *The Ship of the Line*. Vol. 1, *The Development of the Battlefleet, 1650–1850*. London: Conway Maritime, 2003.

Law, Robin. "Jean Barbot as a Source for the Slave Coast of West Africa." *History in Africa* 9 (1982): 155–73.

———. *The Slave Coast of West Africa, 1550–1750: The Impact of the Atlantic Slave Trade on an African Society*. Oxford: Clarendon, 1991.

Leong, Elaine. *Recipes and Everyday Knowledge: Medicine, Science, and the Household in Early Modern England*. Chicago: University of Chicago Press, 2018.

Lightfoot, Natasha. *Troubling Freedom: Antigua and the Aftermath of British Emancipation*. Durham, NC: Duke University Press, 2015.

Lincoln, Margarette. *London and the 17th Century: The Making of the World's Greatest City.* New Haven, CT: Yale University Press, 2021.

Lindsey, Treva B., and Jessica Marie Johnson. "Searching for Climax: Black Erotic Lives in Slavery and Freedom." *Meridians* 12 (2014): 169–95.

Linebaugh, Peter, and Marcus Rediker. *The Many-Headed Hydra: Sailors, Slaves, Commoners, and the Hidden History of the Revolutionary Atlantic.* New York: Beacon, 2000.

Litten, Julian. *The English Way of Death: The Common Funeral since 1450.* London: Robert Hale, 1991.

Livesay, Daniel. *Children of Uncertain Fortune: Mixed-Race Jamaicans in Britain and the Atlantic Family, 1733–1833.* Chapel Hill: Omohundro Institute for Early American History and Culture and the University of North Carolina Press, 2018.

Lorimer, Douglas A. "Black Slaves and English Liberty: A Reexamination of Racial Slavery in England." *Immigrants and Minorities* 3 (1984): 121–50.

Lovejoy, Paul E. "The African Diaspora: Revisionist Interpretations of Ethnicity, Culture and Religion under Slavery." *Studies in the World History of Slavery, Abolition and Emancipation* 2 (1997).

———. *Transformations in Slavery: A History of Slavery in Africa.* 3rd ed. Cambridge: Cambridge University Press, 2012.

Lynch, Kathleen. "Whatever Happened to Dinah the Black? And Other Questions about Gender, Race, and the Visibility of Protestant Saints." In *Conversions: Gender and Religious Change in Early Modern Europe*, edited by Simon Ditchfield and Helen Smith, 258–80. Manchester: Manchester University Press, 2017.

Machado, Maria Helena P. T. "Between Two Beneditos: Enslaved Wet-Nurses amid Slavery's Decline in Southeast Brazil." *Slavery and Abolition* 38 (2017): 320–36.

Mangan, Jane E. *Transatlantic Obligations: Creating the Bonds of Family in Conquest-Era Peru and Spain.* New York: Oxford University Press, 2016.

Marquez, John C. "Witnesses to Freedom: Paula's Enslavement, Her Family's Freedom Suit, and the Making of a Counterarchive in the South Atlantic World." *Hispanic American Historical Review* 101 (2021): 231–63.

Marsh, Christopher. "Attitudes to Will-Making in Early Modern England." In *When Death Do Us Part: Understanding and Interpreting the Probate Records of Early Modern England*, edited by Tom Arkell, Nesta Evans, and Nigel Goose, 158–75. Oxford: Oxford University Press, 2000.

McClure, Ruth K. *Coram's Children: The London Foundling Hospital in the Eighteenth Century.* New Haven, CT: Yale University Press, 1981.

McDougall, Sara, and Sarah M. S. Pearsall. "Introduction: Marriage's Global Past." *Gender and History* 29 (2017): 505–28.

Meldrum, Tim. *Domestic Service and Gender, 1660–1750: Life and Work in the London Household.* London: Routledge, 2014.

Menard, Russell. *Sweet Negotiations: Sugar, Slavery, and Plantation Agriculture in Early Barbados.* Charlottesville: University of Virginia Press, 2006.

Miles, Tiya. *Ties That Bind: The Story of an Afro-Cherokee Family in Slavery and Freedom.* Berkeley: University of California Press, 2005.

Miller, Joseph C. "A Historical Appreciation of the Biographical Turn." In *Biography and the Black Atlantic*, edited by Lisa A. Lindsay and John Wood Sweet, 19–47. Philadelphia: University of Pennsylvania Press, 2014.

Mintz, Sidney W. *Sweetness and Power: The Place of Sugar in Modern History*. New York: Viking, 1985.

Mitchell, David, ed. *Goldsmiths, Silversmiths and Bankers: Innovation and the Transfer of Skill, 1550 to 1750; A Collection of Working Papers Given at a Study Day Held Jointly by the Centre for Metropolitan History and the Victoria and Albert Museum*. Stroud: Alan Sutton, 1995.

Mitchell, Elise A. "Morbid Crossings: Surviving Smallpox, Maritime Quarantine, and the Gendered Geography of the Early Eighteenth-Century Intra-Caribbean Slave Trade." *William and Mary Quarterly* 79 (2022): 117–210.

Molineux, Catherine. *Faces of Perfect Ebony: Encountering Atlantic Slavery in Imperial Britain*. Cambridge, MA: Harvard University Press, 2012.

Morales, R. Isabela. *Happy Dreams of Liberty: An American Family in Slavery and Freedom*. New York: Oxford University Press, 2022.

Morgan, Edward S. *American Slavery, American Freedom: The Ordeal of Colonial Virginia*. New York: W. W. Norton, 1975.

Morgan, Jennifer L. *Laboring Women: Reproduction and Gender in New World Slavery*. Philadelphia: University of Pennsylvania Press, 2004.

———. "*Partus Sequitur Ventrem*: Law, Race, and Reproduction in Colonial Slavery." *Small Axe* 55 (2018): 1–17.

———. *Reckoning with Slavery: Gender, Kinship, and Capitalism in the Early Black Atlantic*. Durham, NC: Duke University Press, 2021.

Morgan, Philip D. *Slave Counterpoint: Black Culture in the Eighteenth-Century Chesapeake and Low Country*. Chapel Hill: Omohundro Institute of Early American History and Culture and the University of North Carolina Press, 1998.

Mossiker, Frances. *Pocahontas: The Life and Legend*. New York: Alfred A. Knopf, 1976.

Muldrew, Craig. "'Th'Ancient Distaff' and 'Whirling Spindle': Measuring the Contribution of Spinning to Household Earnings and the National Economy in England, 1550–1770." *Economic History Review* 65 (2012): 498–526.

Mulry, Kate. *An Empire Transformed: Remolding Bodies and Landscapes in the Restoration Atlantic*. New York: Oxford University Press, 2021.

Mustakeem, Sowande' M. *Slavery at Sea: Terror, Sex, and Sickness in the Middle Passage*. Urbana-Champaign: University of Illinois Press, 2016.

Naylor, Celia E. *Unsilencing Slavery: Telling Truths about Rose Hall Plantation, Jamaica*. Athens: University of Georgia Press, 2022.

Neal, Martha Ashcraft. *The Ashcraft Family: Descendants of Daniel*. Baltimore: Gateway, 1994.

Newell, Margaret Ellen. *Brethren by Nature: New England Indians, Colonists, and the Origins of American Slavery*. Ithaca, NY: Cornell University Press, 2015.

Newman, Brooke N. *A Dark Inheritance: Blood, Race, and Sex in Colonial Jamaica*. New Haven, CT: Yale University Press, 2018.

Newman, Simon P. *Freedom Seekers: Escaping from Slavery in Restoration London*. London: University of London Press, 2022.

———. *A New World of Labor: The Development of Plantation Slavery in the British Atlantic*. Philadelphia: University of Pennsylvania Press, 2013.

Newton, Gill. "Clandestine Marriage in Early Modern London: When, Where and Why?" *Continuity and Change* 29 (2014): 151–80.

Newton, Melanie J. *The Children of Africa in the Colonies: Free People of Color in Barbados in the Age of Emancipation*. Baton Rouge: Louisiana State University Press, 2008.

———. "Returns to a Native Land: Indigeneity and Decolonization in the Anglophone Caribbean." *Small Axe* 41 (2013): 108–22.

Norton, Mary Beth. *Founding Mothers and Fathers: Gendered Power and the Forming of American Society*. New York: Alfred A. Knopf, 1996.

Nussbaum, Felicity A. *The Limits of the Human: Fictions of Anomaly, Race, and Gender in the Long Eighteenth Century*. New York: Cambridge University Press, 2003.

O'Brien, Grant. *Ruckers: A Harpsicord and Virginal Building Tradition*. Cambridge: Cambridge University Press, 2008.

O'Day, Rosemary. *The Professions in Early Modern England*. London: Routledge, 2000.

O'Gorman, Frank. *The Long Eighteenth Century: British Political and Social History, 1688–1832*. London: Bloomsbury, 1997.

Olusoga, David. *Black and British: A Forgotten History*. London: Pan Books, 2017.

Osborn, Emily Lynn. *Our New Husbands Are Here: Households, Gender, and Politics in a West African State from the Slave Trade to Colonial Rule*. Athens: Ohio University Press, 2011.

Otele, Olivette. *African Europeans: An Untold History*. New York: Basic Books, 2021.

Owens, Deidre Cooper. *Medical Bondage: Race, Gender, and the Origins of American Gynecology*. Athens: University of Georgia Press, 2017.

Owens, Emily A. *Consent in the Presence of Force: Sexual Violence and Black Women's Survival in Antebellum New Orleans*. Chapel Hill: University of North Carolina Press, 2022.

———. "Promises: Sexual Labor in the Space between Slavery and Freedom." *Journal of the Louisiana Historical Association* 58 (2017): 179–216.

Page, William, ed. "Industries: Silk-Weaving." In *A History of the County of Middlesex*. Vol. 2, *General; Ashford, East Bedfont with Hatton, Feltham, Hampton with Hampton Wick, Hanworth, Laleham, Littleton*. London: Victoria County History, 1911.

Painter, Nell Irvin. "Soul Murder and Slavery: Toward a Fully Loaded Cost Accounting." In *Southern History across the Color Line*, edited by Nell Irvin Painter, 12–39. Chapel Hill: University of North Carolina Press, 2002.

Palmer, Colin. "From Africa to the Americas: Ethnicity in Early Black Communities of the Americas." *Journal of World History* 6 (1995): 223–36.

Palmer, Jennifer L. *Intimate Bonds: Family and Slavery in the French Atlantic*. Philadelphia: University of Pennsylvania Press, 2016.

Paton, Diana. "The Driveress and the Nurse: Childcare, Working Children and Other Work under Caribbean Slavery." *Past and Present* 246, no. S15 (2020): S27–53.

———. "Gender History, Global History, and Atlantic Slavery: On Racial Capitalism and Social Reproduction." *American Historical Review* 127 (2022): 726–54.

———. "Mary Williamson's Letter, or, Seeing Women and Sisters in the Archives of Atlantic Slavery." *Transactions of the Royal Historical Society* 29 (2019): 153–79.

———. "Maternal Struggles and the Politics of Childlessness under Pronatalist Caribbean Slavery." *Slavery and Abolition* 38 (2017): 251–68.

Patterson, Orlando. *Slavery and Social Death: A Comparative Study.* Cambridge, MA: Harvard University Press, 1982.

Paugh, Katherine. *The Politics of Reproduction: Race, Medicine, and Fertility in the Age of Abolition.* Oxford: Oxford University Press, 2017.

Pearsall, Sarah M. S. *Atlantic Families: Lives and Letters in the Later Eighteenth Century.* New York: Oxford University Press, 2008.

———. *Polygamy: An Early American History.* New Haven, CT: Yale University Press, 2019.

Peck, Linda Levy. *Women of Fortune: Money, Marriage, and Murder in Early Modern England.* New York: Cambridge University Press, 2018.

Perry, Ruth. "Colonizing the Breast: Sexuality and Maternity in Eighteenth-Century England." *Journal of the History of Sexuality* 2 (1991): 204–34.

Pettigrew, William. *Freedom's Debt: The Royal African Company and the Politics of the Atlantic Slave Trade, 1672–1752.* Chapel Hill: Omohundro Institute of Early American History and Culture and the University of North Carolina Press, 2014.

Picard, Lisa. *Restoration London.* London: Weidenfeld and Nicholson, 1997.

Plummer, Alfred. *The London Weavers' Company, 1600–1970.* Boston: Routledge, 1972.

Pollock, Linda. "Childbearing and Female Bonding in Early Modern England." *Social History* 22 (1997): 286–306.

———. "Embarking on a Rough Passage: The Experience of Pregnancy in Early Modern Society." In *Women as Mothers in Pre-industrial England,* edited by Valerie Fildes, 39–67. London: Routledge, 1990.

Power, M. J. "The Social Topography of Restoration London." In *London 1500–1700: The Making of a Metropolis,* edited by A. L. Beier and Roger Finlay, 199–223. London: Longman, 1986.

Price, Richard, and Sally Price. "Saramaka Onomastics: An Afro-American Naming System." *Ethnology* 11 (1972): 341–67.

Puckett, Newbell Miles. "Names of American Negro Slaves." In *Mother Wit from the Laughing Barrel: Readings in the Interpretation of Afro-American Folklore,* edited by Alan Dundes, 158–74. Oxford: University of Mississippi Press, 1973.

Ramsey, William P. M. *The Worshipful Company of Glass Sellers of London.* London: Thomas Connor, 1898.

Rath, Richard Cullen. "African Music in Seventeenth-Century Jamaica: Cultural Transit and Transition." *William and Mary Quarterly* 50 (1993): 700–726.

Rediker, Marcus. *The Slave Ship: A Human History.* New York: Viking, 2007.

Reinke-Williams, Tim. *Women, Work and Sociability in Early Modern London.* Basingstoke: Palgrave Macmillan, 2014.

Richardson, R. C. *Household Servants in Early Modern England.* Manchester: Manchester University Press, 2010.

Robinson, Cedric. *Black Marxism.* 2nd ed. Chapel Hill: University of North Carolina Press, 2000.

Robinson, Charles John *A History of the Mansions and Manors of Herefordshire*. London: Longmans, 1873.

Rodger, N. A. M. *The Command of the Ocean: A Naval History of Britain, 1649–1815*. London: W. W. Norton, 2004.

———. *The Wooden World: An Anatomy of the Georgian Navy*. New York: W. W. Norton, 1996.

Roth, Cassia. "From Free Womb to Criminalized Woman: Fertility Control in Brazilian Slavery and Freedom." *Slavery and Abolition* 38 (2017): 269–86.

Rothenberg, Elizabeth Anne. "'The Diligent Hand Maketh Rich': Commercial Advice for Retailers in Late Seventeenth- and Early Eighteenth-Century England." In *Cultures of Selling: Perspectives on Consumption and Society since 1700*, edited by John Benson and Laura Ugolini, 215–36. Aldershot: Ashgate, 2006.

Rothschild, Emma. *The Inner Life of Empires: An Eighteenth-Century History*. Princeton, NJ: Princeton University Press, 2004.

Rothstein, Natalie. "Canterbury and London: The Silk Industry in the Late Seventeenth Century." *Textile History* 20 (1989): 33–47.

Sackett, Emily. "'Greater Numbers of Fair and Lovely Women': White Women and the Barbadian Demographic Crisis, 1673–1715." *Early American Studies* 20 (2022): 640–52.

Salmon, Marylynn. *Women and the Law of Property in Early America*. Chapel Hill: University of North Carolina Press, 1986.

Schiebinger, Londa. "Agnotology and Exotic Abortifacients: The Cultural Production of Ignorance in the Eighteenth-Century Atlantic World." *Proceedings of the American Philosophical Society* 149 (2005): 316–43.

———. *Plants and Empire: Colonial Bioprospecting in the Atlantic World*. Cambridge, MA: Harvard University Press, 2006.

Schwartz, Marie Jenkins. *Birthing a Slave: Motherhood and Medicine in the Antebellum South*. Cambridge, MA: Harvard University Press, 2006.

Schwarz, L. D. *London in the Age of Industrialisation: Entrepreneurs, Labour Force and Living Conditions, 1700–1850*. Cambridge: Cambridge University Press, 1992.

Scott, Rebecca. *Degrees of Freedom: Louisiana and Cuba after Slavery*. Cambridge, MA: Harvard University Press, 2005.

Seeman, Erik R. *Death in the New World: Cross-Cultural Encounters, 1492–1800*. Philadelphia: University of Pennsylvania Press, 2010.

Shaw, Jenny. "Birth and Initiation on the Peers Plantation: The Problem of Creolization in Seventeenth-Century Barbados." *Slavery and Abolition* 39 (2018): 290–314.

———. *Everyday Life in the Early English Caribbean: Irish, Africans, and the Construction of Difference*. Athens: University of Georgia Press, 2013.

———. "In the Name of the Mother: The Story of Susannah Mingo, a Woman of Color in the Early English Atlantic." *William and Mary Quarterly* 77 (2020): 177–210.

Shumway, Rebecca. *The Fante and the Transatlantic Slave Trade*. Rochester, NY: University of Rochester Press, 2011.

Shyllon, Follarin. "The Black Presence and Experience in Britain: An Analytical Overview." In *Essays on the History of Blacks in Britain: From Roman Times to the Mid-twentieth Century*, edited by Jagdish S. Gundara and Ian Duffield, 202–24. Aldershot: Avebury, 1992.

Smallwood, Stephanie. *Saltwater Slavery: A Middle Passage from Africa to American Diaspora*. Cambridge, MA: Harvard University Press, 2007.

Smith, Cassander L. *Black Africans in the British Imagination: English Narratives of the Early Atlantic World*. Baton Rouge: Louisiana State University Press, 2016.

Smith, Simon S. *Slavery, Family, and Gentry Capitalism in the British Atlantic: The World of the Lascelles, 1648–1834*. Cambridge: Cambridge University Press, 2006.

Snyder, Terri L. "Sexual Consent and Sexual Coercion in Seventeenth Century Virginia." In *Sex without Consent: Rape and Sexual Coercion in America*, edited by Merrill D. Smith, 46–60. New York: New York University Press, 2001.

———. "The Trafficking of Elisha Webb: Black Freedom Claims in British North America." *William and Mary Quarterly* 79 (2022): 211–40.

Soares, Carlos Eugênio Líbano, and Raíza Cristina Canuta da Hora. "African Mothers in the City of Bahia, 1734–99." *Women's History Review* 27 (2018): 875–91.

Sparks, Randy J. *Where the Negroes Are Masters: An African Port in the Era of the Slave Trade*. Cambridge, MA: Harvard University Press, 2013.

Spillers, Hortense J. "Mama's Baby, Papa's Maybe: An American Grammar Book." *Diacritics*, 17 (1987): 64–81.

Steckel, Richard H. "Birth Weights and Infant Mortality among American Slaves." *Explorations in Economic History* 23 (1986): 173–98.

Stevenson, Brenda. *What Sorrows Labour in My Parent's Breast? A History of the Enslaved Black Family*. London: Rowman and Littlefield, 2023.

Stoler, Ann Laura. *Carnal Knowledge and Imperial Power*. Berkeley: University of California Press, 2002.

———. "Intimidations of Empire: Predicaments of the Tactile and Unseen." In *Haunted by Empire: Geographies of Intimacy in North American History*, edited by Ann Laura Stoler, 1–22. Durham, NC: Duke University Press, 2006.

Stone, Lawrence. *The Family, Sex, and Marriage in England, 1500–1800*. New York: Harper and Row, 1977.

Sturtz, Linda L. *Within Her Power: Propertied Women in Colonial Virginia*. New York: Routledge, 2002.

Styles, John. "Spinners and the Law: Regulating Yarn Standards in the English Worsted Industries, 1550–1800." *Textile History* 44 (2013): 145–70.

Sweet, James H. "Defying Social Death: The Multiple Configurations of African Slave Family in the Atlantic World." *William and Mary Quarterly* 70 (2013): 251–72.

———. *Domingo Álvares, African Healing, and the Intellectual History of the Atlantic World*. Chapel Hill: University of North Carolina Press, 2011.

———. *Recreating Africa: Culture, Kinship, and Religion in the African-Portuguese World, 1441–1770*. Chapel Hill: University of North Carolina Press, 2003.

Swingen, Abigail L. *Competing Visions of Empire: Labor, Slavery, and the Origins of the British Atlantic Empire*. New Haven, CT: Yale University Press, 2015.

Taylor, Lou. *Establishing Dress History*. Manchester: Manchester University Press, 2005.

Thirsk, Joan. "Younger Sons in the Seventeenth Century." *History* 54 (1961): 358–77.

Thornbury, Walter. *Old and New London: A Narrative of Its History, Its People, and Its Places*. London, 1878.

Thornton, John K. *Africa and Africans in the Making of the Atlantic World, 1400–1800.* 2nd ed. Cambridge: Cambridge University Press, 1998.

———. "Central African Names and African-American Naming Patterns." *William and Mary Quarterly* 50 (1993): 727–42.

———. "Sexual Demography: The Impact of the Slave Trade on Family Structure." In *Women and Slavery in Africa,* edited by Claire C. Robertson and Martin A. Klein, 39–48. Madison: University of Wisconsin Press, 1983.

Thornton, Peter. *Seventeenth-Century Interior Decoration in England, France, and Holland.* New Haven, CT: Yale University Press, 1978.

Tomalin, Claire. *Samuel Pepys: The Unequalled Self.* London: Penguin, 2002.

Townsend, Camilla. *Pocahontas and the Powhatan Dilemma.* New York: Hill and Wang, 2005.

Trahey, Erin. "Among Her Kinswomen: Legacies of Free Women of Color in Jamaica." *William and Mary Quarterly* 76 (2019): 257–88.

Trouillot, Michel Rolph. *Silencing the Past: Power and the Production of History.* New York: Beacon, 1995.

Turner, Sasha. *Contested Bodies: Pregnancy, Childrearing, and Slavery in Jamaica.* Philadelphia: University of Pennsylvania Press, 2017.

———. "The Nameless and the Forgotten: Maternal Grief, Sacred Protection, and the Archives of Slavery." *Slavery and Abolition* 38 (2017): 232–50.

Velasco, Sherry. *The Lieutenant Nun: Transgenderism, Lesbian Desire, and Catalina de Erauso.* Austin: University of Texas Press, 2000.

Vermeulen, Heather V. "Thomas Thistlewood's Libidinal Linnaean Project: Slavery, Ecology, and Knowledge Production." *Small Axe* 22 (2018): 18–38.

Vickery, Amanda. "An Englishman's Home Is His Castle? Thresholds, Boundaries and Privacies in the Eighteenth-Century London House." *Past and Present* 199 (2008): 147–73.

Vigarello, Georges. *A History of Rape: Sexual Violence in France from the 16th to the 20th Century.* Translated by Jean Birrell. Cambridge: Cambridge University Press, 2001.

Walker, Christine. *Jamaica Ladies: Female Slaveholders and the Creation of Britain's Atlantic Empire.* Chapel Hill: Omohundro Institute of Early American History and Culture and the University of North Carolina Press, 2020.

Walvin, James. *Black and White: The Negro and English Society, 1555–1945.* London: Allen Lane / Penguin, 1973.

Ward, Joseph P. "The Taming of the Thames: Reading the River in the Seventeenth Century." *Huntington Library Quarterly* 71 (2008): 55–75.

Warren, Frederick E., trans. *The Sarum Missal in English.* 2 vols. London: A. R. Mowbray, 1913.

Weissbourd, Emily. "'Those in Their Possession': Race, Slavery, and Queen Elizabeth's 'Edicts of Expulsion.'" *Huntington Library Quarterly* 78 (2015): 1–19.

Welch, Pedro. *Slave Society in the City: Bridgetown Barbados, 1680–1807.* Kingston: Ian Randle, 2003.

West, Emily, and R. J. Knight. "Mothers' Milk: Slavery, Wet-Nursing, and Black and White Women in the Antebellum South." *Journal of Southern History* 83 (2017): 37–68.

West, Emily, and Erin Shearer. "Fertility Control, Shared Nurturing, and Dual Exploitation: The Lives of Enslaved Mothers in the Antebellum United States." *Women's History Review* 27 (2018): 1006–20.

Wheat, David. *Atlantic Africa and the Spanish Caribbean 1570–1640*. Chapel Hill: Omohundro Institute of Early American History and Culture and the University of North Carolina Press, 2016.

Whiting, Gloria McCahon. "Power, Patriarchy, and Provision: African Families Negotiate Gender and Slavery in New England." *Journal of American History* 103 (2016): 583–605.

———. "Race, Slavery, and the Problem of Numbers in Early New England: A View from Probate Court." *William and Mary Quarterly* 77 (2020): 405–40.

White, Deborah Gray. *Ar'n't I A Woman: Female Slaves in the Plantation South*. 2nd ed. New York: W. W. Norton, 1999.

White, Sophie. *Voices of the Enslaved: Love, Labor, and Longing in French Louisiana*. Chapel Hill: Omohundro Institute of Early American History and Culture and the University of North Carolina Press, 2020.

Whyman, Susan E. *Sociability and Power in Late-Stuart England: The Cultural Worlds of the Verneys, 1660–1720*. New York: Oxford University Press, 1999.

Whyte Christine. "Mothering Solidarity: Infant-Feeding, Vulnerability and Poverty in West Africa since the Seventeenth Century." *Past and Present* 246, no. S15 (2020): S54–92.

Williams, Eric. *Capitalism and Slavery*. Chapel Hill: University of North Carolina Press, 1994.

Wilson, Adrian. "The Ceremony of Childbirth and Its Interpretation." In *Women as Mothers in Pre-industrial England*, edited by Valerie Fildes, 68–107. London: Routledge, 1990.

Wilson, Kathleen. *The Island Race: Englishness, Empire, and Gender in the Eighteenth Century*. New York: Routledge, 2002.

———. "The Performance of Freedom: Maroons and the Colonial Order in Eighteenth-Century Jamaica and the Atlantic Sound." *William and Mary Quarterly* 66 (2009): 45–86.

Winer, Rebecca Lynn. "The Enslaved Wet Nurse as Nanny: The Transition from Free to Slave Labor in Childcare in Barcelona after the Black Death (1348)." *Slavery and Abolition* 38 (2017): 303–19.

Wood, Betty. "Servant Women and Sex in the Seventeenth-Century Chesapeake." In *Women in Early America*, edited by Thomas A. Foster, 95–117. New York: New York University Press, 2015.

Wulf, Karin. "Women and Families in Early (North) America and the Wider (Atlantic) World." *History Compass* 8 (2010): 238–47.

Young, Jason R. *Rituals of Resistance: African Atlantic Religion in Kongo and the Lowcountry South in the Era of Slavery*. Baton Rouge: Louisiana State University Press, 2007.

Zacek, Natalie A. *Settler Society in the English Leeward Islands, 1670–1776*. Cambridge: Cambridge University Press, 2010.

Zahedieh, Nuala. *The Capital and the Colonies: London and the Atlantic Economy, 1660–1700*. Cambridge: Cambridge University Press, 2010.

Index

Page numbers in italics refer to illustrations.

158–84 passim, 187, 189, 219n27, 219n29, 226n57; in Barbados, 149, 150, 151; and bills of answer, 139, 220n34; and bills of complaint, 135; and depositions, 119, 121, 134, 139, 170, 171, 174, 221n51

Chaplin, Ann. *See* Tomkyns, Ann

Chaplin, Robert, 22, 67, 145, 153, 174, 182; death of, 149, *176, 180*; as factor, 129, 132, 136; home on St Swithin's Lane, 119, 145, 155; and John's children, 67, 162, 169, 170, 172, 177, 179, 181; as legal defendant, 130, 138, 139, 150, 167, *175*

Charles I, 20, 21, 99, 131

Charles II, 21, 43, 99, 109, 131, 188, 202n10

Chelsea, Jack (runaway), 113

childbirth. *See* birth

childhood, 15, 54, 61, 62, 68, 153, 165, 171

chocolate, 18, 107

Christ Church College, Oxford, 171

Christ Church Parish (Barbados), 17, 21, 38, 72, 75, 85, 88, 94, 190, 191; and baptism register, 2, 3, *14*, 47, 60, 73, 74, 147

churching. *See* birth

Church of England, 72, 73, 75, 79, 80, 93, 96, 148, 152

clandestine marriage. *See* marriage

clothing, 26, 37, 45, 145; in England, 107, 108, 109, 120, 121, 124, 144, 162, 163; for enslaved people, 29, 92, 127; for white colonists, 82, 143. *See also* liveries; osnaburg cloth

coaches, 87, 89; and coach houses, 115; and coachmen, 122, 125

coerced sex, 37, 41, 43, 44–50, 51, 52, 68, 72, 87, 90. *See also* consent; rape; sexual violence

coffeehouses, 107, 108

collars, 10, 100, 109–10, *111*, 113–14, 127, 163, 213n5, 216n53

colonialism, 7, 8, 9, 10, 11, 12, 105, 190, 191

Colston, Edward, 190

Compagnie du Senegal, 26

conjugal relationships, 71, 72, 79–87, 211n60. *See also* marriage

consent, 11, 43, 46, 50, 51, 201n6. *See also* coerced sex; rape; sexual violence

contraception, 51–52. *See also* pregnancy

cookmaid. *See* "Black Cookmaid"

Cormantee, 29–30

cotton, 6, 17, 18, 29, 104, 160

Cozens, William, 160

Cromwell, Oliver, 21

Crow, Rev. Francis, 143

Cubenhah / Nell (enslaved at Rendezvous), 62

Cuffee, Charles, 148

Cuffy (enslaved by Hester's John), 178

Daniel, John, 33, 34, 35

Dean, Elizabeth, 103

death: in England, 118, 128–29, 130, 134–35, 137, 139, 144, 145, 149, 153, 155, 162, 167–84 passim, *186*, 187, 188; of English colonists, 1, 2, 11, 12, 17, 19, 20, 22, 23, 53, 68, 71, 72, 82, 87–89, 95, 96, 142, 152; of enslaved Africans, 31, 32, 34, 40, 71, 72, 90–91, 92–93, 95; and manumission, 148, 149; and Middle Passage, 1, 27; of West Africans, 91–92, 208n8

deathbed. *See* death

deathways. *See* death

debt, 128, 132, 135, 137, 138, 150, 176, 177, 178, 190

depositions. *See* Chancery Court

Dinah (enslaved in Bristol, England), 146

disease, 26, 27, 29, 51, 77, 90; and Benjamin, 87, 90; and John, 115, 117; malaria, 51; plague, 9, 106; smallpox, 27, 90; Tunbridge water as cure for, 131–32

docks: in Bridgetown, 28–29, 102, 104, 165; in London, 10, 16, 97, 99, 100, 104–6, 107, 163, 164, 167

Doll (enslaved by Samuel Pepys), 109

domestic labor: in Barbados, 4, 37–38, 39, 43, 54, 55, 58, 60, 61, 64, 66, 149, 206n88; drudgery of, 37, 58, 124; in London, 160, 162, 173; in Streatham, 117, 118, 119, 121–23, 125–26, 127, 158, 174, 216nn59–61; and surveillance, 39–40, 58, 61. *See also* enslaved children; enslaved men; enslaved women; servants

Dorothy's Ann, 3, *48*, 78, 114, 145, 168

Dorothy's Frances, *48*, 78, 114, 145, 168

feather beds, 37, 38, 56, 69, 119, 122, 123, 124, 127

fetishes. *See* power objects

field workers. *See* enslaved children; enslaved men; enslaved women; servants

food: in England, 107, 118–19, 127, 138, 145, 162; as grave goods, 92, 94; on plantations, 6, 31, 34, 36, 37, 45, 58, 61, 76, 80–81; on ships, 27, 103. *See also* feasts

Forrest, Mr. (coachmaker), 125

Frances's Ann, 48, 70, 77–78, 169, 171, 172, 177, 181, 203n28, 207n1, 225nn45–46

Frances's Elizabeth, 48, 70, 73, 77, 114, 169, 171, 177, 179, 203n28

Frances's Frances, 4, 70, 73, 77, 114, 169, 177, 183, 187, 225n46; death of, 185, 186; education of, 171–72; in later life, 179–81, 226n67; will of, 225n46, 226n63

Franke (enslaved at Bully Gibbons and Rendezvous), 53, 82, 83–84, 87, 89

Fredericksburg (West Africa), 52, 76

freedom, 2, 5, 12, 39, 45, 105, 110, 113, 130, 146, 147, 149, 152, 154, 158, 183, 187, 189, 190; de facto, 135, 146, 153; politics of, 75, 130–31, 218n5; whiteness as reproduction of, 7, 8, 71, 96, 147, 188, 191. *See also* baptisms; free people of color; manumission

free people of color, 146–47, 147–48, 191, 218n7, 221n55, 221n57, 221n59. *See also* freedom; manumission

"French maid" (at Streatham manor house), 117, 118, 119, 121

French people, 26, 34, 92, 108, 117, 170, 171, 172. *See also* Huguenots

fruit, 28, 36–37, 81, 126

Fuentes, Marisa, xii, 195n29, 198n28, 199n52

funerals, 71, 87–89, 91–92, 93–95, 179

furnishings, 107; at Rendezvous, 37, 38; at Streatham, 100, 117, 119–21, 122–25

gardens, 115, 117, 125–26

Garden Tenement, 36–37, 40

Ghana, 23, 26, 77

Godwyn, Morgan, 93

Gold Coast (West Africa), 23–24, 29–30, 52, 59, 76, 77, 78, 84, 91, 92, 197n24

goldsmiths, 107, 160–61, 173, 183, 184, 187

Goodyeare, Moses, 113

"gossips" (women attending births) 56–57, 118. *See also* birth

Great Newes from the Barbadoes (anonymous), 36

Gregory, William, 129–30, 132, 218n13

Guinea Company, 132

Guy, Richard, 137

Hall, Florence, 24, 26, 27

Hall, William, 48, 172, 225n46

Hannah (free person of color, Bridgetown), 149

Hannah's John, 151, 157, 158, 181, 183, 186, 187, 190

Hawley, Henry, 19–20, 22

Hawley, James, 22

Hawley, Susan (Richard Peers I's wife), 19, 20

Hay, Peter, 18

Henrietta Marie (Charles I wife), 131

Herefordshire (England), 15, 21, 37, 54, 55, 98, 135, 140, 157, 179, 180, 181

Hester (enslaved woman on Rendezvous), 74, 79, 90–91, 93, 94, 95

Hester's Elizabeth I, 48, 70, 77, 203n27, 207n1

Hester's Elizabeth II, 48, 70, 77, 203n27, 207n1

Hester's John, 66, 77, 159, 172, 179, 226n57; and baptism, 54, 203n27; death of, 177–78; depositions of, 174, 175, 176; education of, 67, 139, 170–71, 225n40; return to Barbados, 149–51, 177; will of, 178

Hester's Mary, 22, 67, 77, 118, 129–30, 132, 134, 169; birth of, 54, 55, 203n27; death of, 179, 180; education of, 171–72

Hester's Richard, 77, 100, 162, 179, 183; as "able seaman," 164; birth of, 203n27; death of, 150, 152, 177, 213n102; marriage of, 157, 158, 172–77; as primary inheritor, 119–21, 123, 127, 149–51, 159, 170, 177, 178, 181, 184, 187; relationship with Robert Chaplin, 67, 137, 169–71, 173, 176, 226n57; return to Barbados, 150, 177; will of, 225n46, 226n63

145; pursuit of in Chancery Court, 130, 182, 183. *See also* annuities; bequeathals; inheritances

Legacies of British Slavery database, 190

Ligon, Richard, 18, 22, 23, 35, 37, 74, 92, 93; racist views of people of African descent, 44–45, 59, 60, 81, 84–85; on sugar production, 17, 30, 32–33, 34

linens, 37, 120, 121, 124; childbed, 54, 55–56; for shrouds, 87, 91

literacy, 121, 162, 164, 167, 223n23; cultural, 107, 162

Littleton, Edward, 34

liveries, 100, 110, *111*, 113, 162, 215n43, 216n65, 223n18

Livers Ocle (Herefordshire, England), 21, *98*

London, 2, 16, 18, 20, 24, 30, 37, 54, 74, 93, 108, 115, *116*, 118, 120, 125, 131, 138, 150, 165, 179, 188, 190; Aldersgate Street, 182; Chancery Lane, 108; Cheapside, 106, 107, 108, *112*; Cornhill, 107, *112*; Covent Garden, 107, 108, 132, 137, 152, 168; diversity of, 10, 12, 99, 100, 104–5, 108, 109–14, 117, 119, 122, 143–44, 147, 160, 184; education in, 169–70, 179; Essex Street, 107, 108, *112*, 115, 125, 139; Exeter Exchange, 99, 106–7, *112*, 115; expansion of, 100, 105–7; Fleet Street, 107, *112*, 167; George Street, 160; Great Fire of, 106, 107, 132, 140; industry in, 106–7, 140, 160–64, 187; Lothbury, *112*, 155, *156*, 163, 164; Old Bailey, 139; Ormond Street, 181; population of, 9, 159, 189; Royal Exchange, 140, 178; Southwark, 167, 168; Spitalfields, *112*, 155, 160, 161, 189; St. Andrews Holborn, 181; St. Ann and St. Agnes, 168; St. Bride's Fleet Street, 167; St. Christopher Le Stocks, 155, *156*, 168; St. Clement Danes, 19, 108, 152, 155, *156*, 168, 182; St. Dunstan Stepney, 160; St. Leonard's, x, *48*, 115, *157*, 185, *186*; St. Martin in the Fields, 172; St. Mary's Lambeth, *157*, 173; St. Mary's Southwark, 167; St. Nicholas Cole Abbey, 20; St. Paul's Cathedral, 107, *112*, 140, 155; St. Swithin's Lane, *112*, 118, 119, 140, 144, 145, 155, 171,

174; travel to, 5, 10, 96, 97–99, 101, 102, 104, 152, 155; West End, 5, 99, 100, 106; western suburbs of, 168

luxury, 18, 88, 123, 161, 162, 184

"Mancon House" (Rendezvous), 3, 4, 15, 17, 29, 38, 40, 56, 64, 68, 76, 97, 127, 191, 194n7

manumission, 5, 75, 135, 188

Marees, Pieter de, 52, 77, 91

marriage, 47, 71, 72, 132, 138, 169, 188; clandestine, 167, 224n32, 225n51; and coverture, 202n7; of enslaved peopled, 85–86, 208n5, 208n8; of Frances to Benjamin, 79–82, 89; of Frances to John, 68, 70, 82, 83, 84, 89, 95, 96; of Hester to John, 22, 40, 55, 78; of John's children, 168–68, 172–76, 179, 182, 224n33; potential of, for social advancement, 82–83, 141–42, 158, 172; of Richard Peers I, 15–16, 20. *See also* conjugal relationships; dowries

Martin, Frances. *See* Dorothy's Frances

Mason, Sandra, 190

Masque of Blackness (Jonson), 99

maternal inheritance, 7, 8, 194n17, 202n7

Maydwell, James, 160

Mayers, John Pollard, 190

merchants, 93, 188; in Barbados, 89, 150, 183; in London, 9, 107, 132, 137, 140, 155, 161, 173, 178; and slave trade, 26, 28; in Streatham, 100, 115, 117, 126

Middle Passage, 1–2, 4, 7, 24–28, 62, 71, 84, 90, 102

midwives, 54, 55, 56, *57*, 60, 78

Milman, Elizabeth, 181, 226n65, 226n67

Milman, William, 181, 226n65, 226n67

Mingo, Hester. *See* Susannah's Hester

Mingo, Judith. *See* Susannah's Judith

Mingo, Richard. *See* Susannah's Richard

Mingo, Susannah, 1–2, *48*, 72, *156*, 191–92; and baptism, 44, 47, 74, 75, 79, 91, 96, 193n5; in Barbados, 2, 4, 145–52; and childbirth, 49, 50, 51, 52, 54, 59–61, 69, 90; and children's baptism, 3, 50, 53, 72, 74, 76, 96, 147; and conjugal relationship, 86–87;

sexual violence, 46, 201n6. *See also* consent; coerced sex; rape

Sharp, Jane, 56, *57*

ships: commercial, 28, 96, 97, 99, 101–4, 105, 142, 146, 183; Royal Navy, 103, 147, 163–64, 165, 223n21; slave, 1–2, 6, 10, 23, 24, *25*, 26–28, 41, 165

Shobdon (Herefordshire, England), 179, *180*

'Sibell (enslaved in Barbados), 24, 26, 27, 28, 198n34

silk, 108, 110, 120, 123, 143, 160, 161, 162, 163

single women. *See* spinsters

slave revolt, Barbados (1675), 29–30, 39, 74

slavery, 2, 7, 8, 13, 170, 184; acknowledgment of, in modern times, 188, 189, 190; in Barbados, 12, 31, 52, 58, 61, 84, 92, 93, 147, 191; critiques of by contemporaries, 31, 52, 58, 141; in England, 10, 11, 99, 109, 146, 159, 188, 189. *See also* enslavement; slave society; society with slaves

slave society, 3, 6, 10, 12, 17, 40, 45, 52, 61, 62, 74, 135, 146

Sloane, Hans, 35, 56, 65, 94, 210n44

Smith, Venture, 24, 26, 27

social death, 71, 92, 194n17

society with slaves, 10, 12, 135, 159, 184, 187, 188, 195n26

soul value, 72, 76, 218n7

Southerne, Thomas, 141, 142

spa towns, 115, 131–32

Spendlove, Ann. *See* Dorothy's Ann

Spendlove, Dorothy, 2, 4, 6, 48, 191–92, 194n11; in Barbados, 4, 147; and childbirth, 3, 49, 50, 52, 69, 72, 83, 90; and children's baptism, 3, 48, 50, 53; as creole, 100, 142, 143, 144; and domestic labor, 38, 39, 40, 58, 118; financial savvy of, 130, 135; as heir, 5, 8, 53, 117–18, 134, 135–36; likely place of birth, 38, 102, 220n39; as litigant, 12, 53–54, 130, 134, 138–41, 144–45, 150, 153, 160, 167, 189, 218n5; in London, 12, 97, 99, 107, 108, 109, 114, 145, 152; as mother, 8, 41, 64, 66, 68, 69, 78, 136, 145, 159, 168; relationship with

Elizabeth, 39, 49, 53, 66, 67, 68, 99, 118, 134, 135, 138, 143, 144; relationship with Hester and Frances, 38, 43, 53, 55, 56, 64, 66, 67; relationship with John, 6, 43, 46–47, 48, 49, 50, 82–83, 142; relationship with Susannah, 39, 49, 53, 66, 67, 68, 118, 138; in Streatham, 115, 117, 118, 124, 125, 126, 127, 128–29, 137; and whiteness, 43, 50, 68, 69, 99, 100, 143, 188–89

Spendlove, Frances. *See* Dorothy's Frances

Spendlove, John. *See* Dorothy's John

Spendlove and Ashcroft v. Chaplin, 138–45

spinsters, 158, 161, 163, 164, 167, 168, 179, 223n20

stables, 36, 115, 122, 125

Staple Grove, 14, *19*, 64, 91, 135, 146, 149, 150, 151, 158, 159, 176, 177, 178, 179, 183, 184, 190, 196n12, 226n57

stillbirth, 51. *See also* birth

Strand, the (London), 106, 107, 108, *111*, 155

Streatham (England), 150, 155, 165, 169, 173, 189; Dorothy as mistress of, 100, 117–18, 126; furnishings at, 119–21, 122–24, 125; household in, 117, 129, 161, 162, 164, 168; inventory at, 118, 120, 162; location of, 5, 115, *116*; manor house in, 5, 100, 118, 122, 123, 127, 128, 130, 132, 136, 137, 139, 145, 174; as merchant retreat, 100, 108, 115, 117, 131; servants working in, 119–23, 124, 125–26, 127, 158, 174; and St. Leonard's, 115, 185, *186*; Susannah as "Black Cook-maid" in, 100, 119

sugar, 103, 117, 142, 153, 191; and boom, 9, 18, 182; as funding English empire, 100, 107, 187, 190; as grave good, 94; production of, 4, 16, 17–19, 22, 30–34, 36, 40, 83, 90, 114, 199n58; Rendezvous profits from, 127, 136, 138, 142, 158; as valuable commodity, 2, 6–7, 16, 18, 28, 40, 102, 104, 107, 119, 126

Sunbury (England), *116*, 152, 182, 183

Susannah's Hester, 2, 78, 79, 101, 103, 105, 168; and baptism, 3; death of, 155, *156*; and relationships with half siblings, 61, 64, 68, 114, 121

Susannah's Judith, 2, 12, 53, 78–79, 101, 103, 105, 155, *156*, 159, 165, 168, 188, 223n27, 224n33; and baptism, 3, 76; as mother, 182, 183; and relationships with half siblings, 61, 64, 67, 68, 69, 114, 121; as spinster, 158, 160, 161–63, 164

Susannah's Richard, 2, 78, 79, 101, 103, 105, 109; and baptism, 3; death of, *156*, 158; and relationships with half siblings, 61, 64, 68, 69, 100, 114, 119, 121, 127, 162; as sailor, 147, 163–65, 223n21, 224n24; will of, 163, 165, 167

taverns, 107, 108, 149, 151
Taylor, John, 93–94
tea, 18, 104
Thames: estuary, *98*, 104; river, 9, 97, *98*, 100, 105, 106, 107, 108, *111*, *115*, 152, 153, 163, 167, 173
Thrayle, John, 161, 173
tobacco, 6, 16, 17, 18, 28, 94, 104, 106
Tomkyns, Ann, 22, 54, 55, 67, 169, 170, 177, 180, 207n100, 218n13
Tomkyns, Hester, 3, 4, 10, 12, 72, 76, 77, 191, 192; in Barbados, 11, 15–16, 22–23, 29, 30, 33, 34, 36, 37; and childbirth, 40, 54–56; and children's baptism, 54; death of, 3–4, 68, 90, 95, 142, 177, 194n9; likely place of birth, 15, 21, 38; and marriage to John, 72; as mother, 64–65, 66, 67, 68, 70, 169; relationship with Dorothy, Susannah, and Elizabeth, 5, 6, 38–40, 41, 43, 49, 52, 53, 56, 58, 67, 69, 147; relationship with John, 6, 22, 47, 52, 80; as reproducer of whiteness and freedom, 8, 12–13, 43, 188; temperament of, 64, 83–84
Tomlinson, Henry, *48*, 167, 224n31, 224n33
Tomlinson, Joseph, 183, 224n31
Toney (runaway), 113
Tower of London, 97, 113
Town Misse, 109, 215n39
transatlantic slave trade, 7, 9, 12, 23, 26, 99, 100, 102, 109, 165, 182, 185, 190, 197n24, 198n47
A Trip to Jamaica (Ward), 142

Tryon, Thomas, 31, 35, 52, 58, 60, 124
Tunbridge (England), 125, 131–32
Turnor, Edward, 169, 174, 176

Uffenbach, Zacharias Conrad von, 144, 221n47
Ulshiemer, Andreas, 91–92
University College London, 190
unnamed boy (runaway, enslaved by Thomas Dymock), 113

Villault, Nicolas, 92
violence, 103; toward enslaved people, 27, 34–35, 40, 43, 64, 66, 93, 94, 147. *See also* coerced sex; rape; sexual violence
Vokins, Joan, 102–3

Walduck, Thomas, 66
Walrond, Thomas, 89, 212n68
Wane, Daniel, 160
Ward, John, 162
Ward, Ned, 142–43
weather, 59, 119, 126; in Atlantic Ocean, 102, 103, 104
weddings, 71, 80, 81, 82, 83, 84, 86, 92, 173, 176, 182, 211n48, 225n51
Weobley (England), 15, 54, 55, 132
West Africa: coast of, 1, 23, 26, 100; cultural practices in, changed by slavery, 62, 71–72, 79, 84, 90, 92–93, 94, 95; and ethnicities, 23–24, 29–30, 62; initiation practices in, 72, 76–77, 78–79; journey to Barbados from, 24–28, 198n47; marriage in, 84; mortuary practices in, 91–92, 94; population from, in Barbados, 16, 23–24, 35, 94; reproductive practices in, 44, 50–52, 54, 59, 69; slave trade in, 28–29, 99; Susannah as born in, 62, 78–79. *See also* Gold Coast
West African captives, 1, 7, 12, 17, 22, 23–24, 26–30, 41, 84, 85, 90, 99, 102, 165, 197n24; origins of, 23–24
West Indies, 2, 9, 16, 21, 59, 65, 82, 142, 146, 147, 152, 163, 165, 188
Westminster (London), 100, 107, 108
wet nurses, 55, 64–67

White, John (runaway), 113, 115

whiteness: and connection to freedom, 147,
    188, 191; and legitimacy, 83, 96, 188; pro-
    tections afforded women by, 43, 47, 50, 53,
    67, 69, 99, 100, 136; and racial hierarchy,
    136, 142, 143, 188–89; reproduction of, 8,
    11. *See also* Blackness; mixed race, people
    of; racism

white women, 65, 69, 81, 83, 108, 109, 203n25,
    203n29; as enslavers, 40, 69, 81, 82, 204n6;
    as reproducing freedom, 7, 8, 202n8. *See*
also Knights, Frances; Spendlove, Dorothy;
    Tomkyns, Hester

widows, 12, 81, 82, 88, 89, 141, 158,
    181, 187

Willoughby, Francis Lord, 21

Windrush generation, 187

wool, 120, 161, 163, 168

Wren, Christopher, 97, 107, 108

Yorke-Talbot case, 152, 153, 188

Yorkshire (England), 71, 98